AS-Level No

Biology

for OCR

D1407324

CGP

The Complete Course for OCR

Contents

How to use this book

Learning Objectives

- These tell you exactly what you need to learn, or be able to do, for the exam.
- There's a specification reference at the bottom that links to the OCR specification.

Examples

- These are here to help you understand the theory.
- You don't need to learn them unless it says so in the text.

Tips

These are here to help you understand the theory.

How Science Works

- How Science Works is a big part of AS Biology. There's a whole section on it at the front of the book.
- How Science Works is also covered throughout the book wherever you see this symbol.

Exam Tips

There are tips throughout the book to help with all sorts of things to do with answering exam questions.

(Sample right page)

Learning Objectives:
- Be able to calculate the linear magnification of an image.
- Be able to explain the difference between magnification and resolution.
- Be able to state the resolution and magnification that can be achieved by a light microscope, a transmission electron microscope and a scanning electron microscope.
- Be able to explain the need for staining samples for use in light microscopy and electron microscopy.

Specification Reference 1.1.1

Exam Tip
If you find rearranging formulas hard you can use a formula triangle to help. This is the formula triangle for magnification:

All you do is put your finger over the one you want and read off the formula. E.g. if you want the length of specimen you put your finger over that and it leaves behind length of image ÷ magnification.

4. Studying Cells — Microscopes

Investigating cells, and what's in them, involves donning your lab coat and digging out your trusty microscope.

Magnification and resolution of microscopes

We all know that microscopes produce a magnified image of a sample, but resolution is just as important...

Magnification

Magnification is how much bigger the image is than the specimen (the sample you're looking at). It's calculated using this formula:

$$\text{magnification} = \frac{\text{length of image}}{\text{length of specimen}}$$

In the exam, you might be told the actual and magnified size of an object and then be asked to calculate the magnification. You can do this by using the formula above.

— Examples —

Calculating magnification
If you have a magnified image that's 5 mm wide and your specimen is 0.05 mm wide the magnification is:

$$\text{magnification} = \frac{\text{length of image}}{\text{length of specimen}}$$
$$= \frac{5}{0.05} = \times 100$$

5 mm

Calculating length of image
If your specimen is 0.1 mm wide and the magnification of the microscope is × 20, then the length of the image is:
length of image = magnification × length of specimen
= 20 × 0.1 = 2 mm

Calculating length of specimen
If you have a magnified image that's 5 mm wide and the magnification is × 50, then the length of the specimen is:

$$\text{length of specimen} = \frac{\text{length of image}}{\text{magnification}}$$
$$= \frac{5}{50} = 0.1 \text{ mm}$$

When you're calculating magnification you need to make sure that all lengths are in the same unit, e.g. all in millimetres. When dealing with microscopes these units can get pretty tiny. The table below shows common units:

Unit	How many millimetres it is:	To convert
Millimetre (mm)	1 mm	÷ 1000
Micrometre (μm)	0.001 mm	÷ 1000
Nanometre (nm)	0.000001 mm	

(Sample left page)

Tip: The phospholipid bilayer is ~ 7 nm thick.

Tip: For more on models and theories, see p. 1.

Tip: A polar molecule has one end with a slightly positive charge and one end with a slightly negative charge. These charges are nowhere near as strong as the positive or negative charge on an ion, but they do help polar molecules to dissolve in water. Non-polar substances have no charges.

Tip: Water is actually a polar molecule, but it can diffuse (by osmosis) through the cell membrane because it's so small (see page 29).

Tip: There's more on phospholipids and cholesterol on pages 116-117.

Figure 3: A computer model of the fluid mosaic model.

Membrane structure

The structure of all membranes is basically the same. They're all composed of lipids (mainly a type called phospholipids), proteins and carbohydrates (usually attached to proteins or lipids).

In 1972, the **fluid mosaic model** was suggested to describe the arrangement of molecules in the membrane — see Figure 2. In the model, phospholipid molecules form a continuous, double layer (called a bilayer). This bilayer is 'fluid' because the phospholipids are constantly moving. Protein molecules are scattered through the bilayer, like tiles in a mosaic. Some proteins have a polysaccharide (carbohydrate) chain attached — these are called **glycoproteins**. Some lipids also have a polysaccharide chain attached — these are called **glycolipids**. Cholesterol molecules are also present within the bilayer.

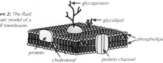

Figure 2: The fluid mosaic model of a cell membrane.

glycoprotein
glycolipid
phospholipids
protein
cholesterol
protein channel

Membrane components

There are five main components you need to know about:

Phospholipids
Phospholipid molecules form a barrier to dissolved (water-soluble) substances. Phospholipids have a 'head' and a 'tail'. The head is **hydrophilic** — it attracts water. The tail is **hydrophobic** — it repels water. The molecules automatically arrange themselves into a bilayer — the heads face out towards the water on either side of the membrane (see Figure 4).

The centre of the bilayer is hydrophobic so the membrane doesn't allow water-soluble substances (like ions and polar molecules) to diffuse through it. Small, non-polar substances (e.g. carbon dioxide) and water can diffuse through the membrane (see p. 29).

phospholipid head
phospholipid tail
phospholipid bilayer

Figure 4: Phospholipid bilayer.

Cholesterol
Cholesterol gives the membrane stability. It is a type of lipid (fat) that's present in all cell membranes (except bacterial cell membranes). Cholesterol fits between the phospholipids (see Figure 5).

Cholesterol binds to the hydrophobic tails of the phospholipids, causing them to pack more closely together. This makes the membrane less fluid and more stable. Cholesterol also has hydrophobic regions, so it's able to create a further barrier to polar substances moving through the membrane.

phospholipid
cholesterol

Figure 5: Cholesterol in the membrane.

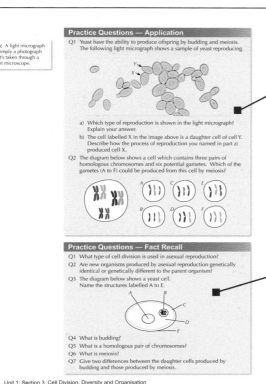

Practice Questions — Application

- Annoyingly, the examiners expect you to be able to apply your knowledge to new situations — these questions are here to give you plenty of practice at doing this.
- All the answers are in the back of the book (including any calculation workings).

Practice Questions — Fact Recall

- There are a lot of facts to learn for AS Biology — these questions are here to test that you know them.
- All the answers are in the back of the book.

Glossary

There's a glossary at the back of the book full of all the definitions you need to know for the exam, plus loads of other useful words.

Exam-style Questions

- Practising exam-style questions is really important — you'll find some at the end of each section.
- They're the same style as the ones you'll get in the real exams — some will test your knowledge and understanding, some will test that you can apply your knowledge and some will test How Science Works.
- All the answers are in the back of the book, along with a mark scheme to show you how you get the marks.

Exam Help

There's a section at the back of the book stuffed full of things to help with your exams.

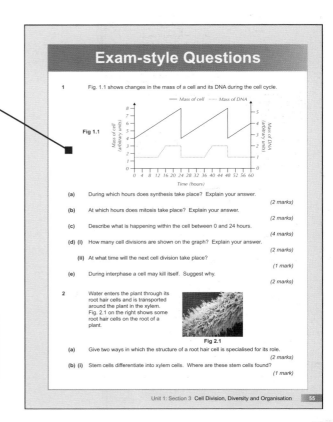

Published by CGP

Editors:
Charlotte Burrows, Emma Elder, Ceara Hayden, Rosie McCurrie, Rachael Rogers,
Hayley Thompson, Jane Towle and Megan Tyler.

Contributors:
Gloria Barnett, James Foster, Barbara Green, Liz Masters, Stephen Phillips, Adrian Schmit, Sophie Watkins,
Anna-Fe Williamson.

ISBN: 978 1 84762 789 6

With thanks to Janet Cruse-Sawyer, Philip Rushworth and Karen Wells for the proofreading.
With thanks to Anna Lupton for the copyright research.

Groovy website: www.cgpbooks.co.uk

Printed by Elanders Ltd, Newcastle upon Tyne.
Jolly bits of clipart from CorelDRAW®

How Science Works

1. The Scientific Process

Science tries to explain how and why things happen. It's all about seeking and gaining knowledge about the world around us. Scientists do this by observing things, developing theories and then testing them to see if they're correct — this is the scientific process. There are five main stages...

1. Developing theories

A **theory** is a possible explanation for something. Theories usually come about when scientists observe something and wonder why or how it happens. Scientists also sometimes form a **model** too — a simplified picture of what's physically going on.

Examples

- Darwin came up with his theory of evolution by natural selection after observing wildlife (e.g. finches) and fossils during a trip around South America and the Galapagos Islands.

- The theory that smoking causes lung cancer was developed after it was observed that many people who contracted lung cancer also smoked.

- John Snow came up with the theory that cholera is transmitted in water, rather than air, after observing lots of cases of cholera clustered around a water pump.

- Edward Jenner came up with the idea that being infected with cowpox protected you from getting smallpox after observing that milkmaids didn't get smallpox.

Tip: A theory is only scientific if it can be tested.

***Figure 1:** Drawings of finches that Darwin made in the Galapagos Islands.*

Tip: Sometimes data from one experiment can be the starting point for developing a new theory.

2. Testing the theories

The next step is to make a **prediction** or **hypothesis** — a specific testable statement, based on the theory, about what will happen in a test situation. Then an experiment or study is carried out to provide evidence that will support the prediction (or help to disprove it). If it's disproved it's back to the drawing board — the theory is modified or a completely new one is developed.

Examples

- Louis Pasteur designed an experiment to test his idea that 'germs' in the air caused disease and decomposition. He boiled two flasks of broth, both of which were left open to the air. One of the flasks had a curved neck (see Figure 2) to trap any airborne bacteria so they couldn't get into the broth. The broth in the flask with the curved neck stayed fresh, whereas the other broth went off. This provided evidence to support his theory. (After more evidence like this modern microbiology was born.)

- Edward Jenner tested his idea that getting cowpox protected people from getting smallpox by infecting a boy with cowpox, then exposing him to smallpox. The boy didn't get smallpox, which provided evidence to support his theory. (Eventually this led to the development of a smallpox vaccine.)

Tip: The results of one experiment can't prove that a theory is true — they can only suggest that it's true. They can however disprove a theory — show that it's wrong.

***Figure 2:** Pasteur's experiment — the flask with the curved neck stayed fresh.*

3. Communicating the results

The results are then published — scientists need to let others know about their work. Scientists publish their results in **scientific journals**. These are just like normal magazines, only they contain scientific reports (called papers) instead of the latest celebrity gossip.

Scientific reports are similar to the lab write-ups you do in school. And just as a lab write-up is reviewed (marked) by your teacher, reports in scientific journals undergo **peer review** before they're published. The report is sent out to peers — other scientists who are experts in the same area. They examine the data and results, and if they think that the conclusion is reasonable it's published. This makes sure that work published in scientific journals is of a good standard.

But peer review can't guarantee the science is correct — other scientists still need to reproduce it. Sometimes mistakes are made and flawed work is published. Peer review isn't perfect but it's probably the best way for scientists to self-regulate their work and to publish quality reports.

4. Validating the theory by more testing

Other scientists read the published theories and results, and try to test the theory themselves in order to validate it (back it up). This involves:

- Repeating the exact same experiments.
- Using the theory to make new predictions and then testing them with new experiments.

┌ **Examples** ─────────────────────────────────

- In 1998 a study was published that linked the MMR vaccine to autism (a developmental disorder). Other scientists then conducted different studies to try to find the same link, but their results didn't back up (validate) the theory.
- In the 1940s a study was published linking smoking and lung cancer. After this many more studies were conducted all over the world that validated the conclusion of the first study.

5. The theory is rejected, or accepted

If multiple experiments show a theory to be incorrect then scientists either have to modify the theory or develop a new one, and start the testing again. If all the experiments in all the world provide good evidence to back a theory up, the theory is thought of as scientific 'fact' (for now) — see Figure 3. But it will never become totally indisputable fact. Scientific breakthroughs or advances could provide new ways to question and test the theory, which could lead to new evidence that conflicts with the current evidence. Then the testing starts all over again... And this, my friend, is the tentative nature of scientific knowledge — it's always changing and evolving.

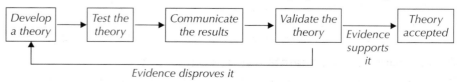

Figure 3: *Flow diagram summarising the scientific process.*

Tip: Some well known biological journals are Nature, The Lancet and the British Medical Journal.

Tip: Scientific findings are also communicated at conferences around the world.

Tip: Other scientists need to reproduce results to make sure they're reliable — see the next page for more.

Tip: Even negative results are communicated — knowing that something is wrong improves scientific knowledge.

Tip: Once an experimental method is found that gives good evidence it becomes a protocol — an accepted method to test that particular thing that all scientists can use.

Tip: 'Good evidence' means reliable evidence — see the next page.

2. Scientific Evidence

So scientists need good evidence to back up their theories. A lot of scientific evidence comes from laboratory experiments, but there are things you can't investigate in a lab (e.g. whether stress causes heart attacks) — so you have to do a study instead. Good evidence basically means reliable evidence...

Reliable evidence

Scientific evidence needs to be **reliable**. This means that it can be consistently reproduced in independent experiments.

┌─ **Example** ───

Experiment 1 result = 15 ⎫ Reliable   Experiment 1 result = 15 ⎫ Unreliable
Experiment 2 result = 16 ⎬ evidence   Experiment 2 result = 200 ⎬ evidence
Experiment 3 result = 15 ⎭   Experiment 3 result = 79 ⎭

If the results are reproducible they're more likely to be true. If the data isn't reliable for whatever reason you can't draw a valid conclusion.

The results of an experiment also need to be as **accurate** and **precise** as possible. Accurate results are those that are really close to the true answer. Precise results are those taken using sensitive instruments that measure in small increments, e.g. using a ruler with a millimetre scale gives more precise data than using a ruler with a scale in centimetres.

Getting reliable evidence

To get reliable evidence you need to do the following things:

1. Control the variables

A **variable** is a quantity that has the potential to change, e.g. weight, temperature, concentration. In an experiment you usually change one variable and measure its effect on another variable:

- The variable you change is called the **independent variable**.
- The variable that you measure is called the **dependent variable**.

Every other variable that could affect the results has to be kept the same (controlled) throughout the experiment. These variables are called **control variables**. If all the variables that could possibly affect the result are controlled then the investigation is said to be a **fair test**.

┌─ **Example** ───

For an investigation into how temperature affects the rate of an enzyme-controlled reaction:

- The independent variable is temperature (as it's the one you change).
- The dependent variable is the rate of reaction (the thing you measure).
- The control variables are the pH of the solution, the concentration of the solution, the volume of the solution etc. (as these could all affect the result if they aren't kept the same throughout).

It's usually straightforward to control all the variables in a lab experiment, but it can be quite tricky when doing studies. You often can't control all the variables, but the more you do control the more reliable the results will be.

2. Use control experiments and control groups

Even if you do manage to keep all the control variables the same, it's still possible that something else you're doing could affect the results. Scientists use control experiments and control groups to eliminate this possibility.

Tip: Evidence is the same thing as data or results.

Exam Tip
Make sure you really understand what reliable means — it crops up in loads of exam questions.

Tip: It's possible to be precise without being accurate. E.g. you could use a pH meter to measure pH of a solution to five decimal places (which would be very precise) — but if you hadn't calibrated the pH meter properly, it wouldn't be an accurate measurement.

Tip: Control variables are also sometimes called confounding variables.

Tip: In a study with human participants, you should try to keep the variables of all the participants the same, e.g. they should all be the same age, sex, etc.

Figure 1: *Well-designed lab experiments where all the variables are controlled give reliable results.*

In lab experiments, controls or **control experiments** are used.

Example

You want to investigate how temperature affects the rate of respiration in yeast. You decide to incubate the yeast at five different temperatures in beakers of liquid growth medium. You then measure the rate at which carbon dioxide is produced at each temperature. The faster the yeast produce CO_2, the greater their rate of respiration.

For each temperature, you'll need to measure the rate of CO_2 production in a beaker of liquid growth medium that doesn't contain any yeast. This will act as a **negative control** and make sure that any changes in the rate of CO_2 production are down to the effect of temperature on the yeast and not the effect of temperature on the liquid growth medium.

Tip: A negative control is not expected to have any effect on the experiment.

In studies, **control groups** are used. The subjects in the study are split into two groups — the experimental group and the control group. The control group is treated in exactly the same way as the experimental group, except for the factor you're investigating.

Example

Say you're investigating the effect of margarine containing omega-3 fish oils on heart disease. You'd have two groups — an experimental group that would be given margarine containing omega-3 fish oils, and a control group that would be given margarine without fish oils. This is done so that you can tell any reduction in heart disease is due to the fish oil, not some other substance in the margarine.

Exam Tip
If you get an exam question asking why a control group is important in a particular experiment make sure your answer is specific to that experiment (not just generally about why control groups are good).

When testing new drugs to see if they work, control groups should always be used. The control group is treated in exactly the same way as the experimental group, except they're given a thing called a **placebo** instead of the drug. A placebo is a dummy pill or injection that looks exactly like the real drug, but doesn't contain the drug. It's used to make sure that people don't improve just because they think they're being treated.

Drug trials also should be **double-blind trials**. This means that the doctor involved doesn't know whether the patient is getting the drug or the placebo, and neither does the patient. This is done to remove **bias**, e.g. doctors who expect the patients on the drugs to get better might report a greater improvement than there was.

Figure 2: The placebo (left) should look identical to the real drug (right).

3. Use a large sample size

Sample size is the number of samples in the investigation, e.g. the number of people in a drug trial. The general rule is the larger the sample size, the more reliable the data is. This is because it reduces the chance of getting a freak result (e.g. if you get the same result twice it might be because of chance, but if you get it 100 times it's much more likely that it's not due to chance).

Annoyingly, there are no rules about how big the sample size has to be to be for the investigation to be considered as 'reliable' — all you need to know is that bigger is always better.

Tip: A large data set is the same thing as a large sample size.

Tip: Scientists can use statistical tests to figure out if a result is likely to be due to chance or not.

4. Collect data carefully

The method used to collect the data can affect how reliable it is. For example, people aren't always truthful when answering questionnaires, which reduces the reliability of the data. Also, if you're using control groups, it's important that subjects are split into the two groups at **random**. This helps to avoid bias, and so makes the data more reliable.

Tip: Bias is when someone intentionally, or unintentionally, favours a particular result.

5. Repeat the measurements

The reliability of a single experiment can be improved by repeating the measurements and calculating the mean. Also, the larger the number of repeats the easier it is to spot **anomalous data** (measurements that fall outside the range of values you'd expect or any pattern you already have).

Tip: Repeating measurements in an experiment improves reliability in the same way as a large sample size — it reduces the likelihood that the results are due to chance.

Drawing conclusions from data

Conclusions need to be **valid**. A conclusion can only be considered as valid if it answers the original question and uses reliable data. It's quite tricky to draw conclusions from data — so scientists need to look out for a couple of things:

Tip: All data will vary a bit, but anomalous results vary a lot from what you'd expect.

Correlations and causal relationships

The results of investigations often show a relationship between two variables, e.g. between smoking and lung cancer. A relationship between two variables is called a **correlation**. There are two types of correlation — **positive correlations** and **negative correlations**.

Positive
As one variable increases the other increases.

Negative
As one variable increases the other decreases.

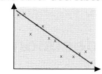

No correlation
There is no relationship between the variables.

Scientists have to be very careful when drawing conclusions from data like this because a correlation between two variables doesn't always mean that a change in one variable causes a change in the other.

Example

There's a correlation between hours spent playing frisbee and skin cancer — the more you play frisbee the higher your risk of getting skin cancer. Playing frisbee doesn't cause skin cancer though — the reason for the correlation is that frisbee is usually played outside in the sun, and excessive exposure to sunlight does cause cancer.

If there's a relationship between two variables and a change in one variable does cause a change in the other (e.g. increased exposure to sunlight does cause an increase in skin cancer) it's called a **causal relationship**. It can be concluded that a correlation is a causal relationship if every other variable that could possibly affect the result is controlled. In reality this is very hard to do — correlations are generally accepted to be causal relationships if lots of studies have found the same thing, and scientists have figured out exactly how one factor causes the other.

Tip: A causal relationship is sometimes called a causal link.

Drawing specific conclusions

Scientists can't make broad generalisations from data — they have to be very specific. They can only conclude what the results show and no more.

Example

The graph shows the results from a study into the effect of penicillin dosage on the duration of fever in men. The only conclusion you can draw is that as the dosage of penicillin increases, the duration of fever in men decreases. You can't conclude that this is true for any other antibiotic, any other symptom or even for female patients — the results could be completely different.

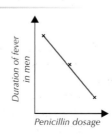

Penicillin dosage

Tip: What conclusion is drawn might be affected by bias, e.g. if someone works for a chemical company they might be more likely to ignore data that showed their product causing environmental problems.

3. Science and Decision Making

Lots of scientific work eventually leads to important discoveries or breakthroughs that could benefit humankind. These results are used by society to make decisions.

How society uses science to make decisions

Scientific knowledge is used by society (that's you, me and everyone else) to make decisions — about the way we live, what we eat, what we drive, etc. All sections of society use scientific evidence to make decisions, e.g. politicians use it to devise policies and individuals use science to make decisions about their own lives.

Examples

- The maximum amount of salt people are advised to eat per day was reduced in government guidelines in 2004, due to the results of a study which showed that reducing salt intake could significantly reduce heart disease.
- Leaded petrol in cars was phased out in many countries after it was found to cause air pollution that damaged the brain.

Factors affecting decision making

Other factors can influence decisions about science or the way science is used:

Economic factors

Society has to consider the cost of implementing changes based on scientific conclusions. Sometimes it decides the cost doesn't outweigh the benefits.

Example

The NHS can't afford the most expensive drugs without sacrificing something else. Sometimes they decide to use a less effective, but less expensive drug, despite evidence showing there's a more effective one.

Social factors

Decisions affect people's lives — sometimes people don't want to follow advice, or are strongly against some recommendations.

Examples

- Scientists may suggest banning smoking and alcohol to prevent health problems, but shouldn't we be able to choose whether we want to smoke and drink or not?
- Scientists may be able to cure many diseases using stem cells, but some people are strongly against the idea of embryonic stem cell research.

Environmental factors

Some scientific research and breakthroughs might affect the environment. Not everyone thinks the benefits are worth the possible environmental damage.

Examples

- Scientists believe unexplored regions like remote parts of rainforests might contain untapped drug resources. But some people think we shouldn't exploit these regions because any interesting finds may lead to deforestation and reduced biodiversity in these areas.
- Scientists have developed genetically modified (GM) crops (e.g. with frost resistance, or high nutrient content), but some people think the possible environmental harm they could do outweighs their benefits.

1. Cells and Organelles

No doubt you learnt about cell structure at GCSE, but there's a lot more to it at AS — as you're about to find out...

Prokaryotes and eukaryotes

There are two main types of organism — eukaryotes and prokaryotes. Prokaryotic organisms are **prokaryotic cells** (i.e. they're single-celled organisms) and eukaryotic organisms are made up of **eukaryotic cells**. Both types of cells contain organelles (see below). Eukaryotic cells are complex and include all animal and plant cells. Prokaryotic cells are smaller and simpler, e.g. bacteria. There's more on prokaryotic cells on page 15.

Organelles

Organelles are parts of cells. Each one has a specific function. If you examine a cell through an electron microscope (see page 18) you can see its organelles and the internal structure of most of them — this is known as the **cell ultrastructure**. Everything you need to know about eukaryotic cell organelles is covered over the next few pages.

Animal and plant cells

Animal and plant cells are both eukaryotic. Eukaryotic cells are generally a bit more complicated than prokaryotic cells and have more organelles. You've probably been looking at animal and plant cell diagrams for years, so hopefully you'll be familiar with some of the bits and pieces...

Animal cells

Figure 1 shows the organelles found in a typical animal cell. You can compare these to the ones found in a typical plant cell on the next page.

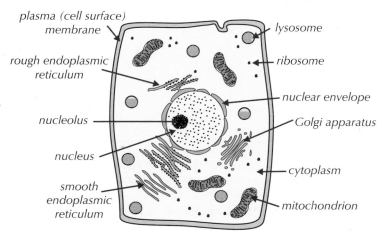

plasma (cell surface) membrane

rough endoplasmic reticulum

nucleolus

nucleus

smooth endoplasmic reticulum

lysosome

ribosome

nuclear envelope

Golgi apparatus

cytoplasm

mitochondrion

Figure 1: *The structure and ultrastructure of a typical animal cell.*

Learning Objectives:

- Be able to compare and contrast, with the aid of diagrams and electron micrographs, the structure and ultrastructure of animal cells and plant cells.

- Be able to describe and interpret drawings and photographs of eukaryotic cells as seen under an electron microscope and be able to recognise the following structures:
  - plasma (cell surface) membrane
  - nucleus
  - nucleolus
  - nuclear envelope
  - lysosomes
  - ribosomes
  - rough and smooth endoplasmic reticulum (ER)
  - Golgi apparatus
  - mitochondria
  - chloroplasts
  - centrioles
  - cilia
  - flagella.
- Be able to outline the functions of the structures listed above.

  Specification Reference 1.1.1

Tip: There are lots of different types of plant and animal cells and they won't all look exactly like the ones shown here or contain exactly the same organelles (e.g. not all plant cells contain chloroplasts). Make sure you know all the distinguishing features for each cell type.

Plant cells

Plant cells have all the same organelles as animal cells, but with a few added extras:

- a cell wall with plasmodesmata (channels for exchanging substances between adjacent cells),
- a vacuole (compartment that contains cell sap),
- and of course good old chloroplasts (the organelles involved in photosynthesis).

These organelles are all shown in Figure 2.

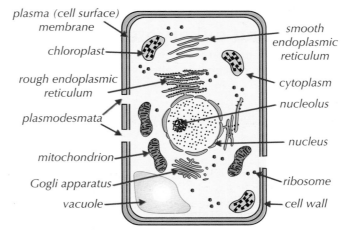

plasma (cell surface) membrane
chloroplast
rough endoplasmic reticulum
plasmodesmata
mitochondrion
Gogli apparatus
vacuole
smooth endoplasmic reticulum
cytoplasm
nucleolus
nucleus
ribosome
cell wall

Figure 2: *The structure and ultrastructure of a typical plant cell.*

Functions of organelles

This table contains a big list of organelles — you need to know the structure and function of them all. Sorry. Most organelles are surrounded by membranes, which sometimes causes confusion — don't make the mistake of thinking that a diagram of an organelle is a diagram of a whole cell. They're not cells — they're parts of cells.

Tip: There's more on the structure and function of the plasma membrane on p. 23.

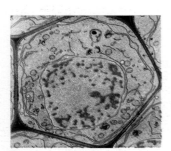

Figure 3: *An electron micrograph of a plant cell. The cell walls appear red/brown.*

Plasma membrane (Also called the cell surface membrane)

Description
The membrane found on the surface of animal cells and just inside the cell wall of plant cells and prokaryotic cells.
It's made mainly of lipids and protein.

Function
Regulates the movement of substances into and out of the cell. It also has receptor molecules on it, which allow it to respond to chemicals like hormones.

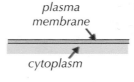

plasma membrane
cytoplasm

Cell wall

Description
A rigid structure that surrounds plant cells. It's made mainly of the carbohydrate cellulose.

Function
Supports plant cells.

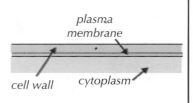

plasma membrane
cell wall
cytoplasm

Nucleus 1

Description

A large organelle surrounded by a nuclear envelope (double membrane), which contains many pores. The nucleus contains chromatin and often a structure called the nucleolus.

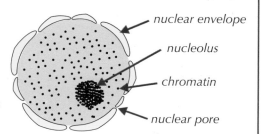

nuclear envelope

nucleolus

chromatin

nuclear pore

Function

Chromatin is made from proteins and DNA (DNA controls the cell's activities). The pores allow substances (e.g. RNA) to move between the nucleus and the cytoplasm. The nucleolus makes ribosomes (see below).

Lysosome -

Description

A round organelle surrounded by a membrane, with no clear internal structure.

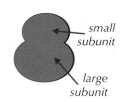

Function

Contains digestive enzymes. These are kept separate from the cytoplasm by the surrounding membrane, and can be used to digest invading cells or to break down worn out components of the cell.

Ribosome 2

Description

A very small organelle that either floats free in the cytoplasm or is attached to the rough endoplasmic reticulum.

small subunit

large subunit

Function

The site where proteins are made.

Rough endoplasmic reticulum (RER) 3

Description

A system of membranes enclosing a fluid-filled space. The surface is covered with ribosomes.

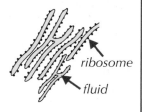

ribosome

fluid

Function *translate mRNA to proteins*

Folds and processes proteins that have been made at the ribosomes.

Smooth endoplasmic reticulum (SER) 4

Description

Similar to rough endoplasmic reticulum, but with no ribosomes.

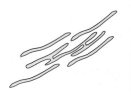

Function

Synthesises and processes lipids.

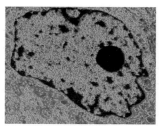

Figure 4: An electron micrograph of a nucleus, showing the nucleolus, nuclear envelope and nuclear pores.

Tip: There's more on DNA and RNA on pages 125-130.

Tip: Organelles in electron micrographs won't always look exactly the same as the ones shown here, e.g. they may vary in size and shape and they can be viewed from different angles, which can affect their appearance.

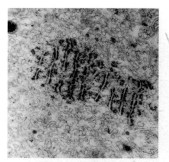

Figure 5: An electron micrograph showing SER (red-brown) and RER (blue).

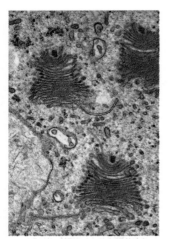

Figure 6: An electron micrograph of Golgi apparatus.

Exam Tip
Never say mitochondria produce energy in the exam — they produce ATP or release energy (energy can't be made).

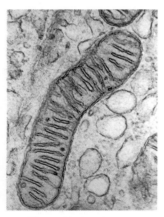

Figure 7: An electron micrograph of a mitochondrion.

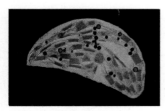

Figure 8: An electron micrograph of a chloroplast.

Vesicle   5

Description
A small fluid-filled sac in the cytoplasm, surrounded by a membrane.

Function
Transports substances in and out of the cell (via the plasma membrane) and between organelles. Some are formed by the Golgi apparatus or the endoplasmic reticulum, while others are formed at the cell surface.

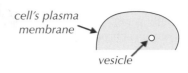

Gogli apparatus   6

Description
A group of fluid-filled flattened sacs. Vesicles are often seen at the edges of the sacs.

Function
It processes and packages new lipids and proteins. It also makes lysosomes.

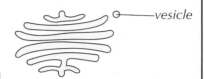

Mitochondrion

Description
It's usually oval-shaped. It has a double membrane — the inner one is folded to form structures called cristae. Inside is the matrix, which contains enzymes involved in respiration.

Function
The site of aerobic respiration, where ATP is produced. Mitochondria are found in large numbers in cells that are very active and require a lot of energy.

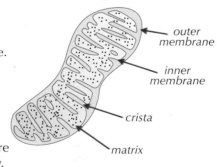

Chloroplast

Description
A small, flattened structure found in plant cells. It's surrounded by a double membrane, and also has membranes inside called thylakoid membranes. These membranes are stacked up in some parts of the chloroplast to form grana. Grana are linked together by lamellae — thin, flat pieces of thylakoid membrane.

Function
The site where photosynthesis takes place. Some parts of photosynthesis happen in the grana, and other parts happen in the stroma (a thick fluid found in chloroplasts).

Centriole

Description

Small, hollow cylinders, containing a ring of microtubules (tiny protein cylinders).

Function

Involved with the separation of chromosomes during cell division (see p. 41).

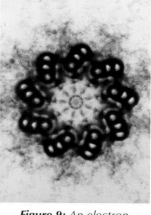

Figure 9: An electron micrograph of centrioles in a tumour cell.

Cilia

Description

Small, hair-like structures found on the surface membrane of some animal cells. In cross-section, they have an outer membrane and a ring of nine pairs of protein microtubules inside, with a single pair of microtubules in the middle.

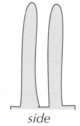
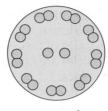

side   *cross-section*

Function

The microtubules allow the cilia to move. This movement is used by the cell to move substances along the cell surface.

Tip: Cilia in the trachea (windpipe) are used to sweep dust and dirt out of the lungs — see page 61.

Flagellum

Description

Flagella on eukaryotic cells are like cilia but longer. They stick out from the cell surface and are surrounded by the plasma membrane. Inside they're like cilia too — two microtubules in the centre and nine pairs around the edge.

Function

The microtubules contract to make the flagellum move. Flagella are used like outboard motors to propel cells forward (e.g. when a sperm cell swims).

Tip: The only example of a flagellum found in humans is the 'tail' of a sperm cell.

Tip: 'Cilium' and 'flagellum' are singular. The plural versions are 'cilia' and 'flagella'.

Practice Questions — Application

Q1 Identify the organelle(s) labelled 'A' in the following electron micrographs. Give the function of each organelle.

a)

b)
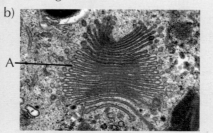

c)

d)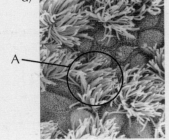

A

Q2 The images below each show a different type of cell.

a) Name organelle X in Image A.

b) Name organelle Y in Image B.

c) Which of the images is a plant cell? Explain your answer.

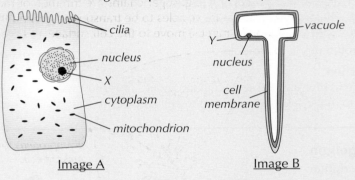

Image A

cilia

nucleus

X

cytoplasm

mitochondrion

Image B

vacuole

Y

nucleus

cell
membrane

Practice Questions — Fact Recall

Q1 Name the organelles labelled A-H on the plant cell below.

Q2 Name three organelles that can be
found in plant cells, but not in animal cells.

Q3 Describe the functions of the nucleus.

Q4 Give one function of a lysosome.

Q5 Describe how the structure of the rough
endoplasmic reticulum is different from
the smooth endoplasmic reticulum.

Q6 What is the function of the smooth
endoplasmic reticulum?

Q7 Which organelle is responsible for making lysosomes?

Q8 Name the organelle responsible for the separation of chromosomes
during cell division.

Q9 Draw a labelled cross-section of a cilium.

2. Organelles Working Together

There are loads of organelles, each with an important role. But it's when they work together that they start to become really impressive.

Protein production

Figure 1 shows the variety of organelles involved in protein production. Each one has a different role. Proteins are made at the ribosomes — the ribosomes on the rough endoplasmic reticulum (ER) make proteins that are excreted or attached to the cell membrane, whereas the free ribosomes in the cytoplasm make proteins that stay in the cytoplasm.

New proteins produced at the rough ER are folded and processed (e.g. sugar chains are added) in the rough ER. Then they're transported from the ER to the Golgi apparatus in vesicles. At the Golgi apparatus, the proteins may undergo further processing (e.g. sugar chains are trimmed or more are added). The proteins enter more vesicles to be transported around the cell. E.g. glycoproteins (found in mucus) move to the cell surface and are secreted.

Learning Objectives:

- Be able to outline the interrelationship between the organelles involved in the production and secretion of proteins.
- Be able to explain the importance of the cytoskeleton in providing mechanical strength to cells, aiding transport within cells and enabling cell movement.

Specification Reference 1.1.1

Tip: Protein production in prokaryotes is slightly different as they don't have the same organelles as eukaryotes.

Tip: Proteins may be stored at the rough endoplasmic reticulum until they are needed by the Golgi apparatus.

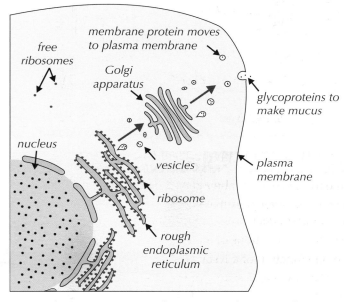

Figure 1: Protein production in a eukaryotic cell.

The cytoskeleton

The organelles in cells are surrounded by the cytoplasm. The cytoplasm is more than just a solution of chemicals though — it's got a network of protein threads running through it. These protein threads are called the cytoskeleton. In eukaryotic cells the protein threads are arranged as **microfilaments** (small solid strands) and **microtubules** (tiny protein cylinders). These are shown in Figure 4 on the next page.

The cytoskeleton has four main functions:

1. The microtubules and microfilaments support the cell's organelles, keeping them in position.

2. They also help to strengthen the cell and maintain its shape.

3. As well as this, they're responsible for the transport of organelles and materials within the cell.

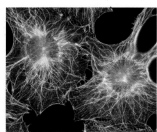

Figure 2: A fluorescent light micrograph of two cells and their cytoskeleton. The microfilaments appear purple, microtubules are shown in yellow and the nuclei are green.

Tip: A cytoskeleton is found in prokaryotes as well as eukaryotes, but the prokaryotic cytoskeleton contains different proteins.

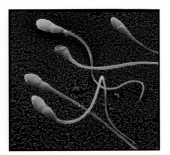

Figure 3: *Sperm cells are propelled by their cytoskeleton.*

Examples

- The movement of chromosomes when they separate during cell division depends on contraction of microtubules in the spindle (see page 41 for more on cell division).
- The movement of vesicles around the cell relies on cytoskeletal proteins.

4. The proteins of the cytoskeleton can also cause the cell to move.

Example

The movement of cilia and flagella is caused by the cytoskeletal protein filaments that run through them. So in the case of single cells that have a flagellum (e.g. sperm cells), the cytoskeleton propels the whole cell.

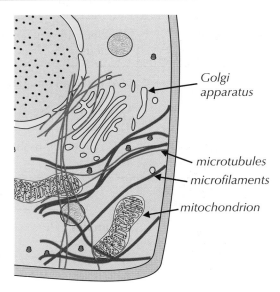

Figure 4: *Diagram showing part of a eukaryotic cell and its cytoplasm.*

Practice Questions — Application

Recent research has shown abnormalities in the Golgi apparatus in some brain cells in Alzheimer's sufferers. The Golgi apparatus in some cells were visualised as small, round, disconnected elements.

Q1 How would the appearance of normal Golgi apparatus differ to the abnormal ones described above?

Q2 Suggest what affect these altered Golgi apparatus might have on protein production.

Q3 Structural abnormalities have also been seen in the cytoskeleton of brain cells in some Alzheimer's sufferers. Suggest how abnormalities in the cytoskeleton may affect protein production.

Practice Questions — Fact Recall

Q1 Describe the role of the ribosomes and RER in protein production.

Q2 Describe the main functions of the cytoskeleton.

3. Prokaryotic Cells

Prokaryotic cells are different from eukaryotic cells.

Prokaryotes vs eukaryotes

The table below summaries the differences between prokaryotic and eukaryotic cells:

Prokaryotic cells	Eukaryotic cells
Extremely small cells (less than 2 µm diameter)	Larger cells (2-200 µm diameter)
DNA is circular	DNA is linear
No nucleus — DNA free in cytoplasm	Nucleus present — DNA is inside nucleus
Cell wall made of a polysaccharide called peptidoglycan	No cell wall (in animals), cellulose cell wall (in plants) or chitin cell wall (in fungi)
No membrane-bound organelles, e.g. no mitochondria	Many membrane-bound organelles
Small ribosomes (20 nm or less)	Larger ribosomes (over 20 nm)
Examples: *E. coli* bacterium, *Salmonella* bacterium	**Examples:** Human liver cell, yeast, amoeba

Bacterial cells

Prokaryotes like bacteria are roughly a tenth the size of eukaryotic cells. This means that normal microscopes aren't really powerful enough to look at their internal structure. The diagram below shows a bacterial cell as seen under an electron microscope (see page 18).

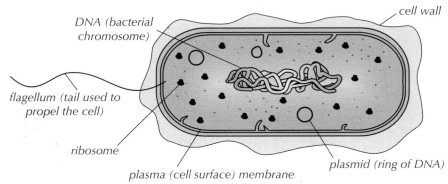

DNA (bacterial chromosome)

cell wall

flagellum (tail used to propel the cell)

ribosome

plasma (cell surface) membrane

plasmid (ring of DNA)

Learning Objective:

- Compare and contrast, with the aid of diagrams and electron micrographs, the structure and function of prokaryotic cells and eukaryotic cells.
  Specification Reference 1.1.1

Tip: A micrometre (µm) is one millionth of a metre, or 0.001 mm.

Tip: Prokaryotes are always single-celled organisms, but eukaryotes can be single-celled or multicellular.

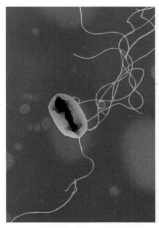

Figure 1: *A prokaryotic cell. The long strands extending from the cell are flagella.*

Tip: Flagella and plasmids aren't always present in prokaryotic cells.

Practice Questions — Fact Recall

Q1 Give three differences between prokaryotes and eukaryotes.

Q2 Give one similarity between prokaryotic and eukaryotic cells.

- Be able to calculate the linear magnification of an image.
- Be able to explain the difference between magnification and resolution.
- Be able to state the resolution and magnification that can be achieved by a light microscope, a transmission electron microscope and a scanning electron microscope.
- Be able to explain the need for staining samples for use in light microscopy and electron microscopy.

Specification Reference 1.1.1

Exam Tip

If you find rearranging formulas hard you can use a formula triangle to help. This is the formula triangle for magnification:

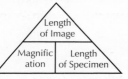

All you do is put your finger over the one you want and read off the formula. E.g. if you want the length of specimen you put your finger over that and it leaves behind length of image ÷ magnification.

4. Studying Cells — Microscopes

Investigating cells, and what's in them, involves donning your lab coat and digging out your trusty microscope.

Magnification and resolution of microscopes

We all know that microscopes produce a magnified image of a sample, but resolution is just as important...

Magnification

Magnification is how much bigger the image is than the specimen (the sample you're looking at). It's calculated using this formula:

$$\text{magnification} = \frac{\text{length of image}}{\text{length of specimen}}$$

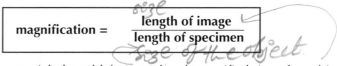

In the exam, you might be told the actual and magnified size of an object and then be asked to calculate the magnification. You can do this by using the formula above.

Examples

Calculating magnification

If you have a magnified image that's 5 mm wide and your specimen is 0.05 mm wide the magnification is:

$$\text{magnification} = \frac{\text{length of image}}{\text{length of specimen}}$$
$$= \frac{5}{0.05} = \times 100$$

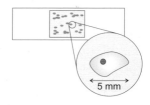

5 mm

Calculating length of image

If your specimen is 0.1 mm wide and the magnification of the microscope is × 20, then the length of the image is:

$$\text{length of image} = \text{magnification} \times \text{length of specimen}$$
$$= 20 \times 0.1 = 2 \text{ mm}$$

Calculating length of specimen

If you have a magnified image that's 5 mm wide and the magnification is × 50, then the length of the specimen is:

$$\text{length of specimen} = \frac{\text{length of image}}{\text{magnification}}$$
$$= \frac{5}{50} = 0.1 \text{ mm}$$

When you're calculating magnification you need to make sure that all lengths are in the same unit, e.g. all in millimetres. When dealing with microscopes these units can get pretty tiny. The table below shows common units:

Unit	How many millimetres it is:	To convert
Millimetre (mm)	1 mm	
Micrometre (µm)	0.001 mm	÷ 1000
Nanometre (nm)	0.000001 mm	÷ 1000

To convert from a smaller unit to a bigger unit you divide by 1000.
E.g. to convert 6 micrometres to millimetres you divide 6 by 1000 = 0.006 mm.
To go from a bigger unit to a smaller unit you times by 1000.

Resolution

Resolution is how detailed the image is. More specifically, it's how well a microscope distinguishes between two points that are close together. If a microscope lens can't separate two objects, then increasing the magnification won't help.

Tip: A microscope can't distinguish between objects that are smaller than its maximum resolution.

┌─ **Example** ─────────────

When you look at a car in the dark that's a long way away you see the two headlights as one light. This is because your eyes can't distinguish between the two points at that distance — your eyes produce a low resolution image. When the car gets a bit closer you can see both headlights — a higher resolution image.

Tip: The maximum resolution you can achieve through a light microscope is 0.2 μm (see next page). That means that any separate objects less than 0.2 μm apart from each other will be seen as one single object.

Practice Questions — Application

Q1 Image A shows a cartilage cell under a × 3150 microscope.

a) What is the diameter of the nucleus (labelled A) in millimetres?

b) What is the diameter of the cell (labelled B) in millimetres?

Q2 A researcher is examining some ribosomes under a microscope. Ribosomes are around 0.00002 mm long. How long will the image appear through a × 40 microscope? Give your answer in millimetres.

Image A

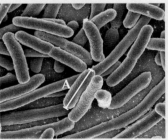

Exam Tip
Don't forget that when you're doing calculations the units need to be the same, e.g. all in millimetres, or all in micrometres.

Image B

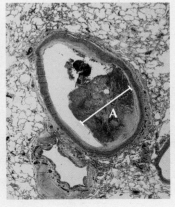

Image C

Q3 Rhinovirus particles are around 0.023 μm in diameter. They appear 0.035 mm under a microscope. What is the magnification of the microscope?

Q4 Image B shows some bacteria. It was taken using a × 7000 microscope. How long is the bacterium labelled A, in micrometres?

Q5 Image C shows a blood clot (labelled A) in an artery. The clot is 2 mm in diameter.

a) What is the magnification of the microscope?

b) The diameter of the artery is 3 mm. If the same specimen was examined under a × 50 microscope, what would the diameter of the artery in the image be?

Q6 A mitochondrion is 10 μm long. In a microscope image it is 10 mm. What is the magnification of the microscope?

Exam Tip
You're allowed a calculator in your exam — make sure you use one in calculation questions like these.

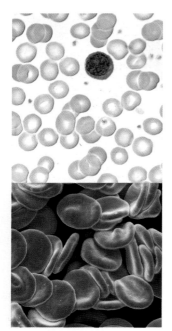

Types of microscope

Light microscopes

They use light (no surprises there). They have a lower resolution than electron microscopes. They have a maximum resolution of about 0.2 micrometres (μm). The maximum useful magnification of a light microscope is about × 1500.

Electron microscopes

Electron microscopes use electrons instead of light to form an image. They have a higher resolution than light microscopes so give more detailed images.

Types of electron microscope

There are two types of electron microscope:

Transmission electron microscope (TEM)

TEMs use electromagnets to focus a beam of electrons, which is then transmitted through the specimen. Denser parts of the specimen absorb more electrons, which makes them look darker on the image you end up with.

TEMs are good because they provide high resolution images, so they can be used to look at very small organelles, e.g. ribosomes. They can also be used to look at the internal structures of organelles in detail. But specimens viewed on TEMs need to be quite thinly sliced. The angle at which specimens are cut can affect how they appear (see Figure 2).

Scanning electron microscope (SEM)

SEMs scan a beam of electrons across the specimen. This knocks off electrons from the specimen, which are gathered in a cathode ray tube to form an image. The images produced show the surface of the specimen and can be 3-D. But they give lower resolution images than TEMs.

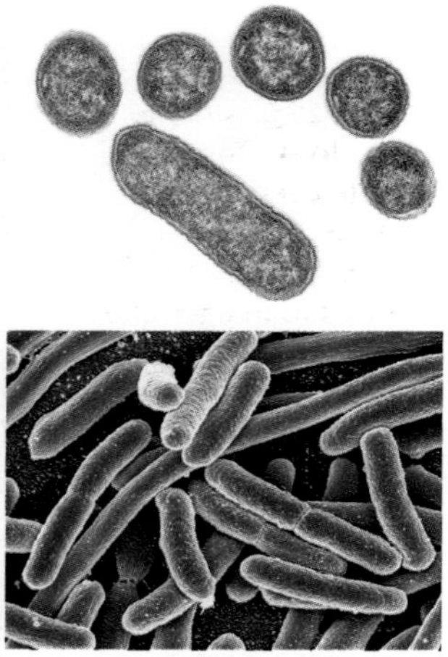

Figure 1: Red blood cells seen under a light microscope (top) and an electron microscope (bottom).

Comparing types of microscope

You need to know about the magnification and resolution of light microscopes and both types of electron microscope. All the important numbers are shown in Figure 3.

	light microscope	TEM	SEM
maximum resolution	0.2 μm	0.0001 μm	0.005 μm
maximum magnification	x 1500	more than x 1 000 000	less than x 1 000 000

Figure 3: Comparison table of light and electron microscope features.

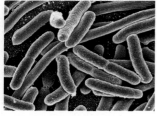

Figure 2: A TEM (top), and SEM (bottom) of E.coli bacteria. The E.coli in the TEM have been cut at different angles.

Staining samples

In light microscopes and TEMs, the beam of light (or electrons) passes through the object being viewed. An image is produced because some parts of the object absorb more light (or electrons) than others. Sometimes the object being viewed is completely transparent. This makes the whole thing look white because the light rays (or electrons) just pass straight through. To get round this, the object can be stained (see next page).

For the light microscope, this means using some kind of dye. Common stains are methylene blue and eosin. The stain is taken up by some parts of the object more than others — the contrast makes the different parts show up (see Figures 4 and 5).

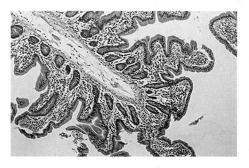

Figure 4: *An eosin stained specimen, as seen through a light microscope.*

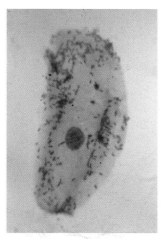

Figure 5: *A cheek cell stained with methylene blue.*

For the electron microscope, objects are dipped in a solution of heavy metals (like lead). The metal ions scatter the electrons, again creating contrast. The image produced is black and white (see Figure 6).

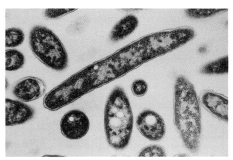

Figure 6: *A black and white electron micrograph image of bacteria.*

Tip: Different dyes are used to stain different and specific parts of the cell. For example, methylene blue stains RNA/DNA whereas eosin is used to highlight the cell membrane. This allows specific parts of the cell to be identified.

Either way, an image is produced because some parts of the object show up darker than others.

Tip: Electron micrograph images are always black and white even when stained. Colour is sometimes artificially added to images after they've been made — don't confuse this with staining.

Practice Questions — Application

Q1 Read the information in the table below.

object	diameter / µm
E.coli bacterium	2.0
nuclear pore	0.05
human egg cell	100
DNA helix	0.002
mitochondrion	0.7
influenza virus	0.1

For each object, state the type of microscope(s) it could be resolved by.

Q2 Two teams of scientists are studying the human immunodeficiency virus (HIV). HIV has a diameter of 0.12 µm. Team One are focusing on HIV surface proteins and how they bind to immune system cells. The second team is studying the internal structure of the virus. Suggest what specific type of microscope each team might use during their studies. Explain your answer.

Exam Tip
If you understand the differences between the types of microscopes, you'll then be able to decide which microscope is the most useful in any given situation.

Exam Tip
Make sure you understand the difference between resolution and magnification — you could be asked to explain it in the exam.

Q1   What is the formula for calculating the magnification of a microscope?

Q2   Explain the difference between magnification and resolution.

Q3   How do transmission electron microscopes work?

Q4   How do scanning electron microscopes work?

Q5   What is the maximum resolution for:

   a) a light microscope,

   b) an transmission electron microscope,

   c) a scanning electron microscope?

Q6   Which has a higher maximum magnification, a TEM or SEM?

Q7   What type of microscope would you use to study an object that is 0.001 µm long?

Q8   Explain why some samples need to be stained before they can be viewed under a microscope.

Section Summary

Make sure you know:

- That eukaryotic cells are more complex than prokaryotic cells. They are larger and contain many more organelles.
- That plant and animal cells are both eukaryotes. Plant cells have the same organelles as animal cells, but they may also contain a cell wall with plasmodesmata, a vacuole and chloroplasts.
- The structure, function and appearance of the following eukaryotic organelles: the plasma membrane, cell wall, nucleus, nucleolus, lysosomes, ribosomes, rough and smooth endoplasmic reticulum, vesicles, Golgi apparatus, mitochondria, chloroplasts, centrioles, cilia and flagella.
- That organelles work together to make proteins. Proteins are made at the ribosomes, transported to the Golgi apparatus in vesicles and are then transported around the cell before being secreted.
- That the cytoplasm contains protein threads known as the cytoskeleton. In eukaryotes, the protein threads are arranged as microfilaments and microtubules.
- That the cytoskeleton is used to support the cell's organelles, strengthen the cell, transport organelles and material within the cell and to move cells.
- That prokaryotes are smaller than eukaryotes and include bacteria. They have a fewer organelles and no nucleus or mitochondria.
- That cells and organelles can be studied using microscopes.
- How to calculate magnification using: magnification = length of image ÷ length of specimen.
- The difference between magnification (how much bigger the sample is) and resolution (how detailed the sample is).
- That a transmission electron microscope (TEM) transmits a beam of electrons through the specimen, and that a scanning electron microscope (SEM) scans a beam of electrons across the specimen.
- That the maximum resolution for a light microscope is 0.2 µm, for TEM it's 0.0001 µm and for SEM it's 0.005 µm.
- That the maximum magnification for a light microscope is x 1500, for TEM it's more than x 1 000 000 and for SEM it's less than x 1 000 000.
- That staining samples is often required before using a microscope in order to see the different cellular structures and organelles.

Exam-style Questions

1   A scientist is studying secretory epithelial cells from the stomach under a light microscope.

        The microscope has a magnification of × 100 and a resolution of 0.2 μm.

(a) (i)   The ribosomes in the epithelial cells are 25 nm in diameter. Will the scientist be able to see them using the light microscope? Explain your answer.

(2 marks)

   (ii) Describe the difference the scientist could expect to see if he compared the ribosomes in the stomach cells to those from bacterial cells.

(1 mark)

  (iii) State **two** differences the scientist would observe if he compared the stomach cell to a plant cell.

(2 marks)

(b)   The scientist sees an image of an epithelial cell that is 4 mm in diameter. Calculate the actual diameter of the cell.

(2 marks)

(c)   One of the main functions of secretory epithelial cells in the stomach is to produce and secrete digestive enzymes.

         Describe the role of each organelle involved in the **production** and **secretion** of extracellular proteins.

         In your answer, you should use appropriate technical terms, spelled correctly.

(6 marks)

2   Abnormal mitochondria have been found in diseased heart tissue, suggesting a link between mitochondria and heart disease. To investigate this further, a group of scientists produced a strain of mice with abnormal mitochondria.

        The abnormal mice developed symptoms of heart disease after just one year. Normal mice showed similar symptoms after two years.

(a)   Suggest why abnormal mitochondria might be problematic in heart tissue.

(2 marks)

(b)   Fig. 2.1 (next page) shows mitochondria in the normal mice and the abnormal mice.

   (i)   Describe **two** differences between the mitochondria found in the abnormal and normal mice.

(2 marks)

   (ii) The mitochondrion labelled **A** in the normal mouse is about 1.5 μm in length. Calculate the magnification of the image.

(2 marks)

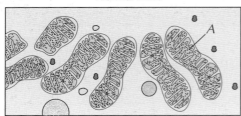
Normal mice

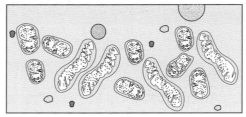
Abnormal mice

Fig. 2.1

(c) "A person's risk of developing heart disease increases with age."
How do the results of this study help to support this statement?

(1 mark)

3 Penicillins are a group of antibiotics that are only effective against prokaryotic cells.
They work by inhibiting cell wall synthesis, leading to cell lysis (bursting).

(a) Explain why penicillin antibiotics can clear bacterial infections in
humans without harming the infected individual's cells.

(2 marks)

(b) The electron micrograph in Fig. 3.1 shows an intact *Staphyloccus aureus*
bacterium (right) and one undergoing lysis (left).

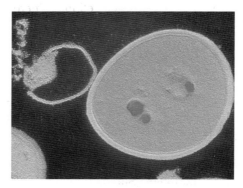

Fig. 3.1

(i) Suggest **one** reason why an electron microscope was used
to view these cells rather than a light microscope.

(2 marks)

(ii) In order to produce an electron micrograph, the specimen is usually dipped in
a solution of heavy metals before being viewed. Explain why this is done.

(3 marks)

(c) Give **two** ways in which you could distinguish between a prokaryotic cell
and a eukaryotic cell in an electron micrograph.

(2 marks)

1. Cell Membranes — The Basics

Cell membranes are the boundaries of cells, but there's an awful lot more to them than that...

Membrane function

Cells (and many of the organelles inside them) are surrounded by membranes that have a wide range of functions. You need to be able to describe the functions of membranes at the cell surface, as well as those within cells.

Membranes at the cell surface (plasma membranes)

Plasma membranes control which substances enter and leave the cell. They're **partially permeable** — they let some molecules through but not others.

Substances can move across the plasma membrane by diffusion, osmosis or active transport (see pages 29-33). Plasma membranes also allow recognition by other cells (e.g. the cells of the immune system, see p. 162) and cell communication (see p. 27).

Membranes within cells

The membranes around organelles (see p. 8-11) divide the cell into different compartments. This makes different functions more efficient.

┌─ **Example** ─────────────────────────────
The substances needed for respiration (like enzymes) are kept together inside mitochondria by the mitochondria's outer membrane.
└──

The membranes of some organelles are folded, increasing their surface area and making chemical reactions more efficient.

┌─ **Example** ─────────────────────────────
The inner membrane of a mitochondrion contains enzymes needed for respiration. It has a large surface area, which increases the number of enzymes present and makes respiration more efficient.
└──

Membranes can form vesicles to transport substances between different areas of the cell (see p. 10).

┌─ **Example** ─────────────────────────────
Proteins are transported in vesicles from the rough endoplasmic reticulum to the Golgi apparatus during protein synthesis.
└──

Membranes within cells are also partially permeable so they can control which substances enter and leave the organelle.

┌─ **Example** ─────────────────────────────
RNA (see page 127) leaves the nucleus via the nuclear membrane (also called the nuclear envelope). DNA is too large to pass through the partially permeable membrane, so it remains in the nucleus.
└──

Learning Objectives:

- Be able to outline the roles of membranes within cells and at the surface of cells.
- Know that plasma (cell surface) membranes are partially permeable barriers.
- Be able to describe, with the aid of diagrams, the fluid mosaic model of membrane structure.
- Be able to describe the roles of the following components of the cell membrane:
  - phospholipids
  - cholesterol
  - proteins
  - glycolipids
  - glycoproteins.
- Be able to outline the effect of changing temperature on membrane structure and permeability.

Specification Reference 1.1.2

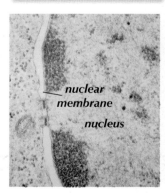

Figure 1: *Electron micrograph showing the nucleus surrounded by the nuclear membrane.*

Membrane structure

The structure of all membranes is basically the same. They're all composed of lipids (mainly a type called phospholipids), proteins and carbohydrates (usually attached to proteins or lipids).

Tip: The phospholipid bilayer is ~ 7 nm thick.

Tip: For more on models and theories, see p. 1.

In 1972, the **fluid mosaic model** was suggested to describe the arrangement of molecules in the membrane — see Figure 2. In the model, phospholipid molecules form a continuous, double layer (called a bilayer). This bilayer is 'fluid' because the phospholipids are constantly moving. Protein molecules are scattered through the bilayer, like tiles in a mosaic. Some proteins have a polysaccharide (carbohydrate) chain attached — these are called **glycoproteins**. Some lipids also have a polysaccharide chain attached — these are called **glycolipids**. Cholesterol molecules are also present within the bilayer.

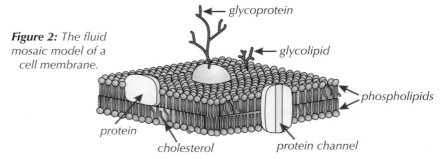

Figure 2: The fluid mosaic model of a cell membrane.

glycoprotein
glycolipid
phospholipids
protein
cholesterol
protein channel

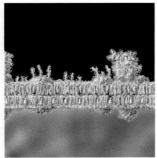

Figure 3: A computer model of the fluid mosaic model.

Membrane components

There are five main components you need to know about:

Phospholipids

Phospholipid molecules form a barrier to dissolved (water-soluble) substances. Phospholipids have a 'head' and a 'tail'. The head is **hydrophilic** — it attracts water. The tail is **hydrophobic** — it repels water.

Tip: A polar molecule has one end with a slightly positive charge and one end with a slightly negative charge. These charges are nowhere near as strong as the positive or negative charge on an ion, but they do help polar molecules to dissolve in water. Non-polar substances have no charges.

The molecules automatically arrange themselves into a bilayer — the heads face out towards the water on either side of the membrane (see Figure 4).

The centre of the bilayer is hydrophobic so the membrane doesn't allow water-soluble substances (like ions and polar molecules) to diffuse through it. Small, non-polar substances (e.g. carbon dioxide) and water can diffuse through the membrane (see p. 29).

phospholipid bilayer
phospholipid head
phospholipid tail

Figure 4: Phospholipid bilayer.

Tip: Water is actually a polar molecule, but it can diffuse (by osmosis) through the cell membrane because it's so small (see page 29).

Cholesterol

Cholesterol gives the membrane stability. It is a type of lipid (fat) that's present in all cell membranes (except bacterial cell membranes). Cholesterol fits between the phospholipids (see Figure 5).

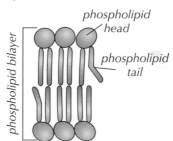

phospholipid
cholesterol

Figure 5: Cholesterol in the membrane.

Cholesterol binds to the hydrophobic tails of the phospholipids, causing them to pack more closely together. This makes the membrane less fluid and more stable. Cholesterol also has hydrophobic regions, so it's able to create a further barrier to polar substances moving through the membrane.

Tip: There's more on phospholipids and cholesterol on pages 116-117.

Proteins

Proteins control what enters and leaves the cell. Some proteins form channels in the membrane (see page 32) — these allow small, charged particles through. Other proteins (called carrier proteins) transport larger molecules and charged particles across the membrane by active transport and facilitated diffusion (see pages 32-33). Proteins also act as receptors for molecules (e.g. hormones) in cell signalling (see page 27). When a molecule binds to the protein, a chemical reaction is triggered inside the cell.

Tip: Charged particles include ions and polar molecules.

Glycolipids and glycoproteins

Glycolipids and glycoproteins stabilise the membrane by forming hydrogen bonds with surrounding water molecules. They act as receptors for messenger molecules in cell signalling and are sites where drugs, hormones and antibodies bind (see pages 27-28). They're also antigens — cell surface molecules involved in self-recognition and the immune response (see page 161).

Tip: A hydrogen bond is a weak bond that forms between a slightly positively-charged hydrogen atom in one molecule and a slightly negatively-charged atom or group in another molecule, e.g. oxygen.

Temperature and membranes

Cell membranes are affected by temperature — it affects how much the phospholipids in the bilayer can move, which affects membrane structure.

Temperatures below 0 °C

The phospholipids don't have much energy, so they can't move very much. They're packed closely together and the membrane is rigid. But channel proteins and carrier proteins in the membrane denature (lose structure and function), increasing the permeability of the membrane (see Point 1, Figure 6). Ice crystals may form and pierce the membrane, making it highly permeable when it thaws.

Tip: Remember, glycolipids are carbohydrates attached to lipids, and glycoproteins are carbohydrates attached to proteins. Glyco is Greek for sweet or sugar and it refers to the carbohydrate bit.

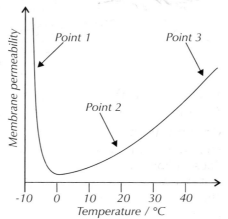

Figure 6: Graph to show the effect of temperature on membrane permeability.

Temperatures between 0 and 45 °C

The phospholipids can move around and aren't packed as tightly together — the membrane is partially permeable (see Point 2, Figure 6). As the temperature increases the phospholipids move more because they have more energy — this increases the permeability of the membrane.

Temperatures above 45 °C

The phospholipid bilayer starts to melt (break down) and the membrane becomes more permeable. Water inside the cell expands, putting pressure on the membrane. Channel proteins and carrier proteins in the membrane denature so they can't control what enters or leaves the cell — this increases the permeability of the membrane (Point 3, Figure 6).

Figure 7: Beetroot can be used to show how temperature affects membrane structure. The amount of red pigment outside of the cell (in the tube) increases as the temperature increases.

Practice Questions — Application

Q1 Suggest a function of each of the following membranes:
 a) the membrane surrounding a chloroplast,
 b) the membranes within chloroplasts,
 c) the membrane surrounding a bacterial cell.

Q2 Chloride ions (Cl⁻) need to pass through the plasma membrane to get inside the cell. How might they move across the membrane?

Q3 The protein content of a typical cell membrane is around 50%. In energy-releasing organelles, such as mitochondria, the amount rises to around 75%. Suggest a reason for this difference.

Q4 A person removes some raspberries from the freezer that have frozen solid and leaves them on a plate to defrost. When he returns, there's a red puddle on the plate around the fruit. Use your knowledge of cell membranes to explain what has happened.

Practice Questions — Fact Recall

Q1 Explain what is meant when a cell membrane is described as being 'partially permeable'.

Q2 Identify the structures labelled A-E in the diagram below.

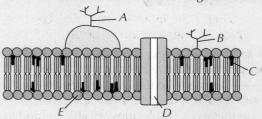

Q3 Explain the meaning of the terms 'hydrophilic' and hydrophobic'.

Q4 Explain why the plasma membrane is an effective barrier against water-soluble substances.

Q5 How does the plasma membrane control what enters and leaves the cell?

Q6 Give the function(s) of the following membrane components:
a) cholesterol,
b) glycoproteins and glycolipids.

Q7 Describe and explain what happens to the plasma membrane at temperatures above 45 °C.

2. Cell Membranes and Signalling

The cells in your body all need to work together — and to do that, they need to communicate. The cell membrane plays a key role in this communication.

Cell signalling

Cells need to communicate with each other to control processes inside the body and to respond to changes in the environment. Cells communicate with each other by cell signalling, which uses messenger molecules.

Cell signalling starts when one cell releases a messenger molecule (e.g. a hormone). This molecule travels to another cell (e.g. in the blood). The messenger molecule is detected by the cell because it binds to a receptor on its cell membrane. The binding then triggers a change in the cell, e.g. a series of chemical signals is set off.

Membrane receptors

The cell membrane is important in the signalling process. Membrane-bound proteins act as receptors for messenger molecules.

Receptor proteins have specific shapes — only messenger molecules with a complementary shape can bind to them. Different cells have different types of receptors — they respond to different messenger molecules. A cell that responds to a particular messenger molecule is called a **target cell**. Figure 1 shows how messenger molecules are able to bind to target cells but not to non-target cells.

Learning Objectives:

- Be able to explain the term cell signalling.
- Be able to explain the role of membrane-bound receptors as sites where hormones and drugs can bind.

Specification Reference 1.1.2

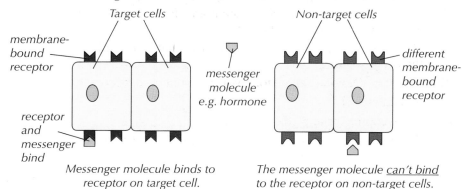

Messenger molecule binds to receptor on target cell.

The messenger molecule can't bind to the receptor on non-target cells.

Figure 1: *Messenger molecules and membrane-bound receptors.*

Tip: Complementary shapes fit together, e.g.

Non-complementary shapes don't fit together, e.g.

Tip: You don't just get a single type of receptor on each cell. Every cell type has a specific combination of many different receptors.

Hormones as messenger molecules

Many messenger molecules are hormones. Hormones work by binding to receptors in cell membranes and triggering a response in the cell.

┌─ **Example 1 — Glucagon** ─────────────

Glucagon is a hormone that's released when there isn't enough glucose in the blood. It binds to receptors on liver cells, causing the liver cells to break down stores of glycogen to glucose.

┌─ **Example 2 — FSH** ─────────────

FSH is a hormone that's released by the pituitary gland during the menstrual cycle. It binds to receptors on cells in the ovaries, causing an egg to mature ready for ovulation.

Tip: A hormone can trigger different responses in different cells. For example, in men, FSH binds to cells in the testes and initiates the production of sperm.

The role of drugs

Many drugs work by binding to receptors in cell membranes.
They either trigger a response in the cell, or block the receptor and prevent it from working.

Example 1 — Morphine

The body produces chemicals called endorphins, to relieve pain.
Endorphins bind to opioid receptors in the brain and reduce the transmission of pain signals. Morphine is a drug used to relieve pain.
It works by binding to the same opioid receptors as endorphins, also triggering a reduction in pain signals.

Example 2 — Antihistamines

Cell damage causes the release of a chemical called histamine. Histamine binds to receptors on the surface of other cells and causes inflammation.
Antihistamines work by blocking histamine receptors on cell surfaces.
This prevents histamine from binding to the cell and stops inflammation.

Practice Questions — Application

The diagrams below show a messenger molecule, its membrane bound receptor and a molecule of an antagonistic drug. The drug inhibits the action of the messenger molecule.

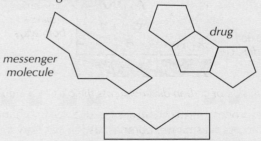

Tip: Don't worry if you're not sure what antagonistic means — all the information you need is given in the question. (But just so you know, an antagonistic molecule blocks the action of another molecule).

Q1 Using the information in the diagrams and your own knowledge, explain how the drug works.

Q2 The diagram on the right shows a mutated version of the membrane-bound receptor. Explain why cells with only the mutated version of the receptor can't respond to the messenger molecule.

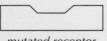

mutated receptor

Q3 The messenger molecule is only able to produce a response in liver cells. Suggest why this is the case.

28   Unit 1: Section 2 Cell Membranes

3. Exchange Across Plasma Membranes

There are many ways substances move in and out of cells across the membrane. First up, diffusion and osmosis.

Diffusion

Diffusion is the net movement of particles (molecules or ions) from an area of higher concentration to an area of lower concentration — see Figure 1. Molecules will diffuse both ways, but the net movement will be to the area of lower concentration. This continues until particles are evenly distributed throughout the liquid or gas. The concentration gradient is the path from an area of higher concentration to an area of lower concentration. Particles diffuse down a concentration gradient.

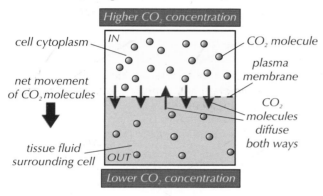

Figure 1: *Diffusion of carbon dioxide across the plasma membrane.*

Diffusion is a passive process — no energy is needed for it to happen. Particles can diffuse across plasma membranes, as long as they can move freely through the membrane.

Examples

- Small, non-polar molecules such as oxygen and carbon dioxide are able to diffuse easily through spaces between phospholipids.

- Water is also small enough to fit between phospholipids, so it's able to diffuse across plasma membranes even though it's polar.

Factors affecting the rate of diffusion

There are three main factors that affect the rate of diffusion:

- The concentration gradient — the higher it is, the faster the rate of diffusion.

- The thickness of the exchange surface — the thinner the exchange surface (i.e. the shorter the distance the particles travel), the faster the rate.

- The surface area — the larger the surface area (e.g. of the plasma membrane), the faster the rate of diffusion.

Osmosis

Osmosis is the diffusion of water molecules across a partially permeable membrane, from an area of higher water potential (i.e. a higher concentration of water molecules) to an area of lower water potential (i.e. a lower concentration of water molecules) — see Figure 2 on the next page.

Learning Objectives:

- Be able to explain what is meant by passive transport and diffusion.

- Be able to explain what is meant by osmosis, in terms of water potential. (No calculations of water potential will be required.)

- Be able to recognise and explain the effects that solutions of different water potentials can have upon animal and plant cells.

- Be able to explain what is meant by facilitated diffusion including the role of membrane proteins.

- Be able to explain what is meant by active transport.

- Be able to explain what is meant by endocytosis and exocytosis.

Specification Reference 1.1.2

Tip: Large molecules, ions and polar substances need help to cross the plasma membrane — see p. 32.

Tip: Water can also move across the membrane through protein channels (see p. 32) called aquaporins.

Water potential is the potential (likelihood) of water molecules to diffuse out of or into a solution.

Pure water has a water potential of zero. Adding solutes to pure water lowers its water potential — so the water potential of any solution is always negative. The more negative the water potential, the stronger the concentration of solutes in the solution.

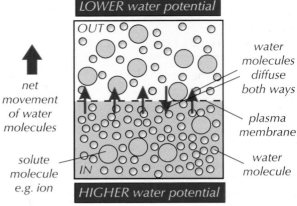

Figure 2: Osmosis across the plasma membrane.

— **Example** —
Glass A contains pure water — it's got a water potential of zero. Glass B contains a solution of orange squash. The orange squash molecules are a solute. They lower the concentration of the water molecules. This means that the water potential of the orange squash is lower than the water potential of pure water.

Water potential and cells

Cells are affected by the water potential of the surrounding solution. Water moves in or out of a cell by osmosis. How much moves in or out depends on the water potential of the surrounding solution. Animal and plant cells behave differently in different solutions.

Isotonic solutions

If two solutions have the same water potential they're said to be isotonic. Cells in an isotonic solution won't lose or gain any water — there's no net movement of water molecules because there's no difference in water potential between the cell and the surrounding solution. Both plant and animal cells will stay the same when placed in an isotonic solution — see Figure 3.

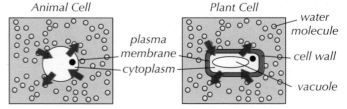

Figure 3: Cells in isotonic solutions.

<u>No</u> net movement of water.

Hypotonic solutions

If a cell is placed in a solution that has a higher water potential, water will move into the cell by osmosis. Solutions with a higher water potential compared with the inside of the cell are called hypotonic. An animal cell in a hypotonic solution will swell and eventually burst (see Figure 4, next page).

If a plant cell is placed in a hypotonic solution, the vacuole will swell and the contents of the vacuole and cytoplasm will push against the cell wall (see Figure 4). This causes the cell to become **turgid** (swollen). The cell won't burst because the inelastic cell wall is able to withstand the increase in pressure.

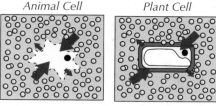

Net movement of water *into* the cell.

Figure 4: *Cells in hypotonic solutions.*

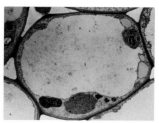

Figure 6a: *A turgid plant cell. The full vacuole (blue) is pushing against the cell wall.*

Hypertonic solutions

If a cell is placed in a solution that has a lower water potential, water will move out of the cell by osmosis. Solutions with a lower water potential than the cell are called hypertonic. If an animal cell is placed in a hypertonic solution it will shrink (see Figure 5). If a plant cell is placed in a hypertonic solution it will become **flaccid** (limp). The cytoplasm and plasma membrane will eventually pull away from the cell wall (again, see Figure 5). This is called **plasmolysis**.

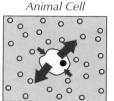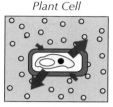

Net movement of water *out of* the cell.

Figure 5: *Cells in hypertonic solutions.*

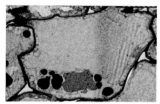

Figure 6b: *A flaccid plant cell. Water has left the vacuole.*

> **Tip:** A hypertonic solution would have a strong concentration of solutes compared to the cell.

Practice Questions — Application

Q1 The photograph on the right shows ink diffusing through a beaker of water. Explain what is happening to the ink molecules.

Q2 Describe the movement of water molecules in each of the following situations:

a) Human cheek cells with a water potential of -300 kPa are placed in a salt solution with a water potential of -325 kPa.

b) Apple slices with a water potential of -750 kPa are placed in a beaker of pure water.

c) Orange squash with a water potential of -450 kPa is sealed in a length of Visking tubing and suspended in a solution of equal water potential.

Q3 Potato cells with a water potential of -350 kPa are placed in sucrose solutions with varying water potentials. The water potential of each solution is shown in the table below.

Solution	Water potential
1	-250 kPa
2	-500 kPa
3	-1000 kPa

a) After 15 minutes, the potato cells in solution 1 have become turgid. Explain why this has happened.

b) Predict what will happen to the cells in solutions 2 and 3. Explain your answers.

> **Tip:** Water potential is usually measured in kilopascals (or kPa). It's actually a unit of pressure.

> **Tip:** Remember, a higher water potential is closer to 0 (the water potential of pure water).

> **Tip:** Visking tubing is a partially permeable membrane — it's used a lot in osmosis and diffusion experiments.

> **Tip:** Remember — small, non-polar substances and water can diffuse directly through the membrane.

> **Exam Tip**
> Always say down the concentration gradient in the exam, not across or along — or you won't get the marks.

> **Tip:** Carrier proteins are sometimes called transport proteins.

Facilitated diffusion

Large molecules, most polar molecules (e.g. glucose) and ions (e.g. sodium ions) can't diffuse directly through the phospholipid bilayer of the cell membrane. Instead they diffuse through carrier proteins or channel proteins in the cell membrane — this is called facilitated diffusion.

Like diffusion, facilitated diffusion moves particles down a concentration gradient, from a higher to a lower concentration. It's also a passive process — it doesn't use energy. But unlike diffusion, there are two types of membrane protein involved — carrier proteins and channel proteins.

Carrier proteins

Carrier proteins move large molecules (including polar molecules and ions) into or out of the cell, down their concentration gradient. Different carrier proteins facilitate the diffusion of different molecules.

Example

GLUT1 is a carrier protein found in almost all animal cells. It specifically helps to transport glucose across the plasma membrane.

Here's how carrier proteins work:

- First, a large molecule attaches to a carrier protein in the membrane.
- Then, the protein changes shape.
- This releases the molecule on the opposite side of the membrane — see Figure 7.

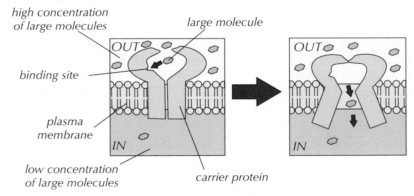

Figure 7: *Movement of a molecule by a carrier protein.*

Channel proteins

Channel proteins form pores in the membrane for smaller ions and polar molecules to diffuse through, down their concentration gradient (see Figure 9). Different channel proteins facilitate the diffusion of different particles.

Figure 8: *Computer model showing a cross section of a protein channel in the phospholipid bilayer.*

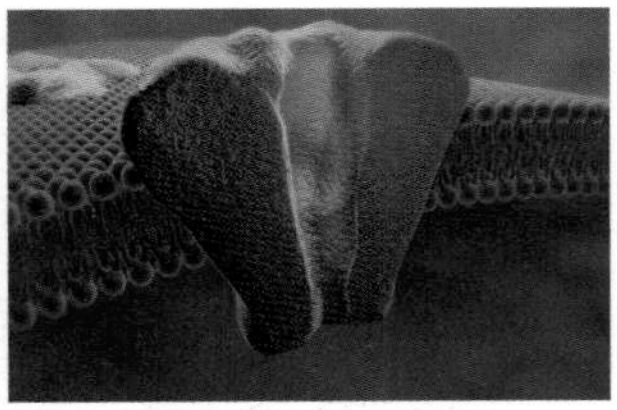

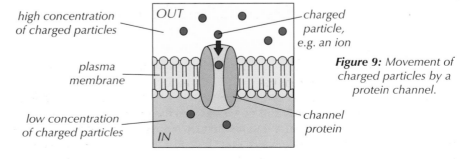

Figure 9: *Movement of charged particles by a protein channel.*

Active transport

Active transport uses energy to move molecules and ions across plasma membranes, against a concentration gradient. This process involves carrier proteins and is pretty similar to facilitated diffusion — see Figure 10. A molecule attaches to the carrier protein, the protein changes shape and this moves the molecule across the membrane, releasing it on the other side. The only difference is that energy is used (from ATP — a common source of energy used in the cell), to move the solute against its concentration gradient.

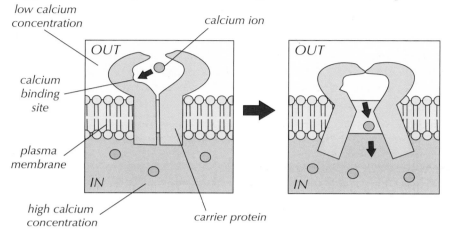

Figure 10: The active transport of calcium ions.

Endocytosis

Some molecules are way too large to be taken into a cell by carrier proteins, e.g. proteins, lipids and some carbohydrates. Instead a cell can surround a substance with a section of its plasma membrane. The membrane then pinches off to form a vesicle inside the cell containing the ingested substance — the substance has been taken in by endocytosis (see Figure 11).

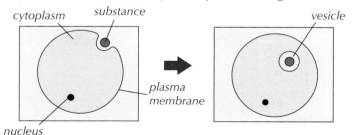

Figure 11: The process of endocytosis.

Some cells also take in much larger objects by endocytosis — for example, some white blood cells (mainly phagocytes, see page 161) use endocytosis to take in things like microorganisms and dead cells so that they can destroy them.

Exocytosis

Some substances produced by the cell (e.g. digestive enzymes, hormones, lipids) need to be released from the cell — this is done by exocytosis (see Figure 13, next page). Vesicles containing these substances pinch off from the sacs of the Golgi apparatus and move towards the plasma membrane. The vesicles fuse with the plasma membrane and release their contents outside the cell. Some substances (like membrane proteins) aren't released outside the cell — instead they are inserted straight into the plasma membrane.

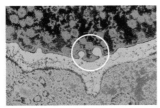

Figure 12: Vesicles containing substances for secretion breaking through the plasma membrane (circled).

Tip: There's more on vesicles and the Golgi apparatus on p. 10.

Exam Tip
Always be specific about which membrane you're talking about in the exam — don't just say, 'fuses with the cell membrane' if what you mean is 'fuses with the cell surface (plasma) membrane'.

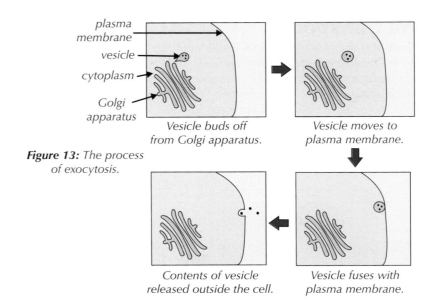

Vesicle buds off from Golgi apparatus.

Vesicle moves to plasma membrane.

Contents of vesicle released outside the cell.

Vesicle fuses with plasma membrane.

Figure 13: The process of exocytosis.

Practice Questions — Application

Q1 The diagram below shows a gap between two neurones. Each neurone is surrounded by a membrane. Chemical messengers are secreted from the membrane of neurone 1 and travel across the gap to the membrane of neurone 2, where they bind with cell surface receptors.

a) Name structure Z.

b) Describe what is happening in steps A to C on the diagram.

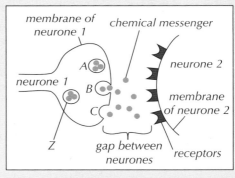

Once the chemical messengers bind to the receptors, they cause sodium ions (Na$^+$) to move across the membrane of neurone 2, down a concentration gradient.

c) Suggest how the sodium ions might travel across the membrane.

Q2 ATP is produced by mitochondria during aerobic respiration. The overall equation for this process can be written as:

glucose + oxygen → carbon dioxide + water + ATP

The graph below shows the relationship between the relative rates of oxygen consumption and the active transport of sodium ions across epithelial cells.

a) Describe the relationship shown by the graph.

b) Suggest an explanation for this relationship.

c) What effect would the rate of the facilitated diffusion of sodium ions have on the rate of oxygen consumption?

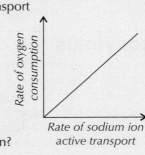

Summary of transport mechanisms

You've covered a lot of different transport mechanisms in this section, so here's a handy table to help you remember the similarities and differences:

Type of transport:	Description
Diffusion (see p. 29)	▪ Net movement of particles from an area of higher concentration to an area of lower concentration. ▪ Passive process — doesn't require energy.
Osmosis (see pages 29-30)	▪ Movement of water molecules across a partially permeable membrane from an area of higher water potential to an area of lower water potential. ▪ Passive process — doesn't require energy.
Facilitated diffusion (see p. 32)	▪ Net movement of particles from an area of higher concentration to an area of lower concentration. ▪ Uses carrier proteins to aid the diffusion of large molecules (including ions and polar molecules) through the plasma membrane. ▪ Uses channel proteins to aid the diffusion of smaller ions and polar molecules through the plasma membrane. ▪ Passive process — doesn't require energy.
Active transport (see p. 33)	▪ Movement of molecules against a concentration gradient. ▪ Uses carrier proteins to transport molecules. ▪ Active process — requires energy (ATP).
Endocytosis (see p. 33)	▪ Movement of large molecules (e.g. proteins) or objects (e.g. dead cells) into a cell. ▪ The plasma membrane surrounds a substance and then pinches off to form a vesicle inside the cell. ▪ Active process — requires energy.
Exocytosis (see pages 33-34)	▪ Movement of molecules out of a cell. ▪ Vesicles fuse with the plasma membrane and release their contents. ▪ Active process — requires energy.

Exam Tip
Make sure you know the definitions of diffusion and osmosis off by heart.

Exam Tip
Make sure you know what types of molecules (e.g. large/small, polar/ non-polar/ionic) are moved by the different types of transport.

Practice Question — Application

Q1 Copy and complete the table to show which kind of transport could be used in each case. The first column has been done for you.

Transport system	A plant cell taking in water	Calcium ions moving into a cell against a concentration gradient	A muscle cell taking in polar glucose molecules	A white blood cell taking in anthrax bacteria
Osmosis	✓			
Facilitated diffusion using channel proteins	✓			
Facilitated diffusion using carrier proteins	✗			
Active transport using carrier proteins	✗			
Endocytosis	✗			
Exocytosis	✗			

Tip: Calcium ions are charged, but relatively small.

Tip: Glucose is a polar molecule, but it's also relatively large.

Tip: If you're struggling with this table, take a look back at pages 29-34. You need to think about the type of substance being transported in each case.

Practice Questions — Fact Recall

Q1 What is diffusion?

Q2 Is diffusion an active or passive process?

Q3 What type of molecules are able to diffuse through the plasma membrane?

Q4 Describe the difference between simple diffusion through a plasma membrane and facilitated diffusion through a plasma membrane.

Q5 Define osmosis.

Q6 Define the term 'water potential'.

Q7 Describe and explain what will happen to each of the following:

a) an animal cell placed in a hypotonic solution,

b) a plant cell placed in a hypotonic solution,

c) a plant cell placed in a hypertonic solution.

Q8 Summarise the similarities and differences between facilitated diffusion and active transport.

Q9 Describe how the following are used to transport substances across the cell membrane:

a) carrier proteins,   b) channel proteins.

Q10 Describe the process of endocytosis.

Tip: A hypotonic solution has a higher water potential than the cell. A hypertonic solution has a lower water potential than the cell.

Section Summary

Make sure you know:

- That plasma membranes have a range of functions including: controlling which substances enter and leave the cell, allowing recognition by other cells and allowing cells to communicate.

- That plasma membranes are partially permeable — they let some molecules through but not others.

- That membranes within cells also have a range of functions including: dividing the cell into different compartments to make different functions more efficient, increasing the surface area of organelles to make chemical reactions more efficient, forming vesicles to transport substances around the cell, controlling what substances enter and leave organelles.

- The 'fluid mosaic' structure of cell membranes — a phospholipid bilayer scattered with proteins.

- The roles of the following components of the cell membrane: phospholipids (form a barrier to dissolved substances), cholesterol (gives the membrane stability), proteins (control what enters and leaves the cell, act as receptors), glycolipids and glycoproteins (stabilise the membrane, act as receptors/antigens).

- That membranes are affected by temperature because it influences how much the phospholipids in the bilayer can move, affecting membrane structure.

- That cells communicate with each other through signalling, using messenger molecules.

- That, in cell signalling, messenger molecules bind to membrane-bound receptors on target cells. Messenger molecules can only bind to receptors with a complementary shape to their own.

- That membrane-bound receptors are sites where hormones and drugs bind.

- That diffusion is the passive movement of particles from an area of high concentration to an area of lower concentration.

- That osmosis is diffusion of water molecules across a partially permeable membrane from an area of higher water potential to lower water potential.

- How animal and plant cells behave in isotonic, hypotonic and hypertonic solutions.

- That facilitated diffusion (a passive process) uses carrier proteins and channel proteins to move molecules down a concentration gradient.

- That large molecules, most polar molecules and ions all travel by facilitated diffusion.

- That active transport uses energy (from ATP) to actively move molecules against a concentration gradient.

- That cells can take in large molecules and substances by endocytosis — the plasma membrane surrounds the substance and then pinches off, forming a vesicle inside the cell.

- That cells can secrete substances by exocytosis — vesicles containing substances for release outside the cell fuse with the plasma membrane, then release their contents.

Exam-style Questions

1   Fig. 1.1 shows normal onion cells under a light microscope. The cytoplasm has been dyed red. Fig. 1.2 shows the same onion cells after they have been placed in a **weak salt solution**. The solution has a lower water potential than the onion cells.

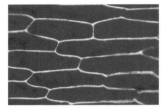
Fig. 1.1

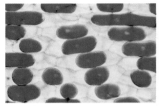
Fig. 1.2

(a) (i) Explain what is meant by the term water potential.

(1 mark)

(ii) Describe and explain the changes seen between Fig. 1.1 and Fig. 1.2.

(3 marks)

(iii) Describe what might happen if animal cells were placed in a solution with a lower water potential than the cell contents.

(2 marks)

(b)   In Fig. 1.2 it is possible to see the cells' plasma membranes.

(i) Describe the **fluid mosaic structure** of the plasma membrane.

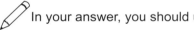In your answer, you should use appropriate technical terms, spelled correctly.

(6 marks)

(ii) State **two** functions of the plasma membrane.

(2 marks)

2   Glucose is a product of digestion. It is also a relatively large polar molecule. Once glucose has been digested, it must be absorbed into the bloodstream from the cells of the small intestine. Part of the absorption process happens by **facilitated diffusion**.

(a) (i) Suggest why glucose must use facilitated diffusion to cross the plasma membranes of the intestinal cells.

(3 marks)

(ii) Does this process require energy? Explain your answer.

(1 mark)

(b)   Another stage of the absorption process happens using **active transport**. Explain what is meant by the term active transport.

(2 marks)

3   A group of students investigated the water potential of potato cells.

They cut cubes of potato of equal size and shape, weighed them and placed a single cube into one of four different concentrations of sucrose solution. One cube was placed in pure water.

They re-weighed each of the cubes every hour and after 12 hours the mass of all the cubes remained constant. The overall change in mass for each cube is shown in Fig. 3.1.

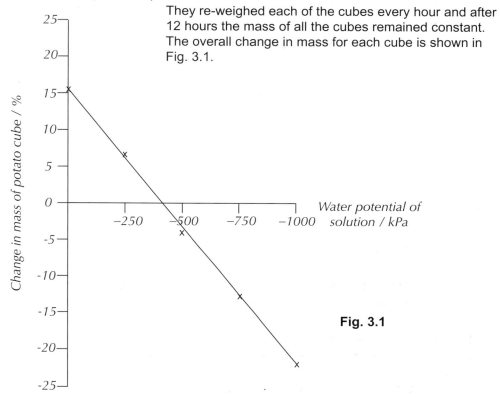

Fig. 3.1

(a)   The students recorded the difference in mass between the cubes at the start and end of the experiment in grams, but plotted the overall change as a percentage. Suggest why the graph was plotted in this way.

(1 mark)

(b)   What was the change in mass for the potato cube placed in **pure water**?

(1 mark)

(c) (i)   Explain why the cubes in the –500, –750 and –1000 kPa solutions lost mass.

(2 marks)

   (ii)   Use Fig. 3.1 to estimate the **water potential** of the potato cells.

(1 mark)

(d)   Suggest how the students could make their results more reliable.

(1 mark)

(e)   If the experiment was repeated with cubes that had a larger surface area would you expect the mass of all the cubes to become constant before 12 hours, at 12 hours or after 12 hours? Explain your answer.

(2 marks)

1. The Cell Cycle and Mitosis

We need new cells for growth and to replace damaged tissue, so our body cells need to be able to make more of themselves. They do this during the cell cycle.

The cell cycle

The cell cycle is the process that all body cells from multicellular organisms use to grow and divide. It starts when a cell has been produced by cell division and ends with the cell dividing to produce two identical cells. The cell cycle consists of a period of cell growth and DNA replication, called **interphase**, and a period of cell division, called **mitosis**.

Mitosis only occupies a small percentage of the cell cycle. Most of the cell cycle is taken up by interphase, which is sub-divided into three separate growth stages called G_1, S and G_2 (see Figure 1). During interphase the genetic material (DNA) is copied and checked for any mutations (errors) that may have occurred. If mutations are found in the DNA, the cell may kill itself. This prevents any mutations from being passed on to daughter cells, which could cause them not to function.

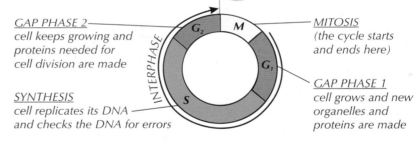

GAP PHASE 2
cell keeps growing and proteins needed for cell division are made

SYNTHESIS
cell replicates its DNA and checks the DNA for errors

MITOSIS
(the cycle starts and ends here)

GAP PHASE 1
cell grows and new organelles and proteins are made

INTERPHASE — G_2 M G_1 S

Figure 1: *Stages of the cell cycle.*

Interphase

During interphase the cell carries out normal functions, but also prepares to divide. The cell's DNA is unravelled and replicated, to double its genetic content. The organelles are also replicated so it has spare ones, and its ATP content is increased (ATP provides the energy needed for cell division).

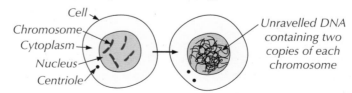

Cell
Chromosome
Cytoplasm
Nucleus
Centriole

Unravelled DNA containing two copies of each chromosome

Mitosis

There are two types of cell division — mitosis and meiosis (see p. 44 for more on meiosis). Mitosis is the form of cell division that occurs during the cell cycle. It's needed for the growth of multicellular organisms (like us) and for repairing damaged tissues. Mitosis is really one continuous process, but it's described as a series of division stages — prophase, metaphase, anaphase and telophase.

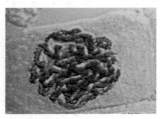

Figure 2: *Interphase in bluebell cells.*

Tip: Mitosis is also important in asexual reproduction — see page 43.

The structure of chromosomes in mitosis

Before we go into the detail of mitosis, you need to know more about the structure of chromosomes. As mitosis begins, the chromosomes are made of two strands joined in the middle by a **centromere**. The separate strands are called **chromatids**. Two strands on the same chromosome are called **sister chromatids**. There are two strands because each chromosome has already made an identical copy of itself during interphase. When mitosis is over, the chromatids end up as one-strand chromosomes in the new daughter cells.

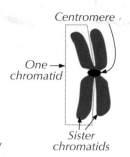

Centromere

One chromatid

Sister chromatids

Tip: You could remember the order of the phases in mitosis (**p**rophase, **m**etaphase, **a**naphase, **t**elophase) by using, 'purple mice are tasty'.

1. Prophase

The chromosomes condense, getting shorter and fatter. Tiny bundles of protein called **centrioles** start moving to opposite ends of the cell, forming a network of protein fibres across it called the **spindle**. The **nuclear envelope** (the membrane around the nucleus) breaks down and chromosomes lie free in the cytoplasm.

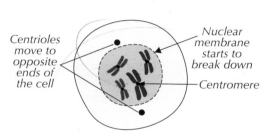

Centrioles move to opposite ends of the cell

Nuclear membrane starts to break down

Centromere

Figure 3: Prophase in bluebell cells.

2. Metaphase

The chromosomes (each with two chromatids) line up along the middle of the cell (at the spindle equator) and become attached to the spindle by their centromere.

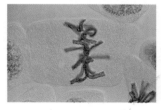

Spindle fibres

Centromeres on spindle equator

Figure 4: Metaphase in bluebell cells.

3. Anaphase

The centromeres divide, separating each pair of sister chromatids. The spindles contract, pulling chromatids to opposite ends of the cell, centromere first.

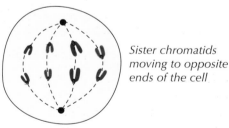

Sister chromatids moving to opposite ends of the cell

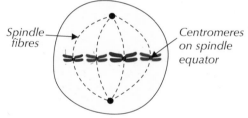

Figure 5: Anaphase in bluebell cells.

4. Telophase

The chromatids reach the opposite poles on the spindle. They uncoil and become long and thin again. They're now called chromosomes again. A nuclear envelope forms around each group of chromosomes, so there are now two nuclei. **Cytokinesis** then occurs — this is the division of the cytoplasm. The cell membrane constricts, pinching the cell into two daughter cells. The daughter cells are genetically identical to the original cell and to each other. Mitosis is finished and each daughter cell starts the interphase part of the cell cycle to get ready for the next round of mitosis.

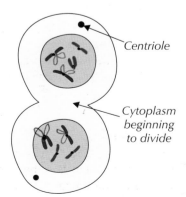

Centriole

Cytoplasm beginning to divide

Figure 6: Telophase in bluebell cells.

Mitosis in plants

Tip: A meristem is a mitotically active plant tissue, found in the areas of a plant that are growing, like the shoots and roots.

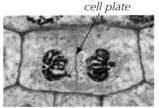

cell plate

***Figure 7:** The cell plate in a dividing onion cell.*

Tip: The chromosomes in the pics on the right have been stained so they can be seen under a microscope.

The process of mitosis described on the previous page takes place in animals. Mitosis in plants is pretty similar, but there are a few differences:

- In animals, most cells can divide by mitosis. In plants, only cells in meristems can divide by mitosis.

- During prophase in animal cells, the spindle forms between centrioles. However, plant cells don't have centrioles so the spindle forms without them.

- Cytokinesis in animals begins at the edge of a cell, where the cell membrane constricts. Cytokinesis is different in plants because they have a cell wall. It begins in the centre of a cell with a **cell plate**. This is a double membrane which secretes materials needed to make two cell walls (one for each daughter cell). The cell walls begin to form in the centre and move outwards until they meet the perimeter.

Practice Questions — Application

The photo below shows mitosis in onion cells.

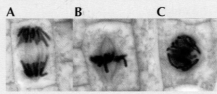

Q1 Which cell (A-C) is undergoing the following:
  a) metaphase,
  b) prophase?
Q2 Describe the stage of mitosis shown by cell A.

Practice Questions — Fact Recall

Q1   What is the cell cycle?
Q2   During which period of the cell cycle does cell growth occur?
Q3   Explain why DNA is checked during interphase.
Q4   Why is mitosis needed?
Q5   Describe what happens during prophase.
Q6   During which stage of mitosis do chromosomes line up along the centre of a cell?
Q7   During which stage of mitosis are chromatids pulled to opposite poles of the cell?
Q8   How many cells are produced during mitosis?
Q9   In mitosis, a parent cell divides to produce genetically different daughter cell. True or false?
Q10 Describe two differences between mitosis in animal and plant cells.

2. Reproduction and Meiosis

Some organisms reproduce using mitosis, e.g. yeast. Other organisms produce offspring through sexual reproduction, so they need gametes — and these are made by meiosis. It's way less confusing than it sounds, promise...

Asexual reproduction

Some organisms (e.g. some plants and fungi) reproduce **asexually** (without sex) using mitosis. This means any new organisms produced are genetically identical to the original, parent organism.

┌─ **Example — Budding in yeast cells** ─────────────

Yeast are single-celled microorganisms and are a type of fungi. Yeast cells are eukaryotic, with all the usual organelles in the cytoplasm (see pages 8-11) and a nucleus containing chromosomes (DNA) — see Figure 1.

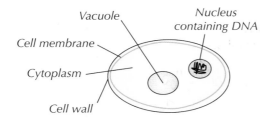

Vacuole *Nucleus containing DNA* *Cell membrane* *Cytoplasm* *Cell wall*

Figure 1: *Diagram of a yeast cell.*

Yeast can reproduce asexually by a process called **budding**. As budding involves mitosis, the offspring produced are genetically identical to the parent cell. It happens like this:

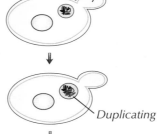

1 The parent yeast cell swells on one side, forming a bud at the surface of the cell.

Bud

2 The cell undergoes interphase — the DNA and organelles are replicated ready for the cell to divide.

Duplicating

3 The cell begins to undergo mitosis — the replicated DNA, cytoplasm and organelles move into the bud.

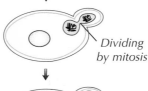

Dividing by mitosis

4 Nuclear division is complete — the budding cell contains a nucleus that has an identical copy of the parent cell's DNA.

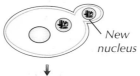

New nucleus

5 Finally, cytokinesis occurs and the bud pinches off from the parent cell, producing a new, genetically identical yeast cell.

Learning Objectives:

- Be able to explain the significance of mitosis for asexual reproduction.
- Be able to outline, with the aid of diagrams and photographs, the process of cell division by budding in yeast.
- Be able to explain the meaning of the term 'homologous pair of chromosomes'.
- Know that cells produced by meiosis are not genetically identical. (Details of meiosis are not required.)

Specification Reference 1.1.3

Exam Tip
If you get a question on budding in the exam, remember to use the right scientific terminology — and that'll be a lot easier if you've got mitosis straight in your head (see pages 40-41).

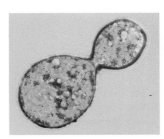

Figure 2: *A Cryptococcus yeast cell budding.*

Sexual reproduction

Gametes are the sperm cells in males and egg cells in females. In sexual reproduction two gametes join together at fertilisation to form a zygote, which divides and develops into a new organism.

Normal body cells have the **diploid number (2n)** of chromosomes — meaning each cell contains two of each chromosome (a pair), one from the mum and one from the dad. The chromosomes that make up each pair are the same size and have the same genes, although they could have different versions of those genes (called alleles). These pairs of matching chromosomes are called homologous pairs.

Exam Tip
Make sure you know what a homologous pair of chromosomes is for the exam.

Tip: Figure 3 on the right shows one-stranded chromosomes. These will become double-stranded chromosomes when the DNA is replicated before cell division.

---Example-----------------------------------

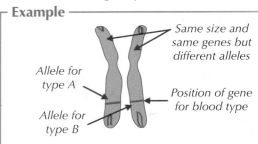

Same size and same genes but different alleles

Allele for type A

Position of gene for blood type

Allele for type B

Figure 3: Diagram showing a pair of homologous chromosomes.

Gametes have a **haploid (n) number** of chromosomes — there's only one copy of each chromosome. At fertilisation, a haploid sperm fuses with a haploid egg, making a cell with the normal diploid number of chromosomes. Half these chromosomes are from the father (the sperm) and half are from the mother (the egg). The diploid cell produced by fertilisation is called a zygote.

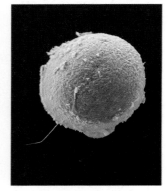

Figure 4: Electron micrograph of a sperm fertilising an egg.

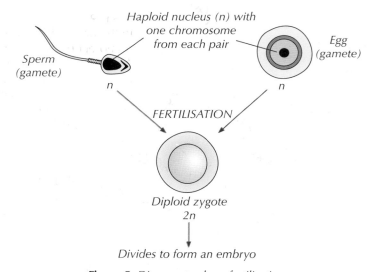

Haploid nucleus (n) with one chromosome from each pair

Sperm (gamete)

Egg (gamete)

n

n

FERTILISATION

Diploid zygote 2n

Divides to form an embryo

Figure 5: Diagram to show fertilisation.

Meiosis

Meiosis is a type of cell division that happens in the reproductive organs to produce gametes. Cells that divide by meiosis are diploid to start with, but the gametes that are formed from meiosis are haploid — the chromosome number halves. Cells formed by meiosis are all genetically different because each new cell ends up with a different combination of chromosomes.

You don't need to learn the details of meiosis, just understand that it produces genetically different cells. The diagram on the next page shows how it happens.

Tip: Mitosis produces new body cells that have the same number of chromosomes as the parent cell. Meiosis produces new sex cells that have half the number of chromosomes as the parent cell.

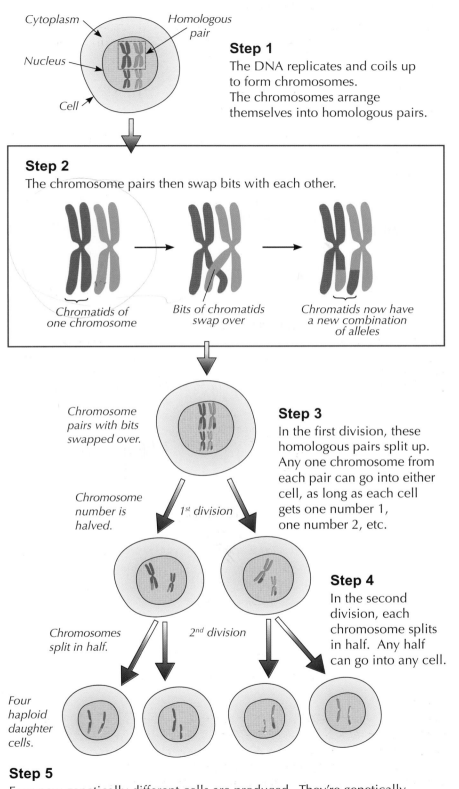

Step 1
The DNA replicates and coils up to form chromosomes.
The chromosomes arrange themselves into homologous pairs.

Cytoplasm

Homologous pair

Nucleus

Cell

Step 2
The chromosome pairs then swap bits with each other.

Chromatids of one chromosome

Bits of chromatids swap over

Chromatids now have a new combination of alleles

Step 3
In the first division, these homologous pairs split up. Any one chromosome from each pair can go into either cell, as long as each cell gets one number 1, one number 2, etc.

Chromosome pairs with bits swapped over.

Chromosome number is halved.

1st division

Step 4
In the second division, each chromosome splits in half. Any half can go into any cell.

Chromosomes split in half.

2nd division

Four haploid daughter cells.

Step 5
Four new genetically different cells are produced. They're genetically different from each other because the chromosomes swap bits during meiosis and each gamete gets a combination of half of them, at random.

Tip: We've only shown 4 chromosomes here for simplicity. Humans actually have 46 (23 homologous pairs).

Exam Tip
You don't need to learn about how chromosome pairs swap bits for your exam, but it's included here to help you understand how meiosis creates genetic variation.

Tip: Take a look back at page 41 to remind yourself what a chromatid is.

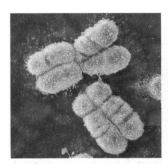

Figure 6: *Condensed double-armed chromosomes.*

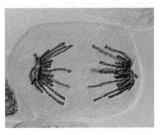

Figure 7: *Chromosomes separating during the second division in meiosis.*

Exam Tip
It's really important you spell meiosis and mitosis correctly in the exam — otherwise you might not get the mark.

Practice Questions — Application

Q1 Yeast have the ability to produce offspring by budding and meiosis. The following light micrograph shows a sample of yeast reproducing.

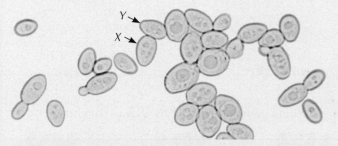

a) Which type of reproduction is shown in the light micrograph? Explain your answer.

b) The cell labelled X in the image above is a daughter cell of cell Y. Describe how the process of reproduction you named in part a) produced cell X.

Q2 The diagram below shows a cell which contains three pairs of homologous chromosomes and six potential gametes. Which of the gametes (A to F) could be produced from this cell by meiosis?

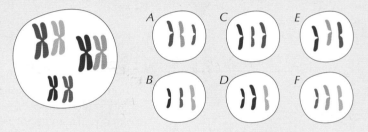

Practice Questions — Fact Recall

Q1 What type of cell division is used in asexual reproduction?

Q2 Are new organisms produced by asexual reproduction genetically identical or genetically different to the parent organism?

Q3 The diagram below shows a yeast cell.
Name the structures labelled A to E.

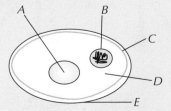

Q4 What is budding?

Q5 What is a homologous pair of chromosomes?

Q6 What is meiosis?

Q7 Give two differences between the daughter cells produced by budding and those produced by meiosis.

Tip: A light micrograph is simply a photograph that's taken through a light microscope.

3. Stem Cells and Differentiation

All multicellular organisms stem from, err, stem cells. Every cell in your body was produced from a stem cell. So was every cell in every other multicellular organism's body. So they're pretty important.

Stem cells

Multicellular organisms are made up of many different cell types that are **specialised** for their function, e.g. liver cells, muscle cells and white blood cells. All these specialised cell types originally came from stem cells. Stem cells are **unspecialised** cells — they can develop into any type of cell. All multicellular organisms have some form of stem cell.

┌─ Example ───

In humans, stem cells are found in early embryos and in a few places in adults. In the first few days of an embryo's life, any of its cells can develop into any type of human cell — they're all stem cells. In adults, stem cells are found in a few places (e.g. bone marrow), but they're not as flexible — they can only develop into a limited range of cells (see below).

Differentiation

Stem cells divide to become new cells, which then become specialised. The process by which a cell becomes specialised for its job is called differentiation (see Figure 1).

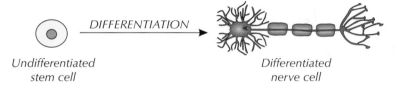

Undifferentiated stem cell   DIFFERENTIATION   *Differentiated nerve cell*

Figure 1: *Diagram showing stem cell differentiation.*

In animals, adult stem cells are used to replace damaged cells.

┌─ Example ───

Bones are living organs, containing nerves and blood vessels. The main bones of the body have marrow in the centres. Here, adult stem cells divide and differentiate to replace worn out blood cells — **erythrocytes** (red blood cells) and **neutrophils** (white blood cells that help to fight infection).

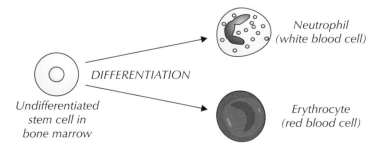

Neutrophil (white blood cell)

DIFFERENTIATION

Undifferentiated stem cell in bone marrow

Erythrocyte (red blood cell)

Figure 2: *Diagram showing how a stem cell in the bone marrow can differentiate into a neutrophil or erythrocyte.*

Learning Objectives:

- Be able to define the term 'stem cell'.

- Be able to define the term 'differentiation', with reference to the production of erythrocytes (red blood cells), neutrophils derived from stem cells in bone marrow, and the production of xylem vessels and phloem sieve tubes from cambium.

- Be able to describe and explain, with the aid of diagrams and photographs, how cells of multicellular organisms are specialised for particular functions, with reference to erythrocytes (red blood cells), neutrophils, epithelial cells, sperm cells, palisade cells, root hair cells and guard cells.

Specification Reference 1.1.3

Exam Tip
Make sure you know this example (of how bone marrow stem cells differentiate into blood cells) for the exam — you could be tested on it.

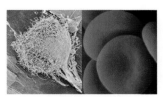

Figure 3: *Bone marrow stem cells (left) can differentiate into red blood cells (right).*

Plants are always growing, so stem cells are needed to make new shoots and roots throughout their lives. Stem cells in plants can differentiate into various plant tissues.

Example

In plants, stem cells are found in the **cambium**. Stem cells of the vascular cambium in the root and shoot divide and differentiate to become **xylem** and **phloem** (see Figure 4).

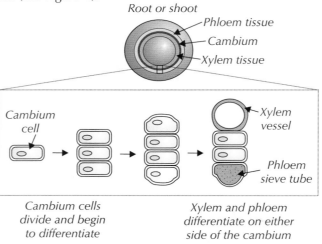

Figure 4: The differentiation of stem cells in the cambium into xylem and phloem.

The vascular cambium forms a ring inside the root and shoots. The cells divide and grow out from the ring, differentiating as they move away from the cambium.

Specialised cells

Once cells differentiate, they have a specific function. Their structure is adapted to perform that function. You need to know how the following cell types are specialised for their functions:

Examples — Animal cells

Erythrocytes (red blood cells) carry oxygen in the blood. The biconcave disc shape provides a large surface area for gas exchange. They have no nucleus so there's more room for haemoglobin (see p. 83), the protein that carries oxygen.

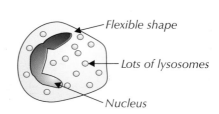

Neutrophils (white blood cells, e.g. phagocytes) defend the body against disease. Their flexible shape allows them to engulf foreign particles or pathogens (see p. 161). The many lysosomes in their cytoplasm contain digestive enzymes to break down the engulfed particles.

Figure 5: A scanning electron micrograph of a white blood cell.

Epithelial cells cover the surfaces of organs. The cells are joined by interlinking cell membranes and a membrane at their base. Some epithelia (e.g. in the lungs) have cilia that beat to move particles away. Other epithelia (e.g. in the small intestine) have microvilli — folds in the cell membrane that increase the cell's surface area.

Tip: Cells that have cilia on them are called ciliated cells — the tissue is called ciliated epithelium.

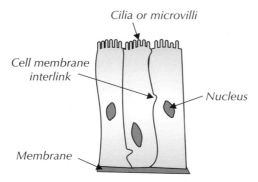

Figure 6: *Epithelial cells (pinkish-brown) with cilia (yellow) in the lungs.*

Sperm cells (male sex cells) have a flagellum (tail) so they can swim to the egg (female sex cell). They also have lots of mitochondria to provide the energy to swim. The acrosome contains digestive enzymes to enable the sperm to penetrate the surface of the egg.

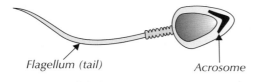

Figure 7: *Scanning electron micrograph of a sperm cell.*

Examples — Plant cells

Palisade mesophyll cells in leaves do most of the photosynthesis. They contain many chloroplasts, so they can absorb a lot of sunlight. The walls are thin, so carbon dioxide can easily diffuse into the cell.

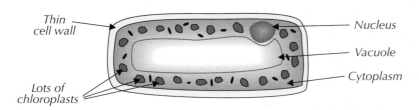

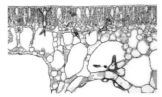

Figure 8: *The band of green cells at the top of this water lily leaf are palisade mesophyll cells.*

Root hair cells absorb water and mineral ions from the soil. They have a large surface area for absorption and a thin, permeable cell wall, for entry of water and ions. The cytoplasm contains extra mitochondria to provide the energy needed for active transport (see p. 33).

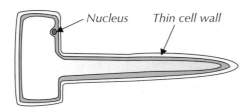

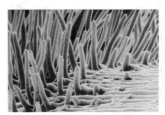

Figure 9: *Scanning electron micrograph of the root hairs on a cress root.*

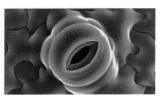

Figure 10: Turgid guard cells (red) open the stoma in a tobacco leaf.

Guard cells line the stomata — the tiny pores in the surface of the leaf used for gas exchange. In the light, guard cells take up water (into their vacuoles) and become turgid. Their thin outer walls and thickened inner walls force them to bend outwards, opening the stomata. This allows the leaf to exchange gases for photosynthesis.

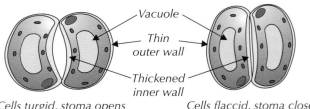

Vacuole

Thin outer wall

Thickened inner wall

Cells turgid, stoma opens   *Cells flaccid, stoma closes*

Practice Question — Application

Q1 The photograph below shows epithelial cells of the small intestine.

With reference to the photograph above, give one way in which epithelial cells are adapted to their function.

Practice Question — Fact Recall

Q1 What is a stem cell?

Q2 Define 'differentiation'.

Q3 a) What are:
    i)   erythrocytes?
    ii) neutrophils?

    b) Where in the body are the stem cells that differentiate into erythrocytes and neutrophils found?

    c) Describe one adaptation of the following to their function:
    i)   erythrocytes,
    ii) neutrophils.

Q4 Briefly describe the formation of xylem and phloem from stem cells in the root of a plant.

Q5 a) Explain why having a flagellum helps a sperm cell to carry out its function.

    b) Give one other way in which sperm cells are adapted to their function.

Q6 What is the function of:
    a) palisade mesophyll cells?
    b) root hair cells?

Q7 Describe how guard cells are adapted to their function.

4. Tissues, Organs and Systems

As you saw on pages 48-50, there are loads of different types of specialised *cells. These cells are grouped together to make up tissues, organs and organ systems, which perform particular functions...*

Tissues

A tissue is a group of cells (plus any extracellular material secreted by them) that are specialised to work together to carry out a particular function. A tissue can contain more than one cell type.

Examples

You need to know the following examples of tissues:

Squamous epithelium tissue is a single layer of flat cells lining a surface. It's found in many places in the body, including the alveoli in the lungs, and provides a thin exchange surface for substances to diffuse across quickly.

Nucleus

Basement membrane

Ciliated epithelium is a layer of cells covered in cilia (see p. 11). It's found on surfaces where things need to be moved — in the trachea for instance, where the cilia waft mucus along (see page 61).

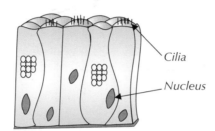

Cilia

Nucleus

Xylem tissue is a plant tissue with two jobs — it transports water around the plant, and it supports the plant. It contains xylem vessel cells and parenchyma cells.

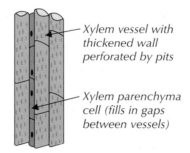

Xylem vessel with thickened wall perforated by pits

Xylem parenchyma cell (fills in gaps between vessels)

Phloem tissue transports sugars around the plant. It's arranged in tubes and is made up of sieve cells, companion cells, and some ordinary plant cells. Each sieve cell has end walls with holes in them, so that sap can move easily through them. These end walls are called sieve plates.

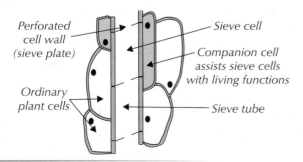

Perforated cell wall (sieve plate)

Sieve cell

Companion cell assists sieve cells with living functions

Ordinary plant cells

Sieve tube

Learning Objectives:

- Be able to explain the meaning of the terms 'tissue', 'organ' and 'organ system'.

- Be able to explain, with the aid of diagrams and photographs, how cells are organised into tissues, using squamous and ciliated epithelia, xylem and phloem as examples.

- Be able to discuss the importance of cooperation between cells, tissues, organs and organ systems.

Specification Reference 1.1.3

Tip: Epithelium is a tissue that forms a covering or a lining.

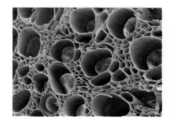

Figure 1: *Xylem tissue in a rootlet. The xylem vessels are brown and the parenchyma cells green.*

Exam Tip
Take a look at pages 90-91 for more on xylem and phloem.

Organs

An organ is a group of different tissues that work together to perform a particular function.

Tip: Gas exchange is the exchange of gases (oxygen and carbon dioxide) between an organism and its environment. There's loads more about it on pages 59-62.

> **Examples**
>
> The **lungs** are an animal organ which carry out gas exchange. They contain squamous epithelium tissue (in the alveoli) and ciliated epithelium tissue (in the bronchi etc.). They also have elastic connective tissue and vascular tissue (in the blood vessels).
>
>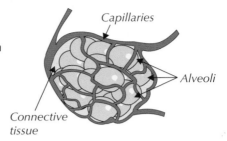
>
> The **leaf** is a plant organ which carries out gas exchange and photosynthesis. It contains palisade tissue, as well as epidermal tissue, and xylem and phloem tissues in the veins.
>
>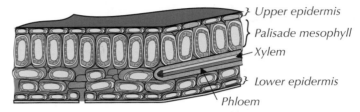

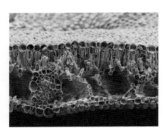

Figure 2: The cross section of a taro leaf. The palisade mesophyll is bright green and the xylem and phloem are grey.

Organ systems

Organs work together to form organ systems — each system has a particular function.

Exam Tip
Make sure you know the definition of tissues, organs and organ systems really well. You could be asked to apply your knowledge to lots of different examples in the exam — and it's easy marks if you've got the definitions straight in your head.

> **Examples**
>
> The **respiratory system** is made up of all the organs, tissues and cells involved in gas exchange. The lungs, trachea, larynx, nose, mouth and diaphragm are all part of the respiratory system.
>
>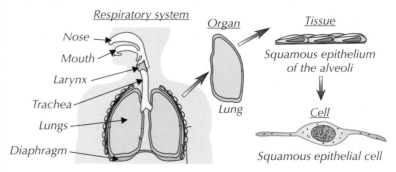
>
> The **circulatory system** is made up of the organs involved in blood supply. The heart, arteries, veins and capillaries are all parts of this system.
>
>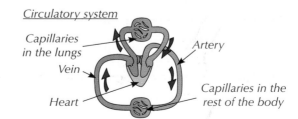

Tip: For more on the function of the circulatory system take a look at page 69.

Cooperation between cells, tissues, organs and organ systems

Multicellular organisms work efficiently because they have different cells specialised for different functions. It's advantageous because each different cell type can carry out its specialised function more effectively than an unspecialised cell could.

Specialised cells can't do everything on their own though. Each cell type depends on other cells for the functions it can't carry out. This means the cells, tissues and organs within multicellular organisms must cooperate with each other to keep the organism alive and running.

Exam Tip
It's common sense that different types of specialised cell need to cooperate to get the things they need — but make sure you know how to explain this. Using an example might help you make your point in the exam.

Examples

- A palisade cell (see p. 49) is good at photosynthesising, but it's no good at absorbing water and minerals from the soil. It depends on root hair cells (see p. 49) for this. And vice versa.

- Muscles cells are great for getting you where you want to go, but to do this they need oxygen. They depend on erythrocytes (red blood cells) to carry oxygen to them from the lungs.

Multicellular organisms have developed different systems of cooperation between different cells:

1. Transport systems

These are used to carry substances between the different cells.

Tip: There's more about the transport systems in plants on page 90.

Examples

- In plants, xylem cells carry water and minerals from the root hair cells to the palisade cells, and phloem cells carry sugars around the plant.

- In humans, the circulatory system helps to move substances around the body in the blood.

2. Communication systems

These allow communication between cells in different parts of the organism. Both plants and animals have chemical communication systems that use messenger molecules such as hormones (see p. 27). Animals also have a nervous system for communication, sending electrical signals to different tissues and organs.

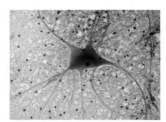

Figure 3: *Nerves like the one shown above send electrical impulses around the body, allowing communication between different parts of an organism.*

Practice Questions — Fact Recall

Q1 What is a tissue?

Q2 Tissues can't contain more than one type of cell. True or false?

Q3 Explain why the following are defined as tissues:
  a) squamous epithelium,
  b) ciliated epithelium.

Q4 Give two examples of plant tissues.

Q5 What is an organ?

Q6 What is an organ system?

Q7 Give an example of an organ system and explain why it is classed as an organ system.

Section Summary

Make sure you know:

- That most of the cell cycle is taken up by interphase — a period of cell growth during which the cell's genetic material is copied and checked for mutations (errors).
- That a small percentage of the cell cycle is taken up by mitosis (a type of cell division that produces two genetically identical daughter cells).
- That mitosis is needed for the growth of multicellular organisms and tissue repair.
- The stages of mitosis — prophase (chromosomes condense, the spindle forms and the nuclear envelope breaks down), metaphase (chromosomes line up along the centre of the cell and attach to the spindle), anaphase (the spindles contract, pulling chromatids to opposite poles of the cell) and telophase (cytokinesis occurs, forming two new cells).
- The differences between mitosis in animal and plant cells — mitosis only occurs in cells in the meristems of plants, plant cells don't have centrioles, and cytokinesis in plants begins in the centre of a cell and involves a cell plate.
- That some organisms, such as yeast, reproduce asexually using mitosis.
- The process of budding in yeast, including the swelling of a yeast cell on one side, the replication of the cell's DNA and organelles, the movement of replicated DNA and organelles into the bud, nuclear division and the separation of the bud from the parent cell.
- That the term 'homologous pair of chromosomes' refers to a pair of matching chromosomes.
- That in sexual reproduction two gametes join together at fertilisation to form a zygote, which divides and develops into a new organism.
- That gametes are produced by meiosis (a type of cell division that produces four genetically different cells).
- That stem cells are unspecialised cells that can develop into any type of cell.
- That differentiation is the process by which a cell becomes specialised.
- That stem cells in the bone marrow of an animal differentiate into erythrocytes (red blood cells) and neutrophils (white blood cells).
- How stem cells in the cambium of a plant differentiate into xylem and phloem.
- How erythrocytes, neutrophils, epithelial cells and sperm cells in animals, and palisade mesophyll cells, root hair cells and guard cells in plants are specialised for their functions.
- That a tissue is a group of cells (plus any extracellular material secreted by them) that are specialised to carry out a particular function.
- These examples of tissues — squamous epithelium, ciliated epithelium, xylem tissue and phloem tissue.
- That an organ is a group of different tissues that work together to perform a particular function.
- That organ systems are organs which work together for a particular function.
- How cells, tissues and organs within multicellular organisms must cooperate with each other to keep the organism alive and running.

Exam-style Questions

1   Fig. 1.1 shows changes in the mass of a cell and its DNA during the cell cycle.

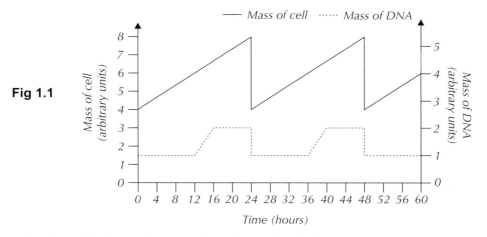

Fig 1.1

(a)   During which hours does synthesis take place? Explain your answer.

(2 marks)

(b)   At which hours does mitosis take place? Explain your answer.

(2 marks)

(c)   Describe what is happening within the cell between 0 and 24 hours.

(4 marks)

(d) (i)   How many cell divisions are shown on the graph? Explain your answer.

(2 marks)

(ii)   At what time will the next cell division take place?

(1 mark)

(e)   During interphase a cell may kill itself. Suggest why.

(2 marks)

2   Water enters the plant through its root hair cells and is transported around the plant in the xylem. Fig. 2.1 on the right shows some root hair cells on the root of a plant.

Fig 2.1

(a)   Give **two** ways in which the structure of a root hair cell is specialised for its role.

(2 marks)

(b) (i)   Stem cells differentiate into xylem cells. Where are these stem cells found?

(1 mark)

(ii) Explain why xylem can be considered a tissue.

(2 marks)

(iii) The xylem is a transport system in a plant that enables cooperation between different types of specialised cells. Explain why cooperation between specialised cells is important in multicellular organisms.

(2 marks)

3 Fig. 3.1 below show cytokinesis in animal, plant and yeast cells.

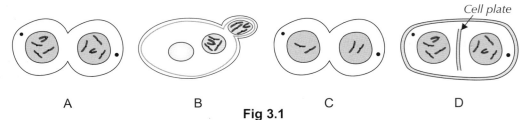

Fig 3.1

(a) In the table on the right, write the letters **A**, **B**, **C** or **D** next to the description which most closely matches the diagram. One has been done for you.

(3 marks)

Description	Letter
Budding in a yeast cell.	
Mitosis in an animal cell.	
Mitosis in a plant cell.	
Meiosis in an animal cell.	C

(b) (i) Telophase is a phase of mitosis. Describe what happens during telophase in animal cells.

In your answer, you should use appropriate technical terms, spelled correctly.

(4 marks)

(ii) The list, E to G, below describes some processes that occur in mitosis in an animal cell.

E	centrioles start moving to opposite ends of the cell
F	the chromatids are pulled to opposite ends of the cell
G	the chromosomes become attached to the spindle

Which process occurs in the phase immediately before telophase?

(1 mark)

(iii) Give **three** reasons why mitosis is important for organisms.

(3 marks)

(c) Describe how daughter cells produced by meiosis differ to their parent cell.

(2 marks)

1. Exchange Surfaces

Every organism has substances it needs to take in and others it needs to get rid of in order to survive. An organism's size and surface area affect how quickly this is done.

Learning Objective:

- Be able to explain, in terms of surface area : volume ratio, why multicellular organisms need specialised exchange surfaces and single-celled organisms do not.

Specification Reference 1.2.1

Exchange of substances with the environment

Every organism, whatever its size, needs to exchange things with its environment. Cells need to take in oxygen (for aerobic respiration) and nutrients (e.g. glucose). They also need to excrete waste products like carbon dioxide and urea. How easy the exchange of substances is depends on the organism's surface area to volume ratio.

Tip: A ratio shows how big one value is <u>in relation</u> to another.

Surface area : volume ratios

Before going into the effects of surface area : volume ratios, you need to understand a bit more about them. Smaller organisms have bigger surface area : volume ratios than larger organisms. This is shown in the example below.

Figure 1: A hippo (top) has a small surface area : volume ratio. A mouse (bottom) has a large surface area : volume ratio.

— **Example** —

A mouse has a bigger surface area relative to its volume than a hippo. This can be hard to imagine, but you can prove it mathematically.

Imagine these animals as cubes...

The mouse could be represented by a cube measuring 1 cm × 1 cm × 1 cm.

Its volume is: $1 \times 1 \times 1 = 1$ cm³

Its surface area is: $6 \times 1 \times 1 = 6$ cm²

So the mouse has a surface area : volume ratio of <u>6 : 1</u>.

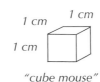

1 cm   1 cm
1 cm

"cube mouse"

Compare this to a cube hippo measuring 2 cm × 4 cm × 4 cm.

Its volume is: $2 \times 4 \times 4 = 32$ cm³

Its surface area is:

$2 \times 4 \times 4 = 32$ cm²
(top and bottom surfaces of cube)

$+ 4 \times 2 \times 4 = 32$ cm²
(four sides of the cube)

Total surface area = 64 cm²

4 cm
4 cm
2 cm

"cube hippo"

So the hippo has a surface area : volume ratio of 64 : 32 or <u>2 : 1</u>.

The cube mouse's surface area is six times its volume, but the cube hippo's surface area is only twice its volume. Smaller animals have a bigger surface area compared to their volume.

Exam Tip
If you're asked to calculate a surface area to volume ratio in the exam, always give your answer in its simplest form, e.g. 2 : 1 rather than 64 : 32.

Specialist exchange organs

An organism needs to supply every one of its cells with substances like glucose and oxygen (for respiration). It also needs to remove waste products from every cell to avoid damaging itself. Single-celled organisms exchange substances differently to multicellular organisms.

Single-celled organisms

In single-celled organisms, substances can diffuse directly into (or out of) the cell across the cell surface membrane. The diffusion rate is quick because of the short distances the substances have to travel and because single-celled organisms have a relatively high surface area : volume ratio.

Multicellular organisms

In multicellular organisms, diffusion across the outer membrane is too slow, for two reasons:

1. Some cells are deep within the body — there's a big distance between them and the outside environment.

2. Larger animals have a low surface area to volume ratio — it's difficult to exchange enough substances to supply a large volume of animal through a relatively small outer surface.

So rather than using straightforward diffusion to absorb and excrete substances, multicellular organisms need specialised **exchange organs** (like lungs, see p. 60).

Tip: Remember, diffusion is the net movement of particles from an area of higher concentration to an area of lower concentration.

Tip: There's more on factors affecting the rate of diffusion on page 29.

Tip: One way to work out surface area of a block is to calculate the area of each side (length × height) then add them all together. To work out volume, calculate the length × width × height.

Tip: To compare two ratios (e.g. 7:2 and 3:1) it's best to get the last figure in each ratio to be 1 (e.g. 7:2 would become 3.5:1). Then you can easily see which ratio is the largest (e.g. 3.5:1 is a bigger ratio than 3:1).

Practice Questions — Application

Below are three blocks of different sizes (not drawn to scale).

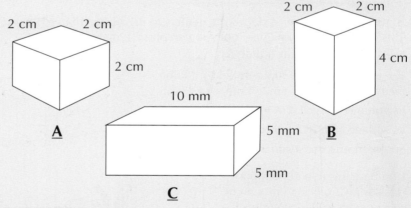

Q1 For each block work out its:
   a) surface area. b) volume. c) surface area : volume ratio.

Q2 Which block has the greatest surface area : volume ratio?

Practice Questions — Fact Recall

Q1 a) Name two substances an animal needs to take in from its environment.

   b) Name two substances an animal needs to release into its environment.

Q2 Explain two reasons why diffusion is too slow in multicellular organisms for them to absorb and excrete substances this way.

2. The Gaseous Exchange System

Multicellular organisms need a gaseous exchange system to survive. The gaseous exchange system in mammals is based around the lungs.

Gas exchange in mammals

In mammals, the lungs are gas exchange organs. They help to get oxygen into the blood (for respiration) and to get rid of carbon dioxide (made by respiring cells) from the body.

Structure of the gaseous exchange system

As you breathe in, air enters the trachea (windpipe). The trachea splits into two bronchi — one bronchus leading to each lung. Each bronchus then branches off into smaller tubes called bronchioles. The bronchioles end in small 'air sacs' called alveoli — see Figure 1. This is where gases are exchanged (see next page). The ribcage, intercostal muscles and diaphragm all work together to move air in and out (see page 63).

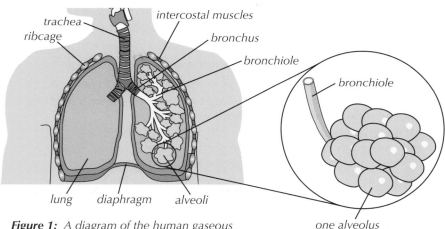

Figure 1: *A diagram of the human gaseous exchange system with the alveoli enlarged.*

Alveoli

Lungs contain millions of alveoli — these form the **gas exchange surface**. Alveoli are arranged in bunches at the end of bronchioles. They're surrounded by a network of capillaries, giving each alveolus its own blood supply — see Figure 2.

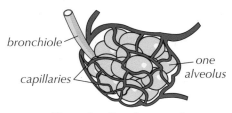

Figure 2: *Alveoli covered in a network of capillaries.*

Alveoli structure

Each alveolus is made from a single layer of thin, flat cells called the alveolar epithelium. The walls of the capillaries are made from capillary endothelium (also a type of epithelium).

The walls of the alveoli contain elastic fibres (see page 61). These help the alveoli to return to their normal shape after inhaling and exhaling air.

Learning Objectives:

- Be able to describe the features of an efficient exchange surface, with reference to diffusion of oxygen and carbon dioxide across an alveolus.

- Be able to describe the features of the mammalian lung that adapt it to efficient gaseous exchange.

- Be able to describe the functions of cartilage, cilia, goblet cells, smooth muscle and elastic fibres in the mammalian gaseous exchange system.

- Be able to describe, with the aid of diagrams and photographs, the distribution of cartilage, ciliated epithelium, goblet cells, smooth muscle and elastic fibres in the trachea, bronchi, bronchioles and alveoli of the mammalian gaseous exchange system.

Specification Reference 1.2.1

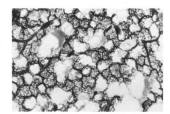

Figure 3: *A light micrograph of capillaries surrounding alveoli.*

Tip: Epithelial tissue is pretty common in the body. It's usually found on exchange surfaces.

Tip: Haemoglobin is a protein found in red blood cells. There's more about it on page 83.

Tip: Don't forget, gases pass through two layers of cells (the alveolar epithelium and the capillary endothelium).

Exam Tip
Be specific in your exam answers — don't just talk about increasing the rate of diffusion for gases, talk about increasing the rate of diffusion for oxygen and carbon dioxide.

Gas exchange in the alveoli

Oxygen (O_2) diffuses out of the alveoli, across the alveolar epithelium and the capillary endothelium, and into haemoglobin in the blood — see Figure 4.

Carbon dioxide (CO_2) diffuses into the alveoli from the blood, crossing the capillary endothelium then the alveolar epithelium. After entering the alveolar space, it's breathed out.

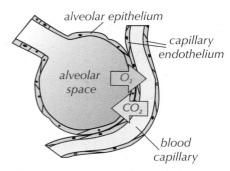

Figure 4: *Gaseous exchange between an alveolus and a capillary.*

Adaptations for gas exchange

All gas exchange surfaces are adapted for efficient gas exchange. Most gas exchange surfaces have two things in common:

- They have a large surface area, which increases the rate of diffusion.
- They're thin (often just one layer of epithelial cells) — this provides a short diffusion pathway across the gas exchange surface, which increases the rate of diffusion.

A steep concentration gradient of oxygen and carbon dioxide is also maintained across the exchange surface, which increases the rate of diffusion.

The lungs

The lungs have the following specific adaptations for gas exchange:

- Many alveoli provide a large surface area for diffusion to occur across.
- The alveolar epithelium and capillary endothelium are each only one cell thick, giving a short diffusion pathway.
- All the alveoli have a good blood supply from capillaries — they constantly take away oxygen and bring more carbon dioxide, maintaining the concentration gradients — see Figure 5.
- The diaphragm and intercostal muscles are involved in ventilation (see p. 63), which also keeps the concentration gradients of oxygen and carbon dioxide high.

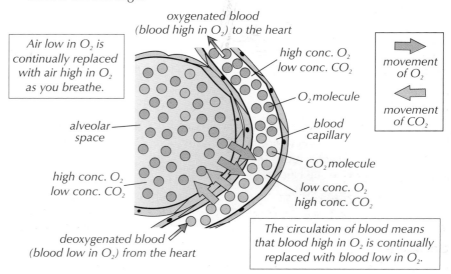

Figure 5: *Diagram showing how O_2 moves from an area of high concentration (inside the alveolus) to low concentration (in the deoxygenated blood).*

Q1 A mountain climber is climbing at altitude, where there's less oxygen. Suggest how this will affect gas exchange in the alveoli.

Q2 One of the effects of severe obesity is that the sufferer cannot fully inhale. Suggest the effect this would have on the rate of diffusion of oxygen.

Q3 The pictures on the right show light micrographs of healthy lung tissue (top) and diseased lung tissue from a patient with emphysema (bottom). The alveoli appear white.

   a) Describe the main difference between the healthy lung tissue and the diseased lung tissue.

   b) Use your answer to part a) to explain why people with emphysema have a lower level of oxygen in the blood than normal.

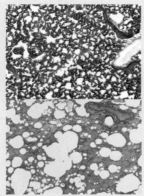

Key features of the gaseous exchange system

The following features all help to increase the efficiency of the gaseous exchange system in mammals:

Goblet cells

Goblet cells secrete mucus (see Figure 6). The mucus traps microorganisms and dust particles in the inhaled air, stopping them from reaching the alveoli.

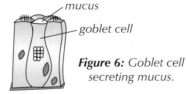

Figure 6: Goblet cell secreting mucus.

Cilia

The cilia are hair-like structures on the surface of epithelial cells. They beat the mucus secreted by the goblet cells — see Figure 7. This moves the mucus (plus the trapped microorganisms and dust) upward away from the alveoli towards the throat, where it's swallowed. This helps prevent lung infections.

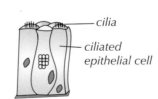

Figure 7: Ciliated epithelium.

Elastic fibres

Elastic fibres help the process of breathing out (see p. 63). On breathing in, the lungs inflate and the elastic fibres are stretched. Then, the fibres recoil to help push the air out when exhaling.

Smooth muscle

Smooth muscle allows the diameter of the airways to be controlled. During exercise the smooth muscle relaxes, making the tubes wider. This means there's less resistance to airflow and air can move in and out of the lungs more easily.

Cartilage

Cartilage in the walls of the trachea and bronchi provides them with support. It's strong but flexible — it stops the trachea and bronchi collapsing when you breathe in and the pressure drops (see p. 63).

Figure 8: An electron micrograph of ciliated cells (pink) and goblet cells (green) in the bronchus.

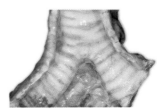

Figure 9: Cartilage rings (cream) in the trachea.

Distribution of features in the gaseous exchange system

You need to know the distribution of the features described on the previous page for the exam. This is illustrated in Figure 11 and summarised in the table below (Figure 12).

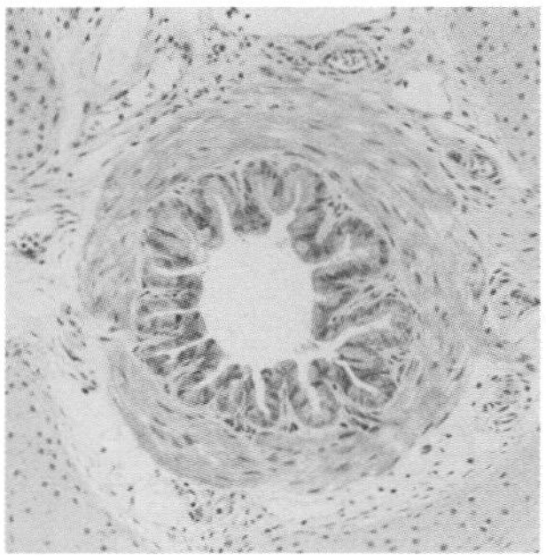

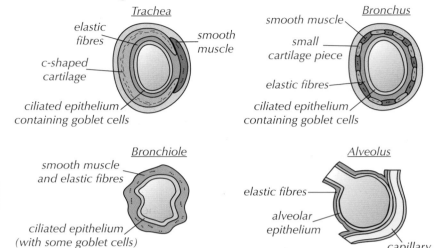

Figure 10: *Cross-section of a bronchiole. The dark pink folds are ciliated epithelium. The pink ring around it is smooth muscle.*

Figure 11: *Cross-sections of structures in the mammalian gaseous exchange system.*

Part of the lung	Cartilage	Smooth muscle	Elastic fibres	Goblet cells	Epithelium
Trachea	large C-shaped pieces	✓	✓	✓	ciliated
Bronchi	smaller pieces	✓	✓	✓	ciliated
Larger bronchiole	none	✓	✓	✓	ciliated
Smaller bronchiole	none	✓	✓	✗	ciliated
Smallest bronchiole	none	✗	✓	✗	no cilia
Alveoli	none	✗	✓	✗	no cilia

Figure 12: *Table summarising the distribution of features in the mammalian gaseous exchange system.*

Practice Questions — Fact Recall

Q1 Describe how oxygen gets from the lungs into the blood.

Q2 Describe the features of the lungs and explain how they affect the rate of diffusion.

Q3 In the mammalian gaseous exchange system, what is the function of:
a) goblet cells? b) cilia?

Q4 Describe the function and distribution of elastic fibres in the gaseous exchange system of mammals.

Q5 Where in the airways is smooth muscle found?

Q6 Describe the difference between the distribution of cartilage in the trachea and in the bronchi.

Exam Tip
If an exam question asks you about the factors that affect diffusion, remember they <u>speed up</u> or <u>slow down</u> the rate of diffusion — don't write about them making diffusion 'better' or 'worse' or else you won't get the marks.

3. Breathing

Breathing is pretty important, both for life and for the exam...

Ventilation

Ventilation consists of inspiration (breathing in) and expiration (breathing out). It's controlled by the movements of the diaphragm, intercostal muscles and ribcage.

Inspiration

- The intercostal and diaphragm muscles contract.
- This causes the ribcage to move upwards and outwards and the diaphragm to flatten, increasing the volume of the thorax (the space where the lungs are).
- As the volume of the thorax increases the lung pressure decreases (to below atmospheric pressure).
- This causes air to flow into the lungs — see Figure 1.
- Inspiration is an active process — it requires energy.

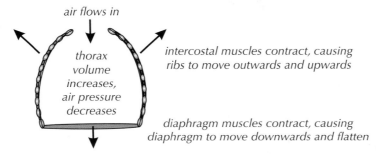

air flows in

thorax volume increases, air pressure decreases

intercostal muscles contract, causing ribs to move outwards and upwards

diaphragm muscles contract, causing diaphragm to move downwards and flatten

Figure 1: *Diagram showing what happens during inspiration.*

Expiration

- The intercostal and diaphragm muscles relax.
- The ribcage moves downwards and inwards and the diaphragm becomes curved again.
- The thorax volume decreases, causing the air pressure to increase (to above atmospheric pressure).
- Air is forced out of the lungs — see Figure 2.
- Expiration is a passive process — it doesn't require energy.

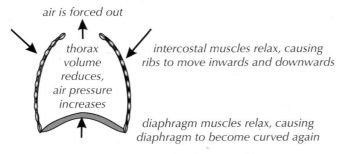

air is forced out

thorax volume reduces, air pressure increases

intercostal muscles relax, causing ribs to move inwards and downwards

diaphragm muscles relax, causing diaphragm to become curved again

Figure 2: *Diagram showing what happens during expiration.*

Tip: Air always flows from areas of <u>high</u> pressure to areas of <u>low</u> pressure.

Tip: It's the movement of the ribcage and diaphragm and the resulting change in lung pressure that causes air to flow in and out — not the other way round.

Tip: Remember, when the diaphragm contracts, it's flat. When it relaxes, it bulges upwards. Think of it like trying to hold your stomach in — you contract your muscles to flatten your stomach and relax to release it.

Spirometers

A spirometer is a machine that can be used to investigate breathing. It can give readings of:

- **Tidal volume** (TV) — the volume of air in each breath. This is usually about 0.4 dm³.
- **Vital capacity** — the maximum volume of air that can be breathed in or out.
- **Breathing rate** — how many breaths are taken per unit time (usually per minute).
- **Oxygen uptake** — the rate at which a person uses up oxygen (e.g. the number of dm³ used per minute).

Tip: dm³ is short for decimetres cubed — it's the same as litres.

Exam Tip
You need to be able to define tidal volume and vital capacity in the exam.

How to use a spirometer

A spirometer has an oxygen-filled chamber with a movable lid (see Figure 4). The person using the spirometer breathes through a tube connected to the oxygen chamber. As the person breathes in and out, the lid of the chamber moves up and down. These movements are recorded by a pen attached to the lid of the chamber — this writes on a rotating drum, creating a **spirometer trace**. The soda lime in the tube the subject breathes into absorbs carbon dioxide.

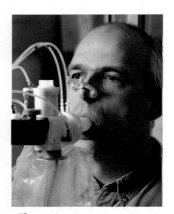

Figure 3: A person using a spirometer.

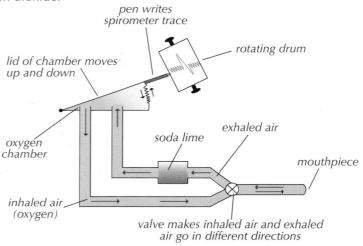

Figure 4: Diagram showing how a spirometer works.

The total volume of gas in the chamber decreases over time. This is because the air that's breathed out is a mixture of oxygen and carbon dioxide. The carbon dioxide is absorbed by the soda lime — so there's only oxygen in the chamber which the subject inhales from. As this oxygen gets used up by respiration, the total volume decreases.

To get a valid reading from a spirometer, the person using it must wear a nose clip — this ensures that they can only breathe in and out through their mouth (and so all the air they breathe goes through the spirometer). The machine must also be airtight with no leaks.

Tip: Using a spirometer can be dangerous as you're continually breathing in the same air that you just breathed out — so you need to make sure there's enough oxygen in the chamber.

Analysing data from spirometers

In the exam, you might have to work out breathing rate, tidal volume, vital capacity and oxygen uptake from a spirometer trace. There's an example of how to do this on the next page.

Example

The graph below shows a spirometer trace.

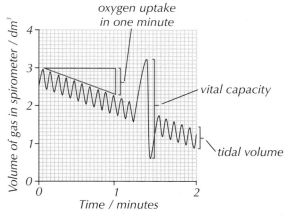

- In this trace, the breathing rate in the first minute is 10 breaths per minute (there are 10 'peaks' in the first minute).

- The tidal volume may change from time to time, but in this trace it's about 0.5 dm³.

- The graph shows a vital capacity of 2.65 dm³.

- Oxygen uptake is the decrease in the volume of gas in the spirometer chamber. It can be read from the graph by taking the average slope of the trace. In this case, it drops by 0.7 dm³ in the first minute — so oxygen uptake is 0.7 dm³/min.

Tip: A line sloping upwards on this spirometer trace indicates that the person using it is breathing out (and so the volume of gas in the spirometer is increasing).

A line sloping down indicates that the person is breathing in.

The longer the line, the deeper the breath in or out.

Practice Questions — Application

Look at the spirometer trace below.
It was recorded from a healthy 17 year old student at rest.

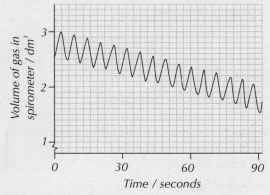

Q1 What is the student's tidal volume?

Q2 Work out the breathing rate of this student.
Give your answer in breaths per minute.

Q3 Explain why the volume of gas in the spirometer drops over time.

The same student then spent 5 minutes exercising vigorously. He stops exercising and immediately records a new spirometer trace. This is shown on the next page.

Exam Tip
Make sure you look carefully at the axes of any graph you get in the exam. For example, it could be the volume of gas in the lungs, not the spirometer, that's plotted on the y-axis.

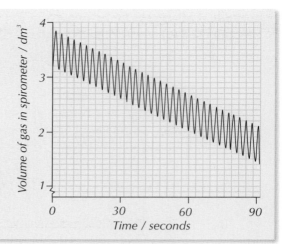

Q4 Describe how exercise has caused the student's tidal volume and breathing rate to change.

Q5 Calculate the student's oxygen uptake in the first minute after exercise.

Q6 The student has a vital capacity of 2.85 dm³. What does this mean?

Section Summary

Make sure you know...

- That single-celled organisms exchange substances with their environment by direct diffusion through their cell surface membranes, and that the rate of diffusion is quick because of the organisms' high surface area : volume ratios.

- That multicellular organisms can't exchange substances by direct diffusion across their outer membranes because it would be too slow — some cells are deep within the body and larger animals have a low surface area : to volume ratio. Instead they have specialist exchange organs.

- That all gas exchange surfaces are adapted for efficient gas exchange. These adaptations increase the rate of diffusion and include having a large surface area and being thin (often only one cell thick). Steep concentration gradients of oxygen and carbon dioxide are also maintained across the exchange surface.

- That the lungs are adapted for efficient gas exchange in the following ways:
  - Many alveoli provide a large surface area for diffusion.
  - The alveolar epithelium and capillary endothelium are each only one cell thick.
  - The alveoli have a good blood supply from the capillaries to maintain the steep concentration gradients of oxygen and carbon dioxide.
  - The intercostal muscles and diaphragm are involved in ventilation, which also keeps the concentration gradients of oxygen and carbon dioxide high.

- That goblet cells lining the airways secrete mucus, and cilia sweep it away from the alveoli (removing trapped microorganisms and dust).

- That elastic fibres in the walls of the airways and the alveoli stretch and recoil to help the process of breathing out.

- That smooth muscle allows the diameter of the airways to be controlled.

- That cartilage provides the trachea and bronchi with support.

- How to describe the distribution of goblet cells, ciliated epithelium, elastic fibres, smooth muscle and cartilage in the mammalian gaseous exchange system.

- How the ribcage, diaphragm and intercostal muscles all work together during ventilation.

- That tidal volume is the volume of air in each breath and that vital capacity is the maximum volume of air that can be breathed in or out.

- How a spirometer can be used to measure tidal volume, vital capacity, breathing rate and oxygen uptake.

- How to interpret data from a spirometer trace.

1 (a)   The lungs are the gaseous exchange organs in mammals.

   (i)   Explain why multicellular organisms such as mammals need specialised gaseous exchange organs.

(3 marks)

   (ii)   Describe and explain **two** adaptations of the lungs for efficient gas exchange.

(4 marks)

(b)   The gills are the gaseous exchange organ in fish. Fig. 1.1 shows a cross section through a dogfish gill. The gill consists of long, thin **primary lamellae**, each of which is covered in hundreds of tiny leaf-like projections called **secondary lamellae.**

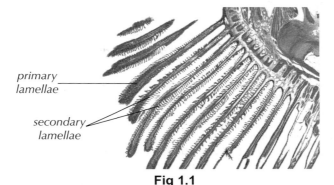

primary lamellae

secondary lamellae

Fig 1.1

   (i)   Suggest how the presence of the lamellae increases the efficiency of gas exchange across the gills.

(2 marks)

   (ii)   Give **one** other possible adaptation of the gills for efficient gas exchange. Explain your answer.

(2 marks)

2 (a)   Use the most appropriate terms to complete the passage on inspiration below.

   During inspiration, the diaphragm and .... muscles ....

   This causes the .... to move upwards and outwards and the diaphragm

   to flatten, increasing the .... of the thorax. As this happens,

   lung .... decreases to below that of the atmosphere, causing air to

   flow into the lungs.

(5 marks)

(b)   The volume of air in each breath is known as the tidal volume.
   What is the **maximum volume** of air that can be breathed in or out known as?

(1 mark)

3   A spirometer is a machine used to investigate breathing.

  (a)   Explain how a spirometer trace may be obtained.

(3 marks)

  (b)   A spirometer trace of a person at rest is shown in Fig 3.1.

    (i)   What happened between points A and B?

(1 mark)

    (ii)   Use Fig 3.1 to work out the person's breathing rate.

(1 mark)

    (iii)   Suggest how the appearance of this trace would differ if the volume of gas in the spirometer was recorded instead of the volume of gas in the lungs. Explain your answer.

(4 marks)

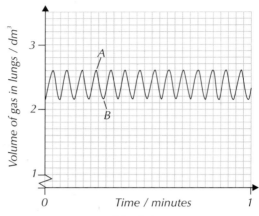

Fig 3.1

  (c)   Suggest **two** things that would need to be done when using the spirometer to obtain a **reliable** measurement of the person's tidal volume.

(2 marks)

4   Fig. 4.1 shows a cross section of the mammalian trachea.

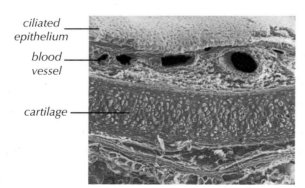

Fig 4.1

  (a)   Describe the function of the cilia on ciliated epithelial cells.

(1 mark)

  (b) (i)   Give **one** function of cartilage in the trachea.

(1 mark)

    (ii)   Where else in the mammalian gaseous exchange system is cartilage found?

(1 mark)

  (c)   Give **one** other feature of the trachea **not** labelled in Fig 4.1 and describe its function.

(2 marks)

1. The Circulatory System

All multicellular organisms need to transport materials around the body. Transport systems can vary depending on the organism — we humans have a transport system called the circulatory system.

Why do multicellular organisms need a transport system?

As you saw on page 58, single-celled organisms can get all the substances they need by diffusion across their outer membrane. If you're multicellular though, it's a bit harder to supply all your cells with everything they need — multicellular organisms are relatively big and they have a low surface area to volume ratio. A lot of multicellular organisms (e.g. mammals) are also very active. This means that a large number of cells are all respiring very quickly, so they need a constant, rapid supply of glucose and oxygen.

To make sure that every cell has a good enough supply, multicellular organisms need a transport system. In mammals, this is the circulatory system, which uses blood to carry glucose and oxygen around the body. It also carries hormones, antibodies (to fight disease) and waste (like CO_2).

Single and double circulatory systems

Not all organisms have the same type of circulatory system — some have a single circulatory system and others have a double circulatory system.

Single circulatory system

In a single circulatory system, blood only passes through the heart once for each complete circuit of the body.

Example

Fish have a single circulatory system. The heart pumps blood to the gills (to pick up oxygen) and then on through the rest of the body (to deliver the oxygen) in a single circuit.

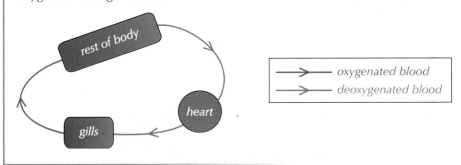

oxygenated blood
deoxygenated blood

Double circulatory system

In a double circulatory system, the blood passes through the heart twice for each complete circuit of the body.

Learning Objectives:

- Be able to explain the need for transport systems in multicellular animals in terms of size, level of activity and surface area : volume ratio.

- Be able to explain the meaning of the terms 'single circulatory system' and 'double circulatory system', with reference to the circulatory systems of fish and mammals.

- Be able to explain the meaning of the terms 'closed circulatory system' and 'open circulatory system', with reference to the circulatory systems of fish and insects.

Specification Reference 1.2.2

Exam Tip
Remember, multicellular organisms have a small surface area to volume ratio — just writing they have a small surface area won't get you full marks in the exam.

Exam Tip
If you're asked to define a single or double circulatory system, writing that the blood travels through the heart once/twice isn't enough. You need to say it does this for each complete circuit of the body too.

Example

Mammals have a double circulatory system. The heart is divided down the middle, so it's really like two hearts joined together. The right side of the heart pumps blood to the lungs (to pick up oxygen). From the lungs it travels to the left side of the heart, which pumps it to the rest of the body. When blood returns to the heart, it enters the right side again.

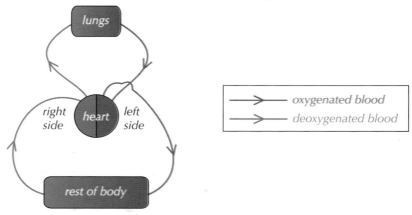

Tip: The right and left sides of the heart are reversed in the diagram because it's the right and left of the person the heart belongs to.

So, our circulatory system is really two linked loops. One sends blood to the lungs — this is called the pulmonary system, and the other sends blood to the rest of the body — this is called the systemic system.

The advantage of the mammalian double circulatory system is that the heart can give the blood an extra push between the lungs and the rest of the body. This makes the blood travel faster, so oxygen is delivered to the tissues more quickly.

Closed and open circulatory systems

Some organisms have a closed circulatory system and some have an open circulatory system.

Closed circulatory system

In a closed circulatory system, the blood is enclosed inside blood vessels.

Tip: Mammals have a closed circulatory system too — see page 80.

Example

Fish have a closed circulatory system. The heart pumps blood into arteries. These branch out into millions of capillaries. Substances like oxygen and glucose diffuse from the blood in the capillaries into the body cells, but the blood stays inside the blood vessels as it circulates. Veins take the blood back to the heart.

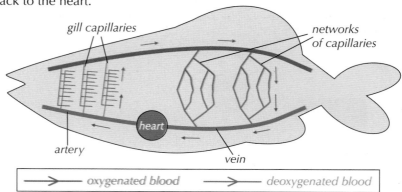

Open circulatory system

In an open circulatory system, blood isn't enclosed in blood vessels all the time. Instead, it flows freely through the body cavity.

Example

Insects have an open circulatory system. The heart is segmented. It contracts in a wave, starting from the back, pumping the blood into a single main artery. That artery opens up into the body cavity. The blood flows around the insect's organs, gradually making its way back into the heart segments through a series of valves.

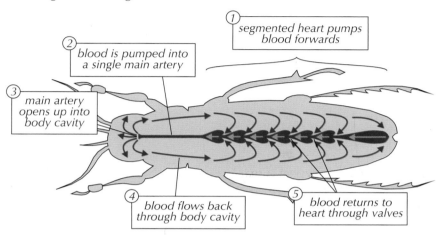

1. segmented heart pumps blood forwards
2. blood is pumped into a single main artery
3. main artery opens up into body cavity
4. blood flows back through body cavity
5. blood returns to heart through valves

The circulatory system supplies the insect's cell with nutrients, and transports things like hormones around the body. It doesn't supply the insect's cells with oxygen though — this is done by a system of tubes called the tracheal system.

Practice Questions — Fact Recall

Q1 Give two reasons why multicellular organisms need transport systems.

Q2 a) Name a group of animals that has a double circulatory system.

b) For the group of animals you named in a), briefly describe how their double circulatory system works.

Q3 Explain why the circulatory system of a fish is described as:

a) a single circulatory system,

b) a closed circulatory system.

Q4 Explain why the insect circulatory system is described as an open circulatory system.

Exam Tip
Make sure you read the question properly — if you're asked what a closed circulatory system is, don't answer with the definition of a double circulatory system because you've misread the question.

- Be able to describe, with the aid of diagrams and photographs, the external and internal structure of the mammalian heart.

- Be able to explain, with the aid of diagrams, the differences in the thickness of the walls of the different chambers of the heart in terms of their functions.

- Be able to describe the cardiac cycle, with reference to the action of the valves in the heart.

Specification Reference 1.2.2

Figure 2: The external structure of a pig's heart.

Tip: There's more about how the atrioventricular valves and semi-lunar valves work on the next page.

2. Heart Basics

So, you've seen on page 70 that mammals like you and I have a double circulatory system. Well, now you need to know about the pump that keeps the blood flowing nicely through the system. Introducing the heart...

External and internal structure of the heart

Figures 1 and 3 below show the external and internal structure of the heart. The heart consists of two muscular pumps. The right side of the heart pumps deoxygenated blood to the lungs and the left side pumps oxygenated blood to the rest of the body.

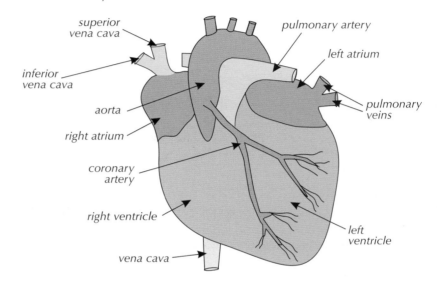

Figure 1: The external structure of the heart.

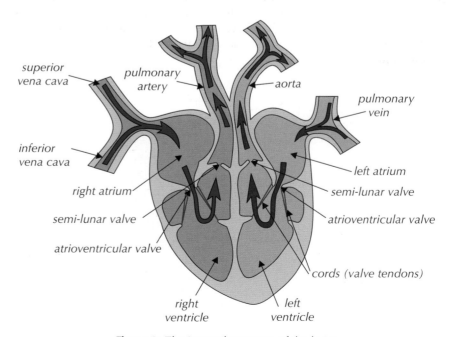

Figure 3: The internal structure of the heart.

Heart valves

The **atrioventricular** (**AV**) **valves** link the atria to the ventricles, and the **semi-lunar** (**SL**) **valves** link the ventricles to the pulmonary artery and aorta — they all stop blood flowing the wrong way.

The valves only open one way — whether they're open or closed depends on the relative pressure of the heart chambers. If there's higher pressure behind a valve, it's forced open. If pressure is higher in front of the valve, it's forced shut — see Figure 4.

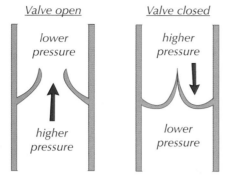

Figure 4: Diagram showing how heart valves open and close.

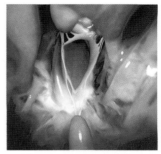

Figure 5: A heart valve.

Thickness of heart chamber walls

The heart is mainly **cardiac muscle**. When it contracts it creates high pressure — enough to force blood all the way around the body.

Each of the four chambers of the heart has a different function. The more work that a heart chamber has to do, the more muscle it needs — so, the thicker its wall is. The left ventricle of the heart has thicker, more muscular walls than the right ventricle, because it needs to contract powerfully to pump blood all the way round the body. The right side only needs to get blood to the lungs, which are nearby. The ventricles have thicker walls than the atria, because they have to push blood out of the heart whereas the atria just need to push blood a short distance into the ventricles. This is shown in Figure 6 below.

Tip: To demonstrate the differences in thickness between the chamber walls — the left ventricle wall is 8-15 mm thick, the right ventricle wall is 4-5 mm thick and the right atrium wall is about 2 mm thick.

Tip: Blood leaving the heart in the arteries is under high pressure due to the contraction of the ventricle walls. This pressure is called <u>hydrostatic pressure</u>.

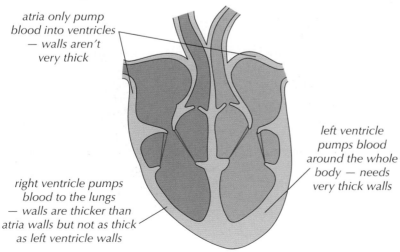

atria only pump blood into ventricles — walls aren't very thick

left ventricle pumps blood around the whole body — needs very thick walls

right ventricle pumps blood to the lungs — walls are thicker than atria walls but not as thick as left ventricle walls

Figure 6: Diagram showing the different thicknesses of the heart chamber walls.

The cardiac cycle

The cardiac cycle is an ongoing sequence of contraction and relaxation of the atria and ventricles that keeps blood continuously circulating round the body. The volume of the atria and ventricles changes as they contract and relax, altering the pressure in each chamber. This causes valves to open and close, which directs the blood flow through the heart. The cardiac cycle can be simplified into three stages:

Tip: Cardiac contraction is also called systole, and relaxation is called diastole.

1. Ventricles relax, atria contract

The ventricles are relaxed. The atria fill with blood, which decreases their volume and increases the pressure. The higher pressure in the atria causes the atrioventricular valves to open, allowing the blood to flow into the ventricles.
The atria then contract, decreasing their volume and increasing the pressure even further — forcing the remaining blood out.

Tip: Muscle contraction, of the atria or the ventricles, creates pressure inside the heart chambers.

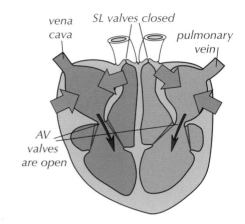

vena cava
SL valves closed
pulmonary vein
AV valves are open

2. Ventricles contract, atria relax

The ventricles contract and the atria relax. The pressure is higher in the ventricles than the atria, so the atrioventricular valves close to prevent backflow. The high pressure in the ventricles opens the semi-lunar valves — blood is forced out into the pulmonary artery and aorta.

Tip: Remember that if there's a higher pressure in front of a valve it's forced shut and if there's a higher pressure behind a valve it's forced open (see page 73).

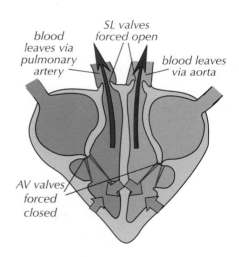

blood leaves via pulmonary artery
SL valves forced open
blood leaves via aorta
AV valves forced closed

3. Ventricles relax, atria relax

The ventricles and atria both relax, increasing their volume and lowering the pressure in the heart chambers. The higher pressure in the pulmonary artery and aorta causes the semi-lunar valves to close, preventing backflow. Then the atria fill with blood again due to the higher pressure in the vena cava and pulmonary vein, and the cycle starts over again.

Exam Tip
In questions where you gain marks for quality of written communication (see p. 222), you need to write out the full names of structures (not just their abbreviations) and spell them correctly. For example, you'd need to write 'atrioventricular valve' rather than just 'AV valve'.

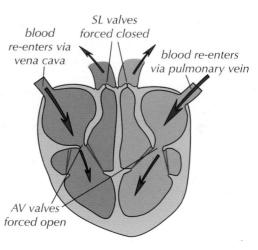

blood re-enters via vena cava
SL valves forced closed
blood re-enters via pulmonary vein
AV valves forced open

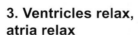

Practice Questions — Application

The diagram below shows pressure changes in one cardiac cycle.

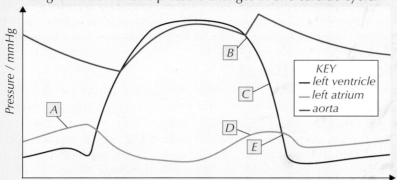

KEY
— left ventricle
— left atrium
— aorta

Tip: mmHg is a unit of measurement for pressure. It means millimetres of mercury.

Q1 Why is the atrial pressure increasing at point A?

Q2 Is the semi-lunar valve open or closed at point B?
Explain your answer.

Q3 Why is the ventricular pressure decreasing at point C?

Q4 Why is the atrial pressure increasing at point D?

Q5 Is the atrioventricular valve open or closed at point E?
Explain your answer.

Tip: To answer the questions on the left you need to be able to link the pressure changes in the left ventricle, left atrium and aorta to each of the three stages of the cardiac cycle.

Practice Questions — Fact Recall

Q1 Which side of the heart pumps deoxygenated blood?

Q2 a) The diagram below (left) shows the external structure of the heart.
Name the structures labelled A to H.

b) The diagram below (right) shows the internal structure of the heart.
Name the structures labelled A to H.

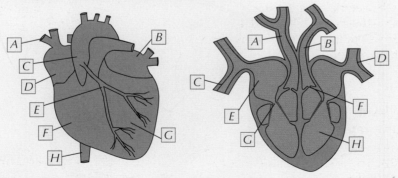

Q3 Why does the left ventricle of the heart have thicker, more muscular
walls than the right ventricle?

Q4 a) Name the valves that link the ventricles to the aorta and
pulmonary artery.

b) What is the function of these valves?

Q5 What is the cardiac cycle?

Q6 When the atria contract, describe the pressure and volume changes
that take place in the atria.

Tip: To answer Q3 on the left, think about where the left and right ventricles are pumping blood to.

3. Electrical Activity of The Heart

You don't have to remember to send electrical impulses to your heart muscle to make it contract — it happens automatically. This electrical activity can be captured on electrocardiograms, which can help to diagnose heart problems.

Control of heartbeat

Cardiac muscle is 'myogenic' — this means that it can contract and relax without receiving signals from nerves. This pattern of contractions controls the regular heartbeat.

The process starts in the **sino-atrial node (SAN)**, which is in the wall of the right atrium. The SAN is like a pacemaker — it sets the rhythm of the heartbeat by sending regular waves of electrical activity over the atrial walls. This causes the right and left atria to contract at the same time. A band of non-conducting collagen tissue prevents the waves of electrical activity from being passed directly from the atria to the ventricles. Instead, these waves of electrical activity are transferred from the SAN to the **atrioventricular node (AVN)**.

The AVN is responsible for passing the waves of electrical activity on to the bundle of His. But, there's a slight delay before the AVN reacts, to make sure the ventricles contract after the atria have emptied. The **bundle of His** is a group of muscle fibres responsible for conducting the waves of electrical activity to the finer muscle fibres in the right and left ventricle walls, called the **Purkyne tissue**. The Purkyne tissue carries the waves of electrical activity into the muscular walls of the right and left ventricles, causing them to contract simultaneously, from the bottom up.

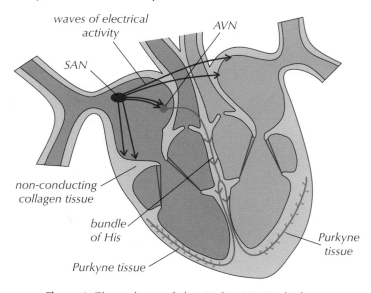

Figure 1: The pathway of electrical activity in the heart.

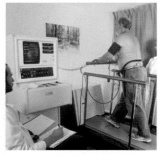

Figure 2: A patient exercising whilst linked up to an electrocardiograph.

Electrocardiographs

A doctor can check someone's heart function using an electrocardiograph — a machine that records the electrical activity of the heart. The heart muscle depolarises (loses electrical charge) when it contracts, and repolarises (regains charge) when it relaxes. An electrocardiograph records these changes in electrical charge using electrodes placed on the chest.

Electrocardiograms (ECGs)

The trace produced by an electrocardiograph is called an electrocardiogram, or ECG. A normal ECG looks like this:

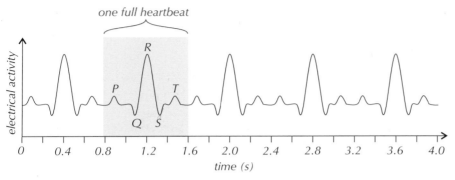

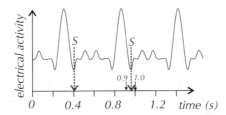

Figure 3: *An ECG of a healthy heartbeat.*

The **P wave** is caused by contraction (depolarisation) of the atria. The main peak of the heartbeat, together with the dips at either side, is called the **QRS complex** — it's caused by contraction (depolarisation) of the ventricles. The **T wave** is due to relaxation (repolarisation) of the ventricles.

Calculating heart rate

Your heart rate is the number of beats per unit time — usually beats per minute (bpm). You can use an ECG to work out a person's heart rate by using the following equation:

> heart rate (bpm) = 60 ÷ time taken for one heartbeat (s)

Exam Tip
This formula only works if the time taken for one heartbeat is in seconds — check the units of any values you're given in the exam.

┌─ **Example 1** ──────────────

To find out the heart rate shown on the ECG below, first you need to find the time taken for one heartbeat. You can do this by working out the time between one wave (e.g. the R wave) and the next.

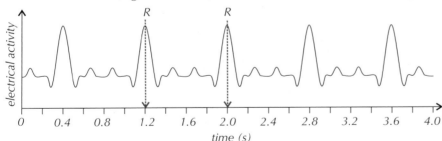

Here, one heartbeat lasts (2 − 1.2) = 0.8 s

Heart rate = 60 ÷ time taken for one heartbeat

= 60 ÷ 0.8 = 75 bpm

Exam Tip
The normal heart rate range for an adult at rest is 60 to 100 beats per minute (bpm). So if you work out heart rate in the exam and get a value way outside this range (e.g. 5 bpm), you know you need to do your calculation again.

┌─ **Example 2** ──────────────

Here, the time taken for one heartbeat is worked out using the time between one S wave and the next.

One heartbeat lasts
(0.95 − 0.4) = 0.55 s

Heart rate = 60 ÷ 0.55 = 109 bpm

Tip: This resting heart rate is outside the normal range (see above) — it's too fast. If a person's heart rate is consistently too fast, it may mean they have a heart problem — see the next page.

Diagnosing heart problems

Doctors compare their patients' ECGs with a normal trace. This helps them to diagnose any heart problems.

Examples

Heart rate too fast

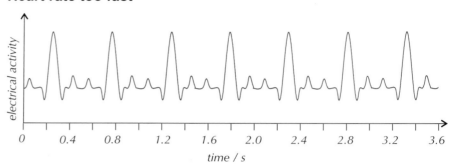

This heartbeat is too fast — around 120 beats per minute. That might be OK during exercise, but at rest it shows that the heart isn't pumping blood efficiently.

Ventricles not contracting properly

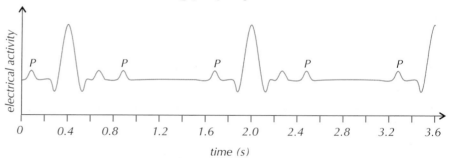

Here, the atria are contracting but sometimes the ventricles are not (some P waves aren't followed by a QRS complex). This might mean there's a problem with the AVN — impulses aren't travelling from the atria through to the ventricles.

Fibrillation

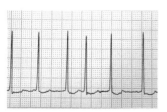

Figure 4: An ECG showing atrial fibrillation.

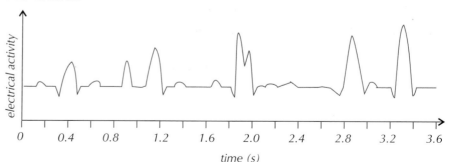

This is fibrillation — a really irregular heartbeat. The atria or ventricles completely lose their rhythm and stop contracting properly. It can result in anything from chest pain and fainting to lack of pulse and death.

Practice Questions — Application

Below are an ECG of a person with a normal heart rate (A) and an ECG of a person with an abnormal heart rate (B).

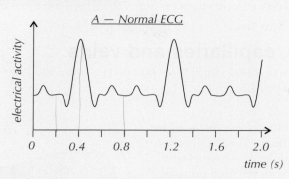

A — Normal ECG

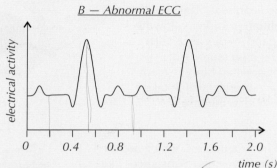

B — Abnormal ECG

Q1 Work out the heart rate shown on ECG A.

Q2 Work out the heart rate shown on ECG B.

Q3 Describe two differences between the heartbeats shown by ECG A and ECG B.

Exam Tip
Always show your working for calculation questions — you can still pick up marks for correct working, even if you get the final answer wrong or misread values off a graph.

Tip: Remember, the units for heart rate are usually beats per minute (bpm).

Practice Questions — Fact Recall

Q1 a) What does SAN stand for, in relation to the heart?

b) What is the function of the SAN?

Q2 Name the tissue that prevents electrical signals passing directly from the atria to the ventricles.

Q3 Describe the role of the bundle of His.

Q4 Describe the role of the Purkyne tissue.

Q5 a) What does ECG stand for?

b) What can an ECG be used to diagnose?

4. Blood Vessels

As you know, mammals have a closed circulatory system, which means our blood is enclosed in blood vessels (see p. 70). There are three different types of blood vessels...

Arteries, capillaries and veins

The three types of blood vessel that you need to know about are arteries, capillaries and veins.

Arteries

Arteries carry blood from the heart to the rest of the body. Their walls are thick and muscular and have elastic tissue to cope with the high pressure produced by the heartbeat. The inner lining (**endothelium**) is folded, allowing the artery to expand — this also helps it to cope with high pressure. All arteries carry oxygenated blood except for the pulmonary arteries, which take deoxygenated blood to the lungs.

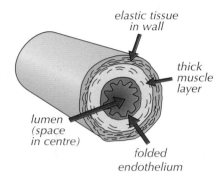

Capillaries

Arteries branch into capillaries, which are the smallest of the blood vessels. Substances like glucose and oxygen are exchanged between cells and capillaries, so they're adapted for efficient diffusion, e.g. their walls are only one cell thick. Capillaries connect to veins.

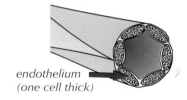

Veins

Veins take blood back to the heart under low pressure. They're wider than equivalent arteries, with very little elastic or muscle tissue. Veins contain valves to stop the blood flowing backwards (see p. 73). Blood flow through the veins is helped by contraction of the body muscles surrounding them. All veins carry deoxygenated blood (because oxygen has been used up by body cells), except for the pulmonary veins, which carry oxygenated blood to the heart from the lungs.

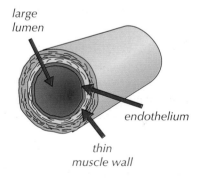

Tissue fluid

Tissue fluid is the fluid that surrounds cells in tissues. It's made from substances that leave the blood, e.g. oxygen, water and nutrients. Cells take in oxygen and nutrients from the tissue fluid, and release metabolic waste into it. In a **capillary bed** (the network of capillaries in an area of tissue), substances move out of the capillaries, into the tissue fluid, by pressure filtration (see the next page).

Tip: Arteries don't contain any valves, unlike veins.

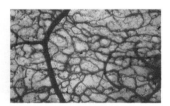

Figure 1: A light micrograph of capillaries.

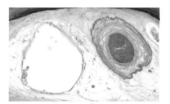

Figure 2: A light micrograph of a vein (left) artery (right).

Tip: Arteries are the 'way art' (way out) of the heart, and veins are the 'vey in' (way in).

Pressure filtration

At the start of the capillary bed, nearest the arteries, the hydrostatic pressure inside the capillaries is greater than the pressure in the tissue fluid. This difference in pressure forces fluid out of the capillaries and into the spaces around the cells, forming tissue fluid. As fluid leaves, the pressure reduces in the capillaries — so the pressure is much lower at the end of the capillary bed that's nearest to the veins. Due to the fluid loss, the water potential at the end of the capillaries nearest the veins is lower than the water potential in the tissue fluid — so some water re-enters the capillaries from the tissue fluid at the vein end by osmosis (see Figure 3).

Unlike blood, tissue fluid doesn't contain red blood cells or big proteins, because they're too large to be pushed out through the capillary walls.

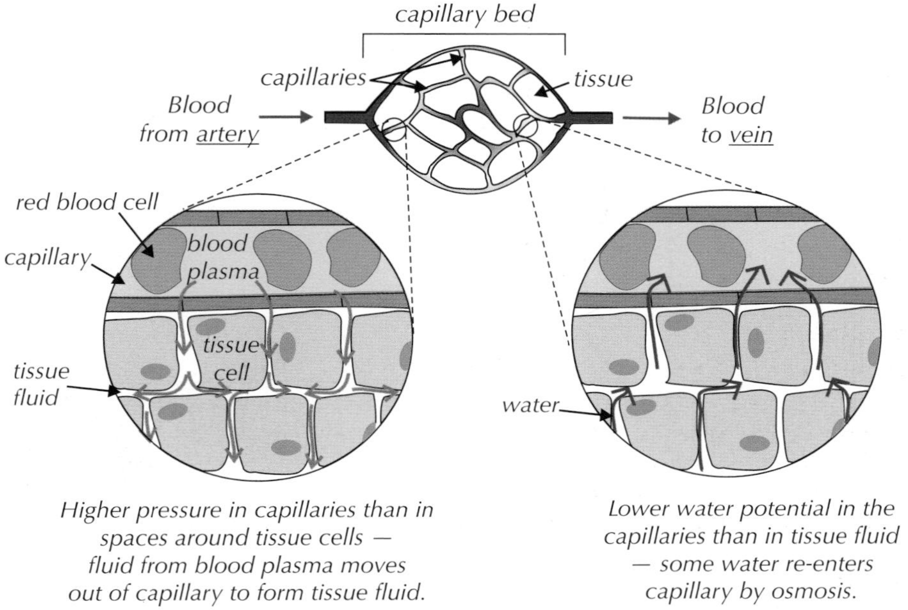

Tip: Don't get the effect of hydrostatic pressure and that of osmosis mixed up — at the artery end of a capillary bed, the fluid is forced out of the capillaries by hydrostatic pressure (pressure exerted by a liquid). Whereas at the vein end of a capillary bed, water moves into the capillaries by osmosis. See p 29-30 for more on osmosis.

Tip: Water potential is the likelihood of water molecules to diffuse out of or into a solution — see page 30.

Tip: Blood plasma is just the liquid that carries everything in the blood.

capillary bed

capillaries — *tissue*

Blood from artery → → *Blood to vein*

red blood cell

capillary

blood plasma

tissue cell

tissue fluid

water

Higher pressure in capillaries than in spaces around tissue cells — fluid from blood plasma moves out of capillary to form tissue fluid.

Lower water potential in the capillaries than in tissue fluid — some water re-enters capillary by osmosis.

Figure 3: *The movement of fluid between capillaries and tissue cells.*

Lymph vessels

Not all of the tissue fluid re-enters the capillaries at the vein end of the capillary bed — some excess tissue fluid is left over. This extra fluid eventually gets returned to the blood through the **lymphatic system** — a kind of drainage system, made up of lymph vessels (see Figure 4).

Tip: The lymphatic system is also part of the immune system.

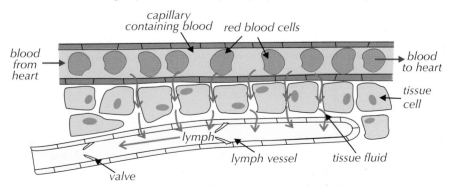

capillary containing blood   *red blood cells*

blood from heart

blood to heart

tissue cell

lymph

lymph vessel   *tissue fluid*

valve

Figure 4: *Diagram to show tissue fluid draining into lymph vessels.*

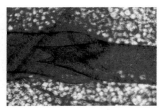

Figure 5: Light micrograph of a lymph vessel containing a valve. The valve allows lymph to move from right to left only.

The smallest lymph vessels are the lymph capillaries. Excess tissue fluid passes into lymph vessels. Once inside, it's called **lymph**. Valves in the lymph vessels stop the lymph going backwards — see Figure 5. Lymph gradually moves towards the main lymph vessels in the thorax. Here, it's returned to the blood, near the heart.

Blood, tissue fluid and lymph

Blood, tissue fluid and lymph are all quite similar — tissue fluid is formed from blood, and lymph is formed from tissue fluid. The main differences are shown in the table.

	Blood	Tissue fluid	Lymph	Comment
Red blood cells	✓	✗	✗	Red blood cells are too big to get through capillary walls into tissue fluid.
White blood cells	✓	very few	✓	Most white blood cells are in the lymph system. They only enter tissue fluid when there's an infection.
Platelets	✓	✗	✗	Only present in tissue fluid if the capillaries are damaged.
Proteins	✓	very few	only antibodies	Most plasma proteins are too big to get through capillary walls.
Water	✓	✓	✓	Tissue fluid and lymph have a higher water potential than blood.
Dissolved solutes	✓	✓	✓	Solutes (e.g. salt) can move freely between blood, tissue fluid and lymph.

Tip: Platelets are small fragments of cells that play an important role in blood clotting.

Practice Question — Application

Tip: For this application question, think about how the concentration of protein in the blood affects the water potential of the capillary.

Q1 Albumin is a protein found in the blood. Hypoalbuminemia is a condition where the level of albumin in the blood is very low. It causes an increase in tissue fluid, which can lead to swelling. Explain how hypoalbuminemia causes an increase in tissue fluid.

Practice Questions — Fact Recall

Tip: A transverse section is a cross-section through a structure, at a right angle to its length.

Q1 The diagrams on the right are transverse sections of three blood vessels (the diagrams are not drawn to scale). Name the blood vessels A - C.

A   B   C

Q2 Describe the structure of an artery.

Q3 a) Name the blood vessels that have valves in them.

    b) What is the function of these valves?

Q4 What is tissue fluid?

Q5 Explain the movement of fluid at the artery end of a capillary bed.

Q6 Where does excess tissue fluid drain into?

Q7 a) Give two differences between blood and tissue fluid.

    b) Give one difference between tissue fluid and lymph.

Tip: To distinguish between different types of blood vessels, you need to think about how thick the walls need to be for each type, how much muscle there will be in the walls, etc.

5. Haemoglobin

Lots of organisms have haemoglobin in their blood to transport oxygen.

Haemoglobin and oxyhaemoglobin

Human haemoglobin is found in red blood cells — its role is to carry oxygen around the body. Haemoglobin is a large protein with a quaternary structure — it's made up of four polypeptide chains. Each chain has a haem group which contains iron and gives haemoglobin its red colour (see Figure 1). Each molecule of human haemoglobin can carry four oxygen molecules.

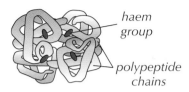

Figure 1: *Human haemoglobin.*

In the lungs, oxygen joins to the iron in haemoglobin to form **oxyhaemoglobin**. This is a reversible reaction — near the body cells, oxygen leaves oxyhaemoglobin and it turns back to haemoglobin (see Figure 2). When an oxygen molecule joins to haemoglobin it's referred to as **association** or **loading**, and when oxygen leaves oxyhaemoglobin it's referred to as **dissociation** or **unloading**.

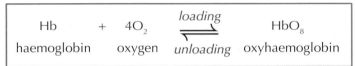

$$\text{Hb} \quad + \quad 4O_2 \quad \underset{unloading}{\overset{loading}{\rightleftharpoons}} \quad HbO_8$$

haemoglobin   oxygen   oxyhaemoglobin

Figure 2: *The association and dissociation of oxyhaemoglobin.*

Affinity for oxygen and pO_2

Affinity for oxygen means the tendency a molecule has to bind with oxygen. Haemoglobin's affinity for oxygen varies depending on the conditions it's in — one of the conditions that affects it is the **partial pressure of oxygen (pO_2)**.

pO_2 is a measure of oxygen concentration. The greater the concentration of dissolved oxygen in cells, the higher the partial pressure. As pO_2 increases, haemoglobin's affinity for oxygen also increases:

- Oxygen loads onto haemoglobin to form oxyhaemoglobin where there's a high pO_2.

- Oxyhaemoglobin unloads its oxygen where there's a lower pO_2.

Oxygen enters blood capillaries at the alveoli in the lungs. Alveoli have a high pO_2 so oxygen loads onto haemoglobin to form oxyhaemoglobin. When cells respire, they use up oxygen — this lowers the pO_2. Red blood cells deliver oxyhaemoglobin to respiring tissues, where it unloads its oxygen. The haemoglobin then returns to the lungs to pick up more oxygen. Figure 3 summarises this process.

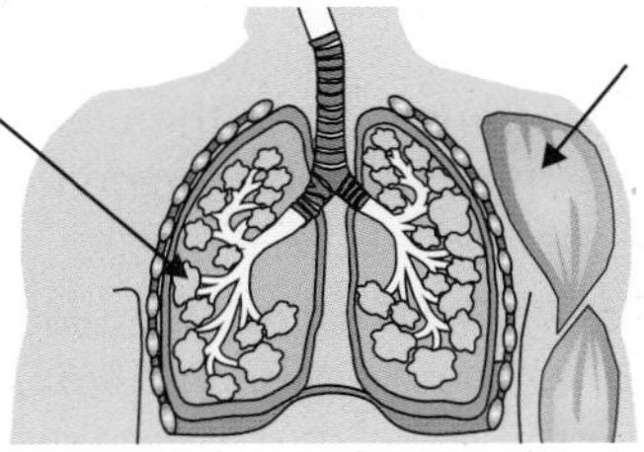

Alveoli in lungs
- *HIGH oxygen concentration*
- *HIGH pO_2*
- *HIGH affinity*
- *Oxygen LOADS*

Respiring tissue
- *LOW oxygen concentration*
- *LOW pO_2*
- *LOW affinity*
- *Oxygen UNLOADS*

Figure 3: *Oxygen loading and unloading in the body.*

Learning Objectives:

- Be able to describe the role of haemoglobin in carrying oxygen and carbon dioxide.

- Be able to explain the significance of the different affinities of fetal haemoglobin and adult haemoglobin for oxygen.

- Be able to describe and explain the significance of the dissociation curves of adult oxyhaemoglobin at different carbon dioxide levels (the Bohr effect).

Specification Reference 1.2.2

Tip: A protein with a quaternary structure just means it's made up of more than one polypeptide — see page 110 for more.

Tip: Haemoglobin is sometimes shortened to Hb.

Dissociation curves

An oxygen dissociation curve shows how saturated the haemoglobin is with oxygen at any given partial pressure. The affinity of haemoglobin for oxygen affects how saturated the haemoglobin is:

Tip: 100% saturation means every haemoglobin molecule is carrying the maximum of 4 molecules of oxygen.

Tip: 0% saturation means none of the haemoglobin molecules are carrying any oxygen.

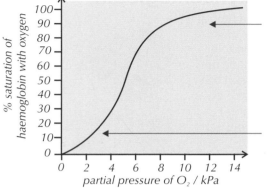

Where pO_2 is high (e.g. in the lungs), haemoglobin has a high affinity for oxygen, so it has a high saturation of oxygen.

Where pO_2 is low (e.g. in respiring tissues), haemoglobin has a low affinity for oxygen, so it has a low saturation of oxygen.

Figure 4: *Dissociation curve for adult haemoglobin.*

Weirdly, the saturation of haemoglobin can also affect the affinity — this is why the graph is 'S-shaped' and not a straight line. When haemoglobin combines with the first O_2 molecule, its shape alters in a way that makes it easier for other molecules to join too. But as the haemoglobin starts to become saturated, it gets harder for more oxygen molecules to join. As a result, the curve has a steep bit in the middle where it's really easy for oxygen molecules to join, and shallow bits at each end where it's harder — see Figure 5. When the curve is steep, a small change in pO_2 causes a big change in the amount of oxygen carried by the haemoglobin.

Tip: kPa (kilopascal) is a unit used to measure pressure.

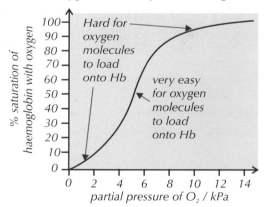

Figure 5: *The S-shaped dissociation curve for haemoglobin.*

Fetal haemoglobin

Adult haemoglobin and fetal haemoglobin have different affinities for oxygen. Fetal haemoglobin has a higher affinity for oxygen than adult haemoglobin (the fetus's blood is better at absorbing oxygen than its mother's blood). This is really important because the fetus gets oxygen from its mother's blood across the placenta.

By the time the mother's blood reaches the placenta, its oxygen saturation has decreased because some has been used up by the mother's body. The placenta has a low pO_2, so adult oxyhaemoglobin will unload its oxygen (adult oxyhaemoglobin will dissociate).

Exam Tip
Make sure you don't get haemoglobin mixed up with oxyhaemoglobin in the exam — fetal haemoglobin has a higher affinity for oxygen, not fetal oxyhaemoglobin.

For the fetus to get enough oxygen to survive its haemoglobin has to have a higher affinity for oxygen than adult haemoglobin. This means fetal haemoglobin takes up oxygen (becomes more saturated) in lower pO_2 than adult haemoglobin — see Figure 6. If its haemoglobin had the same affinity for oxygen as adult haemoglobin, its blood wouldn't be saturated enough.

Tip: The placenta acts like a fetus's lungs — the fetal haemoglobin has a higher affinity for oxygen (than adult haemoglobin), so it becomes more saturated with O_2 at the placenta.

Exam Tip
If you're asked to draw a dissociation curve for fetal haemoglobin, make sure you draw it to the left of adult haemoglobin curve.

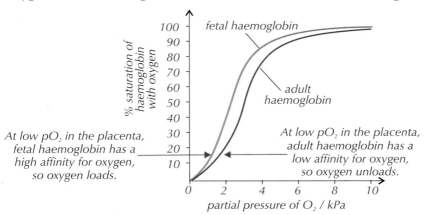

Figure 6: The dissociation curve for adult haemoglobin and fetal haemoglobin.

Carbon dioxide concentration

The **partial pressure of carbon dioxide (pCO_2)** is a measure of the concentration of CO_2 in a cell. To complicate matters, pCO_2 also affects oxygen unloading. Haemoglobin gives up its oxygen more readily at a higher pCO_2. It's a cunning way of getting more O_2 to cells during activity.

When cells respire they produce carbon dioxide, which raises the pCO_2. This increases the rate of oxygen unloading — the dissociation curve 'shifts' right. The saturation of blood with oxygen is lower for a given pO_2, meaning that more oxygen is being released — see Figure 7. This is called the **Bohr effect**.

Tip: Active cells need more oxygen for aerobic respiration. The word equation for aerobic respiration is: glucose + oxygen → carbon dioxide + water + energy.

Tip: When dissociation curves are being compared, the further left the curve is, the higher the haemoglobin's affinity for oxygen is.

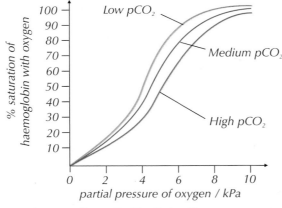

Figure 7: The Bohr effect.

Tip: The Bohr effect shifts the oxygen dissociation curve to the right.

Explanation of the Bohr effect

The reason for the Bohr effect is linked to how CO_2 affects blood pH. Most of the CO_2 from respiring tissues diffuses into red blood cells and is converted to **carbonic acid** by the enzyme **carbonic anhydrase**. (The rest of the CO_2, around 10%, binds directly to haemoglobin and is carried to the lungs.) The carbonic acid splits up to give hydrogen ions and hydrogencarbonate ions — see Figure 8 on the next page.

PLASMA		*RED BLOOD CELLS*		
carbon dioxide (+ water) CO_2 *(+* H_2O*)*	→ *carbonic anhydrase* →	*carbonic acid* H_2CO_3	→	*hydrogen ions* + *hydrogencarbonate ions* H^+ HCO_3^-

Figure 8: *The formation and splitting of carbonic acid.*

Tip: pH is a measure of the H^+ ion concentration of a solution. An acidic solution has a low pH and a high concentration of H^+ ions.

This increase in hydrogen ions causes oxyhaemoglobin to unload its oxygen so that haemoglobin can take up the hydrogen ions. This forms a compound called **haemoglobinic acid** — see Figure 9. (This process also stops the hydrogen ions from increasing the cell's acidity — the haemoglobin 'mops up' the hydrogen ions.) The hydrogencarbonate ions diffuse out of the red blood cells and are transported in the blood plasma.

RED BLOOD CELLS

hydrogen ions + oxyhaemoglobin ⟶ *haemoglobinic acid + oxygen*

H^+ + HbO_8 ⟶ HHb + $4O_2$

Figure 9: *The formation of haemoglobinic acid and unloading of oxygen.*

Tip: More CO_2 is released from actively respiring tissues, which causes the dissociation of more O_2.

When the blood reaches the lungs the low pCO_2 causes the hydrogencarbonate and hydrogen ions to recombine into CO_2 (and water). The CO_2 then diffuses into the alveoli and is breathed out.

Practice Questions — Application

The graph on the right shows a dissociation curve for adult haemoglobin.

Q1 Copy the graph and draw another dissociation curve to represent fetal haemoglobin.

Q2 Explain why you have drawn the dissociation curve for fetal haemoglobin in this way.

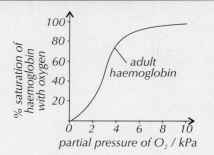

Practice Questions — Fact Recall

Q1 Where is haemoglobin found in humans?

Q2 What does oxygen load onto haemoglobin to form?

Q3 What is meant by 'haemoglobin's affinity for oxygen'?

Q4 Where in the body would you find cells with a high pO_2? Explain your answer.

Q5 What is shown on an oxygen dissociation curve?

Q6 State the main advantage of the Bohr effect.

Q7 Describe the shift that the Bohr effect would have on a dissociation curve for normal adult haemoglobin.

Q8 Name the enzyme that converts CO_2 to carbonic acid.

Q9 a) What happens to carbonic acid in red blood cells?

b) How does this lead to the unloading of oxygen?

Exam Tip

You could get a quality of written communication (QWC) question on this topic — so make sure you can spell words like 'haemoglobin', 'oxyhaemoglobin', 'dissociation curve' and 'Bohr effect' correctly.

Section Summary

Make sure you know...

- That multicellular organisms need a transport system to supply their cells with everything they need because they're big in size, have a small surface area to volume ratio and are usually very active.

- That fish have a single circulatory system (blood only passes through the heart once for each complete circuit of the body) and that mammals have a double circulatory system (blood passes through the heart twice for each complete circuit of the body).

- That fish have a closed circulatory system (the blood is enclosed inside blood vessels) and that insects have an open circulatory system (the blood isn't enclosed in blood vessels all the time).

- The internal and external structures of the heart, including the superior and inferior vena cava, pulmonary artery, aorta, pulmonary vein, right atrium, left atrium, semi-lunar valves, atrioventricular valves, cords, right ventricle, left ventricle and coronary artery.

- How heart valves work — if there's a higher pressure behind a valve it's forced open, but if pressure is higher in front of the valve it's forced shut.

- That the left ventricle has a thicker wall than the right ventricle and that ventricles have thicker walls than atria, as well as the reasons for these differences.

- The cardiac cycle, including the semi-lunar and atrioventricular valve movements.

- The roles of the following structures in controlling the heartbeat: sino-atrial node (sets the heartbeat rhythm), atrioventricular node (passes on the waves of electrical activity to the bundle of His), bundle of His (passes on the waves of electrical activity to the Purkyne tissue), Purkyne tissue (passes on the waves of electrical activity to the muscular walls of the right and left ventricles).

- How to interpret and explain electrocardiogram (ECG) traces of normal and abnormal heart activity.

- The differences in the structures of arteries, capillaries and veins.

- That the function of arteries is to carry blood away from the heart (under high pressure), that capillaries are the site for the exchange of substances between the cells and the blood, and that veins carry blood back to the heart under low pressure.

- That tissue fluid is formed from blood plasma by the action of pressure filtration at the artery end of a capillary bed.

- That tissue fluid is formed from blood, and lymph is formed from tissue fluid — and the differences between blood, tissue and lymph.

- That the role of haemoglobin is to carry oxygen around the body.

- That affinity for oxygen means the tendency a molecule has to bind with oxygen.

- That as partial pressure of oxygen (pO_2) increases, haemoglobin's affinity for oxygen increases.

- That a dissociation curve shows how saturated haemoglobin is at any given partial pressure.

- That fetal haemoglobin has a higher affinity for oxygen than adult haemoglobin, allowing it to pick up the oxygen from adult oxyhaemoglobin at the placenta.

- That an increase in carbon dioxide concentration (pCO_2) increases the rate of oxygen unloading and the dissociation curve shifts right — this is called the Bohr effect.

- The explanation behind the Bohr effect — CO_2 in red blood cells is converted to carbonic acid by carbonic anhydrase, carbonic acid splits into hydrogen ions and hydrogencarbonate ions, and this increase in hydrogen ions causes oxyhaemoglobin to unload oxygen so that haemoglobin can take up the hydrogen ions (forming haemoglobinic acid).

Exam-style Questions

1   Fig. 1.1 is a diagram
of the internal structure
of the heart. The valves
are shown but not labelled.

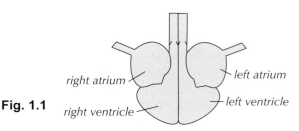

Fig. 1.1

(a)   Describe **and** explain where the blood is flowing **into** in Fig. 1.1.

(3 marks)

(b)   Name the valves that connect the atria to the ventricles
and describe their function.

(2 marks)

(c) (i)   Fig. 1.2 is a simplified
diagram of a transverse
section of an atrium.

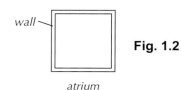

Fig. 1.2

Draw a similar diagram to show the relative thickness of the wall of a ventricle.

(1 mark)

(ii) Explain the difference between the thickness of the atrial and ventricular walls.

(2 marks)

2   Fig. 2.1 shows two oxygen dissociation
curves for the same man.

One curve was produced based on blood
tests when he was watching television
and the other was produced based on
blood tests immediately after a bike ride.

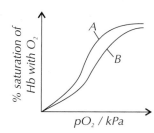

Fig. 2.1

(a)   Which curve was produced after the bike ride?
Explain your answer.

(3 marks)

(b) (i)   What name is given to the effect shown on the graph?

(1 mark)

(ii) Explain how this effect happens.

(6 marks)

3 Some people suffer from a disease called third-degree atrioventricular block — the waves of electrical activity from the sino-atrial node (SAN) are not relayed to the atrioventricular node (AVN). A pacemaker can be fitted to take over this role. Fig. 3.1 shows a heart with a pacemaker attached.

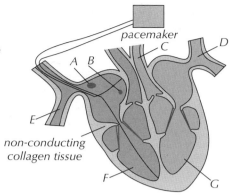

Fig. 3.1

(a) From Fig. 3.1, identify which labels correspond to the following structures by writing a letter from A to G in the table.

AVN	
Right ventricle	
Pulmonary vein	

(3 marks)

(b) What is the purpose of the non-conducting collagen tissue shown on the diagram?

(1 mark)

(c) Explain why the pacemaker must be programmed to have a delay between receiving waves of electrical activity from the SAN and activating the AVN.

(2 marks)

(d) Describe the passage of the waves of electrical activity from the AVN to rest of the heart, causing the ventricles to contract.

In your answer, you should use appropriate technical terms, spelled correctly.

(4 marks)

4 Fig 4.1 shows part of the circulatory system of a mammal. The arrows show the direction of blood flow.

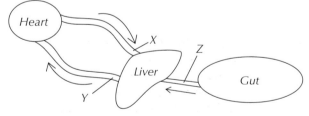

Fig. 4.1

(a) (i) Which vessel in Fig 4.1, **X**, **Y** or **Z**, transports blood at the highest pressure? Explain your answer.

(2 marks)

(ii) State **three** ways in which the structure of blood vessel X differs from the structure of blood vessel Y.

(3 marks)

(b) The liver is surrounded by a capillary bed and tissue fluid.
Describe how tissue fluid is formed.

(2 marks)

(c) State **two** ways in which blood is different from lymph.

(2 marks)

1. Xylem and Phloem

Humans have one transport system — the circulatory system. Plants go one better and have two transport systems — the xylem and the phloem...

Why do plants need transport systems?

Plant cells need substances like water, minerals and sugars to live. They also need to get rid of waste substances. Like animals, plants are multicellular so have a small surface area : volume ratio (see page 57). Plants could exchange substances by direct diffusion (from the outer surface to the cells), but that would be too slow. So plants need transport systems to move substances to and from individual cells quickly.

Location of xylem and phloem tissues

There are two types of tissue involved in transport in plants. Xylem tissue transports water and mineral ions up a plant's stem to the leaves. Phloem tissue transports dissolved substances, like sugars, up and down a plant.

Xylem and phloem are found throughout a plant — they transport materials to all parts. Where they're found in each part is connected to the xylem's other function, which is support. The locations of xylem and phloem in a plant's roots, stem and leaves are shown below:

Roots

In a root, the xylem and phloem are in the centre to provide support for the root as it pushes through the soil — see Figure 1.

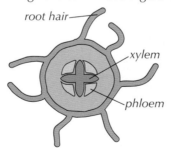

Figure 1: *Cross-section of a root.*

Stem

In the stems, the xylem and phloem are near the outside to provide a sort of 'scaffolding' that reduces bending — see Figure 2.

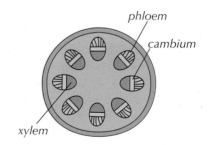

Figure 2: *Cross-section of a stem.*

Leaves

In a leaf, xylem and phloem make up a network of veins which support the thin leaves — see Figure 3.

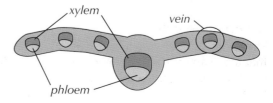

Figure 3: *Cross-section of a leaf.*

Learning Objectives:

- Be able to explain the need for transport systems in multicellular plants in terms of size and surface area : volume ratio.
- Be able to describe, with the aid of diagrams and photographs, the distribution of xylem and phloem tissue in roots, stems and leaves of dicotyledonous plants.
- Be able to describe, with the aid of diagrams and photographs, the structure and function of xylem vessels, sieve tube elements and companion cells.

Specification Reference 1.2.3

Tip: Plants also need carbon dioxide, but this enters at the leaves (where it's needed).

Tip: The cambium is a plant tissue that contains stem cells which differentiate into xylem and phloem — see p. 48.

Tip: One of the learning objectives mentions dicotyledonous plants — don't worry, this is just a category of plant that includes most green and non-woody plants, bushes and trees.

Adaptations of xylem vessels

Xylem is a tissue made from several different cell types (see page 51). You need to learn about xylem vessels — the part of xylem tissue that's adapted for transporting water and mineral ions.

Xylem vessels are very long, tube-like structures formed from cells (vessel elements) joined end to end — see Figure 4. There are no end walls on these cells, making an uninterrupted tube that allows water to pass up through the middle easily. The cells are dead, so they contain no cytoplasm.

The cell walls are thickened with a woody substance called **lignin**, which helps to support the walls and stops them collapsing inwards. The lignin is present in spiral patterns, which allows flexibility and prevents the stem from breaking. The amount of lignin increases as the cell gets older.

Water and mineral ions move into and out of the vessels through small **pits** in the walls where there's no lignin. This is how other types of cells are supplied with water.

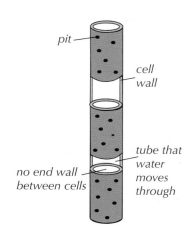

Figure 4: A xylem vessel with internal detail showing.

Figure 5: An SEM image of a xylem vessel in a bamboo plant with lignin (grey loops) in the walls.

Exam Tip
Remember to write that lignin supports the xylem <u>walls</u>, not the whole plant.

Adaptations of phloem tissue

Phloem tissue transports sugars like sucrose, round plants. Like xylem, phloem is formed from cells arranged in tubes. But, unlike xylem, it's purely a transport tissue — it isn't used for support as well. Phloem tissue contains phloem fibres, phloem parenchyma, sieve tube elements and companion cells. Sieve tube elements and companion cells are the most important cell types in phloem for transport (see Figure 6).

Tip: Phloem tissue also transports small amounts of amino acids, certain ions and plant hormones — but mainly sugars (the sugars it transports are dissolved).

Sieve tube elements

These are living cells that form the tube for transporting sugars through the plant. They are joined end to end to form sieve tubes. The 'sieve' parts are the end walls, which have lots of holes in them to allow sugars to pass through. Unusually for living cells, sieve tube elements have no nucleus, a very thin layer of cytoplasm and few organelles. The cytoplasm of adjacent cells is connected through the holes in the sieve plates.

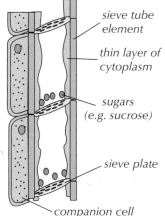

Figure 6: Phloem tissue.

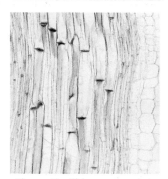

Figure 7: Phloem vessels in a Cucurbita plant. The sieve cells are stained blue and the sieve plates are dark green.

Companion cells

The lack of a nucleus and other organelles in sieve tube elements means that they can't survive on their own. So there's a companion cell for every sieve tube element. Companion cells carry out the living functions for both themselves and their sieve cells. For example, they provide the energy for the active transport of sugars.

Tip: The active transport of sugars requires energy — see p. 33 for more details.

Practice Questions — Application

Q1 Below is a light micrograph of a root cross-section.

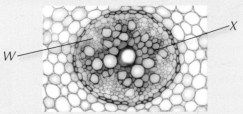

   a) Is structure W xylem or phloem?

   b) Is structure X xylem or phloem?

Q2 Figure A below is an SEM of phloem tissue in a plant stem.
   Figure B below is an SEM of xylem vessels in an ash tree.

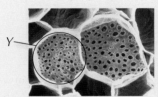 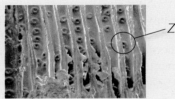

   Figure A   **Figure B**

   a) Name structure Y in Figure A.

   b) Name structure Z in Figure B and describe its function.

Tip: Microscopes pop up everywhere in Biology — SEM stands for scanning electron microscope. (You learnt about these on page 18.)

Practice Questions — Fact Recall

Q1 Explain why plants can't exchange substances by direct diffusion.

Q2 The outline on the right represents a cross-section of a plant's stem. Copy the outline and draw in the position of the xylem and phloem.

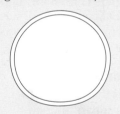

Tip: It's easy to get the location of the xylem and phloem mixed up, so make sure you learn the diagrams on p. 90.

Q3 The diagram below shows the cross-section of a leaf.

   Name the structures labelled A to C.

Q4 What do xylem vessels transport?

Q5 Name the substance present in the xylem vessel walls that prevents them collapsing.

Q6 How do substances move in and out of the xylem vessels?

Q7 What is the main substance phloem tissue transports?

Q8 a) Are sieve tube elements living cells or dead cells?

   b) Give two ways that sieve tube elements differ from normal plant cells.

2. Water Transport

Plants are pretty clever when it comes to transporting water. They can take it up from their roots to their leaves against the force of gravity. Let's see how they manage that...

How does water enter a plant?

Water has to get from the soil, through the root and into the xylem to be transported around the plant. Water enters through root hair cells and then passes through the root **cortex**, including the **endodermis**, to reach the xylem — see Figure 1.

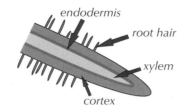

Figure 1: Cross-section of a root.

Water always moves from areas of higher water potential to areas of lower water potential — it goes down a **water potential gradient**. The soil around roots generally has a high water potential (i.e. there's lots of water there) and leaves have a lower water potential (because water constantly evaporates from them). This creates a water potential gradient that keeps water moving through the plant in the right direction, from roots (high) to leaves (low) — see Figure 2.

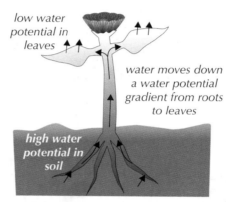

Figure 2: Water potential gradient up a plant.

Water transport through the root

Water travels through the roots (via the root cortex) into the xylem by two different pathways:

The symplast pathway

The symplast pathway (see Figure 3) goes through the living parts of cells — the cytoplasm. The cytoplasm of neighbouring cells connect through **plasmodesmata** (small channels in the cell walls).

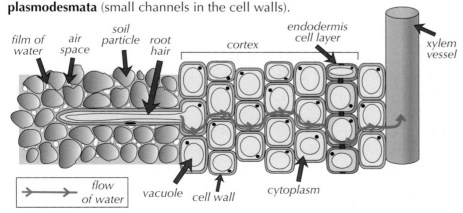

Figure 3: The symplast pathway.

Learning Objectives:

- Be able to explain, in terms of water potential, the movement of water between plant cells, and between plant cells and their environment. (No calculations involving water potential will be set.)

- Be able to describe, with the aid of diagrams, the pathway by which water is transported from the root cortex to the air surrounding the leaves, with reference to the Casparian strip, apoplast pathway, symplast pathway, xylem and the stomata.

- Be able to define the term transpiration.

- Be able to explain the mechanism by which water is transported from the root cortex to the air surrounding the leaves, with reference to the transpiration stream, cohesion and adhesion.

Specification Reference 1.2.3

Tip: Water moves into a root hair cell by osmosis. There's more about osmosis and water potential on pages 29-31.

Figure 4: Root hairs on a cress root.

The apoplast pathway

The apoplast pathway (see Figure 5) goes through the non-living parts of the cells — the cell walls. The walls are very absorbent and water can simply diffuse through them, as well as passing through the spaces between them.

When water in the apoplast pathway gets to the endodermis cells in the root, its path is blocked by a waxy strip in the cell walls, called the **Casparian strip**. Now the water has to take the symplast pathway. This is useful, because it means the water has to go through a cell membrane. Cell membranes are able to control whether or not substances in the water get through (see p. 23). Once past this barrier, the water moves into the xylem.

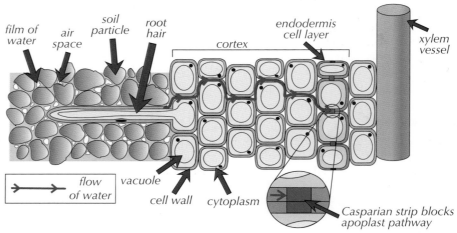

Figure 5: The apoplast pathway.

Water transport through the leaves

Xylem vessels transport the water all around the plant. At the leaves, water leaves the xylem and moves into the cells mainly by the apoplast pathway. Water evaporates from the cell walls into the spaces between cells in the leaf. When the **stomata** (tiny pores in the surface of the leaf) open, water moves out of the leaf as vapour (down the water potential gradient) into the surrounding air — see Figure 6. The loss of water vapour from a plant's surface is called **transpiration** (see p. 96).

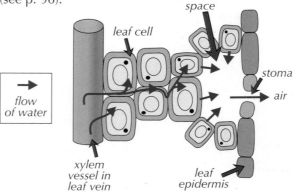

Figure 6: Water loss from a leaf.

Water movement up a plant

The movement of water from roots to leaves is called the **transpiration stream**. The mechanisms that move the water include cohesion, tension and adhesion.

Cohesion and tension

Cohesion and tension help water move up plants, from roots to leaves, against the force of gravity (see Figure 7).

1. Water evaporates from the leaves at the 'top' of the xylem (transpiration).

2. This creates a tension (suction), which pulls more water into the leaf.

3. Water molecules are cohesive (they stick together) so when some are pulled into the leaf others follow. This means the whole column of water in the xylem, from the leaves down to the roots, moves upwards.

4. Water enters the stem through the root cortex cells.

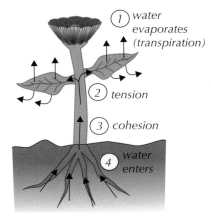

Figure 7: *Water movement up a plant.*

Tip: Air bubbles can form in the xylem, which block the column of water, preventing water from reaching the cells. Without enough water the cells become flaccid (see page 31) and the plant wilts.

Tip: Water movement up a plant increases as the transpiration rate increases — see page 96.

Adhesion

Adhesion is also partly responsible for the movement of water. As well as being attracted to each other, water molecules are attracted to the walls of the xylem vessels. This helps water to rise up through the xylem vessels.

Practice Questions — Application

The diagram below shows a section through a root.

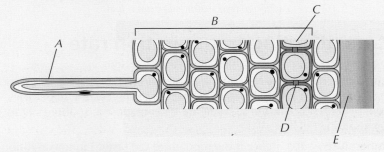

Answer the following questions about the diagram.

Q1 What type of cell is cell A?

Q2 Which cell layer is the endodermis — B or C?

Q3 Name structure D.

Q4 If structure E was blocked, suggest what effect this may have on the plant.

Practice Questions — Fact Recall

Q1 Briefly describe the pathway of water from the soil into the xylem.

Q2 Describe how water moves through the symplast and apoplast pathways.

Q3 What is transpiration?

Q4 What is the transpiration stream?

Q5 Explain adhesion in terms of water movement in the xylem.

Exam Tip
Don't get transpiration mixed up with the transpiration stream — they are two different processes.

- Be able to explain why transpiration is a consequence of gaseous exchange.

- Be able to describe the factors that affect transpiration rate.

- Be able to describe, with the aid of diagrams, how a potometer is used to estimate transpiration rates.

- Be able to describe, with the aid of diagrams and photographs, how the leaves of some xerophytes are adapted to reduce water loss by transpiration.

Specification Reference 1.2.3

Tip: Water moves from areas of higher water potential to areas of lower water potential — it moves down the water potential gradient.

Tip: The rate of transpiration can fluctuate at different times of day, e.g. because the humidity is higher or lower.

Tip: Transpiration rate isn't exactly the same as water uptake by a plant — some water is used for photosynthesis and to support the plant, and some water is produced during respiration.

3. Transpiration

Transpiration was introduced on the previous couple of pages, but unfortunately there's loads more you need to know about it...

Why does transpiration happen?

So you know that transpiration is the evaporation of water from a plant's surface, especially the leaves. But I bet you didn't know it happens as a result of **gas exchange**.

A plant needs to open its stomata to let in carbon dioxide so that it can produce glucose (by photosynthesis). But this also lets water out — there's a higher concentration of water inside the leaf than in the air outside, so water moves out of the leaf down the water potential gradient when the stomata open. So transpiration's really a side effect of the gas exchange needed for photosynthesis.

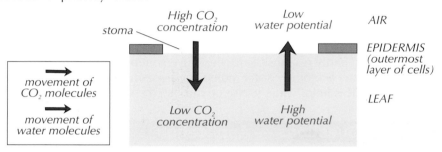

Figure 1: Simplified diagram to show gas exchange and water loss from a leaf.

Factors affecting transpiration rate

There are four main factors that affect transpiration rate:

1. **Light** — the lighter it is the faster the transpiration rate. This is because the stomata open when it gets light (the lighter it gets, the wider they open). When it's dark the stomata are usually closed, so there's little transpiration.

2. **Temperature** — the higher the temperature the faster the transpiration rate. Warmer water molecules have more energy so they evaporate from the cells inside the leaf faster. This increases the water potential gradient between the inside and outside of the leaf, making water diffuse out of the leaf faster.

3. **Humidity** — the lower the humidity, the faster the transpiration rate. If the air around the plant is dry, the water potential gradient between the leaf and the air is increased, which increases transpiration.

4. **Wind** — the windier it is, the faster the transpiration rate. Lots of air movement blows away water molecules from around the stomata. This increases the water potential gradient, which increases the rate of transpiration.

Estimating transpiration rate — potometers

A potometer is a special piece of apparatus used to estimate transpiration rates. It actually measures water uptake by a plant, but it's assumed that water uptake by the plant is directly related to water loss by the leaves. You can use it to estimate how different factors affect the transpiration rate.

Using a potometer

The steps involved in using a potometer are listed below and shown in Figure 2.

1. Cut a shoot underwater to prevent air from entering the xylem. Cut it at a slant to increase the surface area available for water uptake.

2. Assemble the potometer in water and insert the shoot under water, so no air can enter.

3. Remove the apparatus from the water but keep the end of the capillary tube submerged in a beaker of water.

4. Check that the apparatus is watertight and airtight.

5. Dry the leaves, allow time for the shoot to acclimatise and then shut the tap.

6. Remove the end of the capillary tube from the beaker of water until one air bubble has formed, then put the end of the tube back into the water.

7. Record the starting position of the air bubble.

8. Start a stopwatch and record the distance moved by the bubble per unit time, e.g. per hour.

9. Remember, the conditions need to be kept constant throughout the experiment, e.g. the temperature and the air humidity.

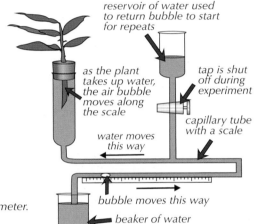

reservoir of water used to return bubble to start for repeats

as the plant takes up water, the air bubble moves along the scale

tap is shut off during experiment

capillary tube with a scale

water moves this way

bubble moves this way

beaker of water

Figure 2: *A potometer.*

Tip: You can use a potometer to test the effect of different factors on transpiration rate, e.g. by using a fan to increase air movement or a lamp to increase light etc.

Tip: When estimating the rate of transpiration by measuring water uptake, you need to carry out repeats to increase the reliability of your data and to help identify any anomalies in your data. (See page 5 for more.)

Adaptations in xerophytic plants

Xerophytes are plants like cacti, pine trees and prickly pears, which are adapted to live in dry climates. Their adaptations prevent them losing too much water by transpiration.

┌─ **Examples** ─────────────────

Examples of xerophytic adaptations include:

1. **Stomata are sunk in pits** — the pits trap water vapour, reducing transpiration by lowering the water potential gradient.

2. **A layer of 'hairs' on the epidermis** — this traps moist air round the stomata, which reduces the water potential gradient between the leaf and the air, slowing transpiration down.

3. **Curled leaves** — this traps moist air, slowing down transpiration. This also lowers the exposed surface area for losing water and protects the stomata from wind.

4. **A reduced number of stomata** — this means there are fewer places where water vapour can diffuse out of the leaf.

5. **Thick, waxy layer on the epidermis** — this reduces water loss by evaporation because the layer is waterproof (water can't move through it).

Tip: The first three examples of adaptations reduce transpiration by reducing the water potential gradient between the air spaces in the leaf and the air outside the leaf.

Tip: Remember, water is lost from a leaf as water vapour.

Tip: The thick, waxy layer on the epidermis of a plant is called a cuticle.

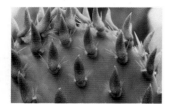

Figure 3: *Spines on a xerophyte.*

6. **Spines instead of leaves** (e.g. cactus) — this reduces the surface area for water loss.

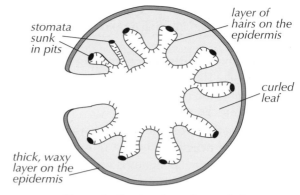

Figure 4: *Section through a curled leaf of a xerophyte.*

Practice Questions — Application

Q1 The photographs below show sections of leaves from two different plants.

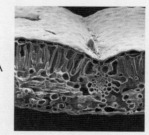 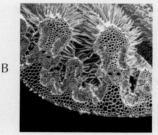

A   B

Which leaf belongs to a xerophyte? Explain your answer.

Q2 A potometer was used to test the effect of temperature on transpiration rate. The test was repeated 3 times. The results are shown in the table.

Temperature (°C)	Distance moved by the bubble in 10 minutes (mm)		
	Test 1	Test 2	Test 3
10	15	12	14
20	19	16	19
30	25	22	23

a) Calculate the mean result for each temperature. Give your answers to one decimal place.

b) Plot a graph of the mean results and use it to estimate the distance the bubble would move in ten minutes at 25 °C.

c) Describe and explain the results of the experiment.

Exam Tip
If you're asked in the exam to give your answer to one decimal place, make sure you round it up or down correctly — otherwise you won't get the marks.

Practice Questions — Fact Recall

Q1 What process is transpiration a consequence of?
Q2 Explain how wind affects transpiration rate.
Q3 Other than wind, give three factors that affect transpiration rate.
Q4 When using a potometer to estimate transpiration rate, what assumption is made?

4. Translocation

The phloem transports dissolved substances (like sugars) around the plant to where they're needed. Scientists still aren't sure exactly how this movement works, but they do have a hypothesis...

What is translocation?

Translocation is the movement of **assimilates** (e.g. sugars like sucrose) to where they're needed in a plant. It's an energy-requiring process that happens in the phloem.

Translocation moves assimilates from 'sources' to 'sinks'. The **source** is where assimilates are produced (so they're at a high concentration there). The **sink** is where assimilates are used up (so they're at a lower concentration there).

> **Example**
>
> The source for sucrose is the leaves (where it's made), and the sinks are the other parts of the plant, especially the food storage organs and the meristems (areas of growth) in the roots, stems and leaves.

Enzymes maintain a concentration gradient from the source to the sink by changing the dissolved substances at the sink (e.g. by breaking them down or making them into something else). This makes sure there's always a lower concentration at the sink than at the source.

> **Example**
>
> In potatoes, sucrose is converted to starch in the sink areas, so there's always a lower concentration of sucrose at the sink than inside the phloem. This makes sure a constant supply of new sucrose reaches the sink from the phloem.

The mass flow hypothesis

Scientists still aren't certain exactly how the assimilates are transported from source to sink by translocation. The best supported theory is the mass flow hypothesis:

1. Source

Active transport is used to actively load the assimilates (e.g. sucrose from photosynthesis) into the sieve tubes of the phloem at the source (e.g. the leaves). This lowers the water potential inside the sieve tubes, so water enters the tubes by osmosis. This creates a high pressure inside the sieve tubes at the source end of the phloem — see Figure 1 on the next page.

2. Sink

At the sink end, assimilates are removed from the phloem to be used up. This increases the water potential inside the sieve tubes, so water also leaves the tubes by osmosis. This lowers the pressure inside the sieve tubes — see Figure 1.

3. Flow

The result is a pressure gradient from the source end to the sink end. This gradient pushes assimilates along the sieve tubes to where they're needed.

Learning Objectives:

- Be able to explain translocation as an energy-requiring process transporting assimilates, especially sucrose, between sources (e.g. leaves) and sinks (e.g. roots, meristems).
- Be able to describe, with the aid of diagrams, the mechanism of transport in phloem involving active loading at the source and removal at the sink, and the evidence for and against this mechanism.

Specification Reference 1.2.3

Tip: Assimilates are substances that become incorporated into the plant tissue.

Exam Tip
Make sure you learn what the terms 'source' and 'sink' mean — you could be tested on them in the exam.

Tip: There's more about active transport on page 33.

Tip: The phloem transports assimilates up and down a plant, from sources to sinks. (See pages 90-91 for more on the phloem.)

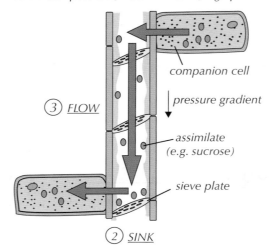

Tip: Companion cells contain many mitochondria, which means they can make lots of ATP. ATP is needed to actively load the assimilates into the phloem at the source.

① SOURCE

low water potential, water moves in, high pressure

companion cell

③ FLOW

pressure gradient

assimilate (e.g. sucrose)

sieve plate

② SINK

high water potential, water moves out, low pressure

Figure 1: *How the mass flow hypothesis works.*

Tip: There's more about sieve plates and companion cells on page 91.

Mass flow evidence

There is evidence both for and against mass flow.

Supporting evidence

Tip: There's more about carrying out experiments to support (or disprove) hypotheses on page 1.

1. If you remove a ring of bark (which includes the phloem, but not the xylem) from a woody stem a bulge forms above the ring — see Figure 2. If you analyse the fluid from the bulge, you'll find it has a higher concentration of sugars than the fluid from below the ring. This is because the sugars can't move past the area where the bark has been removed — this is evidence that there's a downward flow of sugars.

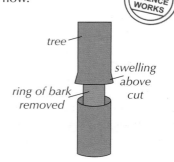

tree

swelling above cut

ring of bark removed

Figure 2: *Diagram to show the effect of removing a ring of bark from a tree.*

Tip: Sugars are made in the leaves, so that's why there's a downward flow of sugars (from source to sink) in this case.

Tip: The build up of sugars above the ring causes a decrease in water potential, so water moves into the cells — adding to the bulge.

2. You can investigate pressure in the phloem using aphids (they pierce the phloem, then their bodies are removed leaving the mouthparts behind, which allows the sap to flow out... gruesome). The sap flows out quicker nearer the leaves than further down the stem — this is evidence that there's a pressure gradient.

3. If you put a metabolic inhibitor (which stops ATP production) into the phloem then translocation stops — this is evidence that active transport is involved.

4. There's an experimental model for mass flow (see the next page).

Objections

1. Sugar travels to many different sinks, not just to the one with the highest water potential, as the model would suggest.

2. The sieve plates would create a barrier to mass flow. A lot of pressure would be needed for the assimilates to get through at a reasonable rate.

Experiment showing mass flow hypothesis

The mass flow hypothesis can be modelled in this experiment:

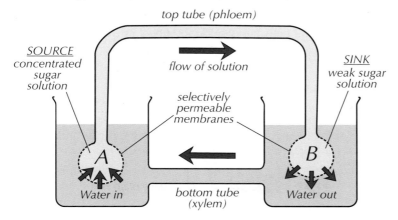

Tip: A selectively permeable membrane is one with very small holes in it. This means only tiny molecules (like water) can pass through it, but bigger molecules (like sucrose) can't.

A and B are two containers, each lined with a selectively permeable membrane just like cells have. The top tube connecting A and B represents the phloem, and the bottom tube represents the xylem. A represents the source end and contains a concentrated sugar solution. B represents the sink end and contains a weak sugar solution.

Water enters A by osmosis, increasing the pressure, which causes the sugar solution to flow along the top tube (phloem). Pressure increases in B, forcing water out and back through the bottom tube (xylem), which just transports water.

Practice Questions — Application

The diagram on the right shows the translocation of sucrose from the roots (where it was stored as starch) to a sink. This process happens in the Spring.

Q1 Suggest a sink for the sucrose shown on the diagram.

Q2 Using the mass flow hypothesis:

a) explain why water enters the sieve tubes in the roots,

b) explain why water leaves the sieve tubes at the sink.

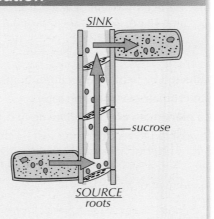

Practice Questions — Fact Recall

Q1 Define translocation.

Q2 What is the difference between a source and a sink in a plant?

Q3 Describe one piece of evidence in support of the mass flow hypothesis.

Q4 Describe one piece of evidence against the mass flow hypothesis.

Exam Tip
Practise spelling words like 'translocation', 'assimilates' and 'phloem' — you can pick up extra marks for correct spelling.

Section Summary

Make sure you know...

- That plants are multicellular and have a small surface area to volume ratio, so they need a transport system to move substances to and from individual cells because direct diffusion would be too slow.
- That plants have two transport systems — the xylem (which transports water and mineral ions) and the phloem (which mainly transports sugars).
- The distribution of xylem and phloem tissue in roots, stems and leaves of a plant.
- How xylem vessels are adapted for transporting water and mineral ions — they're made up of cells with no end walls (so water can easily pass up through the middle), the cells are dead (so they contain no cytoplasm), their walls are lignified (which helps to support the xylem walls and give flexibility) and they contain pits (which is how other types of cell are supplied with water).
- How sieve tube elements in phloem tissue are adapted for transporting sugars — they're joined end to end (to form sieve tubes), they have no nucleus, a thin layer of cytoplasm and few organelles, and they contain sieve plates with holes (which allow sugars to pass through from one cell to another).
- That companion cells in phloem tissue carry out the living functions for both themselves and their sieve cells.
- That water enters a root through root hair cells.
- That water always moves from an area of higher water potential (in the soil around the roots) to an area of lower water potential (in the leaves).
- How water moves through the symplast pathway (via the cytoplasm of cells) and the apoplast pathway (via the cell walls).
- That the Casparian strip is a waxy strip in the cell walls of the root endodermis that blocks that path of water in the apoplast pathway, so that it has to travel through the symplast pathway into the xylem.
- How water passes out of the leaves — down a water potential gradient through the stomata.
- That transpiration is the evaporation of water from a plant's surface.
- That the transpiration stream is the movement of water from roots to leaves.
- How cohesion and tension, and adhesion move water up the xylem.
- That transpiration occurs as a result of gas exchange — as stomata open to let carbon dioxide in, water is let out.
- How transpiration rate is affected by light, temperature, humidity and wind.
- How a potometer is used to estimate transpiration rate.
- That a xerophytic plant is a plant that's adapted to living in dry climates.
- How xerophytic plants are adapted to reduce water loss — they may have reduced numbers of stomata that are sunk in pits, a layer of hairs on the epidermis, a thick, waxy layer on the epidermis and curled leaves or spines.
- That translocation is the movement of assimilates (e.g. sugars like sucrose), to where they're needed in a plant.
- That translocation moves assimilates from their source (where they're produced) to their sink (where they're used up).
- That the mass flow hypothesis is the best supported theory for translocation.
- That the mass flow hypothesis involves assimilates being actively loaded at the source and removed at the sink, resulting in a pressure gradient from source to sink. This gradient pushes assimilates along the sieve tubes to where they're needed.
- Evidence for and against the mass flow hypothesis.
- How the mass flow hypothesis can be demonstrated in an experiment.

Exam-style Questions

1   A student used a potometer to investigate the effect of light intensity on transpiration rate. Her results are shown in Fig. 1.1.

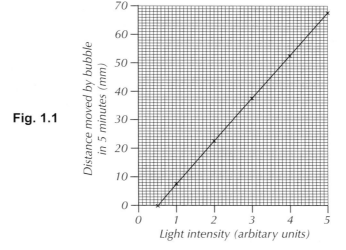

Fig. 1.1

(a) (i)   Using the graph, work out the rate of bubble movement for a light intensity of **1.5 arbitrary units**. Give your answer in mm/minute.

(2 marks)

(ii)   Describe and explain the results shown by the graph.

(3 marks)

(iii)   Suggest what **control** should be used for this investigation.

(1 mark)

(b)   Explain how and why transpiration occurs.

(2 marks)

2   Fig 2.1 shows a section of the phloem in a plant.

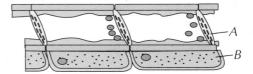

Fig. 2.1

(a) (i)   Name structure **A** and describe its function.

(2 marks)

(ii)   Describe and explain the function of cell **B**.

(2 marks)

(b)   Sucrose is transported from the leaves to the meristems of a plant via the phloem. Explain, using the **mass flow hypothesis**, how this process works.

(6 marks)

3 (a) Fig 3.1 shows the passage of water through part of a plant's root.

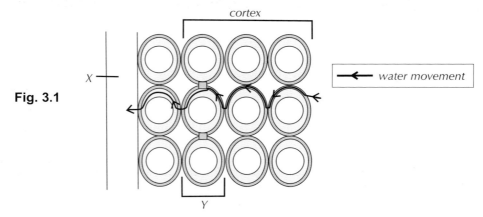

Fig. 3.1

(i) Name the structure marked **X** and the cell layer marked **Y** on Fig 3.1.

(2 marks)

(ii) Describe and explain the movement of the water in Fig. 3.1.

(3 marks)

(b) Explain how water moves up the plant by cohesion and tension.

(4 marks)

(c) Would the speed at which water moves up the plant be **faster** or **slower** on humid days? Explain your answer.

(2 marks)

(d) Explain, in terms of temperature, why a plant's transpiration rate increases during the summer.

 In your answer, you should use appropriate technical terms, spelled correctly.

(5 marks)

4 Table 4.1 describes some of the adaptations of a xerophyte.
Complete the table to explain how each adaptation reduces water loss.
The first row has been done for you.

Adaptation of xerophyte	How adaptation reduces water loss from the plant
Stomata are sunk in pits	The pits trap water vapour, lowering the water potential gradient.
Spines	
Curled leaves	
Reduced number of stomata	
Thick, waxy layer on the epidermis	

Table 4.1

(4 marks)

1. Water

Water is essential for life. The next few pages will show you what it is about water that makes it so important.

Functions of water

Water is vital to living organisms. It makes up about 80% of a cell's contents and has loads of important functions, inside and outside cells, such as:

- Water is a reactant in loads of important chemical reactions, like photosynthesis and hydrolysis reactions (see p. 108).
- Water transports substances. The fact that it's a liquid, a solvent (see p. 107) and cohesive (see p. 106) means it can easily transport all sorts of materials, like glucose and oxygen, around plants and animals.
- Water helps with temperature control because it has a high specific heat capacity (see p. 106) and a high latent heat of evaporation (see p. 106).
- Water is a habitat. The fact that it helps with temperature control, is a solvent and becomes less dense when it freezes (see p. 106) means many organisms can survive and reproduce in it.

Structure of water

To understand the structure of water, you need to know a bit about the chemistry involved in holding water molecules together.

Polarity of water

A molecule of water (H_2O) is one atom of oxygen (O) joined to two atoms of hydrogen (H_2) by shared electrons — see Figure 1.

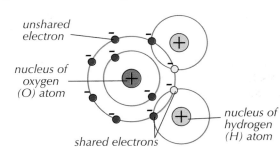

Figure 1: The structure of a water molecule.

Because the shared negative hydrogen electrons are pulled towards the oxygen atom, the other side of each hydrogen atom is left with a slight positive charge ($\delta+$). The unshared negative electrons on the oxygen atom give it a slight negative charge ($\delta-$). This makes water a polar molecule — it has a slight (partial) negative charge on one side and a slight (partial) positive charge on the other (see Figure 2).

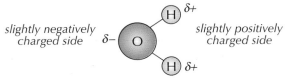

Figure 2: The slight charges on a water molecule.

Learning Objectives:

- Be able to describe how hydrogen bonding occurs between water molecules.
- Be able to relate hydrogen bonding between water molecules and other properties of water to the roles of water in living organisms.

Specification Reference 2.1.1

Exam Tip
Examiners like asking you to relate structure to properties and function, so make sure you're clear on the structure of water.

Tip: $\delta+$ is pronounced delta positive and $\delta-$ is delta negative.

Exam Tip
Be careful not to write that a water molecule has a positive and a negative side — you must make it clear that one side has a partial positive charge and the other side has a partial negative charge.

Hydrogen bonding

Hydrogen bonds are weak bonds
between a slightly positively
charged hydrogen atom in one
molecule and a slightly negatively
charged atom in another molecule.
Hydrogen bonds form between
water molecules because the
slightly negatively charged oxygen
atoms of water attract the slightly
positively charged hydrogen atoms
of other water molecules. This
hydrogen bonding gives water
some of its useful properties.

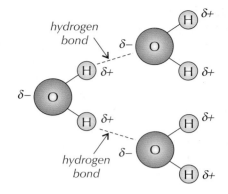

Figure 3: *Diagram showing how hydrogen bonds hold water molecules together.*

Properties of water

The structure of a water molecule gives it some useful properties, and these
help to explain many of its functions:

High specific heat capacity

Hydrogen bonds give water a high **specific heat capacity** — this is the
energy needed to raise the temperature of 1 gram of a substance by 1 °C.
When water is heated, a lot of the heat energy is used to break the hydrogen
bonds between the water molecules. This means there is less heat energy
available to actually increase the temperature of the water. So water has
a high specific heat capacity — it takes a lot of energy to heat it up.
This is useful for living organisms because it stops rapid temperature changes,
allowing them to keep their temperature fairly stable.

High latent heat of evaporation

Water evaporates when the hydrogen bonds holding water molecules together
are broken. This allows the water molecules on the surface of the water
to escape into the air as a gas. It takes a lot of energy (heat) to break the
hydrogen bonds between water molecules, so a lot of energy is used up when
water evaporates. This means water has a high latent heat of evaporation —
lots of heat is used to change it from a liquid to a gas. This is useful for living
organisms because it means water's great for cooling things — it carries away
heat energy when it evaporates from a surface, which cools the surface and
helps to lower the temperature.

Very cohesive

Cohesion is the attraction between molecules of the same type (e.g. two water
molecules). Water molecules are very cohesive (they tend to stick together)
because they're polar. This helps water to flow, making it great for transporting
substances.

Lower density when solid

At low temperatures water freezes — it turns from a liquid to a solid.
Water molecules are held further apart in ice than they are in liquid water,
which makes ice less dense than liquid water — this is why ice floats on top
of water. This is useful for living organisms because, in cold temperatures,
ice forms an insulating layer on top of water — the water below doesn't
freeze. This means the organisms that live in water do not freeze and can still
move around.

Good solvent

A lot of important substances in biological reactions are ionic (like salt, for example). This means they're made from one positively charged atom or molecule and one negatively charged atom or molecule (e.g. salt is made from a positive sodium ion and a negative chloride ion).

Because water is polar, the slightly positively charged end of a water molecule will be attracted to the negative ion, and the slightly negatively charged end of a water molecule will be attracted to the positive ion. This means the ions will get totally surrounded by water molecules — in other words, they'll dissolve (see Figure 4). So water's polarity makes it useful as a solvent (a substance capable of dissolving another substance). This means living organisms can take up useful substances (e.g. mineral ions) dissolved in water and these dissolved substances can be transported around the organism's body.

Tip: Most biological reactions take place in solution, so water's pretty essential.

Tip: Remember — a molecule is polar if it has a slightly negatively charged side and a slightly positively charged side.

Tip: Polar molecules, such as glucose, dissolve in water because hydrogen bonds form between them and the water molecules.

Figure 4: A positive ion (left) and a negative ion (right) dissolved in water.

Practice Questions — Fact Recall

Q1 Give three functions of water that are important to living organisms.

Q2 Why is water classed as a polar molecule?

Q3 Label this diagram of a water molecule showing the name and charge on each atom.

Q4 What is a hydrogen bond?

Q5 Draw a diagram showing four water molecules hydrogen bonded together.

Q6 Explain why water has a high specific heat capacity.

Q7 Explain why water is good for cooling things.

Q8 Give two reasons why the polarity of water makes it good for transporting substances.

Q9 The diagrams on the right show molecular models of liquid water and ice.

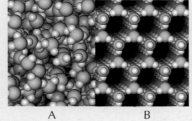

a) Which diagram, A or B, is a molecular model of ice? Give a reason for your answer.

b) Explain how the formation of ice can be beneficial for organisms.

A   B

Q10 Describe how an Mg^{2+} ion dissolves in water.

Exam Tip
If you're asked in the exam about how a particular ion dissolves in water, don't get put off by the ion itself — just figure out if it's positively charged or negatively charged. E.g. in Q10 here Mg^{2+} is a positively charged magnesium ion.

2. Proteins

Proteins have lots of useful functions in organisms. Their function is related to their structure, which is determined by the basic units they're made from and the bonds between them.

What are proteins made from?

Proteins are polymers. These are large, complex molecules composed of long chains of monomers — small basic molecular units. The monomers of proteins are amino acids. A **dipeptide** is formed when two amino acids join together. A **polypeptide** is formed when more than two amino acids join together. Proteins are made up of one or more polypeptides.

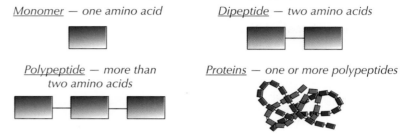

Figure 1: *Amino acids join together to form peptides and proteins.*

Amino acid structure

All amino acids have the same general structure — a carboxyl group (-COOH) and an amino group ($-NH_2$) attached to a carbon atom. The difference between different amino acids is the variable (or residual) group they contain (shown as R on diagram).

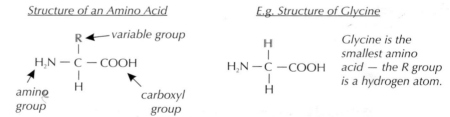

Polypeptide formation

Amino acids are linked together by **condensation reactions** to form dipeptides and polypeptides. A molecule of water is released during the reaction. The bonds formed between amino acids are called **peptide bonds**. A peptide bond forms between the amino group of one amino acid and the carboxyl group of another amino acid. The reverse reaction adds a molecule of water to break the peptide bond — this is called a **hydrolysis** reaction.

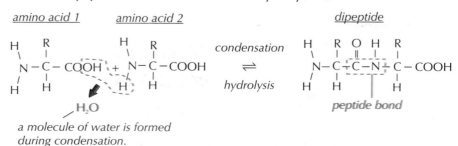

Tip: Condensation reactions <u>form</u> a water molecule, hydrolysis reactions <u>use</u> a water molecule.

Q1 Look at the following amino acid structures.

<table>
<tr><td>Glycine</td><td>Alanine</td><td>Valine</td></tr>
</table>

Glycine

$$H_2N - \overset{\overset{\displaystyle H}{|}}{\underset{\underset{\displaystyle H}{|}}{C}} - COOH$$

Alanine

$$H_2N - \overset{\overset{\displaystyle CH_3}{|}}{\underset{\underset{\displaystyle H}{|}}{C}} - COOH$$

Valine

$$\begin{array}{cc} CH_3 & CH_3 \\ \diagdown & \diagup \\ & CH \\ & | \end{array}$$
$$H_2N - \overset{}{\underset{\underset{\displaystyle H}{|}}{C}} - COOH$$

Draw the dipeptides and polypeptide that would be formed from a condensation reaction between:

a) glycine and valine.

b) alanine and glycine.

c) glycine, alanine and valine.

Q2 Draw the amino acids produced from the hydrolysis of the dipeptide below.

$$H_2N - \overset{\overset{\displaystyle H}{|}}{\underset{\underset{\displaystyle H}{|}}{C}} - \overset{\overset{\displaystyle O}{\|}}{C} - \overset{\overset{\displaystyle H}{|}}{N} - \overset{\overset{\displaystyle CH_2OH}{|}}{\underset{\underset{\displaystyle H}{|}}{C}} - COOH$$

Tip: If you compare these amino acids to the basic amino acid structure on p. 108 you can spot the R groups, e.g. for alanine it's -CH$_3$.

Exam Tip
Remember that in hydrolysis a molecule of water is used, so for Q2 you need to make sure you've added two Hs and one O.

Protein structure

Proteins are big, complicated molecules. They're much easier to explain if you describe their structure in four 'levels'. These levels are a protein's primary, secondary, tertiary and quaternary structures. The four structural levels of a protein are held together by different kinds of bonds.

Primary structure

This is the sequence of amino acids in the polypeptide chain. It is held together by the peptide bonds between the amino acids.

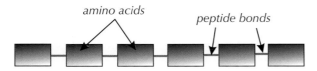

Figure 2: A protein's primary structure.

Secondary structure

The polypeptide chain doesn't remain flat and straight. Hydrogen bonds form between the –NH and –CO groups of the amino acids in the chain. This makes it automatically coil into an alpha (a) helix or fold into a beta (b) pleated sheet — this is the secondary structure.

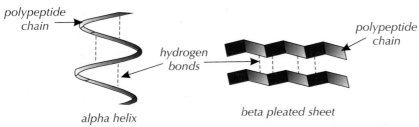

Figure 3: A protein's secondary structure.

Tip: In a polypeptide chain the –NH and –CO groups are polar. The H atom in the N–H bond has a slightly positive charge and the O atom in the C=O bond has a slightly negative charge. This means hydrogen bonds can form between different amino acids in a chain.

$$\underset{\diagup}{\overset{\diagdown}{N}} - \overset{\delta-}{H} \cdots \overset{\delta-}{O} = \underset{\diagup}{\overset{\diagdown}{C}}$$

Tertiary structure

The coiled or folded chain of amino acids is often coiled and folded further. More bonds form between different parts of the polypeptide chain such as:

- **Ionic interactions** — these are weak attractions between negatively charged R groups and positively charged R groups on different parts of the molecule — see Figure 5.

- **Disulfide bonds** — whenever two molecules of the amino acid cysteine come close together, the sulfur atom in one cysteine bonds to the sulfur in the other cysteine, forming a disulfide bond — see Figure 4.

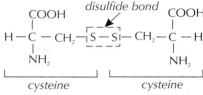

Figure 4: A disulfide bond.

- **Hydrophobic and hydrophilic interactions** — when hydrophobic (water-repelling) R groups are close together in the protein, they tend to clump together. This means that hydrophilic (water-attracting) R groups are more likely to be pushed to the outside, which affects how the protein folds up into its final structure — see Figure 5.

- **Hydrogen bonds** — these weak bonds form between slightly positively charged hydrogen atoms in some R groups and slightly negatively charged atoms in other R groups on the polypeptide chain — see Figure 5.

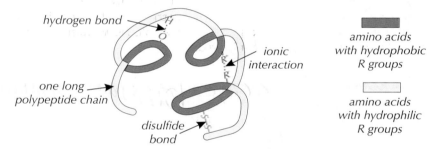

Figure 5: Examples of bonding in a protein's tertiary structure.

For proteins made from a single polypeptide chain, the tertiary structure forms their final 3D structure.

Quaternary structure

Some proteins are made of two or more polypeptide chains held together by bonds. The quaternary structure is the way these polypeptide chains are assembled together. It tends to be determined by the tertiary structure of the individual polypeptide chains. Because of this, it can be influenced by all the bonds mentioned above. For proteins made from more than one polypeptide chain, the quaternary structure is the protein's final 3D structure.

Example

Haemoglobin is a protein made up of four polypeptide chains — two α chains and two β chains. Each polypeptide chain has a **prosthetic group** — a non-polypeptide structure needed for the activity of the protein. The prosthetic groups in a haemoglobin molecule are haem groups, which each contain an iron (Fe^{2+}) ion.

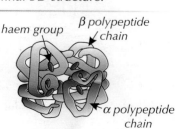

Figure 6: Haemoglobin's quaternary structure.

Tip: Remember, an R group is an amino acid's variable group. It's also called an amino acid's 'side chain'.

Exam Tip
Make sure you spell the name of a bond correctly in the exam, otherwise you won't get the mark.

Tip: Heating a protein to a high temperature will break up the weak bonds/interactions in the protein, i.e. the ionic interactions, hydrogen bonds and hydrophobic/hydrophilic interactions. In turn this will cause a change in the protein's 3D shape.

Tip: Not all proteins have a quaternary structure — some are made of only <u>one</u> polypeptide chain.

Tip: Don't get the α and β polypeptide chains in a haemoglobin molecule confused with the α helices and β pleated sheets that form a protein's secondary structure — they're not the same thing.

Functions of proteins

A protein's shape relates to its function. You need to know about fibrous proteins and globular proteins.

Fibrous proteins

Fibrous proteins are tough and rope-shaped. They tend to be found in connective tissue e.g. tendons.

> ### Example — Collagen
>
> Collagen is a fibrous protein that forms supportive tissues in animals, so it needs to be strong and flexible. It's made of three polypeptide chains that are tightly coiled into a strong triple helix — see Figure 7. The chains are interlinked by strong covalent bonds. Minerals can bind to the triple helix to increase its rigidity.

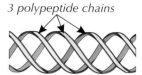

3 polypeptide chains

Figure 7: *The structure of a collagen molecule.*

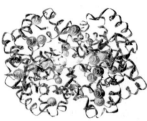

Figure 8: *A molecular model of collagen.*

Globular proteins

Globular proteins are round and compact. They're soluble, so they're easily transported in fluids.

> ### Example — Haemoglobin
>
> Haemoglobin is a globular protein that carries oxygen around the body. Its structure is curled up so that hydrophilic (water-attracting) side chains are on the outside of the molecule and hydrophobic (water-repelling) side chains face inwards. This makes haemoglobin soluble in water, which makes it good for transport in the blood.

Exam Tip
You need to learn how the proteins collagen and haemoglobin are adapted for their function.

Figure 9: *A molecular model of haemoglobin.*

Tip: It's the iron-containing haem groups in haemoglobin that bind to oxygen.

Practice Questions — Fact Recall

Q1 What are the monomers of proteins?

Q2 What is a polypeptide?

Q3 Draw the general structure of an amino acid.

Q4 What sort of reaction:

    a) links amino acids together?   b) breaks amino acids apart?

Q5 What is the name of the bond that forms between amino acids?

Q6 Describe how the secondary structure of a protein is formed.

Q7 Look at the diagram of the polypeptide chain on the right.

    a) What level of a protein's structure does it show?

    b) Name the bonds labelled A-C.

    c) Describe how the bond labelled C is formed.

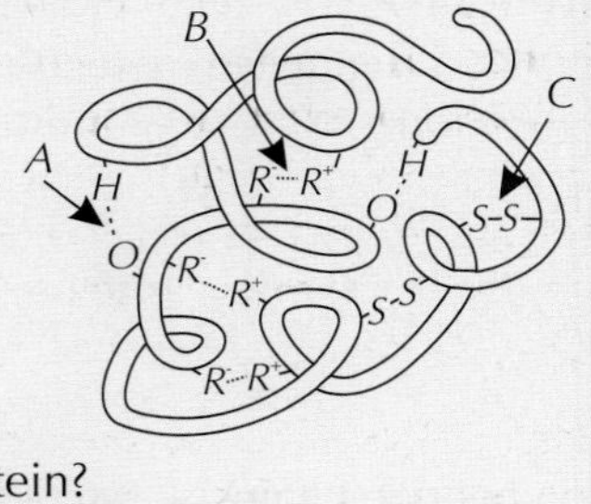

Q8 What is the quaternary structure of a protein?

Q9 Describe the quaternary structure of haemoglobin.

Q10 What is the function of collagen?

Q11 Explain how the globular structure of haemoglobin makes it suited to its function.

Carbohydrates are needed by living organisms for things like energy storage and support — their function is related to their structure.

What are carbohydrates made from?

Most carbohydrates are polymers. The monomers of carbohydrates are **monosaccharides**. Single monosaccharides are also called carbohydrates though.

Example

Glucose is a monosaccharide with six carbon atoms in each molecule. There are two forms of glucose — **alpha (α) glucose** and **beta (β) glucose**:

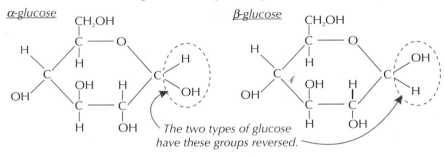

The two types of glucose have these groups reversed.

Glucose's structure is related to its function as the main energy source in animals and plants. Its structure makes it soluble so it can be easily transported. Its chemical bonds contain lots of energy.

Polysaccharide formation

Monosaccharides are joined together by **glycosidic bonds**. During synthesis, a hydrogen atom on one monosaccharide bonds to a hydroxyl (OH) group on the other, releasing a molecule of water — this is a **condensation** reaction. Just like with the polypeptides on p. 108, the reverse of this reaction is **hydrolysis**. A molecule of water reacts with the glycosidic bond, breaking it apart.

A **disaccharide** is formed when two monosaccharides join together and a **polysaccharide** is formed when more than two monosaccharides join together.

Examples

- Two α-glucose molecules are joined together by a glycosidic bond to form maltose — a disaccharide.

  synthesis
  hydrolysis
  $+ H_2O$

  H_2O is removed

  glycosidic bond

- Lots of α-glucose molecules are joined together by glycosidic bonds to form amylose — a polysaccharide.

  glycosidic bonds

Q1 Look at the following monosaccharides.

α-glucose   galactose   fructose

Draw the disaccharide that would be formed from a condensation reaction between:

a) α-glucose and galactose   b) α-glucose and fructose

Q2 Draw the monosaccharides produced from hydrolysis of the polysaccharides shown below.

a)

b)

Exam Tip
All you need to remember for questions like Q2 is to split them at the glycosidic bond and add an 'H' to either side.

Functions of carbohydrates

You need to know about the relationship between the structure and function of three polysaccharides — starch, glycogen and cellulose.

Starch

Starch is the main energy storage material in plants. Cells get energy from glucose and plants store excess glucose as starch (when a plant needs more glucose for energy it breaks down starch to release the glucose). Starch is insoluble in water so it doesn't cause water to enter cells by osmosis, which would make them swell (see p. 29). This makes it good for storage. Starch is a mixture of two polysaccharides of alpha-glucose — amylose and amylopectin:

- **Amylose** is a long, unbranched chain of α-glucose. The angles of the glycosidic bonds are different between two α-glucose molecules than they are between two β-glucose molecules. This gives amylose a coiled structure, almost like a cylinder. This makes it compact, so it's really good for storage because you can fit more in to a small space.

- **Amylopectin** is a long, branched chain of α-glucose. Its side branches allow the enzymes that break down the molecule to get at the glycosidic bonds easily. This means that the glucose can be released quickly.

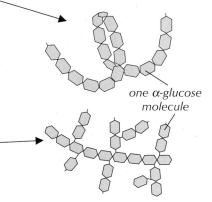

one α-glucose molecule

Figure 1: *The structures of amylose (top) and amylopectin (bottom).*

Tip: You can test for the presence of starch using the iodine test (see page 121).

Tip: Hydrogen bonds between α-glucose molecules help to hold amylose in its helical structure.

Exam Tip
Always specify whether you're talking about α-glucose or β-glucose — you won't get a mark for only saying glucose.

Glycogen

Glycogen is the main energy storage material in animals. Animal cells get energy from glucose too, but animals store excess glucose as glycogen — another polysaccharide of alpha-glucose. Its structure is very similar to amylopectin, except that it has loads more side branches coming off it — see Figure 2. Loads of branches means that stored glucose can be released quickly, which is important for energy release in animals. It's also a very compact molecule, so it's good for storage.

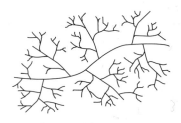

Figure 2: *The structure of glycogen.*

Cellulose

Cellulose is the major component of cell walls in plants. It's made of long, unbranched chains of beta-glucose. The bonds between the sugars are straight, so the cellulose chains are straight. The cellulose chains are linked together by **hydrogen bonds** to form strong fibres called **microfibrils** — see Figure 3. The strong fibres mean cellulose provides structural support for cells (e.g. in plant cell walls).

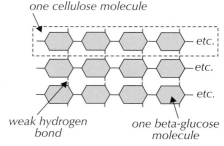

one cellulose molecule

weak hydrogen bond

one beta-glucose molecule

Figure 3: *The structure of a cellulose microfibril.*

Figure 4: *Coloured scanning electron micrograph (SEM) of cellulose microfibrils in a plant cell wall.*

Exam Tip
If you're asked about the function of glycogen in the exam, make sure you say it acts as an energy store or reserve — you won't get marks just for saying it 'contains energy'.

Exam Tip
Don't panic if you're asked to draw a diagram in the exam — you don't have to be the best artist in the world, but make sure you add labels to point out all the important bits.

Practice Questions — Fact Recall

Q1 Draw the structure of:

    a) an α-glucose molecule,   b) a β-glucose molecule.

Q2 Name the bond that forms between two monosaccharides to make a disaccharide.

Q3 What is the main energy storage material in:

    a) plants,   b) animals?

Q4 a) Is starch soluble or insoluble?

    b) Use your answer to a) to describe why starch is good for storage.

Q5 a) Name the structures shown below:

A

B

    b) Explain an advantage of structure A that makes it suitable for energy storage.

Q6 Describe the structure of glycogen and explain how its structure makes it suited to its function.

Q7 a) Which carbohydrate is the major component of plant cell walls?

    b) Describe the structure of this carbohydrate, and explain how its structure makes it suited to its function in cell walls.

Q8 Sketch and label a diagram of a microfibril.

4. Lipids

Lipids are commonly known as fats or oils. They're found in plants and animals, and have a variety of different functions.

What are lipids made from?

Lipids are different from proteins and carbohydrates because they're not polymers formed from long chains of monomers. Lipids are made from a variety of different components, but they all contain **hydrocarbons** (molecules that contain only hydrogen and carbon atoms). The components they're made from relates to the lipid's function. There are three types of lipid you need to know about — triglycerides, phospholipids and cholesterol.

Triglycerides

Triglycerides have one molecule of glycerol with three fatty acids attached to it. Each fatty acid is joined to the glycerol molecule by an **ester bond**. Fatty acid molecules have long 'tails' made of hydrocarbons. The tails are 'hydrophobic' (they repel water molecules). These tails make lipids insoluble in water.

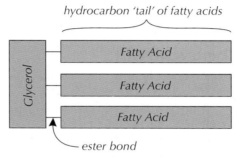

Figure 1: Structure of a triglyceride.

Fatty acids

All fatty acids consist of the same basic structure, but the hydrocarbon tail varies — see Figure 2. There are two kinds of fatty acids — saturated and unsaturated. The difference is in their hydrocarbon tails:

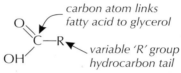

Figure 2: Structure of a fatty acid.

- **Saturated fatty acids** don't have any double bonds between their carbon atoms. The fatty acid is 'saturated' with hydrogen.

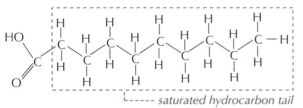

Figure 3: Saturated fatty acid.

- **Unsaturated fatty acids** do have double bonds between carbon atoms, which cause the chain to kink.

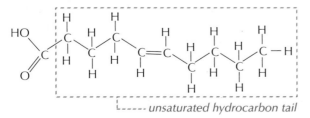

Figure 4: Unsaturated fatty acid.

Tip: One triglyceride molecule has three ester bonds:

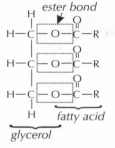

Tip: The variable R group can be any hydrocarbon.

Tip: Most animal fats are saturated — the fatty acids in these lipids are saturated so they have no double bonds.

Tip: Most plant fats are unsaturated — some of the fatty acids in these lipids are unsaturated meaning they have double bonds.

Phospholipids

The lipids found in cell membranes aren't triglycerides — they're phospholipids. Phospholipids are pretty similar to triglycerides except one of the fatty acid molecules is replaced by a phosphate group. The phosphate group is ionised (electrically charged), which makes it attract water molecules (see p. 107). So the phosphate part of the phospholipid molecule is hydrophilic (water-attracting) while the rest (the fatty acid tails) is hydrophobic (water-repelling).

Tip: Remember, a phospholipid has a phosphate group.

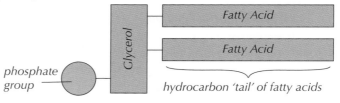

Figure 5: Structure of a phospholipid.

Cholesterol

Cholesterol is a type of lipid often found in cell membranes. It's also used to make other things like steroids.

It has a hydrocarbon ring structure attached to a hydrocarbon tail. The hydrocarbon ring structure has a polar hydroxyl group attached to it, which makes cholesterol slightly soluble in water. However, it's insoluble in blood, so is carried around the body by proteins called lipoproteins (see page 148).

Tip: Examples of steroids made by the body include bile acids, some hormones and vitamin D.

Tip: In a hydrocarbon ring structure, the carbon atoms are literally arranged in a ring-like shape instead of a long chain.

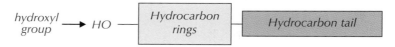

Figure 6: Structure of cholesterol.

Functions of lipids

You need to know how the structures of triglycerides, phospholipids and cholesterol are related to their functions:

Triglycerides

Triglycerides are mainly used as energy storage molecules. They're good for this because the long hydrocarbon tails of the fatty acids contain lots of chemical energy — a load of energy is released when they're broken down. Because of these tails, lipids contain about twice as much energy per gram as carbohydrates.

Also, they're insoluble, so they don't cause water to enter the cells by osmosis (which would make them swell). The triglycerides bundle together as insoluble droplets in cells because the fatty acid tails are hydrophobic (water-repelling) — the tails face inwards, shielding themselves from water with their glycerol heads — see Figure 7.

Tip: Foods with a high fat content provide lots of energy. Having a diet high in fat is linked to the development of obesity (see page 147).

Tip: Storage molecules need to be insoluble otherwise they'd just dissolve (and release whatever they were storing) whenever they came into contact with water.

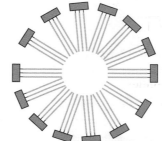

Figure 7: Diagram showing an insoluble triglyceride droplet.

Phospholipids

Phospholipids make up the bilayer of cell membranes (see p. 24). Cell membranes control what enters and leaves a cell.

Phospholipid heads are hydrophilic and their tails are hydrophobic, so they form a double layer with their heads facing out towards the water on either side. The centre of the bilayer is hydrophobic, so water-soluble substances can't easily pass through it — the membrane acts as a barrier to those substances.

Tip: You learnt how the structure of phospholipids and cholesterol relate to their function in Unit 1: Section 2, but you need to know it for this unit too.

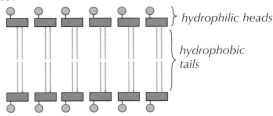

Figure 8: A phospholipid bilayer.

Cholesterol

Cholesterol molecules help strengthen the cell membrane by interacting with the phospholipid bilayer. The small size and flattened shape allows cholesterol to fit in between the phospholipid molecules in the membrane. They bind to the hydrophobic tails of the phospholipids, causing them to pack more closely together. This helps to make the membrane less fluid and more rigid.

Tip: There's more about cholesterol on page 148.

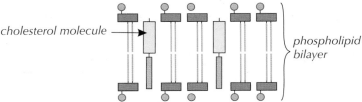

Figure 9: Cholesterol molecules within a cell membrane.

Practice Questions — Fact Recall

Q1 What are the components of a triglyceride?

Q2 Explain the difference between a saturated fatty acid and an unsaturated fatty acid.

Q3 Name the structures A-D in the diagram of a phospholipid below.

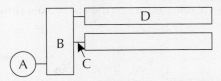

Q4 Describe the structure of a cholesterol molecule.

Q5 Give two reasons why triglycerides are used as energy storage molecules.

Q6 a) What is the function of phospholipids?

    b) Explain how the structure of phospholipids make them suited to their function.

Q7 a) Where are cholesterol molecules found in cell membranes?

    b) Describe the role cholesterol molecules have in cell membranes.

5. Biochemical Tests for Molecules

The next few pages are all about tests you can do to find out if a substance contains proteins, carbohydrates or lipids. You never know when you might need to find out exactly what is in a food sample...

The biuret test for proteins

If you needed to find out if a substance contained protein you'd use the biuret test. There are two stages to this test.

1. The test solution needs to be alkaline, so first you add a few drops of sodium hydroxide solution.
2. Then you add some copper(II) sulfate solution.

If protein is present, the solution turns purple. If there's no protein, the solution will stay blue — see Figure 1. The colours can be fairly pale, so you might need to look carefully.

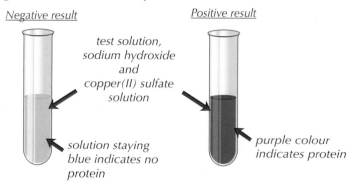

Negative result

Positive result

test solution, sodium hydroxide and copper(II) sulfate solution

solution staying blue indicates no protein

purple colour indicates protein

Figure 1: *A positive and negative biuret test result.*

Figure 2: *A negative (left) and positive (right) biuret test result.*

Practice Questions — Application

A biuret test was carried out to determine which liquids contained protein. The results of the experiment are shown in the table below.

Liquid	Result
De-ionised water	Blue
Cow's milk	Blue
Orange juice	Purple
Orange squash	Blue
Goat's milk	Purple

Q1 Which of the liquids in the table gave a positive test result?

Q2 Suggest why the scientist tested de-ionised water.

Q3 The scientist measured the pH of each liquid after the test. The pH of the cow's milk was below 7, so the scientist marked the test result as void.

a) Why did they mark the result as void?

b) Suggest what mistake the scientist might have made during the experiment.

The Benedict's test for sugars

Sugar is a general term for monosaccharides and disaccharides. All sugars can be classified as reducing or non-reducing. To test for sugars you use the Benedict's test. The test differs depending on the type of sugar you are testing for.

Reducing sugars

Reducing sugars include all monosaccharides (e.g. glucose) and some disaccharides (e.g. maltose). You add Benedict's reagent (which is blue) to a sample and heat it. Make sure the solution doesn't boil. If the test's positive it will form a coloured precipitate — solid particles suspended in the solution. The colour of the precipitate changes as shown in Figure 3.

Tip: If the substance you want to test is a solid, you may have to prepare a solution of it before testing. You could do this by first crushing the solid with water and then filtering out the solid.

Heat sample with Benedict's reagent.

sample stays **blue**   sample forms **green**→*yellow*→*orange*→**brick red precipitate**

no reducing sugar present   **reducing sugar present**

Figure 3: Benedict's test for reducing sugars.

The higher the concentration of reducing sugar, the further the colour change goes — you can use this to compare the amount of reducing sugar in different solutions. A more accurate way of doing this is to filter the solution and weigh the precipitate.

Exam Tip
Be careful with your wording when you're describing the Benedict's test — you need to say you <u>heat</u> the sample, you won't get a mark for saying you warm it.

Non-reducing sugars

If the result of the reducing sugars test is negative, there could still be a non-reducing sugar present. To test for non-reducing sugars, like sucrose, first you have to break them down into monosaccharides. You do this by getting a new sample of the test solution (i.e. not the same one you've already added Benedict's reagent to) and boil it with dilute hydrochloric acid. Then you neutralise it by adding sodium hydrogencarbonate. Finally just carry out the Benedict's test as you would for a reducing sugar — see Figure 4.

Tip: Always use an excess of Benedict's solution — this makes sure that all the sugar reacts.

Heat sample with Benedict's reagent.

sample stays **blue**   sample forms **green**→*yellow*→*orange*→**brick red precipitate**

no reducing sugar present   **reducing sugar present**

Boil a new sample with dilute hydrochloric acid then neutralise sample by adding sodium hydrogencarbonate. Heat sample with Benedict's reagent.

sample stays **blue**   sample forms **green**→*yellow*→*orange*→**brick red precipitate**

no non-reducing (or reducing) sugar present   **non-reducing sugar present**

Figure 4: Benedict's test for non-reducing sugars.

Figure 5: A blue colour (left) indicates a negative Benedict's test result and a brick red colour (right) indicates a positive result.

Q1 The table shows data from four different Benedict's tests. What conclusions can you draw from each test?

Test	Procedure	Result
1	Sample heated with Benedict's reagent.	Blue
2	Sample heated with Benedict's reagent, (remained blue), then boiled with hydrochloric acid and neutralised. Finally heated with Benedict's reagent.	Red
3	Sample heated with Benedict's reagent, (remained blue), then boiled with hydrochloric acid and neutralised. Finally heated with Benedict's reagent.	Blue
4	Sample heated with Benedict's reagent.	Red

Quantitative version of the Benedict's test

A quantitative version of the Benedict's test allows you to estimate how much glucose (or other reducing sugar) there is in a solution by using a colorimeter.

What is a colorimeter?

A colorimeter is a device that measures the strength of a coloured solution by seeing how much light passes through it — see Figure 7. It measures absorbance (the amount of light absorbed by the solution). The more concentrated the colour of the solution, the higher the absorbance is.

Figure 7: A colorimeter is used to measure the amount of light absorbed by a substance.

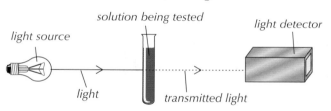

Figure 6: A diagram showing how a colorimeter works.

It's pretty difficult to measure the concentration of the coloured precipitate formed in the Benedict's test, so when you're estimating glucose concentration you measure the concentration of the blue Benedict's solution that's left after the test (the paler the solution left, the more glucose there was). So, the higher the glucose concentration, the lower the absorbance of the solution.

✳ Making a calibration curve

First you need to make a calibration curve. To do this you need to:

- Make up several glucose solutions of different, known concentrations, e.g. 10 mM, 20 mM and 30 mM. There should be the same volume of each.

- Do a Benedict's test on each solution. Use the same amount of Benedict's reagent in each case — it has to be a large enough volume to react with all the sugar in the strongest solution and still have some reagent left over.

- Remove any precipitate from the solutions — either leave the test tubes for 24 hours (so that the precipitate settles out) or centrifuge them.

- Use a colorimeter with a red filter to measure the absorbance of the Benedict's solution remaining in each tube.

- Use the results to make the calibration curve, showing absorbance against glucose concentration.

Tip: A calibration curve may look like this:

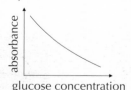

There's more about them on the next page.

Tip: In a centrifuge solutions are spun at high speed so the precipitate is separated from the solution.

Finding an unknown glucose concentration

Once you've made a calibration curve, you can test an unknown solution in the same way as the solutions of known concentrations and use the calibration curve to find its concentration.

Example

An unknown solution gives an absorbance value of 0.80. Reading across this calibration graph from an absorbance value of 0.8 shows that the concentration of glucose in the unknown solution is 20 mM.

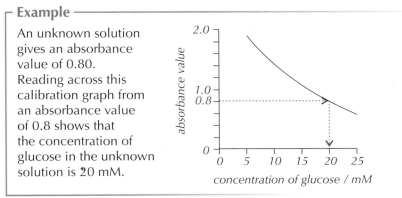

The iodine test for starch

If you want to test for the presence of starch in a sample, you'll need to do the iodine test. Just add iodine dissolved in potassium iodide solution to the test sample. If there is starch present, the sample changes from browny-orange to a dark, blue-black colour — see Figure 9. If there is no starch, it stays browny-orange.

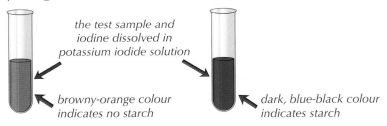

the test sample and iodine dissolved in potassium iodide solution

browny-orange colour indicates no starch

dark, blue-black colour indicates starch

Figure 8: *A negative (left) and positive (right) iodine test result.*

Figure 9: *A dark blue-black colour indicates the presence of starch in an iodine test.*

The emulsion test for lipids

If you want to test for the presence of lipids in a sample, you'll need to do the emulsion test. To do this you shake the test substance with ethanol for about a minute, then pour the solution into water. Any lipid will show up as a milky emulsion — see Figures 10 and 11. The more lipid there is, the more noticeable the milky colour will be. If there's no lipid, the solution will stay clear.

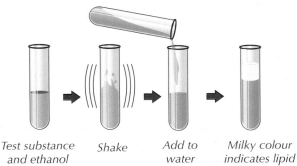

Test substance and ethanol *Shake* *Add to water* *Milky colour indicates lipid*

Figure 10: *The emulsion test for lipids.*

Figure 11: *A positive result using the emulsion test.*

Q1 The biuret test is used to test for proteins.

    a) What is added to the test solution to make it alkaline?

    b) What is added next to the solution?

    c) What would a positive test result look like?

Q2 Describe how to test for reducing sugars and say what a positive and a negative result would look like.

Q3 a) What is a colorimeter?

    b) Assuming a calibration curve had already been created, describe how you would use a colorimeter and the calibration curve to measure the glucose concentration of an unknown solution.

Q4 Name a test to find out if starch is present in a sample or not.

Section Summary

Make sure you know...

- That water molecules are polar (they have a slight negative charge on one side and a slight positive charge on the other).

- That a hydrogen bond is a weak bond between a slightly positively charged hydrogen atom in one molecule and a slightly negatively charged atom in another molecule.

- The properties of water (high specific heat capacity, high latent heat of evaporation, very cohesive, lower density when solid, good solvent) and how they relate to the functions of water.

- The structure of an amino acid (carboxyl group, amino group and R group).

- That peptide bonds are formed between amino acids during condensation reactions (to form dipeptides and polypeptides) and broken during hydrolysis reactions.

- That a protein's primary structure is the sequence of amino acids, held together by peptide bonds.

- That a protein's secondary structure is an alpha (α) helix or beta (β) pleated sheet, held together by hydrogen bonding between the -NH and -CO groups of amino acids in the chain.

- That a protein's tertiary structure is the further coiling or folding of the polypeptide chain, held together by ionic interactions, disulfide bonds, hydrophobic and hydrophilic interactions, and hydrogen bonds.

- That a protein's quaternary structure is the way in which two or more polypeptide chains are assembled together and how this applies to haemoglobin.

- That collagen is a fibrous protein and how its structure relates to its function.

- That haemoglobin is a globular protein and how its structure relates to its function.

- The molecular structures of the monosaccharides α-glucose and β-glucose, and how they differ.

- That glycosidic bonds are formed between monosaccharides during condensation reactions to form disaccharides (e.g. maltose) and polypeptides (e.g. amylose), and broken during hydrolysis reactions.

- The structure of starch (amylose and amylopectin), glycogen (long, branched chains of α-glucose) and cellulose (long, unbranched chains of β-glucose held together by hydrogen bonds to form microfibrils), and how their structures are related to their functions.

- The structure of a triglyceride (one molecule of glycerol with three fatty acids), a phospholipid (one molecule of glycerol, two fatty acids and a phosphate group) and cholesterol (hydrocarbon ring structure, hydrocarbon tail and hydroxyl group) and how their structures are related to their functions.

- How to test a substance for the presence of proteins (biuret test), reducing and non-reducing sugars (Benedict's test), starch (iodine test) and lipids (emulsion test).

- How to use a colorimeter to determine the glucose concentration of a solution.

Exam-style Questions

1 Photosynthesis is the process by which plants synthesise glucose from carbon dioxide and water using light as an energy source. Glucose is stored as starch in a plant.

(a) A student investigating photosynthesis kept two plants, A and B, under different conditions. They tested a leaf from each plant for the presence of starch, using the iodine test. The table below shows the results of the test. Complete the table to show the observation from the iodine test on each of the leaves.

	Observation	Starch present
Leaf A		Yes
Leaf B		No

(2 marks)

(b) Amylose is one of the polysaccharides that forms starch.

(i) Name the other polysaccharide present in starch molecules.

(1 mark)

(ii) Describe the structure of amylose and explain how its structure makes it suited to its function.

(3 marks)

(c) Cellulose is also a polysaccharide found in plants.

(i) Describe **three** ways in which cellulose differs from starch.

(3 marks)

Fig. 1.1 shows a glucose molecule that makes up cellulose.

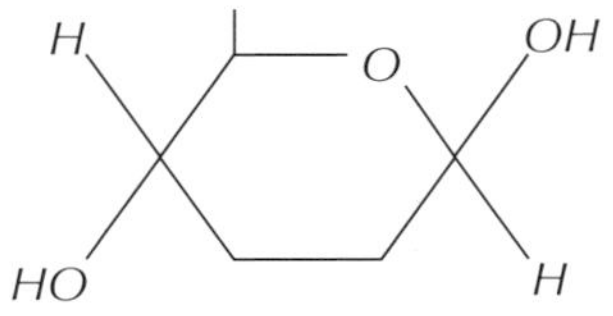

Fig. 1.1

(ii) Draw how two molecules of glucose link together to form part of a cellulose molecule.

(1 mark)

(iii) Describe how a cellulose molecule is broken apart into molecules of glucose.

(3 marks)

2 Fats (lipids) are essential as part of a balanced diet.

(a) Describe a test you could do to find out if a liquidised food sample contains lipids, including what observation would indicate a positive result.

(3 marks)

(b)   There are many different types of lipid in the body, including:

- triglycerides
- phospholipids
- cholesterol

(i)   Describe how the structures of the above types of lipid are related to their functions.

In your answer you must clearly link lipid structure and function.

(7 marks)

(ii) Explain why cholesterol is soluble in water.

(2 marks)

3   The human body contains many different proteins.
Each of these proteins has a primary, secondary and tertiary structure.

(a)   Describe the primary structure of a protein.

(2 marks)

(b)   The tertiary structure of a protein is held in place by different types of bonds.
Complete the following passage by using the most appropriate terms from
the list to fill the gaps. Each term **should not** be used more than once.

ionic	negatively	hydrophobic	disulfate	hydrogen
cysteine	positively	covalent	glycine	disulfide

To form the tertiary structure of a protein, ... interactions form between
negatively and positively charged R groups on different parts of the polypeptide
chain. Whenever two molecules of the amino acid .... come close
together they can become joined by their sulfur atoms to form .... bonds.
Weak bonds called .... bonds also form between slightly ....
charged hydrogen atoms in some R groups and slightly .... charged
atoms in other R groups on the polypeptide chain.

(6 marks)

(c)   Collagen and haemoglobin are examples of two proteins in the human body.
Complete the table below to give three differences between the structures of
collagen and haemoglobin.

Collagen	*Haemoglobin*

(3 marks)

(d)   The biuret test can be used to test for the presence of protein in a urine sample.
Describe how this test would be carried out, including what observations would
indicate positive and negative results.

(4 marks)

1. DNA and RNA

DNA and RNA are both nucleic acids — and they're both essential for the function of living organisms...

DNA function

Your **DNA** (**deoxyribonucleic acid**) contains your genetic information — that's all the instructions needed to grow and develop from a fertilised egg to a fully grown adult. There's more on the role of DNA on page 130.

DNA structure

DNA has a **double-helix** structure. This means that a DNA molecule is formed from two separate strands which wind around each other to form a spiral (see Figure 1). The strands are polynucleotides. They're made up of lots of nucleotides joined together in a long chain.

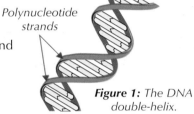

Polynucleotide strands

Figure 1: The DNA double-helix.

DNA molecules are really long and are coiled up very tightly, so a lot of genetic information can fit into a small space in the cell nucleus.

Nucleotide structure

Each nucleotide is made from a phosphate group, a pentose sugar (with 5 carbon atoms) and a nitrogenous (nitrogen-containing) **base**.

The sugar in DNA nucleotides is a **deoxyribose sugar**. Each nucleotide has the same sugar and phosphate. The base on each nucleotide can vary though. There are four possible bases — adenine (A), thymine (T), cytosine (C) and guanine (G). Adenine and guanine are a type of base called a **purine**. Cytosine and thymine are **pyrimidines**. The structure of a nucleotide is illustrated in Figure 2.

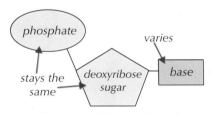

phosphate

stays the same

deoxyribose sugar

varies

base

Figure 2: A DNA nucleotide.

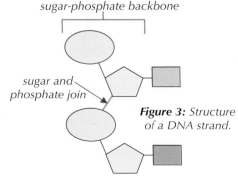

sugar-phosphate backbone

sugar and phosphate join

Figure 3: Structure of a DNA strand.

Polynucleotide strands

Many nucleotides join together to form the polynucleotide strands. The nucleotides join up between the phosphate group of one nucleotide and the sugar of another, creating a **sugar-phosphate backbone** — see Figure 3.

There's more on the role of DNA on page 130.

Learning Objectives:

- Know that deoxyribonucleic acid (DNA) is a polynucleotide, it's usually double stranded and it's made up of nucleotides containing the bases adenine (A), thymine (T), cytosine (C) and guanine (G).

- Be able to describe, with the aid of diagrams, how hydrogen bonding between complementary base pairs (A to T, G to C) on two antiparallel DNA polynucleotides leads to the formation of a DNA molecule, and how the twisting of DNA produces its 'double-helix' shape.

- Know that ribonucleic acid (RNA) is a polynucleotide, it's usually single stranded and it's made up of nucleotides containing the bases adenine (A), uracil (U), cytosine (C) and guanine (G).

   Specification Reference 2.1.2

Tip: The pyrimidines are cytosine and thymine.

Tip: A polynucleotide is a polymer made up of nucleotide monomers.

Complementary base pairing

Two DNA polynucleotide strands join together by hydrogen bonds between the bases. Each base can only join with one particular partner — this is called complementary base pairing. Adenine always pairs with thymine (A - T) and guanine always pairs with cytosine (G - C) — see Figure 4. This means that a purine (A or G) always pairs with a pyrimidine (T or C). Two hydrogen bonds form between A and T, and three hydrogen bonds form between C and G.

Tip: If you're struggling to remember which base pairs with which, just think — you eat Apple Turnover with Gloopy Custard.

Tip: The two ends of a polynucleotide strand are different — one end has a phosphate group and the other has a hydroxyl (OH) group attached to the sugar. That's how you can tell which direction a strand is running in.

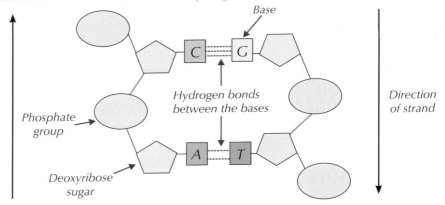

Figure 4: Complementary base pairing in DNA molecules.

The two polynucleotides strands are antiparallel — they run in opposite directions. Two antiparallel strands twist to form a DNA double-helix.

Summary

If you tie all this information together, you end up with a DNA molecule that looks like the one in Figure 6.

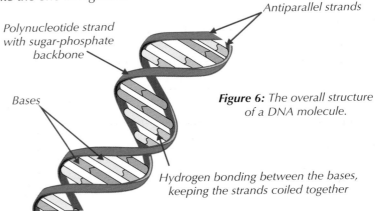

Figure 6: The overall structure of a DNA molecule.

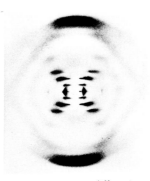

***Figure 5:** X-ray diffraction picture of DNA. The cross of bands shows that the molecule is a helix.*

Tip: The structure of a nucleotide and the arrangement of the DNA double helix is the same in all living organisms.

Practice Questions — Application

Q1 Here are the base sequences of two short stretches of DNA. For each one, write down the sequence of bases they would pair up with:

   a) ACTGTCGTAGTCGATGCTA

   b) TGCACCATGTGGTAAATCG

Q2 Scientists analysed a section of double stranded DNA. There were 68 bases in total (34 base pairs) and 22 of the bases were adenine. How many of the bases were:

   a) thymine?   b) cytosine?   c) guanine?

RNA function

The nucleic acid **RNA** (**ribonucleic acid**) is similar in structure to DNA. There are several different types of RNA, each with a different function. One of the main types is **mRNA** — it's used to make proteins from the instructions contained within DNA (see page 130).

(see page 130)

Tip: <u>m</u>RNA stands for messenger RNA. It acts as a messenger by carrying genetic information between DNA and the cytoplasm.

RNA structure

Like DNA, RNA is made of nucleotides that contain one of four different bases. The nucleotides also form a polynucleotide strand with a sugar-phosphate backbone. But the structure of RNA differs from DNA in three main ways:

- The sugar in RNA nucleotides is a **ribose** sugar (not deoxyribose). It's still a pentose sugar though.
- The nucleotides form a single polynucleotide strand (not a double one).
- **Uracil** (U, a pyrimidine) replaces thymine as a base. Uracil always pairs with adenine in RNA.

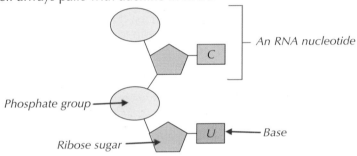

Figure 7: *Structure of an RNA strand.*

DNA and RNA comparison

Questions asking you to compare the structure of DNA and RNA are a regular feature in the exam. Luckily for you, the main points are summarised in the table below:

	DNA	mRNA
Shape	Double-stranded — twisted into a double-helix and held together by hydrogen bonds	Single-stranded
Sugar	Deoxyribose sugar	Ribose sugar
Bases	A, T, C, G	A, U, C, G

Practice Questions — Fact Recall

Q1 The diagram shows a DNA nucleotide. Name parts A, B and C.

Q2 Name the purines in DNA.

Q3 Describe how a DNA double-helix is formed from two polynucleotide strands.

Q4 How would the structure in the diagram above be different if it was an RNA nucleotide?

Q5 Name the pyrimidines in RNA.

Exam Tip
Questions on the structure of DNA and RNA are easy marks in the exam — and they come up a lot. Make sure you know the structures inside out.

Learning Objective:
- Be able to outline, with the aid of diagrams, how DNA replicates semi-conservatively, with reference to the role of DNA polymerase.

Specification Reference 2.1.2

2. DNA Replication

DNA is able to replicate itself and it does so on a regular basis. Clever thing.

Why does DNA replicate?

DNA copies itself before cell division (see page 40) so that each new cell has the full amount of DNA. This is important for making new cells and for passing genetic information from generation to generation (see pages 44-45).

How is DNA replicated?

A DNA molecule has a paired base structure (see page 126), which makes it easy for DNA to copy itself. Here's how it works:

Exam Tip
If you're asked to describe the process of semi-conservative replication in the exam, you need to make sure you do it in the <u>correct order</u> or you won't get all the marks. Get the sequence clear in your head now.

1 The hydrogen bonds between the two polynucleotide DNA strands break. The helix unzips to form two single strands.

Hydrogen bonds break

Helix

2 Each original single strand acts as a template for a new strand. Free-floating DNA nucleotides join to the exposed bases on each original template strand by complementary base pairing — A with T and C with G.

Bases match up using complementary base pairing.

3 The nucleotides on the new strand are joined together by the enzyme **DNA polymerase**. Hydrogen bonds form between the bases on the original and new strand.

Each new DNA molecule contains one strand from the original DNA molecule and one new strand.

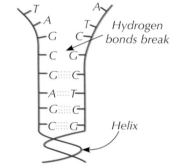

DNA polymerase joins the nucleotides. Hydrogen bonds form between strands.

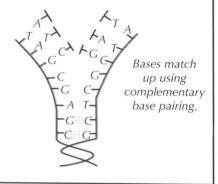

New strand   *Original DNA strand*

This type of copying is called **semi-conservative replication** because half of the new strands of DNA are from the original piece of DNA.

Practice Questions — Application

Tip: Have a look back at page 126 if you're struggling to remember which base pairs with which.

Q1 The diagram on the right shows a molecule of DNA. Draw the original and replicated strands after semi-conservative replication.

Q2 The evidence that DNA replicated semi-conservatively came from an experiment carried out by Meselson and Stahl. Their experiment used two isotopes of nitrogen — heavy nitrogen (^{15}N) and light nitrogen (^{14}N).

Two samples of bacteria were grown — one in a nutrient broth containing light nitrogen, and one in a broth with heavy nitrogen. As the bacteria reproduced, they took up nitrogen from the broth to help make new DNA.

The bacteria that had been grown in the heavy nitrogen broth were then grown in a light nitrogen broth and left for one round of DNA replication.

At each stage of the experiment, the composition of the bacterial DNA was analysed. The results are shown in the table below.

	Bacteria grown in light nitrogen broth only	Bacteria grown in heavy nitrogen broth only	Bacteria grown in heavy nitrogen broth, then in light nitrogen broth
% of heavy nitrogen in one DNA molecule	0	100	50
% of light nitrogen DNA molecule	100	0	50

a) Explain why the bacteria need to take in nitrogen to make DNA.

b) i) DNA is copied by semi-conservative replication. What is meant by this?

ii) Explain how the results shown in the table above provide evidence that DNA replicates semi-conservatively.

c) Scientists predicted that DNA could replicate semi-conservatively because of the paired base structure of a double-stranded DNA molecule. Explain how a paired base structure helps DNA to replicate semi-conservatively.

d) Suggest one way in which Meselson and Stahl may have made sure that their results were reliable.

Tip: To answer Q2 a) you need to know about the structure of a DNA nucleotide. Flick back to page 125 if you need a cheeky little reminder.

Practice Questions — Fact Recall

Q1 Which bonds need to break in a DNA molecule before replication can begin?

Q2 Describe the role of DNA polymerase in DNA replication.

DNA and RNA having starring roles in protein synthesis. Here's why...

Genes

DNA contains genes. A gene is a sequence of DNA nucleotides that codes for a protein (polypeptide). Proteins are made from amino acids. Different proteins have a different number and order of amino acids. It's the order of nucleotide bases in a gene that determines the order of amino acids in a particular protein. Each amino acid is coded for by a sequence of three bases in a gene. Different sequences of bases code for different amino acids.

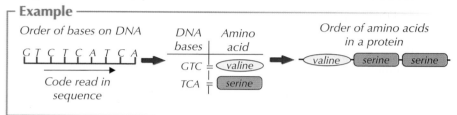

— Example —
Order of bases on DNA

GTCTCATCA

Code read in sequence

DNA bases	Amino acid
GTC	valine
TCA	serine

Order of amino acids in a protein

valine — serine — serine

Gene mutations

Mutations are changes in the base sequence of an organism's DNA. If the sequence of bases in a gene changes, the sequence of amino acids in the protein it codes for may also change. This may affect the way the protein folds up and so its overall 3D shape. As a result, a different or non-functional protein could be produced.

— Example —
All enzymes are proteins. If there's a mutation in a gene that codes for an enzyme, then that enzyme may not fold up properly. This may produce an active site that's the wrong shape and so a non-functional enzyme.

DNA, RNA and protein synthesis

All the reactions and processes in living organisms need proteins. DNA carries the instructions (as genes) to make proteins so it's obviously vital for protein synthesis — but RNA also plays a key role.

DNA molecules are found in the nucleus of the cell. The organelles that assemble proteins are called **ribosomes** — they're found in the cytoplasm. DNA is too large to move out of the nucleus, so a section is copied into a molecule called **mRNA** (a type of RNA, see p. 127). The mRNA leaves the nucleus and joins with a ribosome in the cytoplasm, where it can be used to synthesise a protein. Figure 1 summarises this.

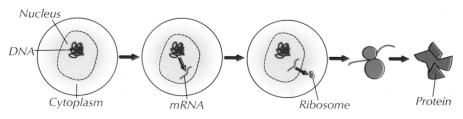

Nucleus

DNA

Cytoplasm   *mRNA*   *Ribosome*   *Protein*

Figure 1: *Making a protein from DNA.*

Q1 The table below shows five amino acids and some of the DNA sequences that code for them.

Amino Acid:	His	Arg	Gly	Tyr	Cys
DNA sequence:	CAT	AGA	GGC	TAC	TGC

Tip: His, Arg, Gly, etc. are all just abbreviated names for amino acids. You don't need to know what they stand for.

Use the table to:

a) determine the DNA sequence that would code for the following amino acid sequence:

His - Arg - His - Gly - Cys - Arg - Tyr - Tyr - Gly - Arg

b) determine the amino acid sequence coded for by the following DNA sequence:

GGC - TAC - GGC - CAT - AGA - AGA - TGC - TAC - CAT

Q2 The flow chart below illustrates how coloured pigment is produced in a certain type of flower:

White protein substrate →(Enzyme A)→ Pink Pigment →(Enzyme B)→ Red Pigment →(Enzyme C)→ Purple Pigment

a) What colour would you expect the flower to be if a mutation occurred that made:

i) Enzyme A non-functional?

ii) Enzyme B non-functional?

b) Explain how a mutation could make one of these enzymes non-functional.

Section Summary

Make sure you know...

- That DNA (deoxyribonucleic acid) is a polynucleotide, made up of nucleotides that contain deoxyribose sugar, a phosphate group and a nitrogenous base — either adenine (A), thymine (T), cytosine (C) or guanine (G).

- That DNA molecules usually have a double-stranded structure held together by hydrogen bonding between complementary base pairs.

- That in complementary base pairing, A always pairs with T and G always pairs with C — so a purine (A or G) always pairs with a pyrimidine (T or C).

- That antiparallel DNA strands twist together to form the DNA double-helix.

- That RNA (ribonucleic acid) is a polynucleotide with a similar structure to DNA, but that RNA is usually single-stranded, the sugar in the nucleotides is ribose sugar and uracil (U) replaces thymine as a base.

- How to describe the sequence of semi-conservative replication in DNA, including the role of DNA polymerase.

- That a gene is a sequence of DNA nucleotides that codes for a protein (polypeptide).

- The roles of DNA and RNA in living organisms — DNA stores genetic information in the form of genes and mRNA carries copies of genes from the nucleus to the cytoplasm for protein synthesis.

Exam-style Questions

1 (a)   DNA is a polynucleotide.
What **three** components make up a DNA nucleotide?

(3 marks)

  (b) (i)   Urea is a weak alkali. Adding urea to a solution of double-stranded DNA will severely disrupt the hydrogen bonding in the DNA.
Explain what effect this will have on the structure of the DNA.

(2 marks)

   (ii)   Depurination of DNA results in the loss of purine bases.
Name the **two** DNA bases that would be lost during depurination.

(2 marks)

  (c) (i)   Use the most appropriate terms to complete the passage on DNA replication below.

Hydrogen bonds between the two polynucleotide strands break and the DNA

double-helix .... to form to two separate strands. Each original strand

acts as a .... for the new strand. Free-floating DNA nucleotides join on

to the exposed bases by .... base pairing — for example, thymine pairs

with .... The nucleotides on the new strands are then joined together

by the enzyme .... and bonds form between the new and

original strands.

(5 marks)

   (ii)   What is the name given to the method by which DNA replicates itself?

(1 mark)

2   RNA and DNA both play important roles in protein synthesis.
  (a)   Give **three** ways in which the structure of RNA is different to the structure of DNA.

(3 marks)

  (b)   Describe the role of mRNA in protein synthesis.

(2 marks)

  (c)   DNA contains genes.
   (i)   Give the definition of a **gene**.

(1 mark)

   (ii)   Suggest how changes to a gene could affect protein production.

(3 marks)

1. Action of Enzymes

Enzymes are proteins that speed up the rate of chemical reactions.
Without enzymes, bodily processes such as digestion would not happen.

Enzymes as biological catalysts

Enzymes speed up chemical reactions by acting as biological catalysts.
A catalyst is a substance that speeds up a chemical reaction without being used up in the reaction itself — biological catalysts are those found in living organisms.

Enzymes catalyse the metabolic reactions in your body, such as digestion and respiration. Enzyme action can be **intracellular** (occur within cells), or **extracellular** (occur outside cells, e.g. in the blood).

Enzyme structure

Enzymes are globular proteins (see p. 111). They have an **active site**, which has a specific shape determined by the enzyme's tertiary structure (see p. 110). The active site is the part of the enzyme where the **substrate** molecules (the substance that the enzyme interacts with) bind to.

For the enzyme to work, the substrate has to fit into the active site (its shape has to be complementary). If the substrate shape doesn't match the active site, the reaction won't be catalysed (see Figure 1). This means that enzymes are very specific and work with very few substrates — usually only one. When a substrate binds to an enzyme's active site, an **enzyme-substrate complex** is formed.

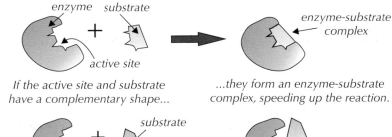

enzyme *substrate*   *enzyme-substrate complex*

active site

If the active site and substrate have a complementary shape...   *...they form an enzyme-substrate complex, speeding up the reaction.*

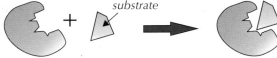

substrate

*If the active site and substrate **do not** have a complementary shape...*   *...the substrate can't fit into the active site so the reaction **can't** be catalysed.*

Figure 1: *An enzyme's active site has a complementary shape to the substrate.*

How enzymes speed up reactions

In a chemical reaction, a certain amount of energy needs to be supplied to the chemicals before the reaction will start. This is called the **activation energy** — it's often provided as heat. Enzymes reduce the amount of activation energy that's needed (see Figure 2 on the next page), often making reactions happen at a lower temperature than they could without an enzyme. This speeds up the rate of reaction.

Learning Objectives:

- Know that enzyme action may be intracellular or extracellular.

- Know that enzymes are globular proteins with a specific tertiary structure, which catalyse metabolic reactions in living organisms.

- Be able to describe, with the aid of diagrams, the mechanism of action of enzyme molecules, with reference to:

  - the active site,
  - specificity,
  - the enzyme-substrate complex,
  - lowering of activation energy,
  - the enzyme-product complex,
  - the lock and key hypothesis,
  - the induced-fit hypothesis.

  Specification Reference 2.1.3

Tip: Metabolic reactions are reactions that occur in living cells.

Exam Tip
When describing enzyme action you need to say the active site and the substrate have a <u>complementary</u> shape, rather than the <u>same</u> shape.

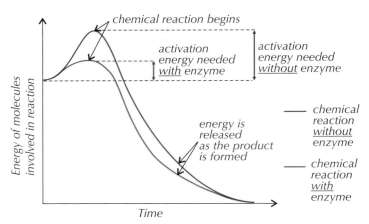

Figure 2: A graph to show the activation energy needed for a reaction with and without an enzyme.

Figure 3: Computer model of an enzyme-substrate complex. The substrate (yellow) has bound to the enzyme's active site.

Tip: Imagine you have to get to the top of a mountain to start a chemical reaction. It would take a lot of energy to get to the top. An enzyme effectively reduces the height of the mountain, so it doesn't take as much energy to start the reaction.

When a substance binds to an enzyme's active site, an enzyme-substrate complex is formed (see previous page) — it's this that lowers the activation energy. Here are two reasons why:

- If two substrate molecules need to be joined, attaching to the enzyme holds them close together, reducing any repulsion between the molecules so they can bond more easily.

- If the enzyme is catalysing a breakdown reaction, fitting into the active site puts a strain on bonds in the substrate. This strain means the substrate molecule breaks up more easily.

Models of enzyme action

Scientists now have a pretty good understanding of how enzymes work. As with most scientific theories, this understanding has changed over time.

The 'lock and key' model

Enzymes are a bit picky — they only work with substrates that fit their active site. Early scientists studying the action of enzymes came up with the 'lock and key' model. This is where the substrate fits into the enzyme in the same way that a key fits into a lock — the active site and substrate have a complementary shape.

Tip: An enzyme-product complex is formed when the substrate has been converted into its products, but they've not yet been released from the active site.

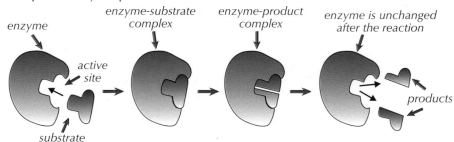

Figure 4: The 'lock and key' model.

Scientists soon realised that the lock and key model didn't give the full story. The enzyme and substrate do have to fit together in the first place, but new evidence showed that the enzyme-substrate complex changed shape slightly to complete the fit. This locks the substrate even more tightly to the enzyme. Scientists modified the old lock and key model and came up with the 'induced fit' model (see next page).

The 'induced fit' model

The 'induced fit' model helps to explain why enzymes are so specific and only bond to one particular substrate. The substrate doesn't only have to be the right shape to fit the active site, it has to make the active site change shape in the right way as well. This is a prime example of how a widely accepted theory can change when new evidence comes along. The 'induced fit' model is still widely accepted — for now, anyway.

Tip: The 'lock and key' model can also be called the 'lock and key' hypothesis, and the 'induced fit' model can also be called the 'induced fit' hypothesis.

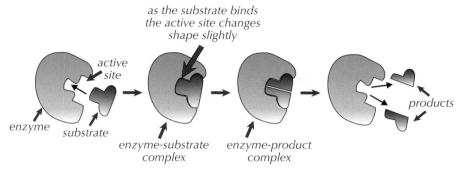

Figure 5: The 'induced fit' model.

Tip: The diagrams on this page and the previous page show how enzymes break substrates down (e.g. one substrate molecule goes into the active site and two products come out). Enzymes can also catalyse <u>synthesis</u> reactions (e.g. two substrate molecules go into the active site, bind together and one product comes out).

Practice Questions — Fact Recall

Q1 What is a catalyst?

Q2 What term is used to describe an enzyme that acts:
  a) within cells?
  b) outside cells?

Q3 What determines the shape of an enzyme's active site?

Q4 What is formed when a substrate binds with an active site?

Q5 Why will an enzyme only bind with one substrate?

Q6 Look at the graph below.

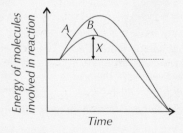

  a) Which line shows a reaction with the presence of an enzyme?
  b) What does the line labelled X represent?

Q7 Explain, in terms of activation energy, why an enzyme enables reactions to happen at lower temperatures than they could without an enzyme.

Q8 Describe the 'lock and key' model of enzyme action.

Q9 What is the main difference between the 'lock and key' model and the 'induced fit' model?

Tip: Every enzyme has an optimum temperature. For most human enzymes it's around 37 °C but some enzymes, like those used in biological washing powders, can work well at 60 °C.

Tip: High temperatures break the weak bonds in an enzyme's tertiary structure, e.g. hydrogen bonds and ionic bonds. See p. 110 for more on protein bonds.

Exam Tip
Make sure you don't say the enzyme's killed by high temperatures — it's <u>denatured</u>.

Exam Tip
Don't forget — both a pH that's too high and one that's too low will denature an enzyme, not just one that's too high.

2. Factors Affecting Enzyme Activity

Enzymes are great at speeding up reactions, but there are several factors that affect how fast they work.

Temperature

Like any chemical reaction, the rate of an enzyme-controlled reaction increases when the temperature's increased. More heat means more kinetic energy, so molecules move faster. This makes the substrate molecules more likely to collide with the enzymes' active sites. The energy of these collisions also increases, which means each collision is more likely to result in a reaction. The rate of reaction continues to increase until the enzyme reaches its **optimum temperature** — this is the temperature at which the rate of an enzyme-controlled reaction is at its fastest.

But, if the temperature gets too high, the reaction stops. The rise in temperature makes the enzyme's molecules vibrate more. If the temperature goes above a certain level, this vibration breaks some of the bonds that hold the enzyme in shape. The active site changes shape and the enzyme and substrate no longer fit together. At this point, the enzyme is **denatured** — it no longer functions as a catalyst (see Figures 1 and 2).

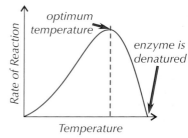

Figure 1: *Effect of temperature on the rate of an enzyme-controlled reaction.*

 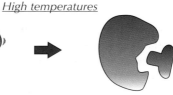

Low temperatures   *High temperatures*

At low temperatures the substrate fits into the active site.

At high temperatures the enzyme vibrates more. This breaks some of the bonds that hold it in shape.

The active site changes shape and the substrate can no longer fit. The enzyme is denatured.

Figure 2: *Effect of temperature on enzyme activity.*

pH

All enzymes have an optimum pH value — this is the pH at which the rate of an enzyme-controlled reaction is at its fastest. Most human enzymes work best at pH 7 (neutral), but there are exceptions. Pepsin, for example, works best at acidic pH 2, which is useful because it's found in the stomach. Above and below the optimum pH, the H^+ and OH^- ions found in acids and alkalis can break the ionic bonds and hydrogen bonds that hold the enzyme's tertiary structure in place. This makes the active site change shape, so the enzyme is denatured.

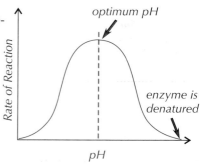

Figure 3: *Effect of pH on the rate of an enzyme-controlled reaction.*

Enzyme concentration

The more enzyme molecules there are in a solution, the more likely a substrate molecule is to collide with one and form an enzyme-substrate complex. So increasing the concentration of the enzyme increases the rate of reaction.

But, if the amount of substrate is limited, there comes a point when there's more than enough enzyme molecules to deal with all the available substrate, so adding more enzyme has no further effect.

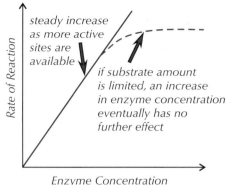

steady increase as more active sites are available

if substrate amount is limited, an increase in enzyme concentration eventually has no further effect

Figure 4: *A graph to show the rate of an enzyme-controlled reaction against enzyme concentration.*

Substrate concentration

The higher the substrate concentration, the faster the reaction. More substrate molecules means a collision between substrate and enzyme is more likely, so more active sites will be used and more enzyme-substrate complexes will be formed. This is only true up until a 'saturation' point though. After that, there are so many substrate molecules that the enzymes have about as much as they can cope with (all the active sites are full), and adding more makes no difference — the enzyme concentration becomes the limiting factor (see Figures 5 and 6).

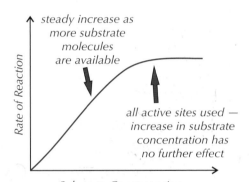

steady increase as more substrate molecules are available

all active sites used — increase in substrate concentration has no further effect

Figure 5: *A graph to show the rate of an enzyme-controlled reaction against substrate concentration.*

Tip: These graphs show the <u>rate</u> of reaction (i.e. the speed of the reaction). When the line on the graph levels off it doesn't mean the reaction has stopped, just that it isn't going any faster.

Tip: A limiting factor is a variable that can slow down the rate of a reaction.

Exam Tip
Don't ever say that the enzymes are used up — say that all the <u>active sites</u> are <u>occupied</u>.

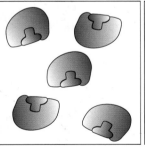

Low substrate concentration — not all active sites are occupied.

Saturation point — all active sites are occupied.

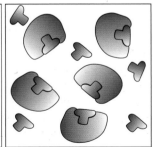

Beyond saturation point — all active sites are occupied and there are spare substrate molecules.

Figure 6: *Effect of substrate concentration on occupation of active sites.*

Q1 Hyperthermophillic bacteria are found in hot springs where temperatures reach 80 °C. Psychrotropic bacteria are found in very cold environments. The graph on the right shows the rate of reaction for an enzyme from three different bacteria.

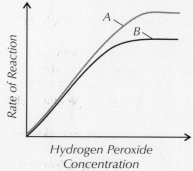

a) Explain which curve on the graph shows the enzyme from:

  i) hyperthermophillic bacteria? ii) psychrotropic bacteria?

b) Explain what would happen to enzyme activity for each type of bacteria shown on the graph if they were put into an environment with a temperature range of 60-75 °C.

Q2 The graph on the left shows the rate of reaction for the enzyme catalase under two different conditions. Catalase is found in the liver.

a) Explain which curve on the graph represents the reaction with the greatest concentration of catalase.

b) Both of the curves flatten out. Explain why this is.

Measuring the rate of an enzyme-controlled reaction

HOW SCIENCE WORKS

You need to be able to describe how the effects of pH, temperature, enzyme concentration and substrate concentration can be investigated experimentally. Here are two ways of measuring the rate of an enzyme-controlled reaction:

1. You can measure how fast the product of the reaction appears and use this to compare the rate of reaction under different conditions.

┌─ **Example** ─────────────────────────────

Catalase catalyses the breakdown of hydrogen peroxide into water and oxygen. It's easy to collect the oxygen produced and measure how much is given off in a set period of time, e.g. a minute (see diagram below). You can then compare the rate at which oxygen is produced in different tests.

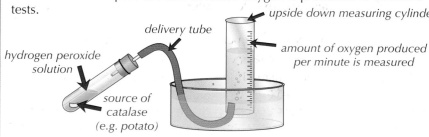

Tip: If you're measuring the <u>rate</u> of a reaction you need to time how quickly something is produced or used up.

2. You can also measure the disappearance of the substrate over time and use this to compare the rate of reaction under different conditions.

Tip: Which method you use to measure the rate of a reaction will normally depend on whether the product or the substrate is easier to test for.

┌─ **Example** ─────────────────────

The enzyme amylase catalyses the breakdown of starch to maltose. It's easy to detect starch using a solution of potassium iodide and iodine. You can time how long it takes for the starch to disappear by regularly adding samples of the starch solution to the iodine solution. When the iodine solution no longer turns blue-black the starch has disappeared. You can then use the times to compare rates between different tests.

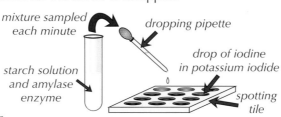
mixture sampled each minute — dropping pipette — drop of iodine in potassium iodide — starch solution and amylase enzyme — spotting tile

Exam Tip
You might have learnt different methods for measuring the rate of an enzyme-controlled reaction to those shown here and on the previous page — it doesn't matter which ones you revise, so long as you know them well enough to describe in the exam.

Here are some general tips on what to include when describing an experiment:

1. Describe the method and the apparatus you'd use.
2. Say what you're measuring (the dependent variable), e.g. the volume of gas produced per minute.
3. Describe how you'd vary the independent variable, e.g. if your independent variable is enzyme concentration you might test five different concentrations of enzyme.
4. Describe what variables you're keeping constant, e.g. temperature, pH, volume of solution, substrate concentration, etc.
5. Say that you need to repeat the experiment at least twice, to make the results more reliable.
6. Say that you need a control, e.g. a test tube containing the substrate solution but no enzyme.

Tip: See pages 222-223 for more on describing experiments.

Practice Questions — Application

A scientist investigated the effect of enzyme concentration on the rate of breakdown of lactose. She prepared different concentrations of lactase solution using sterile water.

$$\text{lactose} \xrightarrow{\text{lactase}} \text{galactose} + \text{glucose}$$

Q1 Suggest one variable she could measure to determine the rate of the reaction.

Q2 Give three variables she should keep constant for a fair test.

Q3 Suggest a control for the experiment.

Tip: The names of enzymes usually end with '-ase'.

Practice Questions — Fact Recall

Q1 Explain why an increase in temperature increases the rate of enzyme activity.

Q2 Explain how a very high temperature can stop an enzyme from working.

Q3 Give a factor other than temperature that can denature an enzyme.

Q4 Explain the effect of increasing the enzyme concentration on the rate of an enzyme-controlled reaction.

Q5 Explain what happens to the rate of an enzyme-controlled reaction when the substrate concentration is increased after the saturation point.

3. Cofactors and Inhibitors

Some substances might need to be present for an enzyme to work. But other substances can slow enzymes down or stop them working altogether.

Learning Objectives:

- Be able to explain the importance of cofactors and coenzymes in enzyme-controlled reactions.
- Be able to explain the effects of competitive and non-competitive inhibitors on the rate of enzyme-controlled reactions, with reference to reversible and non-reversible inhibitors.
- Know that metabolic poisons may be enzyme inhibitors, and be able to describe the action of one named poison.
- Know that some medicinal drugs work by inhibiting the activity of enzymes.

Specification Reference 2.1.3

Cofactors and coenzymes

Some enzymes will only work if there is another non-protein substance bound to them. These non-protein substances are called cofactors.

Inorganic cofactors

Some cofactors are inorganic molecules. They work by helping the enzyme and substrate to bind together (see Figure 1). They don't directly participate in the reaction so aren't used up or changed in any way. For example, manganese ions are cofactors found in hydrolase (enzymes that catalyse the hydrolysis of chemical bonds).

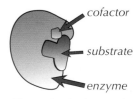

Figure 1: An inorganic cofactor bound to an enzyme and substrate.

Organic cofactors (coenzymes)

Some cofactors are organic molecules — these are called coenzymes. They participate in the reaction and are changed by it (they're just like a second substrate, but they aren't called that). They often act as carriers, moving chemical groups between different enzymes. They're continually recycled during this process (see Figure 2).

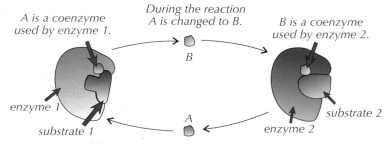

A is a coenzyme used by enzyme 1.

During the reaction A is changed to B.

B is a coenzyme used by enzyme 2.

enzyme 1

B

substrate 1

A

enzyme 2

substrate 2

During the reaction B is changed to A (i.e. the coenzyme is recycled by enzyme 2)

Figure 2: The recycling of coenzymes.

Tip: Organic molecules contain carbon and hydrogen atoms, whereas inorganic molecules don't.

Figure 3: The chemical reaction that makes fireflies glow is catalysed by the enzyme luciferase and an organic cofactor, ATP.

Enzyme inhibitors

Enzyme activity can be prevented by enzyme inhibitors — molecules that bind to the enzyme that they inhibit. Inhibition can be competitive or non-competitive.

Competitive inhibition

Competitive inhibitor molecules have a similar shape to that of the substrate molecules. They compete with the substrate molecules to bind to the active site, but no reaction takes place. Instead they block the active site, so no substrate molecules can fit in it (see Figure 4). How much the enzyme is inhibited depends on the relative concentrations of the inhibitor and substrate. If there's a high concentration of the inhibitor, it'll take up nearly all the active sites and hardly any of the substrate will get to the enzyme.

Exam Tip
Don't say that the inhibitor molecule and the substrate have the same shape — they have a <u>similar</u> shape.

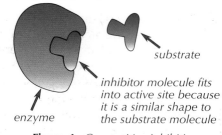

substrate

inhibitor molecule fits into active site because it is a similar shape to the substrate molecule

enzyme

Figure 4: Competitive inhibition.

Non-competitive inhibition

Non-competitive inhibitor molecules bind to the enzyme away from its active site. This causes the active site to change shape so the substrate molecules can no longer bind to it (see Figure 5). They don't 'compete' with the substrate molecules to bind to the active site because they are a different shape. Increasing the concentration of the substrate won't make any difference — enzyme activity will still be inhibited.

Exam Tip
When you're talking about shape change, always refer to the active site — don't just say the enzyme's changed shape.

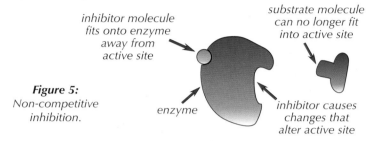

inhibitor molecule fits onto enzyme away from active site

substrate molecule can no longer fit into active site

Figure 5:
Non-competitive inhibition.

enzyme

inhibitor causes changes that alter active site

Tip: If you have a competitive inhibitor, increasing the concentration of the substrate will reverse it's effects — the substrate will out-compete the inhibitor for the active site.

Reversible and non-reversible inhibition

Inhibitors can be reversible (not bind permanently to an enzyme) or non-reversible (bind permanently to an enzyme). Which one they are depends on the strength of the bonds between the enzyme and the inhibitor.

- If they're strong, covalent bonds, the inhibitor can't be removed easily and the inhibition is irreversible.

- If they're weaker hydrogen bonds or weak ionic bonds, the inhibitor can be removed and the inhibition is reversible.

Tip: A covalent bond is formed between two atoms that share electrons.

Metabolic poisons

Metabolic poisons interfere with metabolic reactions (the reactions that occur in cells), causing damage, illness or death — they're often enzyme inhibitors. In the exam you might be asked to describe the action of one named poison.

┌─ **Examples** ─────────────────────
- Cyanide is a non-competitive inhibitor of cytochrome c oxidase, an enzyme that catalyses respiration reactions. Cells that can't respire die.

- Malonate is a competitive inhibitor of succinate dehydrogenase (which also catalyses respiration reactions).

- Arsenic is a non-competitive inhibitor of pyruvate dehydrogenase, yet another enzyme that catalyses respiration reactions.

Exam Tip
It doesn't matter which metabolic poison you learn for the exam, so long as you know an example and can describe how it works.

Drugs

Some medicinal drugs are enzyme inhibitors, for example:

┌─ **Examples** ─────────────────────
- Some antiviral drugs (drugs that stop viruses) — e.g. reverse transcriptase inhibitors are a class of antiviral developed to treat HIV. They work by inhibiting the enzyme reverse transcriptase, which catalyses the replication of viral DNA. This prevents the virus from replicating.

- Some antibiotics — e.g. penicillin inhibits the enzyme transpeptidase, which catalyses the formation of proteins in bacterial cell walls. This weakens the cell wall and prevents the bacterium from regulating its osmotic pressure. As a result the cell bursts and the bacterium is killed.

Tip: Human Immunodeficiency virus (HIV) is a virus that causes AIDS (see pages 172-173).

Q1 Methanol is broken down in the body into formaldehyde. The build up of formaldehyde can cause death. The enzyme that hydrolyses the reaction is alcohol dehydrogenase. The enzyme-substrate complex formed is shown on the right.

a) A diagram of ethanol is shown on the right. If someone had been poisoned with methanol, they could be helped by being given ethanol as soon as possible. Explain why.

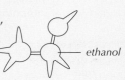

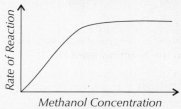

b) The graph shows the rate of the reaction with no ethanol present. Sketch a graph with the same axis showing the rate of reaction with the presence of ethanol.

Q2 Scientists have identified a substance (substance A) that inhibits the enzyme glycogen phosphorylase. This enzyme is responsible for the breakdown of glycogen into glucose. Substance A inhibits glycogen phosphorylase by binding to it away from the active site.

a) Is substance A a competitive or non-competitve inhibitor? Explain your answer.

The scientists test the effect of substance A in a solution containing glycogen and glycogen phosphorylase. The graph on the right shows the rate of the reaction over time.

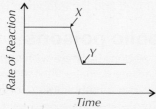

b) At point X the scientists increase the concentration of substance A in the test solution. Describe and explain the shape of the graph between points X and Y.

c) Explain which of the graphs below represents the effect of:

   i) increasing the glycogen concentration at point Z.

   ii) increasing the glycogen phosphorylase concentration at point Z.

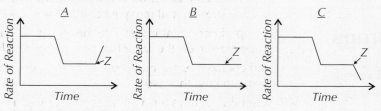

Practice Questions — Fact Recall

Q1 What is a cofactor?

Q2 Describe how a coenzyme is recycled during an enzyme-controlled reaction.

Q3 Where do the following molecules bind to an enzyme:
   a) a non-competitive inhibitor?   b) a competitive inhibitor?
Q4 Explain how non-competitive inhibition prevents enzyme activity.
Q5 State the bonds present between an enzyme and a:
   a) reversible inhibitor.   b) non-reversible inhibitor.
Q6 Name a poison that inhibits enzyme action and describe how it works.

Tip: There are lots of similar sounding words here — look back through the section if you're struggling to remember the difference between them.

Section Summary

Make sure you know:

- That an enzyme is a biological catalyst — a substance that speeds up chemical reactions in living organisms without being used up in the reaction itself.
- That enzyme action may be intracellular (within cells) or extracellular (outside cells).
- That enzymes are globular proteins with a specific tertiary structure.
- That the active site is the part of the enzyme that binds to a substrate to form an enzyme-substrate complex.
- That an enzyme's active site has a specific shape complementary to the shape of the substrate, and so enzymes will usually only work with one substrate.
- That the formation of an enzyme-substrate complex lowers the activation energy needed for a reaction, and the reasons why.
- How to describe the 'lock and key' model and the 'induced fit' model of enzyme action.
- That increasing the temperature increases the rate of an enzyme-controlled reaction by:
  - increasing the kinetic energy of substrate and enzyme molecules, which increases the likelihood of a collision between them.
  - increasing the energy of collisions between substrate and enzyme molecules, which means collisions are more likely to result in a reaction.
- That enzymes have an optimum temperature and an optimum pH at which the rate of an enzyme-controlled reaction is at its fastest.
- That if the temperature becomes too high or the pH too high or too low, the enzyme will become denatured.
- That increasing enzyme concentration will increase the rate of a reaction until the amount of substrate becomes the limiting factor.
- That increasing substrate concentration will increase the rate of a reaction until the saturation point is reached and all active sites are full (enzyme concentration is the limiting factor).
- How to describe experiments that investigate the effects of pH, temperature, enzyme concentration and substrate concentration on the rate of an enzyme-controlled reaction.
- That cofactors and coenzymes are non-protein substances needed to activate some enzymes, and are able to explain how they work.
- That competitive inhibitors have a similar shape to a substrate and inhibit enzymes by binding to the active site.
- That non-competitive inhibitors inhibit enzyme activity by binding to them away from the active site, causing the active site to change shape.
- That some enzyme inhibitors are reversible and some are irreversible, and are able to explain why.
- That some metabolic poisons and medicinal drugs work by inhibiting enzymes, and are able to name and describe a poison that works in this way.

1   Apples contain a substance called catechol and the enzyme catecholase.

When an apple is cut open and exposed to oxygen, the following chemical reaction takes place:

$$\text{catechol} + \tfrac{1}{2}O_2 \xrightarrow{\text{catecholase}} \text{benzoquinone} + H_2O$$

(a) (i) What effect do enzymes have on the activation energy of a reaction?

(1 mark)

(ii) Explain why enzymes have this effect.

(2 marks)

(b) (i) Use the '**induced fit' model** of enzyme activity to explain how catecholase catalyses the reaction shown above.

 In your answer you should make clear how the shape of the enzyme relates to its function.

(7 marks)

(ii) Name **another model** of enzyme action not mentioned in part **(i)** and describe how it differs to the induced fit model.

(2 marks)

(c) Benzoquinone has a brown colour and its production is responsible for the 'browning' of apples once they have been cut.

To reduce the browning of an apple once it has been cut, would it be best to store the apple at room temperature or in a fridge? Explain your answer.

(4 marks)

(d) Catecholase uses copper as a cofactor.

(i) Describe how copper enables catecholase to function.

(3 marks)

(ii) Give **two** differences between organic and inorganic cofactors.

(2 marks)

(e) Copper binds more easily to a chemical called PTU than it does to catecholase.

Suggest why the rate of apple browning would be **lower** in the presence of PTU.

(3 marks)

2   Triglycerides are a type of fat found in foods. In the stomach, gastric lipase acts as a catalyst to break triglycerides down into diglycerides and fatty acids.

gastric
lipase
triglyceride ──────→ diglyceride + fatty acid

(a)   Fig. 2.1 shows the rate of reaction for gastric lipase at different pH values.

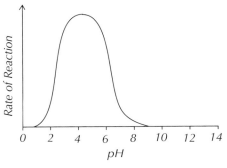

Fig. 2.1

(i)   What is the **optimum pH** of gastric lipase?

(1 mark)

(ii)   At what pH value(s) is gastric lipase **denatured**? Give a reason for your answer.

(2 marks)

(iii) Explain what happens when an enzyme is denatured by an extreme pH value.

(3 marks)

(iv) Suggest **two** variables you would control if you were investigating the activity of gastric lipase at different pH values.

(2 marks)

(b)   The weight-loss drug, orlistat, stops triglycerides from being broken down. Orlistat is a competitive inhibitor of gastric lipase.

Fig. 2.2 shows the reaction with and without orlistat present.

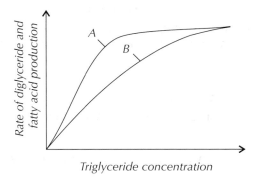

Fig. 2.2

(i)   Which curve on Fig 2.2 shows the reaction **without** the presence of orlistat? Give a reason for your answer.

(1 mark)

(ii)   Explain the action of orlistat in this reaction.

(3 marks)

Learning Objectives:

- Be able to define the term 'balanced diet'.

- Be able to explain how consumption of an unbalanced diet can lead to malnutrition, with reference to obesity.

- Be able to discuss the possible links between diet and coronary heart disease.

- Be able to discuss the possible effects of a high blood cholesterol level on the heart and circulatory system, with reference to low density lipoproteins (LDLs) and high density lipoproteins (HDLs).

  Specification Reference 2.2.1

1. A Balanced Diet

Having a balanced diet is all about getting the right nutrients. But having too little or too much of some nutrients can lead to serious health problems...

What is a balanced diet?

To stay healthy it's important you have a balanced diet. A balanced diet gives you the right amount of all the nutrients you need, plus fibre and water. There are five important nutrients — **carbohydrates**, **proteins**, **fats**, **vitamins** and **mineral salts**. Each nutrient has different functions in the body:

Nutrients	Functions
Carbohydrates	Provide energy.
Fats (lipids)	Act as an energy source, provide insulation, make up cell membranes and physically protect organs.
Proteins	Needed for growth, the repair of tissues and to make enzymes.
Vitamins	Different vitamins have different functions, e.g. vitamin D is needed for calcium absorption, vitamin K is needed for blood clotting.
Mineral salts	Different mineral salts have different functions, e.g. iron is needed to make haemoglobin in the blood, calcium is needed for bone formation.

Fibre and **water** also have important functions, as fibre aids the movement of food through the gut and water is used in chemical reactions. You need a constant supply of water to replace that which is lost through urinating, breathing and sweating.

Malnutrition

Malnutrition is caused by having too little or too much of some nutrients in your diet. There are three causes:

1. Not having enough food, so you get too little of every nutrient.

    > **Example**
    > In many third world countries people have very little food to eat, which makes them malnourished.

2. Malabsorption — this is where your body isn't able to absorb the nutrients from digestion into your bloodstream properly. This causes deficiency illnesses.

    > **Example**
    > Coeliac disease reduces absorption of nutrients from the small intestine, which can lead to deficiency illnesses.

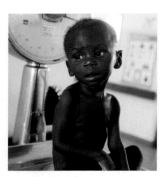

Figure 1: *A boy with malnutrition caused by having too little food.*

Tip: A deficiency illness is an illness caused by not getting enough of a specific nutrient (usually a vitamin or mineral) in the diet.

3. Having an unbalanced diet. An unbalanced diet may contain too little of a nutrient and this can lead to deficiency illnesses. A diet may also be unbalanced if it provides too much of a nutrient, and this can also lead to health problems.

Examples
- Too little iron in your diet can lead to iron deficiency anaemia.
- Too many carbohydrates or fats in your diet can lead to obesity.

Tip: Iron deficiency anaemia is a disease where the blood has less haemoglobin (p. 83) than normal because of a lack of iron (the body needs iron to produce haemoglobin).

Obesity

Over-nutrition (getting too many of some nutrients) can lead to obesity — a condition defined as being 20% (or more) over the recommended body weight. It is a serious condition as it can increase the risk of developing Type 2 diabetes, arthritis, high blood pressure, coronary heart disease (see the next page) and even some forms of cancer.

The main causes of obesity are eating too much sugary or fatty food (which contain a lot of energy) and getting too little exercise. This means that the body takes in more energy than it uses up — and the excess energy is stored as fat which increases body weight. People can also be obese due to an underactive thyroid gland (a gland in your neck that releases certain hormones).

Tip: Diabetes is where the body's blood glucose level can't be controlled properly. There are two types of diabetes, but obesity is mainly linked with an increased risk of developing Type 2.

Tip: Obesity is a bigger problem in developed countries.

Body Mass Index

The Body Mass Index (BMI) is used as a guide to help decide whether someone is underweight, normal, overweight or obese. It's calculated from their height and weight:

$$BMI = \frac{\text{body mass (kg)}}{\text{height (m)}^2}$$

Exam Tip
Don't worry, you don't need to remember this equation for your exam.

The BMI value is then used to classify someone's weight using the table shown below.

Body Mass Index	Weight Description
below 18.5	underweight
18.5 – 24.9	normal
25 – 29.9	overweight
30 – 40	moderately obese
above 40	severely obese

Example

A person weighs 62 kg and is 1.52 m tall. So their BMI is:

$$BMI = \frac{\text{body mass (kg)}}{\text{height (m)}^2} = \frac{62}{1.52^2} = \frac{62}{2.3} = \mathbf{27}$$

This means they are classed as 'overweight'.

However, BMI isn't always reliable as it doesn't take into account how much of a person's body mass is made of up fat. For example, athletes have lots of muscle, which weighs more than fat. This means they could have a high BMI even though they're not overweight.

Figure 2: *Having lots of muscle may affect a person's BMI.*

Coronary heart disease

Coronary heart disease (CHD) is the result of reduced blood flow to the heart and can lead to chest pain (angina) and heart attacks. It's caused by **atherosclerosis** — the narrowing and hardening of the coronary arteries (the blood vessels that supply the heart). Diets that are high in cholesterol and salt can increase the risk of atherosclerosis and CHD.

Blood cholesterol level

Cholesterol is a lipid made in the body (mainly in the liver), but we also get some from our diet. Some cholesterol is needed for the body to function normally. Cholesterol needs to be attached to a protein to be moved around, so the body forms **lipoproteins** — substances composed of both protein and lipid. The body is able to regulate its total blood cholesterol level using lipoproteins. There are two types:

1. Low density lipoproteins (LDLs)

LDLs are mainly lipid. They transport cholesterol from the liver to the blood, where it circulates until needed by cells. Their function is to increase blood cholesterol when the level is too low.

However, a diet high in saturated fat raises LDL level — so more cholesterol is transported to the blood, increasing total blood cholesterol. This increases the build up of fatty deposits in the artery walls (called atheromas — see Figure 3) at places where they've been damaged. This causes atherosclerosis and can lead to CHD.

2. High density lipoproteins (HDLs)

HDLs are mainly protein. They transport cholesterol from body tissues to the liver where it's recycled or excreted. Their function is to reduce blood cholesterol when the level is too high.

A diet high in polyunsaturated fat raises HDL level — so more cholesterol is transported from the blood to the liver, decreasing total blood cholesterol and decreasing the risk of CHD.

Salt

A diet high in salt can cause high blood pressure. This can increase the risk of damage to artery walls. Damaged walls have an increased risk of atheroma formation, which causes atherosclerosis and increases the risk of CHD.

Tip: There's more about atherosclerosis and CHD on pages 175-176.

Tip: A high blood cholesterol level can lead to stroke and high blood pressure as well as CHD.

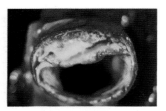

Figure 3: An atheroma (yellow) in an artery.

Tip: Foods like cheese, butter and fatty meats contain a high proportion of saturated fat.

Tip: Foods such as nuts, seeds and many types of fish contain a high proportion of polyunsaturated fat.

Four people had their blood cholesterol levels checked. Their results are shown in the table below, and the desirable levels of LDLs and HDLs are given on the right.

Person	LDL (mmol/L)	HDL (mmol/L)
1	4.9	1.0
2	3.5	1.0
3	3.1	1.7
4	4.9	1.5

Desirable level (mmol/L)

LDL: ≤ 3

HDL: ≥ 1.2

Tip: Remember, LDLs are low density lipoproteins and HDLs are high density lipoproteins.

Tip: The symbol ≤ means 'less than or equal to' and ≥ means 'more than or equal to'.

Tip: High HDL and low LDL levels are desirable because they're the most healthy.

Tip: Use more than one value from the table to support your answer to Q1.

Q1 Based on the information in the table, which person is at most risk of developing coronary heart disease? Explain your answer.

Q2 a) Suggest and explain some dietary advice that Person 2 might be given in relation to their blood cholesterol level.

b) Statins are drugs that reduce the amount of cholesterol the body produces. On average they can lower LDL level by 1.8 mmol/L. Plant stanol esters are compounds that can reduce cholesterol level when eaten. Including 2 g of plant stanol esters in a person's daily diet can reduce their LDL level by 10%.

Based on this information (and assuming that they worked at the same rate) would you expect taking statins or including 2 g of plant stanol esters in their daily diet to produce a greater reduction in Person 2's LDL level? Show your working.

Practice Questions — Fact Recall

Q1 What is a 'balanced diet'?

Q2 Give three causes of malnutrition.

Q3 Give one cause of obesity.

Q4 Give two diseases that obesity can increase the risk of.

Q5 a) What is the Body Mass Index used as?

b) Why is the Body Mass Index not always reliable?

Q6 What are lipoproteins?

Q7 Explain why a diet high in saturated fat may increase the risk of CHD.

Q8 State the function of HDLs.

Q9 Explain why a diet high in salt may increase the risk of CHD.

Exam Tip
You may have heard HDL and LDL being called 'good' and 'bad cholesterol', but you won't get marks for calling them this in the exam.

Learning Objectives:

- Be able to explain that humans depend on plants for food as they are the basis of all food chains. (No details of food chains are required.)

- Be able to describe how the use of fertilisers and pesticides on plants can increase food production.

- Be able to describe how giving antibiotics to animals can increase food production.

- Be able to outline how selective breeding is used to produce crop plants with high yields, disease resistance and pest resistance.

- Be able to outline how selective breeding is used to produce domestic animals with high productivity.

Specification Reference 2.2.1

2. Increasing Food Production

With an ever growing human population we need to produce more and more food. Thankfully there are a range of farming methods that can increase food production — but they're not perfect...

Human food supply

Humans rely on plants for food because plants are at the start of all food chains. Plants use the energy from sunlight to convert carbon dioxide and water into complex organic compounds (such as carbohydrates). Humans and other animals then eat, digest and absorb the compounds, which they use for energy and to grow.

We grow plants both for direct consumption and to feed animals which we then eat. Many modern farming methods aim to maximise productivity by increasing plant and animal growth. Farmers can do this using fertilisers, pesticides, antibiotics and selective breeding.

Fertilisers

Fertilisers are chemicals that increase crop yields by providing minerals (such as nitrate, phosphate and potassium) that plants need to grow. Minerals in the soil are used up during crop growth. Fertilisers replace these minerals so that a lack of minerals doesn't limit growth of the next crop. There are two different types of fertiliser:

- **Natural fertilisers** are organic matter — they include manure and sewage sludge (that's "muck" to you and me).

- **Artificial fertilisers** are inorganic — they contain pure chemicals (e.g. ammonium nitrate) as powders or pellets.

Pesticides

Pesticides are chemicals that increase crop yields by killing pests that feed on the crops. This means fewer plants are damaged or destroyed. Pests include microorganisms, insects or mammals (e.g. rats). Pesticides may be specific and kill only one pest species, or broad, and kill a range of different species. The advantage of broad spectrum pesticides is that they can kill a wide range of pests in one go. However, this means they may also harm some non-pest species.

Antibiotics

Animals farmed for food are sometimes given antibiotics (chemicals that kill or inhibit the growth of bacteria) to increase food production. There are advantages and disadvantages of using antibiotics.

Tip: Antibiotics <u>don't</u> kill viruses.

Advantages

- Animals normally use energy fighting diseases, which reduces the amount of energy available for growth. Giving them antibiotics means animals can use more energy to grow, increasing food production.

- Antibiotics help to promote the growth of animals. This is thought to be because the antibiotics influence bacteria in the animals' gut, allowing the animals to digest food more efficiently. This can increase both the growth rate of the animal and it's size when mature.

- Giving animals antibiotics makes it less likely bacterial diseases will pass from them to humans.

Tip: Feeding animals antibiotics makes them less likely to get a bacterial disease, but it <u>doesn't</u> make them immune. See pages 166-167 for more on immunity.

Disadvantages

- Using antibiotics in farming can increase the chance of bacteria becoming resistant to them (able to survive being exposed to the antibiotic — see page 216). This would make it more difficult to treat diseases (both in animals and humans) in the future.

- Animals naturally have some bacteria in their body which are useful and could be killed by the antibiotics.

- There's also a chance that the antibiotic may be present in animal products which humans consume (e.g. milk), meaning that the antibiotic could also have unwanted effects in our bodies, too.

Figure 1: The use of antibiotics in farming animals like pigs was banned in the European Union in 2006 due to the risk of it increasing antibiotic resistance.

Selective breeding

Selective breeding involves selecting plants or animals with useful characteristics (e.g. high yield), to reproduce together in order to increase productivity. The general method is the same for both crops and animals:

1. Select plants or animals with useful characteristics that will increase food production.
2. Breed them together.
3. Select the offspring with the best characteristics and breed them together.
4. Continue this over several generations until a high-yielding plant or animal is produced.

Selective breeding of crops

Selective breeding of crops often involves selecting plants with characteristics such as high yield, disease resistance or pest resistance.

┌─ **Examples** ──────────────────────────

Corn

A farmer wants a strain of corn plant that is tall and produces lots of ears, so he breeds a tall corn strain with one that produces multiple ears.

He selects the offspring that are tallest and have most ears, and breeds them together. The farmer continues this until he produces a very tall strain that produces multiple ears of corn.

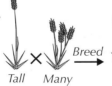

Tall × Many ears → *Breed* → Taller and more ears × → *Breed* → Very tall and many ears

Apples

A farmer wants to produce apples that are resistant to apple scab (a fungal disease that affects some trees). He selects apples with the best taste and breeds them with crab apples that are resistant to apple scab. He then breeds together the offspring that show most resistance and have the best taste. This continues over many generations to produce a tasty apple crop that is resistant to the disease.

Figure 2: Domestic carrots (right) have been selectively bred from wild carrots (left).

Tip: Farmers have to make sure that plants don't naturally cross pollinate (breed together) during selective breeding. This is to make sure that only plants with the desired characteristics breed together.

Selective breeding of animals

Selective breeding of animals involves selecting animals with useful characteristics such as fast growth rate and high meat, milk or egg yields.

┌─ **Example** ──────────────────────────

A farmer wants to produce cows with high meat yields, so he breeds together his largest cows and largest bulls. He selects the offspring that are largest and breeds them together. The farmer continues this over several generations until cows with very high meat yields are produced.

Figure 3: *Selective breeding can increase the meat yield of chickens, but it can also cause them health problems.*

Arguments for and against selective breeding

Selective breeding is a useful way of increasing food production, but it can also raise ethical issues.

Arguments for selective breeding:

- It can produce high-yielding animals and plants.

- It can be used to produce animals and plants that have increased resistance to disease. This means farmers have to use fewer drugs and pesticides.

- Animals and plants could be bred to have increased tolerance of bad conditions, e.g. drought or cold.

Arguments against selective breeding:

- It can cause health problems.

  ┌ **Example** ───────────────
  Some types of chicken have been bred to grow very quickly. However, this has meant their hearts and lungs can't support their increased body mass, causing them distress.

- It reduces genetic diversity. In a selective breeding programme the plants or animals with the best characteristics are usually closely related, so breeding them together can lead to inbreeding. This reduces the gene pool (the number of different alleles in a population) and can make the plant or animal population more susceptible to disease.

Practice Questions — Application

A chicken farmer wants to increase his yield of eggs.

Q1 Describe how the chicken farmer could increase his yield of eggs through selective breeding.

Q2 After a few years of selective breeding the farmer manages to double his egg yield. However, the viral disease, Gumboro, has become much more common in his flock of chickens. Explain how the increased incidence of this disease may have been caused by selective breeding.

Practice Questions — Fact Recall

Q1 Explain why humans rely on plants for food.

Q2 Explain how food production can be increased with the use of:
   a) fertilisers,
   b) pesticides.

Q3 Give three advantages of the use of antibiotics in farming animals.

Q4 What is selective breeding?

Q5 Briefly describe how selective breeding is used to increase food production.

Q6 Give two advantages of the use of selective breeding.

3. Microorganisms and Food

Used in the right way, some microorganisms can be really helpful when it comes to food production. But left to grow uncontrolled, they can cause disease and spoil our food.

Microorganisms in food production

Microorganisms such as bacteria, yeast and other fungi are used in the production of many foods and drinks. Some microorganisms can convert sugar into other substances that humans can then use for food production.

Examples

Bread
Bread is made by mixing yeast (a fungus), sugar, flour and water into a dough. The yeast turn the sugar into ethanol and carbon dioxide — it's the carbon dioxide that makes the bread rise.

Wine
Wine is made by adding yeast to grape juice. The yeast turn the sugar in the grape juice into ethanol (alcohol) and carbon dioxide.

Cheese
Cheese is made by adding bacteria to milk. The bacteria turn the sugar in the milk into lactic acid, which causes the milk to curdle. An enzyme is then used to turn the curdled milk into curds and whey. The curds are separated off and left to ripen into cheese.

Yoghurt
Yoghurt is also made by adding bacteria to milk. The bacteria turn the sugar in the milk into lactic acid, causing the milk to clot and thicken into yoghurt.

Advantages

There are many advantages of using microorganisms to make food:

- Populations of microorganisms grow rapidly under the right conditions, so food can be produced quickly.

- Microorganisms can grow on a range of inexpensive materials.

- Their environment can be artificially controlled — so you can potentially grow food anywhere and at any time of the year.

- Optimum conditions for growth are easy to create, e.g. the right temperature, supply of nutrients and pH.

- Some of the food made using microorganisms often lasts longer in storage than the raw product they're made from, e.g. cheese can be stored for longer than milk.

Disadvantages

There are also disadvantages:

- There's a high risk of food contamination. The conditions created to grow the desirable microorganisms are also favourable to harmful microorganisms. They could cause the foods produced to spoil (go off — see the next page), or if eaten, cause illnesses such as food poisoning.

- The conditions required to grow microorganisms can be simple to create, but small changes in temperature or pH can easily kill the microorganisms.

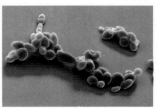

Figure 1: *SEM of Saccharomyces ellipsoideus — a type of yeast used to make wine.*

Exam Tip
There are lots of other foods produced using microorganisms, so don't fret if you get an exam question on one you've not come across before. You should be able to pick up all the marks by applying your scientific knowledge to the information you're given.

Figure 2: The appearance of food can be changed by food spoilage.

Exam Tip
You might need to apply some of your knowledge from other AS topics, e.g. osmosis (p. 29-30), biological molecules (p. 108-117), and enzymes (p. 133-141) to answer questions on food spoilage in the exam.

Tip: Methods that prevent food spoilage and extend the shelf life of food products are also said to <u>preserve</u> the food.

Tip: Food spoils faster when it's warm because microorganisms tend to reproduce more quickly. The enzymes they secrete also have more kinetic energy (see page 136) so food molecules are broken down faster.

Figure 3: Irradiated strawberries (left) have a much longer shelf life than normal strawberries (right).

Food spoilage

Food spoilage is the deterioration of a food's characteristics, e.g. its appearance, taste, texture or odour (see Figure 2). It can be caused by the growth of unwanted microorganisms, such as bacteria and yeast. As the microorganisms multiply they secrete enzymes which break down molecules in the food. For example, proteins are broken down into amino acids, fats into fatty acids and carbohydrates into more simple sugars. It's this breakdown of molecules in food that causes the food to spoil.

Some microorganisms may also produce waste products (toxins) which contribute to food spoilage and could cause food poisoning if the food is eaten. Food poisoning can affect anyone, but some parts of the population are particularly susceptible to it. For example, very young and elderly people, and people who are malnourished, are more likely to be affected by food poisoning because they have a weaker immune system.

Preventing food spoilage

Food spoilage can be prevented by either killing the microorganisms or depriving the microorganisms of the conditions they need to grow — this either slows down or stops their growth.

Salting

Salting is simply adding salt to foods. Salt inhibits the growth of microorganisms by interfering with their ability to absorb water (which they need to survive). Water usually moves into the cells of microorganisms by osmosis. However, salting food lowers the water potential of the environment outside the microbial cells, causing the microorganisms to lose water. Some meats are preserved by salting, and tinned foods are often preserved in brine (a mixture of salt and water).

Adding sugar

Like salting, adding sugar also inhibits the growth of microorganisms by interfering with their ability to absorb water by osmosis (see above). For example, the high sugar content of fruit jams reduces the growth of microorganisms, giving the jam a long shelf life.

Freezing

Freezers keep foods below −18 °C. This slows down enzyme controlled reactions taking place in microorganisms and freezes the water in the food, so the microorganisms can't use it. Freezing can preserve foods for many months.

Pickling in vinegar

Vinegar has a low pH. This denatures enzymes in microorganisms, preventing the enzymes from functioning properly and inhibiting the microorganisms' growth. Vinegar is used to pickle foods like onions.

Heat treatment

Heat treatment involves heating food to a high enough temperature to denature enzymes and kill any microorganisms present. Pasteurisation is one form of heat treatment — it involves raising liquids such as milk to a high temperature.

Irradiation

Irradiation involves exposing foods to radiation, e.g. X-rays or gamma rays. This treatment kills any microorganisms present (by destroying or damaging their DNA) and can extend shelf life considerably.

Practice Questions — Application

Eggs are a popular food choice around the world. However, some eggs contain the bacteria *Salmonella* which can cause food poisoning. A variety of methods are used to protect against poisoning by *Salmonella* and to prolong the shelf life of eggs.

Q1 Suggest three changes you may notice in an egg's characteristics that may indicate it had been spoiled.

Q2 Salted eggs are a popular Asian appetiser, which have a shelf life of up to 40 days. Explain why salting preserves eggs.

Q3 Pickling in vinegar extends the shelf life of eggs. Explain how.

Q4 Many eggs are pasteurised before being sold. Explain how pasteurisation protects against *Salmonella* poisoning.

Tip: Think of the egg without its shell when answering Q1.

Practice Questions — Fact Recall

Q1 Describe an example of the use of microorganisms in food production.

Q2 Discuss two advantages and two disadvantages of the use of microorganisms in food production.

Q3 What is meant by the term 'food spoilage'?

Q4 Explain how microorganisms can cause food spoilage.

Q5 Describe how adding sugar to a food can prevent food spoilage.

Q6 Explain how freezing can preserve food.

Q7 What is the name of the food preservation method that involves exposing food to X-rays or gamma rays?

Section Summary

Make sure you know:

- That a balanced diet gives you the right amount of all the nutrients you need (carbohydrates, fats, proteins, vitamins and mineral salts), plus fibre and water.
- That malnutrition can be caused by not having enough food, by malabsorption (where the body can't absorb nutrients from digestion properly) or by having an unbalanced diet containing too much or too little of a nutrient.
- That obesity is a form of malnutrition defined as being 20% (or more) over the recommended body weight, and that it can increase the risk of Type 2 diabetes, arthritis, high blood pressure, coronary heart disease and some forms of cancer.
- That the main causes of obesity are eating too much sugary or fatty food (which contain a lot of energy) and getting too little exercise.
- That cholesterol is a lipid needed for the body to function normally, but that a high blood cholesterol level can increase the risk of high blood pressure, stroke, atherosclerosis and coronary heart disease (CHD).
- That lipoproteins are substances made up of both lipid and protein.
- That low density lipoproteins (LDLs) are made up mainly of lipids whereas high density lipoproteins (HDLs) are made up mainly of protein.
- That LDLs transport cholesterol from the liver to the blood, and that a high LDL level increases the total blood cholesterol level.
- That a high blood cholesterol level increases the risk of fatty deposits (atheromas) building up in the artery walls, and that this causes atherosclerosis and can lead to CHD.
- That HDLs transport cholesterol from body tissues to the liver, and that high HDL levels decrease total blood cholesterol levels.
- That a diet high in saturated fat increases LDL levels and a diet high in polyunsaturated fat increases HDL levels.
- That a diet high in salt increases the risk of atheroma formation, which increases the risk of CHD.
- That humans rely on plants for food because plants are at the start of all food chains.
- That fertilisers are chemicals which increase crop yields by providing minerals needed for plant growth and that pesticides are chemicals which increase crop yields by killing pests that feed on the crops.
- That antibiotics help to treat or prevent diseases caused by bacteria, and that giving them to animals can increase the animals' growth rate and their size when mature, which can increase food production.
- The advantages and disadvantages of using antibiotics to increase food production.
- That selective breeding involves selecting plants or animals with desirable characteristics to reproduce together in order to increase productivity.
- How to outline the process of selective breeding in order to produce crops with high yields, pest resistance and disease resistance, and animals with high yields.
- The arguments for and against selective breeding.
- The advantages and disadvantages of using microorganisms to make food.
- That food spoilage is the deterioration of a food's characteristics, e.g. its appearance, taste, texture or odour, and how microorganisms cause food spoilage.
- How salting, adding sugar, freezing, pickling in vinegar, heat treatment and irradiation can be used to prevent food spoilage by microorganisms.

Exam-style Questions

1   A dietitian analysed the diets of three men aged 31 – 50. She compared the results to the recommended daily intakes for men of that age, as shown in Table 1.1.

	Recommended daily intake	Average daily intake — Subject 1	Average daily intake — Subject 2	Average daily intake — Subject 3
Energy (kcal)	2500	1840	2423	3150
Protein (g)	55	50	57	55
Carbohydrate (g)	312.5	230	335	480
Total fat (g)	< 97	80	95	110
Saturated fat (g)	< 30.5	15	25	42
Polyunsaturated fat (g)	18	12	18	11
Salt (g)	6	5.2	9.7	6.3

Table 1.1

(a)   The dietitian concluded that **Subject 1** and **Subject 3** could become malnourished if they continue with their current diet.

     (i)   Use evidence from Table 1.1 to suggest why the dietitian believes **Subject 1** is at risk of malnutrition.

(1 mark)

     (ii)   **Subject 3** is currently a healthy body weight, but the dietitian believes he is at risk of becoming obese. Use evidence from Table 1.1 to suggest why the dietitian believes this.

(3 marks)

     (iii) Obesity is associated with an increased risk of developing other medical conditions. State **two** of these conditions.

(2 marks)

(b)   Blood cholesterol level is affected by dietary intake.

     (i)   Describe how the body regulates its **blood cholesterol level**.

      In your answer you should make clear how the blood cholesterol level is raised and lowered.

(6 marks)

     (ii)   Explain why **Subject 3** is most likely to have the highest blood cholesterol level.

(2 marks)

(c)   Use evidence from Table 1.1 to suggest why **Subject 2** may be at risk of CHD.

(4 marks)

(d)   A person may still become malnourished despite having a balanced diet.
Suggest how this is possible.

(1 mark)

2   A pig farmer wants to maximise his farm's productivity. He collects data on three
different breeds of pig as shown in Fig. 2.1 and Table 2.1.

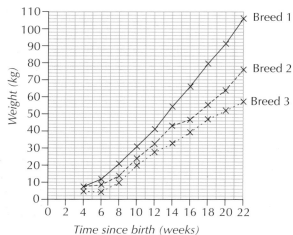

Fig. 2.1

	Meat yield (% of total body weight)
Breed 1	64
Breed 2	73
Breed 3	66

Table 2.1

(a) (i)   Describe the data shown in Fig. 2.1.

(3 marks)

(ii)   Calculate the weight of meat each breed of pig would yield after 22 weeks.
Give your answers to **one decimal place**.

(3 marks)

(b)   The farmer is exploring how he might increase the productivity of his pigs through
selective breeding.

(i)   Which breed(s) of pig should the farmer breed together in order to maximise
productivity? Explain your answer.

(2 marks)

(ii)   Give **two** disadvantages of selective breeding.

(2 marks)

(c)   Antibiotics could also increase the productivity of the pigs, but the farmer is reluctant
to use them.

(i)   Explain **one** way in which antibiotics could increase the productivity of the pigs.

(2 marks)

(ii)   Suggest **three** reasons why the farmer may be reluctant to use antibiotics.

(3 marks)

(d)   The meat from the pigs is irradiated to prevent food spoilage.
Describe how this method helps to prevent food spoilage.

(1 mark)

1. Defining Health and Disease

Learning Objectives:

- Be able to discuss what is meant by the terms 'health' and 'disease'.
- Be able to define and discuss the meanings of the terms 'parasite' and 'pathogen'.

Specification Reference 2.2.2

Before we get on to the really interesting stuff in this section, you need to learn a few key definitions...

What is health?

Health is a state of physical, mental and social well-being, which includes the absence of disease and infirmity (weakness of body or mind).
To be healthy you need to eat nutritious food, so you're not malnourished (see page 146), and have shelter (suitable housing) — these things help to maintain health because they help you to avoid disease.

What is disease?

Disease is a condition that impairs the normal functioning of an organism.
Diseases can be infectious, non-infectious, acute or chronic.

Infectious disease

Infectious diseases can be passed between individuals.
They're caused by infection with pathogens or parasites:

- A **pathogen** is an organism that can cause disease.

- A **parasite** is an organism that lives on or in another organism (the host) and causes damage to that organism. Some parasites cause disease, so they're also pathogens.

Examples — pathogens

- HIV (Human Immunodeficiency Virus) is the virus that causes AIDS — see page 172.
- *Mycobacterium tuberculosis* is the bacterium that causes TB — see page 172.
- *Trichophyton rubrum* is a fungus that causes athlete's foot.

Examples — parasites

- *Plasmodium* species are single-celled parasites that cause malaria (see page 171) — this means they're also pathogens.
- Tapeworms are parasitic worms that live in the digestive system of vertebrates (animals that have a backbone).
- Fleas are parasitic insects which live off the blood of mammals (including humans) and birds.

Non-infectious disease

Non-infectious diseases are caused by genetic defects, nutritional deficiencies, lifestyle and environmental factors (e.g. toxic chemicals).

Examples

- Coronary heart disease (CHD) is a non-infectious disease of the heart (see p.176 for more).
- Emphysema is a type of non-infectious lung disease (see p. 177).

> **Exam Tip**
> Make sure you learn all the definitions on this page and the next. Not only will they feature a fair bit in this section, you could get tested on them directly in the exam.

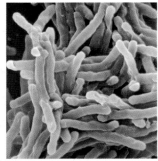

Figure 1: *An SEM of Mycobacterium tuberculosis.*

Figure 2: *The scolex (head-like structure) of a tapeworm.*

Figure 3: An electron micrograph of rhinovirus 14 — a virus which causes the common cold.

Acute and chronic diseases

Diseases can also be classed as acute or chronic:

- Acute diseases usually only cause a problem for a short period of time and the symptoms usually appear rapidly, e.g. a cold.

- Chronic diseases are much more persistent (you can have them your whole life), and the symptoms often appear very slowly but get progressively worse as time goes on, e.g. diabetes and chronic bronchitis (see page 176).

Tip: You'll be vaccinated against yellow fever if you travel to certain countries in Africa or South America. See page 168 for more on vaccinations.

Practice Questions — Application

Q1 Asthma is an inflammatory disease which affects the lungs. It can't be passed from one person to another and usually affects people for long periods of time.

    a) Is asthma an infectious or a non-infectious disease?

    b) Would you describe asthma as acute or chronic?

Q2 Yellow fever is a disease caused by viruses of the Flaviviridae family. Symptoms include fever, headaches and vomiting and last for three or four days.

    a) Is yellow fever an infectious or a non-infectious disease?

    b) Would you describe yellow fever as acute or chronic?

Practice Questions — Fact Recall

Q1 Explain what is meant by the term 'health'.

Q2 What is disease?

Q3 Define the terms 'pathogen' and 'parasite'.

Q4 a) What's the difference between an acute disease and a chronic disease?

    b) Give an example of each.

2. The Immune System

There are loads of different pathogens. The body's primary defences keep most away — but if any sneak through, the immune system keeps us safe.

Primary defences

Your body has a number of primary defences that help prevent pathogens and parasites from entering it. These include the skin and mucous membranes:

The skin

This acts as a physical barrier, blocking pathogens from entering the body. It also acts as a chemical barrier by producing antimicrobial chemicals and can lower pH, inhibiting the growth of pathogens.

Mucous membranes

These protect body openings that are exposed to the environment (such as the mouth, nostrils, ears, genitals and anus). Some mucous membranes secrete **mucus** (note the different spellings) — a sticky substance that traps pathogens and contains antimicrobial enzymes.

The immune response

If a pathogen or parasite gets past the primary defences and enters the body, the immune system will respond. An immune response is the body's reaction to a foreign **antigen**. Antigens are molecules (usually proteins or polysaccharides) found on the surface of cells. When a pathogen (like a bacterium) invades the body, the antigens on its cell surface are identified as foreign, which activates cells in the immune system.

The main stages of the immune response

1. Phagocytosis

A **phagocyte** (e.g. a macrophage) is a type of white blood cell that carries out phagocytosis (engulfment of pathogens). They're found in the blood and in tissues and are the first cells to respond to a pathogen inside the body. Here's how they work:

- A phagocyte recognises the antigens on a pathogen.
- The cytoplasm of the phagocyte moves round the pathogen, engulfing it.
- The pathogen is now contained in a **phagocytic vacuole** (a bubble) in the cytoplasm of the phagocyte.
- A **lysosome** (an organelle that contains digestive enzymes) fuses with the phagocytic vacuole. The enzymes break down the pathogen and it is absorbed into the cytoplasm.

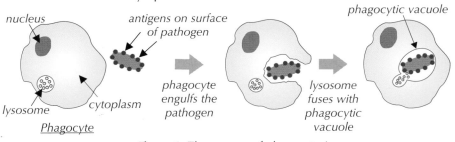

Figure 1: The process of phagocytosis.

The phagocyte then **presents** the pathogen's antigens. It sticks the antigens on its surface to activate other immune system cells.

Learning Objectives:

- Be able to describe the primary defences against pathogens and parasites (including skin and mucous membranes) and outline their importance.
- Be able to define the terms 'immune response' and 'antigen'.
- Be able to describe, with the aid of diagrams and photographs, the structure and mode of action of phagocytes.
- Be able to describe the structure and mode of action of T lymphocytes and B lymphocytes, including the significance of cell signalling.
- Be able to define the term 'antibody'.

Specification Reference 2.2.2

Tip: Macrophages aren't the only type of phagocytic cell, e.g. neutrophils are phagocytic cells too.

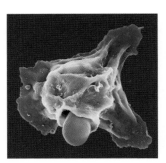

Figure 2: A phagocyte (blue) engulfing a pathogen (red).

2. T lymphocyte activation

A T lymphocyte is another type of white blood cell. Its surface is covered with receptors. The receptors bind to antigens presented by the phagocytes (see Figure 4).

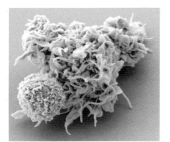

Tip: A complementary antigen means its shape fits into the shape of the receptor.

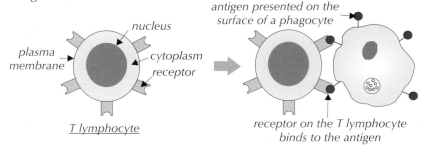

Figure 4: Activation of a T-lymphocyte.

Each T lymphocyte has a different receptor on its surface. When the receptor on the surface of a T lymphocyte meets a complementary antigen, it binds to it — so each T lymphocyte will bind to a different antigen. This process activates the T lymphocyte and is known as **clonal selection**. The activated T lymphocyte then undergoes **clonal expansion** — it divides to produce clones, which then differentiate into different types of T lymphocytes. These T lymphocytes carry out different functions:

- Some activated T lymphocytes, called **helper T cells**, release substances to activate B lymphocytes (see below).
- Some attach to antigens on a pathogen and kill the cell.
- Some become memory cells (see page 166).

Tip: T lymphocytes and B lymphocytes are sometimes just called T cells and B cells.

3. B lymphocyte activation and plasma production

B lymphocytes are also a type of white blood cell (see Figure 5). They're covered with **antibodies** — proteins that bind antigens to form an **antigen-antibody complex**.

Each B lymphocyte has a different shaped antibody on its membrane, so different ones bind to different shaped antigens (see Figure 6).

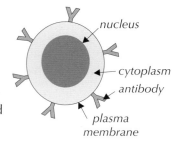

Figure 5: A B lymphocyte.

Antibody A <u>will bind</u> to antigen A, as they have complementary shapes.

Antibody A will <u>not</u> bind to antigen B, as they don't have complementary shapes.

Figure 6: Complementary binding between antibodies and antigens.

Exam Tip
Never say that antigens and antibodies have the 'same shape' or a 'matching shape' — you need to use the phrase 'complementary shape'.

When the antibody on the surface of a B lymphocyte meets a complementary shaped antigen, it binds to it — so each B lymphocyte will bind to a different antigen. This, together with substances released from helper T cells, activates the B lymphocyte. This process is another example of clonal selection. The activated B lymphocyte then divides, by mitosis, into plasma cells (next page) and memory cells (see p. 166). This is another example of clonal expansion.

4. Antibody production

Plasma cells are clones of the B lymphocyte (they're identical to the B lymphocyte). They secrete loads of the antibody, specific to the antigen, into the blood. These antibodies will bind to the antigens on the surface of the pathogen to form lots of antigen-antibody complexes. This is the signal for the immune system to attack and destroy the pathogen. There's lots more on the structure of antibodies and how they help to clear an infection in the next topic (pages 164-165).

Tip: The B lymphocyte divides by mitosis, so that all the cells produced are genetically identical. This means that they all produce identical antibodies specific to the pathogen.

Cell signalling and the immune response

Cell signalling is basically how cells communicate. A cell may release (or present) a substance that binds to the receptors on another cell — this causes a response of some kind in the other cell.

Tip: See page 27 for more on cell signalling.

Cell signalling is really important in the immune response because it helps to activate all the different types of white blood cells that are needed.

— Example —————————————

Helper T cells release substances that bind to receptors on B lymphocytes. This activates the B lymphocytes — the helper T cells are signalling to the B lymphocytes that there's a pathogen in the body.

Practice Questions — Application

Q1 AIDS is an immune system disorder caused by the Human Immunodeficiency Virus. The virus infects and destroys T lymphocytes, so the number that work properly gradually falls. AIDS patients often suffer from opportunistic infections — infections that wouldn't normally cause too much of a problem in a healthy person. Common ones are tuberculosis, pneumonia and an infection of the brain called toxoplasmosis. Explain why AIDS patients suffer from opportunistic infections.

Tip: There's a lot more on AIDS and HIV on pages 172-174.

Q2 Rheumatic fever is a disease where the immune system attacks cells in the heart. It's often triggered by an infection with the bacterium *Streptococcus pyogenes*. Antigens on the surface of *S. pyogenes* have a very similar shape to antigens on the surface of heart cells. Suggest why *S. pyogenes* infection can lead to rheumatic fever.

Tip: Antigens aren't just found on pathogens — your body cells have antigens on them too.

Practice Questions — Fact Recall

Q1 What are the body's two main primary defences against pathogens and parasites?

Q2 What is an immune response?

Q3 What are antigens?

Q4 Define phagocytosis.

Q5 What are the functions of T lymphocytes and plasma cells?

Q6 Draw a flow diagram showing the four main stages of the immune response.

Q7 Give an example of cell signalling being used during an immune response.

Learning Objectives:

- Be able to describe, with the aid of diagrams, the structure of antibodies.
- Be able to outline the mode of action of antibodies, with reference to the neutralisation and agglutination of pathogens.

Specification Reference 2.2.2

Figure 2: A molecular model of an antibody.

Tip: Antibodies need variable regions so that they can recognise and bind to different antigens. If all antibodies recognised the same pathogen they wouldn't be very useful.

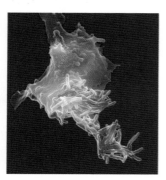

Figure 3: A macrophage (yellow) engulfing a clump of bacteria that has been agglutinated by antibodies.

3. Antibodies

In the previous topic you saw how the presence of a pathogen in the body led to the production of antibodies by B lymphocytes. Now it's time to see how the production of antibodies leads to the destruction of the pathogen.

Antibody structure

Antibodies are proteins — they're made up of chains of amino acid monomers linked by peptide bonds (see p. 108-111 for more on proteins). You need to learn the structure of antibodies (see Figure 1).

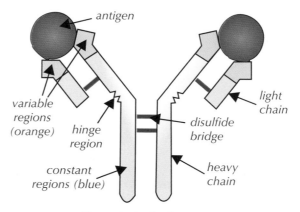

Figure 1: Antibody structure.

The **variable regions** of the antibody form the antigen binding sites. The shape of the variable region is complementary to a particular antigen. The variable regions differ between antibodies. The **hinge region** allows flexibility when the antibody binds to the antigen. The **constant regions** allow binding to receptors on immune system cells, e.g. phagocytes. The constant region is the same in all antibodies. Disulfide bridges (a type of bond) hold the polypeptide chains together.

The role of antibodies in clearing infections

Antibodies help to clear an infection in three main ways:

1. Agglutinating pathogens

Each antibody has two binding sites, so an antibody can bind to two pathogens at the same time — the pathogens become clumped together. Phagocytes then bind to the antibodies and phagocytose a lot of pathogens all at once (see Figure 4).

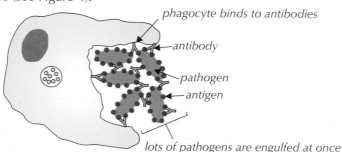

Figure 4: Agglutination of pathogens by antibodies.

2. Neutralising toxins

Antibodies can bind to the **toxins** produced by pathogens. This prevents the toxins from affecting human cells, so the toxins are neutralised (inactivated). The toxin-antibody complexes are also phagocytosed (see Figure 5).

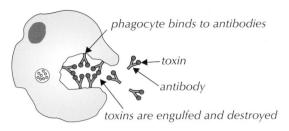

Figure 5: Neutralisation of toxins by antibodies.

3. Preventing the pathogen binding to human cells

When antibodies bind to the antigens on pathogens, they may block the cell-surface receptors that the pathogens need to bind to the host cells. This means the pathogen can't attach to or infect the host cells (see Figure 6).

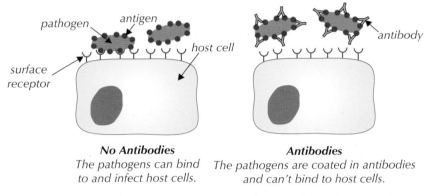

No Antibodies
The pathogens can bind to and infect host cells.

Antibodies
The pathogens are coated in antibodies and can't bind to host cells.

Figure 6: Antibodies preventing pathogens from binding to human cells.

Tip: Different pathogens cause damage in different ways. Not all pathogens produce toxins, so this mode of action will only be useful against some pathogens.

Exam Tip
You need to be able to describe all three ways in which antibodies can work so make sure you read these two pages carefully.

Tip: Host cells are cells in the organism that has been infected by the pathogen.

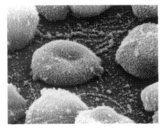

Figure 7: Flu virus particles (blue) attached to red blood cells (red). If these flu virus particles were bound by antibodies they would not be able to bind to the surface of the red blood cells.

Practice Question — Application

Q1 If someone is bitten by a poisonous snake or spider, they will be given antivenom. Antivenom contains antibodies against the toxins in the poison. Using your knowledge of antibodies, explain how antivenom works.

Practice Questions — Fact Recall

Q1 Give the functions of the following regions of an antibody:
   a) The variable region.
   b) The hinge region.
   c) The constant region.

Q2 How many binding sites do antibodies have and why is it useful for them to have this number?

Q3 Give three ways in which antibodies can help defend the body against pathogens.

Learning Objectives:
- Be able to describe the role of memory cells.
- Be able to compare and contrast the primary and secondary immune responses.

Specification Reference 2.2.2

4. Primary and Secondary Immune Responses

There's more than one type of immune response — and you need to know what the similarities and differences between them are...

The primary immune response

When an antigen enters the body for the first time it activates the immune system. This is called the primary response. The primary response is slow because there aren't many B lymphocytes that can make the antibody needed to bind to it. Eventually the body will produce enough of the right antibody to overcome the infection. Meanwhile the infected person will show symptoms of the disease.

After being exposed to an antigen, both T and B lymphocytes produce **memory cells**. These memory cells remain in the body for a long time. Memory T lymphocytes remember the specific antigen and will recognise it a second time around. Memory B lymphocytes record the specific antibodies needed to bind to the antigen. The person is now **immune** — their immune system has the ability to respond quickly to a second infection.

Tip: Being immune doesn't mean you'll never be infected by that pathogen again, it just means that if it gets into your body a second time your immune system quickly kills it before you get ill.

The secondary immune response

If the same pathogen enters the body again, the immune system will produce a quicker, stronger immune response — the secondary response (see Figure 1). Memory B lymphocytes divide into plasma cells that produce the right antibody to the antigen. Memory T lymphocytes divide into the correct type of T lymphocytes to kill the cell carrying the antigen. The secondary response often gets rid of the pathogen before you begin to show any symptoms.

Tip: The secondary response only happens if it's the <u>same pathogen</u>. If it's a different pathogen you just get another primary response.

Tip: The secondary response is always faster than the primary response. This is shown by a steeper line in graphs of blood antibody concentration against time.

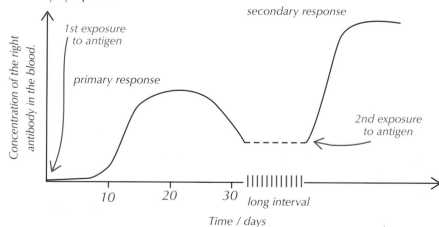

Figure 1: *A graph of antibody concentration against time since antigen exposure.*

Maintaining immunity

Memory B and T lymphocytes only have a limited life-span. This means that someone who is immune to a particular pathogen won't always stay immune forever — once all of the memory B and T lymphocytes have died, that person may be susceptible to attack by the pathogen again. Immunity can be maintained by being continually exposed to the pathogen, so you continue to make more and more memory B and T lymphocytes.

Tip: This is why some vaccines require booster shots — see pages 168-169 for more on vaccines.

People who live in malarial areas and who are constantly exposed to the malaria pathogen will build up a limited immunity to malaria. But if they move away from the malarial area, they'll have no further exposure to the pathogen and eventually they may lose the immunity they have. If they then returned to a malarial area, they would undergo a primary immune response when they encountered the malaria pathogen again.

Tip: See page 171 for loads more on malaria and what causes it.

Comparing the two responses

In the exam you might be asked to compare and contrast the primary and secondary immune response — basically say how they're similar and say how they're different. This is summarised in the table below:

	Primary response	Secondary response
Pathogen	Enters for 1st time	Enters for 2nd time
Speed of response	Slow	Fast
Cells activated	B and T lymphocytes	Memory cells
Symptoms	Yes	No

Exam Tip:
If you're asked to compare and contrast the primary and secondary responses in the exam, make sure you talk about similarities as well as differences. The similarities are, e.g. both are triggered by invasion of the body by a pathogen, both ultimately get rid of the pathogen and both involve the production of antibodies.

Practice Questions — Application

The graph below shows the immune responses of two mice exposed to a pathogen. Both mice were exposed on day 0 of the experiment.

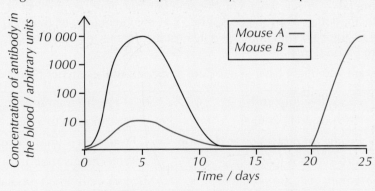

Q1 How much antibody did each mouse have in its blood on day 5?

Q2 Which mouse was already immune to the pathogen? Explain your answer.

Q3 a) On which day was Mouse A exposed to the pathogen again?

b) Describe what happened to Mouse A's immune system after it was exposed again.

Practice Questions — Fact Recall

Q1 Why is the primary immune response slower than a secondary immune response?

Q2 Why does immunity not always last forever?

Q3 Give three differences (other than the speed) between a primary and a secondary immune response.

Tip: Don't get the primary response mixed up with primary defences (see page 161).

Learning Objectives:

- Be able to compare and contrast active, passive, natural and artificial immunity.
- Be able to explain how vaccination can control disease.
- Be able to discuss the responses of governments and other organisations to the threat of new strains of influenza each year.
- Be able to outline possible new sources of medicines, with reference to microorganisms and plants and the need to maintain biodiversity.

Specification Reference 2.2.2

5. Immunity, Vaccinations and Developing Drugs

After you've been infected once by a pathogen you'll be immune to it, but being infected in the first place can be pretty unpleasant. Vaccination can make you immune without the being ill part.

Active and passive immunity

Immunity can be active or passive:

Active immunity

This is the type of immunity you get when your immune system makes its own antibodies after being stimulated by an antigen. There are two different types of active immunity:

1. **Natural** — this is when you become immune after catching a disease.
2. **Artificial** — this is when you become immune after you've been given a vaccination containing a harmless dose of antigen (see below).

Passive immunity

This is the type of immunity you get from being given antibodies made by a different organism — your immune system doesn't produce any antibodies of its own. Again, there are two types:

1. **Natural** — this is when a baby becomes immune due to the antibodies it receives from its mother, through the placenta and in breast milk.
2. **Artificial** — this is when you become immune after being injected with antibodies from someone else. E.g. If you contract tetanus you can be injected with antibodies against the tetanus toxin, collected from blood donations.

In the exam you might have to compare and contrast these types of immunity:

Active Immunity	Passive Immunity
Exposure to antigen	No exposure to antigen
It takes a while for protection to develop	Protection is immediate
Protection is long-term	Protection is short-term
Memory cells are produced	Memory cells aren't produced

Tip: If you get bitten by a poisonous snake or spider, the antivenom you're given will contain antibodies against the poison, so this is another example of artificial, passive immunity.

Tip: Don't get active and passive immunity mixed up. Just remember that in <u>active</u> immunity your body is <u>actively</u> doing something — it's producing antibodies.

Tip: Attenuated viruses have usually been genetically or chemically modified so that they can't produce toxins or attach to and infect host cells.

Vaccination

While your B lymphocytes are busy dividing to build up their numbers to deal with a pathogen (i.e. the primary response — see page 166), you suffer from the disease. Vaccination can help avoid this.

Vaccines contain antigens that cause your body to produce memory cells against a particular pathogen, without the pathogen causing disease. This means you become immune without getting any symptoms. These antigens may be free or attached to a dead or attenuated (weakened) pathogen.

Vaccines may be injected or taken orally. The disadvantages of taking a vaccine orally are that it could be broken down by enzymes in the gut or the molecules of the vaccine may be too large to be absorbed into the blood. Sometimes booster vaccines are given later on (e.g. after several years) to make sure that more memory cells are produced.

If most people in a community are vaccinated, the disease becomes extremely rare. This means that even people who haven't been vaccinated are unlikely to get the disease, because there's no one to catch it from. This is called **herd immunity** — see Figure 1.

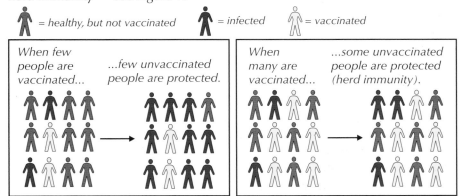

Figure 1: Herd immunity

Figure 2: *A boy being given an oral vaccination for polio.*

Tip: Herd immunity means not everyone needs to be vaccinated. As long as enough people get the vaccine, the pathogen won't be able to spread and even non-vaccinated people will be protected.

Problems with developing vaccinations

Vaccinating against a disease isn't always straightforward. For example, some sneaky pathogens can change their surface antigens. This means that when you're infected, the memory cells produced following a vaccination will not recognise the different antigens. So the immune system has to start from scratch and carry out a primary response against these new antigens.

EXAMPLE: The influenza virus

The influenza virus causes influenza (flu). Proteins (neuraminidase and haemagglutinin) on the surface of the influenza virus act as antigens, triggering the immune system. These antigens can change regularly, forming new strains of the virus.

Exam Tip
You need to learn this example for the exam.

Tip: Pathogens of the same type that have different surface antigens are often referred to as <u>strains</u>.

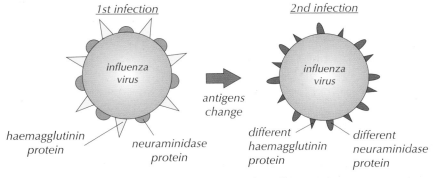

Figure 3: *Changing antigens in the influenza virus.*

Every year there are different strains of the influenza virus circulating in the population, so a different vaccine has to be made. Laboratories collect samples of these different strains, and organisations, such as the WHO (World Health Organisation) and CDC (Centre for Disease Control), test the effectiveness of different influenza vaccines against them.

New vaccines are developed and one is chosen every year that is the most effective against the recently circulating influenza viruses. Governments and health authorities then implement a programme of vaccination using this most suitable vaccine. This is a good example of how society uses science to inform decision making.

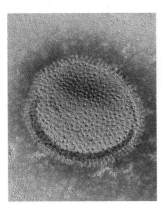

Figure 4: *A TEM of an influenza virus.*

Sources of medicines

Changing antigens also mean that some pathogens can rapidly develop resistance to drugs that are used against them. As a result, scientists need to be constantly developing new drugs to target resistant strains of pathogens, as well as developing drugs for diseases that are currently incurable.

Many medicinal drugs are manufactured using natural compounds found in plants, animals or microorganisms.

┌─ **Examples** ───
- ▪ Penicillin is obtained from a fungus.
- ▪ Some cancer drugs are made using soil bacteria.
- ▪ Daffodils are grown to produce a drug used to treat Alzheimer's disease.

Only a small proportion of organisms have been investigated so far, so it's possible that plants or microorganisms exist that contain compounds that could be used to treat currently incurable diseases, such as AIDS.

Possible sources of drugs need to be protected by maintaining the **biodiversity** (the variety of different species) on Earth. If we don't protect them, some species could die out before we get a chance to study them. Even organisms that have already been studied could still prove to be useful sources of medicines as new techniques are developed for identifying, purifying and testing compounds.

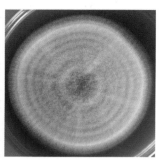

Figure 5: A colony of Penicillium chrysogenum *fungus growing on an agar plate. This fungus produces penicillin.*

Exam Tip
Always pay attention to the units on the axes — on the graph on the right, the y-axis is number of cases in thousands of people, so in 1963 there weren't 6 cases, there were 6000.

Tip: When reading off graphs with multiple scales, double check you've got the right one. If you're struggling to read off the answer, draw lines on the graph to help you.

Practice Questions — Application

Whooping cough is an infection of the respiratory system. The graph below shows the number of cases of whooping cough in Scotland between 1960 and 1999, and the vaccine uptake from the 1970s to 1999.

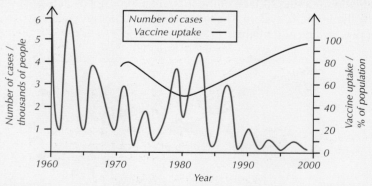

Q1 What percentage of the population were vaccinated in 1990?

Q2 How many cases of whooping cough were there in 1965?

Q3 The whooping cough vaccine was introduced in Scotland in the 1950s. Describe and explain the overall trend in the number of cases of whooping cough after the vaccine was introduced.

Practice Questions — Fact Recall

Q1 Define the terms active and passive immunity.

Q2 How do vaccines give people immunity?

Q3 What is herd immunity?

Q4 Explain why a new vaccine against flu has to be developed every year.

6. Infectious Diseases

There are three infectious diseases you need to know about — malaria, TB and HIV. Make sure you learn what causes them and how they are transmitted.

Malaria

Malaria is a parasitic disease caused by **Plasmodium** — a genus of eukaryotic, single-celled parasites.

Transmission

Plasmodium parasites are transmitted by mosquitoes — insects that feed on the blood of animals, including humans. In particular it's the female **Anopheles** mosquitoes that carry the parasites. The mosquitoes are **vectors** — they don't cause the disease themselves, but they spread the infection by transferring the parasites from one host to another. Mosquitoes transfer the *Plasmodium* parasites into an animal's blood when they feed on them.

Infection

Plasmodium infect the liver cells (hepatocytes) and red blood cells (erythrocytes), and disrupt the blood supply to vital organs. They have a complex life-cycle with multiple different stages (see Figure 1).

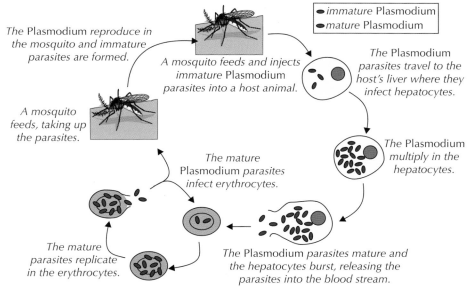

Figure 1: The life-cycle of malaria.

Preventing and treating malaria

There are a number of medicines which can treat malaria but hundreds of thousands of people still die from malaria every year, so scientists are trying really hard to find a way of preventing the disease. The best solution would be to make a vaccine against *Plasmodium*, but this is proving to be a tad tricky for a number of reasons:

- A *Plasmodium* parasite spends most of its life cycle hidden inside human cells. It is only exposed in the bloodstream for a very short period of time, which doesn't give the immune system very long to recognise and destroy it.

- There are four different species of *Plasmodium* that cause malaria. Because of mutation and variation, each species has different antigens — so different species will require different vaccines.

Learning Objectives:

- Be able to describe the causes and means of transmission of malaria, TB and AIDS/HIV (knowledge of the symptoms of these diseases is not required).

- Be able to discuss the global impact of malaria, TB and AIDS/HIV.

Specification Reference 2.2.2

Tip: *Plasmodium* and *Anopheles* are both genus names (see p. 199). There are many species of *Anopheles* mosquito that carry *Plasmodium*, and four species of *Plasmodium* that cause malaria.

Tip: It's specifically the female *Anopheles* that carry the parasite. Male *Anopheles* don't transmit malaria.

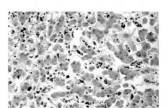

Figure 2: Plasmodium *parasites (dark specks) in the liver.*

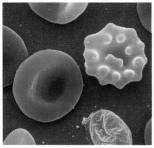

Figure 3: Malaria-infected red blood cell (upper right).

Tip: See page 168 for more on vaccines and how they work.

Tip: Tourists travelling to malarial areas can take anti-malarial drugs to protect themselves, but these are too expensive to use on a large scale.

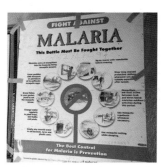

Figure 4: *An educational poster on malaria in Uganda.*

- The *Plasmodium* life-cycle involves more than one stage (a liver stage and a blood stage). Different stages have different antigens, so a vaccine that protects against one stage won't protect against another. The parasite is in each stage for a short amount of time, so there's not much opportunity for the immune system to act on each one.

Although there isn't a vaccine yet, there are other things that can be done to protect against malaria...

┌ **Examples** ─────────────────────────────────

- Mosquito nets and insect repellent can be used to stop people being bitten by the mosquitoes which carry the parasite.
- Pesticides can be used to kill the mosquitoes which carry the parasite.
- People can be educated about the signs and symptoms of malaria so it can be recognised and treated early, before the parasite can spread.

Tuberculosis (TB)

Tuberculosis (TB) is a lung disease caused by the bacterium ***Mycobacterium tuberculosis***.

Transmission

TB spreads by 'droplet infection' — when an infected person coughs or sneezes, tiny droplets of saliva and mucus containing the bacteria are released from their mouth and nose. These droplets are then breathed in by other people. Because of the way it's transmitted, tuberculosis tends to be much more widespread in areas where hygiene levels are poor and where people live in crowded conditions.

Infection

The bacteria invade a type of white blood cell found in the lungs, where they can lay dormant for many years. When someone becomes infected with tuberculosis bacteria, immune system cells build a wall around the bacteria in the lungs. This forms small, hard lumps known as tubercles — see Figure 5. Infected tissue within the tubercles dies and the gaseous exchange surface is damaged, so it becomes difficult to breathe. If the bacteria enter the bloodstream, they can spread to other parts of the body.

Many people with tuberculosis are infected but don't show any symptoms. But if they become weakened, e.g. by another disease or malnutrition, then the infection can become active. They'll show the symptoms and be able to pass on the infection.

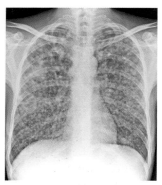

Figure 5: *A coloured X-ray of a patient with tuberculosis. The tubercles are pink.*

Preventing and treating TB

TB can be prevented with the BCG vaccine and treated using antibiotics, but there's a big problem with antibiotic-resistant strains. Improved standards of living and hygiene can also help to prevent TB.

AIDS and HIV

Acquired Immunodeficiency Syndrome (AIDS) is a disease of the immune system caused by the **Human Immunodeficiency Virus** (HIV).

Transmission

HIV is transmitted in three main ways:

- Via unprotected sexual intercourse.
- Via infected bodily fluids (like blood), e.g. sharing needles, transfusions.
- From mother to fetus (through the placenta, breast milk or in childbirth).

Tip: Don't get mixed up between the virus and the disease — HI<u>V</u> is the <u>v</u>irus, AI<u>D</u>S is the <u>d</u>isease.

Infection

The basic structure of HIV is shown in Figure 6. It's made up of a core containing genetic material (RNA) and some proteins (including the enzyme **reverse transcriptase**, which is needed for virus replication). It also has an outer coating of protein called a capsid and an extra outer layer called an envelope. This is made of membrane stolen from the cell membrane of a previous host cell.

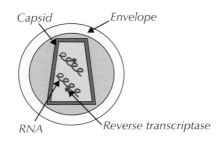

Figure 6: The structure of HIV.

HIV infects human white blood cells (leukocytes). HIV (and all other viruses) can only reproduce inside the cells of the organism it has infected. It doesn't have the equipment (such as enzymes and ribosomes) to replicate on its own, so it uses that of the host cell. Here's the life cycle of HIV:

1. The virus attaches to a receptor molecule on the cell membrane of the host cell.

2. The capsid is released into the cell, where it uncoats and releases the genetic material (RNA) into the cell's cytoplasm.

3. Inside the cell, reverse transcriptase is used to make a complementary strand of DNA from the viral RNA template.

4. From this, double-stranded DNA is made and inserted into the human DNA.

5. Host cell enzymes are used to make viral proteins from the viral DNA found within the human DNA.

6. The viral proteins are assembled into new viruses, which bud from the cell and go on to infect other cells.

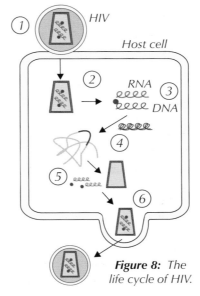

Figure 8: The life cycle of HIV.

Figure 7: An electron micrograph of a cell (blue sphere) infected by HIV (yellow dots).

Tip: See pages 125-127 for loads more on DNA and RNA and how the two are inter-linked.

Tip: When HIV particles emerge from a cell, the cell ruptures and dies.

Tip: It's not the HIV itself which kills people — it's the secondary infections that arise due to loss of cells in the immune system.

HIV infection eventually leads to AIDS, a condition where the immune system deteriorates and eventually fails due to the loss of white blood cells. It makes the sufferer more vulnerable to other infections, like pneumonia.

Preventing and treating HIV

There's no cure or vaccine for HIV. Antiviral drugs can be used to treat HIV. They work by inhibiting virus-specific enzymes (enzymes that only the virus uses), like reverse transcriptase. But these treatments can only slow down the progression of HIV infection and AIDS. Because you can't kill HIV with drugs, the best way to control it is by reducing its spread. This can be done by:

- Using barrier contraceptives, e.g. condoms.
- Screening blood donor volunteers.
- Not sharing hypodermic needles.
- Taking antiviral drugs during pregnancy.

The global impact of malaria, TB and HIV

Malaria, TB and HIV are most common in sub-Saharan Africa and other developing countries. This is because:

- There's limited access to good healthcare — drugs are not always available, people are less likely to be diagnosed and treated, blood donations aren't always screened for infectious diseases and surgical equipment isn't always sterile.

- There's limited health education to inform people how to avoid infectious diseases — e.g. fewer people know about the transmission of HIV and that it can be prevented by safe-sex practices, e.g. using condoms.

- There's limited equipment to reduce the spread of infections — e.g. fewer people have mosquito nets to reduce the chance of infection with malaria.

- There are overcrowded conditions — this increases the risk of TB infection by droplet transmission (see page 172).

The prevalence of malaria, HIV and TB in developing countries, like sub-Saharan Africa, slows down social and economic development because these diseases increase death rates, reduce productivity (fewer people are able to work) and result in high healthcare costs. Studying the global distribution of these diseases is important for many reasons:

- The information can be used to find out where people are most at risk.

- Any data collected can be used to predict where epidemics are most likely to occur.

- It's important for research (e.g. into how it's spread).

- It allows organisations to provide aid where it's needed most.

Tip: In developing countries, the steps that are taken to prevent a disease have to be balanced with the cost. If a vaccine against malaria was developed tomorrow, it might not make much difference because it's likely to cost more than developing countries can afford.

Tip: Infectious diseases can easily spiral out of control. Increased prevalence of the disease means higher health care costs, which means fewer people are treated. As a result more people will be infected and the prevalence will increase even further.

Tip: DEET impregnated clothing is clothing that has DEET soaked into the fabric.

Tip: See pages 168-169 for a recap on vaccines.

Practice Questions — Application

Q1 DEET is a type of insect repellent. Many visitors to malarial areas wear DEET impregnated clothing.
   a) Explain why this may help prevent visitors to the area becoming infected with malaria.
   b) Suggest one other precaution the visitors could take.

Q2 During the life-cycle of HIV, viral RNA is copied into DNA by the enzyme reverse transcriptase. This enzyme is prone to errors and often makes mistakes when copying the viral RNA. Suggest why this makes it difficult to develop a vaccine against HIV.

Q3 The incidence of TB in country X has increased dramatically in the past 20 years. This is thought to be linked to an increase in poverty.
   a) Explain how an increase in poverty could lead to an increase in the incidence of TB.
   b) TB is particularly common in areas where there are high levels of HIV infection. Suggest a reason for this.

Practice Questions — Fact Recall

Q1 Give the genus name of the parasite that causes malaria.

Q2 Describe how tuberculosis is transmitted.

Q3 What does HIV stand for? What disease does HIV cause?

Q4 Give four ways in which the spread of HIV can be controlled.

7. Smoking and Disease

You've probably been told a hundred times that smoking is bad for you. Well this topic explains why...

Damage to the cardiovascular system

Both carbon monoxide and nicotine, found in cigarette smoke, can damage the cardiovascular system and increase the risk of atherosclerosis, coronary heart disease (CHD) and stroke.

Atherosclerosis

Atherosclerosis is the hardening of arteries due to the formation of fibrous plaques called **atheromas** in the arterial wall. Atheromas contain low density lipoprotein (LDL). LDL contains a mixture of protein and cholesterol — this is how cholesterol is transported around the body (see page 148).

     The formation of an atheroma usually begins when damage occurs to the lining of an artery. This allows LDL to enter and collect in the arterial wall. The build up of LDL triggers an immune response, so white blood cells also move into the area. Over time more white blood cells, lipids and connective tissue build up and harden to form a fibrous plaque at the site of damage — the atheroma. The atheroma partially blocks the lumen of the artery and restricts blood flow (see Figure 1).

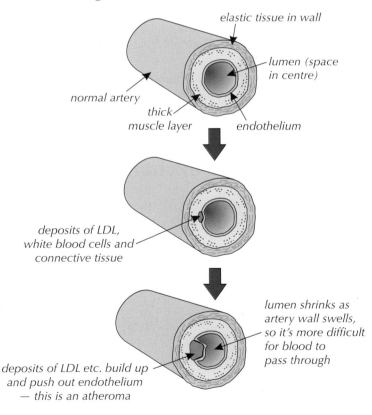

Figure 1: The process of atheroma formation.

Cigarette smoke contains **nicotine** and **carbon monoxide**, which cause an increase in blood pressure. Increased blood pressure can cause damage to the arteries, leading to the formation of more atheromas.

Learning Objectives:

- Be able to describe the effects of nicotine and carbon monoxide in tobacco smoke on the cardiovascular system, with reference to the course of events that lead to atherosclerosis, coronary heart disease and stroke.

- Be able to describe the effects of smoking on the mammalian gas exchange system, with reference to the symptoms of chronic bronchitis, emphysema (chronic obstructive pulmonary disease) and lung cancer.

Specification Reference 2.2.2

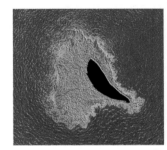

Figure 2: Cross section of an artery viewed under a microscope. The lumen of the artery (black) has narrowed due to the formation of an atheroma (brown).

Tip: It takes a long time for atheromas to build up, so atherosclerosis is described as a chronic disease (see page 160).

Coronary Heart Disease (CHD)

Coronary heart disease is when the coronary arteries (arteries that supply blood to the heart) have lots of atheromas in them. This restricts blood flow to the heart. A reduction in blood flow reduces the amount of oxygen an area of the heart gets and forces the heart muscle to respire anaerobically. This can cause pain (angina) or a heart attack. Smoking increases the risk of CHD for two reasons:

- **Carbon monoxide** in cigarette smoke irreversibly combines with haemoglobin, reducing the amount of oxygen transported in the blood. This reduces the amount of oxygen available to tissues, including the heart.

- **Nicotine** in cigarette smoke makes platelets (cells involved in blood clotting) sticky, increasing the chance of blood clots forming. If clotting happens in the coronary arteries it could cause a heart attack. The presence of atheromas also increases the risk of blood clots forming (and smoking increases atheroma formation — see previous page).

Treatment

CHD can be treated using something called a stent. Stents are tube-like structures which can be placed in obstructed arteries to increase the diameter of the artery and increase blood flow (see Figure 3). This means more oxygen can reach the heart, so the heart muscle can respire aerobically.

Stroke

A stroke is a rapid loss of brain function due to a disruption in the blood supply to the brain. This can be caused by a blood clot in an artery leading to the brain, which reduces the amount of blood, and therefore oxygen, that can reach the brain.

Nicotine increases the risk of stroke because it increases the risk of clots forming (see above). Carbon monoxide also increases the risk of stroke because it reduces the amount of oxygen available to the brain by combining with haemoglobin (see above).

Damage to the gas exchange system

Smoking cigarettes doesn't only damage the cardiovascular system — it can also damage the gas exchange system (i.e. the lungs), increasing the risk of lung cancer, bronchitis and emphysema.

Lung cancer

Cigarette smoke contains many carcinogens (chemicals that can cause a cell to become cancerous). These carcinogens may cause mutations in the DNA of lung cells, which could lead to uncontrolled cell growth and the formation of a malignant (cancerous) tumour.

Malignant tumours grow uncontrollably, blocking air flow to areas of the lung. This decreases gas exchange and leads to a shortness of breath because the body is struggling to take in enough oxygen. The tumour uses lots of nutrients and energy to grow, which causes weight loss.

Chronic bronchitis

Chronic bronchitis is the long-term inflammation of the mucous membrane lining the bronchi. The bronchi are lined with **goblet cells** that produce mucus to trap microorganisms. They're also lined with **cilia** that 'beat' to move the mucus towards the throat so it can be removed (see page 61).

Tip: Smoking isn't the only risk factor for CHD. Obesity (see p. 147) and eating a diet high in saturated fat (p. 148) can also increase the risk of developing CHD.

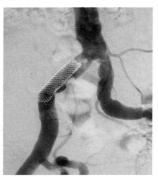

Figure 3: A stent (orange) in a previously obstructed artery (dark blue).

Tip: Aerobic respiration takes place in the presence of oxygen. It's much more efficient than anaerobic respiration, which takes place without oxygen.

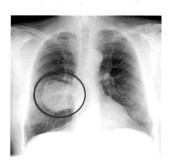

Figure 4: X-ray of an individual with lung cancer. The tumour is circled in red.

The tar in cigarette smoke damages the cilia and causes the goblet cells to produce more mucus. The mucus accumulates in the lungs, which causes increased coughing to try and remove the mucus. Microorganisms multiply in the mucus and cause lung infections that lead to inflammation, which decreases gas exchange.

Chronic bronchitis is a type of **chronic obstructive pulmonary disease** (COPD). COPD is a group of diseases that involve permanent airflow reduction.

Emphysema

Emphysema is a chronic lung disease involving the breakdown of the alveoli. It can be caused by smoking or long-term exposure to air pollution. Emphysema is also a type of COPD.

As with chronic bronchitis, the tar in cigarette smoke causes a build up of mucus, which leads to infection and inflammation of the lungs. This inflammation attracts phagocytes to the area. The phagocytes produce an enzyme that breaks down the protein elastin — an elastic protein found in the walls of the alveoli. Loss of elastin means the alveoli can't recoil to expel air as well (it remains trapped in the alveoli). It also leads to destruction of the alveoli walls, which reduces the surface area of the alveoli — see Figure 5.

an alveolus

less surface area for gas exchange

Figure 5: *Cross-section of healthy alveoli (left) and damaged alveoli (right).*

The loss of elastin and the reduction in the surface area of the alveoli reduce the rate of gas exchange in the alveoli. As a result, less oxygen is absorbed into the blood stream and transported around the body. The lack of oxygen reaching the cells leaves sufferers feeling tired and weak (fatigued).

Other symptoms of emphysema include shortness of breath and wheezing. People with emphysema also have an increased breathing rate as they try to increase the amount of air (containing oxygen) reaching their lungs.

> **Tip:** Don't forget — chronic diseases are persistent (you can have them your whole life), and the symptoms often appear very slowly, but get progressively worse as time goes on. See page ## for more.

> **Tip:** There's more on the structure and function of the alveoli on pages 59-60.

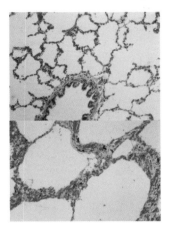

Figure 6: *Light micrographs of healthy lung tissue (top) and diseased lung tissue in a patient with emphysema (bottom).*

Practice Questions — Fact Recall

Q1 What is an atheroma? Describe how one forms.

Q2 Give two effects an atheroma has on the artery it's in.

Q3 Explain how smoking increases the risk of CHD.

Q4 How does smoking contribute to the development of lung cancer?

Q5 What is chronic bronchitis?

Q6 Describe how emphysema can develop as a result of smoking.

Learning Objective:

▪ Be able to evaluate the epidemiological and experimental evidence linking cigarette smoking to disease and early death.

Specification Reference 2.2.2

At AS-level it's not enough to just accept that smoking causes disease — you have to be able to evaluate the evidence linking smoking to disease yourself.

Interpreting data

In the exam, you might have to evaluate evidence linking smoking to disease or death. Here's kind of thing you might get:

Tip: See pages 222-225 for more on interpreting data.

> **Example**
>
> The graph shows the results of a study involving 34 439 male British doctors. Questionnaires were used to find out the smoking habits of the doctors. The number of deaths among the participants from ischaemic heart disease (coronary heart disease) was counted, and adjustments were made to account for differences in age.
>
>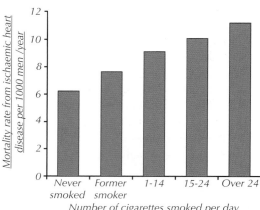

Here are some of the things you might be asked to do:

Describe the data — The graph shows that the number of deaths from ischaemic heart disease increased as the number of cigarettes smoked per day increased. Fewer former smokers and non-smokers died of ischaemic heart disease than smokers.

Tip: Lots of people find describing data difficult, but all you have to do is say what you see.

Draw conclusions — The graph shows a positive correlation between the number of cigarettes smoked per day by male doctors and the mortality rate from ischaemic heart disease. You can't say that smoking more causes an increased risk of dying from ischaemic heart disease though. There could be other factors causing the pattern, e.g. heavier smokers may drink more alcohol and it could be the alcohol (not smoking) that increases the risk of heart disease.

Tip: Always be careful when drawing conclusions — a correlation doesn't necessarily mean that one factor is causing the other (see p. 5).

Evaluate the study — To answer this, you basically need to think about how the study method could affect the results. For example:

▪ A large sample size was used — 34 439. The bigger the sample size the more reliable the results.

▪ People (even doctors) can tell porkies on questionnaires, reducing the reliability of results.

▪ The study only used doctors — this could have swayed the results. Doctors might be more likely to avoid the other risk factors associated with cardiovascular disease (e.g. alcohol, poor diet) and so this might bias the data. All the participants have the same job but they weren't matched otherwise, e.g. they might not be the same weight, or they might do different amounts of exercise a week, etc. This could have affected the results. Just like in an experiment you need to control as many variables as possible.

Figure 1: Questionnaires are often used to collect data, but they're not always reliable sources of information.

The graph below shows the per capita consumption of tobacco and the death rates for COPD (chronic obstructive pulmonary disease, which includes emphysema) from 1945 to 1998 in Australia.

Tip: Per capita basically just means per person.

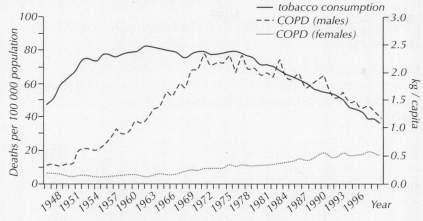

Q1 Describe in detail the trend in male COPD.

Q2 A scientist concludes from this data that COPD in women is not caused by smoking. Discuss this claim.

Section Summary

Make sure you know...

- That health is a state of physical, mental and social well-being, which includes absence of disease and infirmity, and that disease is a condition that impairs the normal functioning of an organism.
- That a pathogen is an organism that can cause damage to the organism it infects (the host) and that a parasite is an organism that lives on or in another organism and causes damage to that organism.
- That the skin and mucous membranes are important primary defences against pathogens.
- That an immune response is the body's reaction to a foreign antigen (a molecule found on the surface of cells).
- The four main stages of the immune response — phagocytosis, T lymphocyte activation, B lymphocyte activation and plasma cell production, and antibody production.
- The structure of antibodies (proteins that bind to antigens), including constant and variable regions.
- How antibodies clear infections by agglutinating pathogens, neutralising toxins and preventing pathogens from binding to cells.
- What memory cells are and their role in secondary immune responses.
- How the primary immune response and secondary immune responses are different.
- The similarities and differences between active, passive, natural and artificial immunity.
- How vaccines make people immune to disease by stimulating memory cell production.
- How governments and other organisations respond to the threat of new strains of influenza each year.
- Why it's important, in terms of drug development, to maintain biodiversity.
- What causes malaria, TB and AIDS/HIV, and how each of these diseases is transmitted.
- The global impacts of malaria, TB and AIDS/HIV.
- How smoking can lead to atherosclerosis, coronary heart disease (CHD) and stroke.
- How smoking can lead to lung cancer, chronic bronchitis and emphysema.
- How to interpret, analyse and evaluate data linking smoking to disease.

Exam-style Questions

1   Tuberculosis (TB) is an infectious disease. More than one million people worldwide die from tuberculosis every year.

(a)   Identify the pathogen which causes TB.

(1 mark)

(b)   Fig. 1.1 shows the number of reported cases of TB in the UK between 2000 and 2009.

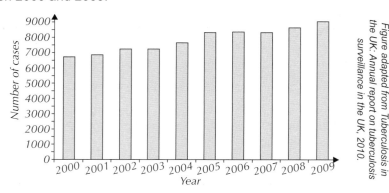

Figure adapted from Tuberculosis in the UK: Annual report on tuberculosis surveillance in the UK, 2010.

Fig. 1.1

(i)   Describe the trend in the number of reported TB cases in the UK between 2000 and 2009.

(1 mark)

(ii)   Calculate the approximate percentage increase in the number of cases of reported TB in the UK between 2003 and 2009. Show your working.

(2 marks)

(iii)   A newspaper headline states that "The number of TB cases in England is predicted to rise by 33% by the year 2018". Discuss this claim using the information in the graph.

(3 marks)

(c)   The incidence of TB in the UK is comparatively **low**. Discuss the reasons why the UK has a comparatively low incidence of TB.

(4 marks)

2   In 1918 there was a worldwide outbreak of influenza called 'Spanish flu'. The virus responsible was the **H1N1** strain — it had type 1 haemagglutinin (H1) and type 1 neuraminidase (N1) antigens on its surface.

(a)   When someone is infected with Spanish flu their immune system responds.

(i)   Describe the sequence of steps in phagocytosis.

 In your answer, you should make clear the correct order of the sequence.

(7 marks)

(ii)   Outline the main stages of the immune response after phagocytosis.

(5 marks)

(b)   Spanish flu circulated the globe for over a year. Explain why survivors of the Spanish flu did not contract it when exposed for a second time.

(2 marks)

(c)   In 1957 there was another outbreak of influenza called 'Asian flu'. It was caused by the **H2N2** strain of influenza. Explain why survivors of the Spanish flu may have contracted Asian flu.

(3 marks)

(d)   Every year new flu vaccines are developed. These contain antigens to multiple strains of influenza. Suggest why this is the case.

(1 mark)

3   Diphtheria is an infectious disease caused by a pathogenic species of bacteria. Cases of diphtheria are now very rare since the introduction of a vaccination in the early 1940's.

(a) (i)   Explain how having a vaccination leads to the formation of memory B lymphocytes.

(3 marks)

(ii)   Explain why individuals who don't have a particular vaccine will still gain some protection from the introduction of the vaccine.

(3 marks)

(b)   Memory B lymphocytes differentiate into plasma cells which produce antibodies.

(i)   Name the **three** main regions of an antibody and give the function of each region.

(6 marks)

(ii)   Tick the boxes to show which **three** of the following are functions of antibodies.

Agglutinating pathogens		Activating memory T lymphocytes	
Killing pathogens directly		Mutating pathogen DNA	
Neutralising toxins		Stopping pathogens binding to cells	

(3 marks)

4   Fig 4.1 shows a scanning electron micrograph of alveoli in a healthy human lung (left) and the effects of emphysema on the alveoli (right).

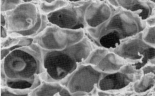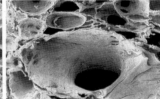

Fig. 4.1

(a)   Describe **one** difference between the healthy alveoli and the diseased alveoli, and explain what effect this would have on gaseous exchange in the alveoli.

(3 marks)

(b) (i)   Name **one** substance in cigarette smoke that causes emphysema.

(1 mark)

(ii)   Sufferers of emphysema often feel **fatigued**. Explain why this is the case.

(4 marks)

Learning Objectives:

- Be able to define the terms 'biodiversity', 'habitat' and 'species'.

- Be able to explain how biodiversity may be considered at different levels: habitat, species and genetic.

- Be able to explain the importance of sampling in measuring the biodiversity of a habitat.

- Be able to describe how random samples can be taken when measuring biodiversity.

- Be able to describe how to measure species richness and species evenness in a habitat.

- Be able to use Simpson's Index of Diversity (*D*) to calculate the biodiversity of a habitat, using the formula:

$$D = 1 - (\Sigma(n/N)^2)$$

- Be able to outline the significance of both high and low values of Simpson's Index of Diversity (*D*).

Specification Reference 2.3.1

1. Investigating Biodiversity

Biodiversity is important — the higher the biodiversity of an area, the healthier that area is. You can work out an area's biodiversity using a bit of data and a nifty little equation...

Biodiversity

The term 'biodiversity' refers to the variety of living organisms in an area. It can be considered at three different levels:

1. Habitat diversity

A habitat is the area inhabited by a species. It includes the physical factors, like the soil and temperature range, and the living (biotic) factors, like availability of food or the presence of predators. Habitat diversity is the number of different habits in an area.

> **Example**
>
> A coastal area could contain many different habitats — beaches, sand dunes, mudflats, salt marshes, etc.

2. Species diversity

A species is a group of similar organisms able to reproduce to give fertile offspring. Species diversity is the number of different species and the abundance of each species in an area.

> **Example**
>
> A woodland could contain many different species of plants, insects, birds and mammals.

3. Genetic diversity

Genetic diversity is the variation of alleles (versions of a gene) within a species or a population of a species.

> **Example**
>
> Human blood type is determined by a gene with three different alleles.

Collecting data on biodiversity

Collecting data on biodiversity usually means finding out the number of different species in a habitat or the number of individuals in each species. In most cases though, it'd be too time-consuming to count every individual organism in a habitat. Instead, a **sample** of the population is taken. Estimates about the whole habitat are based on the sample. Here's how:

1. Choose an area to sample, e.g. a small area within the habitat being studied. To avoid bias in your results, the sample should be chosen at random. This will make it more likely that your sample is representative of the population you're sampling (i.e. the sample shares as many characteristics as possible with the population).

HOW SCIENCE WORKS

If you were looking at plant species in a field, you could pick random sample sites by dividing the field into a grid and using a random number generator and a random letter generator to select coordinates. Then you'd take your samples from these coordinates.

In random sampling every individual has the same chance of being sampled. In non-random sampling, they don't. So if you're studying a field, samples collected only in the corners won't be representative of the whole field because the individuals that only live in the centre and along the edges would be excluded.

2. Record the number of different species or count the number of individuals of each species. How you do this depends on what you're counting.

Examples

For plants you'd use a quadrat (a frame which you place on the ground).

For ground insects you'd use a pitfall trap (a small pit that insects can't get out of).

0.5 m

0.5 m

raised lid
walking insects fall in and are trapped
stone to raise lid
flowerpot or similar container

For flying insects you'd use a sweepnet (a net on a pole).

For aquatic animals you'd use a net.

Make sure you use the appropriate equipment for the organisms you're studying. E.g. a sweepnet won't help you catch millipedes because millipedes can't fly. If you're sampling mobile organisms you should make sure they can't escape before you count them and that you don't count individuals more than once.

3. Repeat the process — take as many samples as possible. Calculating the mean of your repeat results will make your estimate more reliable.

4. The number of individuals for the whole area can then be estimated by taking an average of the data collected in each sample and multiplying it by the size of the whole area.

5. When sampling different habitats and comparing them, always use the same sampling technique.

Example

If you're using a series of pitfall traps you should make sure they're set up in the same way and left for the same length of time.

Tip: You can also make sure your samples are random by taking samples at different times of the day and in different weather conditions.

Tip: When you collect data on biodiversity you can damage the environment (e.g. by trampling plants) and disturb animals. It's a good idea to find ways of minimising this when you plan your investigation. It's also worth having a think about any ethical issues your investigation might raise, e.g. whether catching animals will cause them distress.

Figure 1: *Pitfall traps like this one can be used to catch ground-dwelling insects.*

Tip: For more on reliability see page 3.

Species richness and species evenness

Species richness is the number of different species in an area. The higher the number of species, the greater the species richness. It's measured by taking random samples of a habitat (see previous two pages) and counting the number of different species.

Species evenness is a measure of the relative abundance of each species in an area. The more similar the population size of each species, the greater the species evenness. It's measured by taking random samples of a habitat, and counting the number of individuals of each different species.

The greater the species richness and evenness in an area, the higher the biodiversity. The lower the species richness and evenness, the lower the biodiversity.

Example

Habitat X and habitat Y both contain two different species and 30 individual organisms.

	Habitat X	Habitat Y
No. organisms in species 1	28	15
No. organisms in species 2	2	15
Total	30	30

There are two species in each habitat so the species richness in the two habitats is the same — 2. However, in habitat Y the individual organisms are more evenly distributed between the different species — there are 15 organisms of each species, compared to 28 organisms in species 1 and just 2 organisms in species 2 in habitat X. Habitat Y has greater species evenness. This suggests that habitat Y has a higher biodiversity.

Simpson's Index of Diversity

Species richness and species evenness are simple ways of measuring diversity. But species that are present in a habitat in very small numbers shouldn't be treated the same as those with bigger populations. This is where Simpson's Index of Diversity comes in.

Simpson's Index of Diversity (*D*) is a useful way of measuring species diversity. It's calculated using an equation that takes into account both species richness and species evenness. You calculate Simpson's Index of Diversity using the following formula:

$$D = \left(1 - \sum \left(\frac{n}{N}\right)^2\right)$$

Where...
n = Total number of organisms in one species
N = Total number of all organisms
Σ = 'Sum of' (i.e. added together)

Simpson's Index of Diversity is always a value between 0 and 1. The closer the index is to one, the more diverse the habitat and the greater its ability to cope with change (e.g. the appearance of a new predator). Low index values suggest the habitat is more easily damaged by change, making it less stable.

Exam Tip
If you're asked to define species richness in the exam, you need to say it's the <u>number</u> of species in an area — if you talk about variety or amount you won't get the mark.

Tip: A low species evenness means that one or two species dominate a habitat — other species are only present in low numbers or are not present at all.

Tip: Abundance is the number of individuals. Distribution means where the individuals are found.

Tip: Change has a big effect on habitats with a low index of diversity because there aren't many species present. If one of only a few species gets wiped out, e.g. by a new predator, it makes a much bigger difference to a habitat than if one of many species gets wiped out.

The greater the species richness and evenness, the higher the value of Simpson's Index.

Example

There are 3 different species of flower in this field — a red species, a white and a blue. There are 3 of the red species, 5 of the white and 3 of the blue.

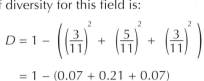

There are 11 organisms altogether, so $N = 11$.

So the index of diversity for this field is:

$$D = 1 - \left(\left(\frac{3}{11}\right)^2 + \left(\frac{5}{11}\right)^2 + \left(\frac{3}{11}\right)^2 \right)$$

$$= 1 - (0.07 + 0.21 + 0.07)$$

$$= 1 - 0.35 = 0.65$$

The field has an index of diversity of 0.65, which is fairly high.

Exam Tip
If you're asked to work out a Simpson's Index of Diversity in the exam, remember that the answer should be between 0 and 1. So if you get a negative number or a number greater than 1, then you've made a mistake.

Calculating the index of diversity can get quite tricky. If you've got a lot of data you might find it easier to plug the numbers into a table — that way you can make sure you don't miss out any steps.

Tip: You need to work out the $(n/N)^2$ bit for each different species and then add them all together.

Example

A student investigates the diversity of fish species in her local pond. She finds 46 fish of 6 different species. To help her calculate the index of diversity for the pond she draws the following table.

Species	n (total number of organisms in species)	$\frac{n}{N}$	$\left(\frac{n}{N}\right)^2$
A	1	0.0217	0.000473
B	6	0.130	0.0170
C	2	0.0435	0.00189
D	15	0.326	0.106
E	3	0.0652	0.00425
F	19	0.413	0.171
N (total number of all organisms) = 46			$\sum\left(\frac{n}{N}\right)^2 = 0.301$

Exam Tip
The numbers in this table have been rounded to 3 significant figures. In the exam, round your answers to the same number of significant figures used in the question (unless you're told otherwise).

She then uses the numbers from the table to calculate the diversity index:

$$D = 1 - 0.301 = 0.699$$

Practice Questions — Application

Q1 An environmental officer is investigating the population of fish in a lake using a net. She sweeps the net through the water to catch fish.

a) Suggest one way in which the environmental officer could standardise the method she uses to collect her data to improve the reliability of her results.

b) Suggest one other way in which the environmental officer could improve the reliability of her results.

Tip: Standardise means make the same. Reliable results can be reproduced in independent experiments (see page 3).

Q2 The table below shows the number of individuals of each species of insect found in two ponds.

Species	Number of individuals found in Pond A	Number of individuals found in Pond B
Damselfly	3	13
Dragonfly	5	5
Stonefly	2	7
Water boatman	3	2
Crane fly	1	18
Pond skater	4	9

a) Which pond has the greatest species evenness? Explain your answer.

b) Use the data provided in the table and the formula given below to calculate the index of diversity to 3 significant figures for:

i) Pond A,

ii) Pond B.

$$D = 1 - (\Sigma(n/N)^2)$$

where N = total number of all organisms
and n = total number of organisms in one species.

c) Would the two ponds be likely to cope with the introduction of a new species of predator? Explain your answer.

Practice Questions — Fact Recall

Q1 Define the following terms:

a) biodiversity,

b) habitat,

c) species.

Q2 Name and describe three levels at which biodiversity can be considered.

Q3 Explain why it is important to take random samples when collecting data on biodiversity.

Q4 Define the following terms:

a) species richness,

b) species evenness.

Q5 Name two things needed to calculate Simpson's Index of Diversity.

Q6 What does a high Simpson's Index of Diversity value indicate?

2. Global Biodiversity

Estimating the Earth's biodiversity is tricky stuff — not least because it's rising in some areas and falling in others. This is partly because of climate change...

Estimating global biodiversity

Global biodiversity is the total number of species on Earth. This includes:

- Named species — scientists have named between 1.5 and 1.75 million species. This figure isn't exact because there's no central database of all species and some scientists have different opinions about the classification of certain species.

- Unnamed species — scientists agree that a large proportion of the species on Earth have not been named — many species are undiscovered, or are known but haven't yet been named.

Scientists estimate that the total number of species on Earth ranges from about 5 million to 100 million. Some of the most recent estimates are around 14 million. There are lots of reasons why scientists have such different ideas:

- Different scientists have used different techniques to make their estimates.

- Relatively little is known about some groups of organisms (e.g. bacteria and insects) — there could be many more than we think.

- Biodiversity varies in different parts of the world — the greatest diversity is near the equator and it decreases towards the poles. Tropical rainforests are largely unexplored — this might mean current estimates of global biodiversity are too low.

- Estimates of global biodiversity change as scientists find out new things — this is an example of the tentative nature of scientific knowledge.

> **Example**
> Genetic research on African Nile crocodiles suggests that they are actually two separate species — not one as originally thought.

Climate change and global biodiversity

Climate change is a significant long-term change in an area's climate, e.g. its average temperature or rainfall patterns. It occurs naturally, but the scientific consensus is that the climate change we're experiencing at the moment is caused by humans increasing emissions of greenhouse gases (such as carbon dioxide). Greenhouse gases cause global warming (increasing global average temperature), which causes other types of climate change, e.g. changing rainfall patterns. Climate change can affect global biodiversity by:

1. Changing environmental conditions

Climate change will affect the environmental conditions in different areas of the world in different ways — some places will get warmer, some colder, some wetter and others drier. All of these changes are likely to affect global biodiversity.

One reason for this is that most species need a particular climate to survive, so a change in climate may mean that an area that was previously inhabitable becomes uninhabitable (and vice versa). This may cause an increase or decrease in the range of some species (the area in which they live). This could increase or decrease biodiversity.

Learning Objectives:
- Be able to discuss current estimates of global biodiversity.
- Be able to discuss the consequences of global climate change on the biodiversity of plants and animals, with reference to changing patterns of agriculture and spread of disease.

Specification Reference 2.3.1 and 2.3.4

Tip: Scientific uncertainty makes biodiversity hard to measure.

Figure 1: *An African Nile crocodile.*

Tip: The Earth is heated by the Sun. Greenhouses gases in the atmosphere absorb most of the energy that would otherwise be radiated out into space, and re-radiate it back to Earth. This keeps us warm. But too much greenhouse gas means too much heat is absorbed and re-radiated back to Earth, so we're getting warmer.

> **Example** ────────────────────────────
>
> The southern range limit of the Sooty Copper Butterfly has moved 60 miles north in recent decades.

Changing environmental conditions may force some species to migrate to a more suitable area, causing a change in species distribution. Migrations usually decrease biodiversity in the areas the species migrate from, and increase biodiversity in the areas they migrate to. If there isn't a suitable habitat to migrate to, the species is a plant and can't migrate, or if the change is too fast, the species may become extinct. This will decrease biodiversity.

> **Example** ────────────────────────────
>
> Corals die if water temperature changes by just one or two degrees.
> In 1998 a coral reef near Panama was badly damaged because the water temperature had increased — at least one species of coral became extinct as a result.

2. Causing the spread of disease

Changing climate may also contribute to the spread of disease. One reason for this is that the ranges of some insects that carry disease might increase.

> **Example** ────────────────────────────
>
> As areas become warmer and wetter insects like mosquitoes, which can carry malaria, will spread into areas that were previously uninhabitable, bringing the disease with them.

Figure 2: *Corals are aquatic organisms. They secrete calcium carbonate which produces coral reefs, like the one shown here.*

This change in distribution could lead to an increase in biodiversity, though the spread of diseases could reduce biodiversity — with some species suffering population decline, or even extinction.

Warmer and wetter conditions may also encourage the spread of fungal diseases. This could also lead to an increase or decrease in biodiversity.

> **Example** ────────────────────────────
>
> *Cryptococcus gattii* is a fungus that can cause disease in humans and other animals. It's normally found in tropical and subtropical areas such as Australia, but since 1999 it's been found in temperate climates like Canada and the USA — possibly because of climate change.

3. Changing agricultural patterns

Changes in temperature, rainfall, the timing of the seasons, and the frequency of flood and drought will affect patterns of agriculture. This may also affect biodiversity. For example, land that was previously unsuitable may become available for agriculture — areas of that were previously too hot or too dry to support much biodiversity can be farmed, increasing the biodiversity in an area.

Also, different crops need different conditions so, as the climate in an area changes, so will the crops grown. This could disrupt food chains — some existing species will be left without a source of food, and new food sources will be provided for other species. This could increase or decrease biodiversity in an area.

It's also possible that extreme weather events and unexpected conditions, such as a flood or a drought or a change in the timing of the seasons, might result in crop failure. This could disrupt food chains and decrease biodiversity.

Figure 3: *Crops damaged by drought in Texas.*

Practice Questions — Application

Q1 Two teams of scientists have produced estimates of global biodiversity. The first team has suggested that there are 16 million species on Earth whereas the second team estimates that there are around 72 million.

Suggest one reason why the second team's estimate is so much higher than the first team's.

Q2 A study was carried out to investigate the effect of temperature on the changing distribution of subtropical plankton species in the north Atlantic. Data collected on global sea surface temperature and plankton distribution are shown in below.

Tip: Plankton are small organisms, such as algae, which are found drifting in water.

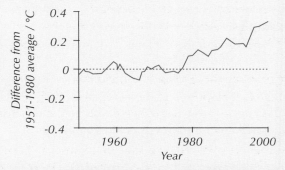

Figure A: Graph to show changing global sea-surface temperature.

Tip: Don't be put off by the question having two different types of data source — just look at each one carefully and compare the trends they show.

Figure B: Diagram to show subtropical plankton distribution.

■ subtropical plankton

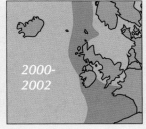

1958-1981

2000-2002

a) Describe the data shown in the graph and diagram.

b) Explain why the study can't conclude that the change in sea-surface temperature caused the change in plankton distribution.

Q3 In 2004, 2007 and 2008 a country experienced unusually high temperatures, drought and wildfires which dramatically reduced the annual crop of barley. The country's government is considering encouraging farmers to grow another crop which might be able to survive these extreme weather events.

Suggest the effect these extreme weather events, and the proposed change in crop, could have on biodiversity.

- Be able to outline the reasons for the conservation of animal and plant species, with reference to economic, ecological, ethical and aesthetic reasons.

- Be able to explain the benefits for agriculture of maintaining the biodiversity of animal and plant species.

- Be able to describe the conservation of plant and animal species, both *in situ* and *ex situ*, with reference to the advantages and disadvantages of these two approaches.

- Be able to discuss the role of botanic gardens in the *ex situ* conservation of rare plant species or plant species extinct in the wild, with reference to seed banks.

- Be able to discuss the significance of environmental impact assessments (including biodiversity estimates) for local authority planning decisions.

- Be able to discuss the importance of international cooperation in species conservation with reference to the Rio Convention on Biodiversity and The Convention in International Trade in Endangered Species (CITES).

Specification Reference 2.3.4

Tip: All these ecological reasons also have knock-on economic effects.

3. Biodiversity and Conservation

As you saw on the previous few pages, climate change could cause the loss of global biodiversity. This isn't a good thing because biodiversity is pretty darn important — but luckily we have ways of conserving species.

The importance of biodiversity

Maintaining biodiversity is important for...

1. Economic reasons

Many species of animals and plants are important to the global economy. Products derived from plant and animal species are traded on a local and global scale.

Examples

- Food and drink — plants and animals are the source of almost all food and some drinks.

- Clothing — a lot of fibres and fabrics are made from plants and animals (e.g. cotton from plants and leather from animals).

- Drugs — many are made from compounds from plants (e.g. the painkiller morphine is made from poppies).

- Fuels — we use a number of organisms to produce renewable fuels, including ethanol and biogas. Fossil fuels are non-renewable (they'll run out), so other sources are of major economic importance.

- Other industrial materials — a huge variety of other materials are produced from plant and animal species, including wood, paper, dyes, adhesives, oils, rubber and chemicals such as pesticides.

It's important to conserve all the organisms we currently use to make products, as well as those we don't currently use — they may provide us with new products in the future, e.g. new drugs for diseases we can't yet cure.

2. Ecological reasons

The ecological reasons for maintaining biodiversity are all down to the complex relationships between organisms and their environments.

Examples

Disruption of food chains
Some species of bear feed on salmon, which feed on herring. If the number of herring decline it can affect both the salmon and the bear populations.

Disruption of nutrient cycles
Decomposers like worms improve the quality of soil by recycling nutrients. If worm numbers decline, soil quality will be affected. This will affect the growth of plants and the amount of food available to animals.

Loss of habitats
Hedgerows are wildlife corridors — they enable organisms to move between different habitats safely. If they're removed species can become isolated and availability of food and nesting sites for many species will be reduced.

Climate change
CO_2 is stored in trees and bogs — the destruction of forests and peat bogs is contributing to climate change (see p. 188).

3. Ethical reasons

Some people believe that we should conserve species simply because it's the right thing to do. Many believe organisms have a right to exist and that they shouldn't become extinct as a result of our activities. Some people believe we have a moral responsibility to conserve biodiversity for future human generations. There are also religious and spiritual reasons for conservation — harmony with the natural world is important to many beliefs and philosophies.

> **Example**
>
> Sacred groves in India are forest patches which are protected by local people for religious reasons. These patches act as 'biodiversity hot spots' and help to conserve rare species and species that are found only in that area.

Tip: Take a look at page 6 in the How Science Works section for how society uses science to make decisions about things like maintaining biodiversity.

4. Aesthetic reasons

Others believe we should conserve biodiversity because it brings joy to millions of people. Areas rich in biodiversity provide a pleasant, attractive environment that people can enjoy and the more biodiversity in an area the more visitors the area is likely to attract — this also has economic advantages.

> **Example**
>
> At the end of the 19th century the National Trust, a conservation charity, was founded with the aim of saving the nation's heritage and open spaces. It now owns and protects many areas of outstanding natural beauty, including parts of the Lake District in Cumbria.

Figure 1: *Wastwater in the Lake District is owned and cared for by the National Trust.*

5. Agricultural reasons

Maintaining biodiversity is important to agriculture because it provides:

Pollinators	Many fruit and vegetable crops are pollinated by insects such as bees and butterflies. The higher the diversity of insects the more pollinators there are.
Protection against disasters	The majority of our food comes from only a few species of plants — if a disease or pest affects these few, our food supply is at risk. E.g. in 1845 only two varieties of potato were planted in Ireland. A disease destroyed both types of potato crop, causing famine. The more crop varieties that are used, the less chance there is that all the crops will be destroyed.
A source of food	Many species are used as food sources for humans and livestock. The more different species there are the more possible sources there are to choose from.
New varieties	Plant varieties are needed for cross-breeding. Wild plants can be bred with domesticated plants to produce new varieties with improved characteristics, e.g. increased disease resistance or faster growth. New varieties of crops can also be bred to cope with climate change. The more varieties of crop there are the more characteristics there are to choose from.
Pest control	A number of animals like frogs, birds and hedgehogs are natural predators of crop pests like slugs. The more of these organisms there are the less pests there will be.

Exam Tip
If you get asked about the agricultural benefits of maintaining biodiversity in the exam, remember that agriculture includes rearing livestock (animals) as well as growing crop plants.

Maintaining biodiversity through conservation

Biodiversity can be maintained through conservation — the protection and management of species and habitats. Conservation is important to ensure the survival of **endangered species** — species which are at risk of extinction because of a low population, or a threatened habitat. A species that is critically endangered is likely to become extinct because its population size is too small.

Types of conservation

There are two main types of conservation:

1. *In situ* conservation

In situ conservation means conservation on site — it involves protecting species in their natural habitat. Methods of *in situ* conservation include:

- Establishing protected areas such as national parks and nature reserves — habitats and species are protected in these areas by restricting urban development, industrial development and farming.

- Controlling or preventing the introduction of species that threaten local biodiversity. For example, grey squirrels are not native to Britain. They compete with the native red squirrel and have caused a population decline (see Figure 2). So they're controlled in some areas.

- Protecting habitats — e.g. controlling water levels to conserve wetlands and coppicing (trimming trees) to conserve woodlands. This allows organisms to continue living in their natural habitat.

- Restoring damaged areas — such as a coastline polluted by an oil spill.

- Promoting particular species — this could be by protecting food sources or nesting sites.

- Giving legal protection to endangered species, e.g. making it illegal to kill them.

Advantages and disadvantages

The advantage of *in situ* conservation is that often both the species and their habitat are conserved. This means that larger populations can be protected and it's less disruptive than removing organisms from their habitats. The chances of the population recovering are also greater than with *ex situ* methods (see next page). But it can be difficult to control some factors that are threatening a species (such as poaching, predators or climate change).

Exam Tip
If you're asked to define 'critically endangered' in the exam, make sure you emphasise that the species is <u>likely</u> to die out.

Figure 2: *The population of red squirrels (top) in the UK has declined due to competition with grey squirrels (bottom).*

Tip: There are lots of laws that help to conserve biodiversity. For example, European Protected Species are legally protected throughout Europe.

2. *Ex situ* conservation

Ex situ conservation means conservation off site — it involves protecting a species by removing part of the population from a threatened habitat and placing it in a new location. *Ex situ* conservation is often a last resort. Methods of *ex situ* conservation include:

- Relocating an organism to a safer area, e.g. five white rhinos were recently relocated from the Congo to Kenya because they were in danger from poachers who kill them for their ivory.

- Breeding organisms in captivity then reintroducing them to the wild when they are strong enough, e.g. sea eagles have been reintroduced to Britain through a captive breeding programme. Breeding is carried out in animal sanctuaries and zoos.

- Botanic gardens are controlled environments used to grow a variety of rare plants for the purposes of conservation, research, display and education. Endangered plant species as well as species that are extinct in the wild can be grown and reintroduced into suitable habitats.

- Seed banks — seeds can be frozen and stored in seed banks for over a century without losing their fertility. Seed banks provide a useful source of seeds if natural reserves are destroyed, for example by disease or other natural disasters.

Advantages and disadvantages

The advantages of *ex situ* conservation are that it can be used to protect individual animals in a controlled environment — things like predation and hunting can be managed more easily. Competition for resources can be reduced, and it's possible to check on the health of individuals and treat them for diseases. Breeding can also be manipulated, e.g. through the use of reproductive hormones and IVF. Finally, it can be used to reintroduce species that have left an area.

But, there are disadvantages — usually only a small number of individuals can be cared for. It can be difficult and expensive to create and sustain the right environment. *Ex situ* conservation is usually less successful than *in situ* methods — many species can't breed successfully in captivity, or don't adapt to their new environment when moved to a new location.

Conservation and EIAs

An **Environmental Impact Assessment** (EIA) is an assessment of the impact a development project (such as building a new shopping centre or power station) might have on the environment.

EIAs involve estimating biodiversity on the project site and evaluating how the development might affect biodiversity. They identify ways that biodiversity could be conserved, any threatened or endangered species on the project site and the laws relating to their conservation. They're then used to deciding on planning stipulations — these are measures that will have to be implemented if the project proceeds. For example, this might involve relocating or protecting endangered species.

Local authorities are often under pressure from conservationists who argue that developments damage the environment and disturb wildlife — they feel that habitats should be left alone. Environmental impact assessments ensure that decision makers consider the environmental impact of development projects — they're used by local authorities to decide if and how projects will proceed.

Figure 3: *Sea eagles have been reintroduced to Britain.*

Figure 4: *Lots of threatened plant species are preserved at the Royal Botanic Gardens.*

Tip: Remember, in *in situ* conservation species stay *in* their natural habitat, whereas in *ex situ* conservation species *ex*it their natural habitat.

Tip: When species are conserved *ex situ*, it's important to make sure that there is enough genetic variation in the population to improve their chances of, e.g. surviving a disease.

Tip: Some developments won't completely destroy a habitat — they may just reduce its size. So an EIA may also look at how much smaller a habitat may become and what impact that will have on the local environment.

Conservation and international cooperation

Conservation is much more likely to be successful when countries work together. For example, some endangered species are found in lots of countries, so it'd be pointless making hunting a species illegal in one country if poachers could just go and hunt them in another. Information about threats to biodiversity needs to be shared and countries need to decide on conservation methods and implement them together. Here are a couple of examples of successful international cooperation:

Rio Convention on Biodiversity

The Rio Convention on Biodiversity is an international agreement that aims to develop international strategies on the conservation of biodiversity and how to use animal and plant resources in a sustainable way. The convention made it part of international law that conserving biodiversity is everyone's responsibility. It also provides guidance to governments on how to conserve biodiversity.

CITES Agreement

CITES (Convention on International Trade in Endangered Species) is an agreement designed to increase international cooperation in regulating trade in wild animal and plant specimens. The member countries all agreed to make it illegal to kill endangered species. The agreement helps to conserve species by limiting trade through licensing, and by making it illegal to trade in products made from endangered animals (such as rhino ivory and leopard skins). It's also designed to raise awareness of threats to biodiversity through education.

Tip: Using resources in a sustainable way means they'll still be around for future generations to use.

Figure 5: *A decline in elephant populations due to hunting for their ivory tusks has led to a ban on the sale of ivory.*

> **Example**
>
> Between 1979 and 1989 the number of African elephants dropped from around 1.3 million to around 600 000 because they were being hunted for their ivory tusks. In 1989, the CITES banned ivory trade to end the demand for elephant tusks so that fewer elephants would be killed for their tusks. The population of elephants in Kenya has doubled since 1989 and elephant populations in some countries, like Botswana, have been downgraded to a less endangered status.

Figure 6: *An Australian Northern Quoll.*

Practice Questions — Application

Q1 The Northern Quoll is an endangered species in Australia. The population has declined due to the cane toad which was introduced to control a pest in sugarcane fields. Some conservations are exploring preserving the Northern Quoll *in situ* by eradicating cane toads, whereas others are considering conserving them in a nature reserve. Sugarcane is an important crop in Australia.

    a) i) Suggest an advantage of *in situ* over *ex situ* conservation of the Northern Quoll.

       ii) Suggest an advantage of *ex situ* over *in situ* conservation of the Northern Quoll.

    b) Suggest the potential economic impact of the *in situ* conservation of the Northern Quoll.

Q2 A development is being planned which will turn an abandoned factory into a block of flats. An Environmental Impact Assessment (EIA) is carried out on the site.

a) What aspects of the site and its development will be considered by the EIA?

b) During the EIA an endangered plant species is discovered on the site. The plant is already conserved in botanical gardens even though it currently has no known agricultural or medicinal uses.

   i)   Suggest an economic reason for why it is being conserved.

   ii) Suggest another *ex situ* method of conservation which could be used to protect the plant species.

Tip: Take a look back at the start of the topic if you need a reminder about economic reasons for conservation.

Practice Questions — Fact Recall

Q1 Give two:

    a) economic reasons for maintaining biodiversity.

    b) ecological reasons for maintaining biodiversity.

    c) ethical reasons for maintaining biodiversity.

Q2 Discuss the reasons why it is important to maintain biodiversity for agriculture.

Q3 What is conservation?

Q4 a) Define *in situ* conservation.

    b) Give two examples of *in situ* conservation.

Q5 a) Define *ex situ* conservation.

    b) Give one disadvantage of *ex situ* conservation over *in situ* conservation.

Q6 What is the Rio Convention on Biodiversity?

Q7 What is the CITES agreement?

Section Summary

Make sure you know:

- The meanings of the terms biodiversity (the variety of living organisms in an area), habitat (the area inhabited by a species) and species (a group of similar organisms able to reproduce to give fertile offspring).

- That biodiversity can be explored at the levels of habitat diversity (the number of different habitats in an area), species diversity (the number of different species and the abundance of each species in an area) and genetic diversity (the variation of alleles within a species or a population of a species).

- How to collect reliable data on biodiversity using random sampling.

- That species richness refers to the number of different species in an area and that species evenness is a measure of the relative abundance of each species in an area.

- How to calculate Simpson's Index of Diversity when given the formula: $D = 1 - (\sum(n/N)^2)$

- That habitats with a high index of diversity (a value close to 1) have a high biodiversity.

- That habitats with a low index of diversity (a value close to 0) are less stable and have a lower ability to cope with change, e.g. the introduction of a new predator, than areas of high biodiversity.

- That current estimates of global biodiversity vary greatly, and the reasons why the estimates vary.

- That climate change has affected the global biodiversity of plants and animals through changing environmental conditions, causing the spread of disease and changing agricultural patterns.

- That maintaining biodiversity is important for economic, ecological, ethical and aesthetic reasons.

- That maintaining biodiversity is important for agriculture because it can provide pollinators, protection against disasters, sources of food, new varieties of plant species and forms of pest control.

- That conservation is the protection and management of species and habitats.

- That *in situ* conservation involves protecting species in their natural habitat, whereas *ex situ* conservation involves protecting a species by moving part of a population from a threatened habitat and placing it in a new location.

- That *in situ* conservation includes establishing protected areas, controlling or preventing the introduction of species that would threaten local biodiversity, protecting habitats, restoring damaged areas, promoting particular species and giving legal protection to endangered species.

- That *ex situ* conservation includes relocating an organism to a safer area, breeding organisms in captivity then reintroducing them to the wild, and conserving organisms in botanic gardens and seed banks.

- The advantages and disadvantages of *in situ* and *ex situ* conservation.

- That an Environmental Impact Assessment is an assessment of the impact a development project might have on the environment.

- That the Rio Convention on Biodiversity is an international agreement that aims to develop international strategies in the conservation of biodiversity and how to use animal and plant resources in a sustainable way.

- That the CITES (Convention on International Trade in Endangered Species) is an agreement designed to increase international cooperation in regulating trade in wild animal and plant specimens.

Exam-style Questions

1 A company wishes to clear part of a wood next to a town and build a new housing estate on the land. An **Environmental Impact Assessment** (**EIA**) is carried out on the development.

(a) What is an EIA?

(1 mark)

(b) A study was conducted on the trees found in the town centre and in the wood. The results are shown in Fig. 1.1.

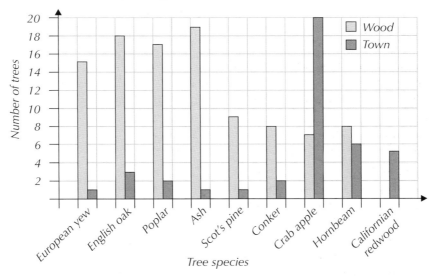

Fig. 1.1

Simpson's Index of Diversity can be calculated using the following equation:

$$D = 1 - (\sum(n/N)^2)$$

where n = Total number of organisms in one species
N = Total number of all organisms

Use the data Fig. 1.1 and the formula provided above to calculate Simpson's Index of Diversity for trees in the wood and in the town.

(6 marks)

(c) Explain what your answers to part **(b)** tell you about the town habitat and the woodland habitat.

(3 marks)

(d) During the EIA it is discovered that the wood supports a small population of red squirrels, which are an endangered species.

Suggest **two** conservation measures that could be undertaken to protect the wood's red squirrel population if the development project goes ahead.

(2 marks)

2   A journalist is investigating global biodiversity for a newspaper article.

He's found a wide range of estimates of the total number of species on Earth produced by environmental researchers. Some of these estimates are shown in Table 2.1.

A	B	C	D	E
15 million	7 million	90 million	120 million	40 million

Table 2.1

(a) (i) What is global biodiversity?

(1 mark)

   (ii) Discuss why these estimates of global biodiversity vary so widely.

(4 marks)

(b)   Climate change may cause changes in patterns of agriculture. The journalist is exploring the impact agricultural changes might have on biodiversity.

Explain how climate change can lead to changing patterns of agriculture, and suggest the impact this might have on global biodiversity.

 In your answer you should make clear the links between climate change, changing patterns of agriculture and global biodiversity.

(7 marks)

(c)   Give **three** reasons why maintaining biodiversity is important for agriculture.

(3 marks)

3   A student is investigating the species diversity of insects in a 500 m² area of woodland.

The student sampled the insect population by arranging a series of covered pitfall traps in the ground. The traps are designed so that insects fall into them while walking along the ground and are unable to escape.

The student arranged the traps in a straight line along the edge of the woodland and left them overnight before coming back to count the insects she had caught.

(a)   Explain what is meant by the term '**species diversity**'.

(2 marks)

(b)   Give **two** reasons why the student did not obtain a representative sample of insects living in the woodland.

(2 marks)

(c)   The student found that the woodland had a **low species evenness**.
What does a low species evenness tell you about a habitat?

(1 mark)

(d)   The student wants to compare the species diversity of insects in the woodland with the species diversity of insects on her local common.

Suggest **one** thing the student must do when sampling insects on the common to ensure that her findings from both habitats are comparable.

(1 mark)

1. Classification Basics

Scientists group organisms together to make them easier to study.

What is classification?

Classification is the act of arranging organisms into groups based on their similarities and differences. This makes it easier for scientists to identify them and to study them. **Taxonomy** is the study of classification. There are a few different classification systems in use, but they all involve placing organisms into groups in a **taxonomic hierarchy**.

In the hierarchy you need to know about, there are eight levels of groups (called taxonomic groups). Similar organisms are first sorted into one of three very large groups called domains, e.g. animals, plants and fungi are in the Eukarya domain. Similar organisms are then sorted into slightly smaller groups called kingdoms, e.g. all animals are in the animal kingdom (Animalia). Similar organisms from that kingdom are then grouped into a phylum. Similar organisms from each phylum are then grouped into a class, and so on down the eight levels of the taxonomic hierarchy. This is illustrated in Figure 1.

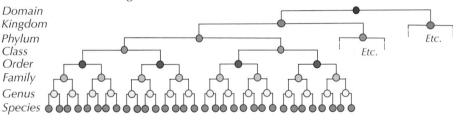

Domain
Kingdom
Phylum
Class
Order
Family
Genus
Species

Etc.
Etc.

Figure 1: *A diagram illustrating the eight taxonomic groups used in classification.*

> **Example — the classification of humans**
> Domain = *Eukarya*, Kingdom = *Animalia*, Phylum = *Chordata*,
> Class = *Mammalia*, Order = *Primates*, Family = *Hominidae*,
> Genus = *Homo*, Species = *sapiens*.

As you move down the hierarchy, there are more groups at each level but fewer organisms in each group. The hierarchy ends with species — the groups that contain only one type of organism (e.g. humans, dog, *E. coli* and about 50 million other living species).

Naming species

The nomenclature (naming system) used for classification is called the **binomial system** — all organisms are given one internationally accepted scientific name in Latin that has two parts.

The first part of the name is the genus name and has a capital letter. The second part is the species name and begins with a lower case letter. Names are always written in *italics* (or they're <u>underlined</u> if they're handwritten).

Learning Objectives:
- Be able to define the terms 'classification' and 'taxonomy'.
- Be able to describe the classification of species into the taxonomic hierarchy of domain, kingdom, phylum, class, order, family, genus and species.
- Be able to outline the binomial system of nomenclature and the use of scientific (Latin) names for species.
- Be able to outline the characteristic features of the following five kingdoms: Prokaryotae (Monera), Protoctista, Fungi, Plantae, Animalia.
- Be able to define the term 'phylogeny'.
- Be able to explain the relationship between classification and phylogeny.

Specification Reference 2.3.2

Exam Tip
You need to learn the names and order of the groups. If you're struggling to remember the order, try this mnemonic...

<u>D</u>aft <u>K</u>ids <u>P</u>refer <u>C</u>hips <u>O</u>ver <u>F</u>loppy <u>G</u>reen <u>S</u>pinach.

The binomial system helps to avoid the confusion of using common names.

┌─ **Example** ──────────────────────────
Americans call a type of bird cockatoos and Australians call them flaming galahs, but it's the same bird. If the correct scientific name is used — *Eolophus roseicapillus* — there's no confusion.

The five kingdoms

Organisms can be placed into one of five kingdoms. You need to know these five kingdoms and the general characteristics of the organisms in each one.

Prokaryotae (Monera)
Example: bacteria
Features: prokaryotic, unicellular (single-celled), no nucleus, less than 5 µm

Protoctista
Examples: algae, protozoa
Features: eukaryotic cells, usually live in water, single-celled or simple multicellular organisms

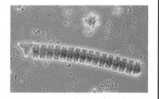

Fungi
Examples: moulds, yeasts, mushrooms
Features: eukaryotic, chitin cell wall, saprotrophic (they secrete extracellular enzymes to digest dead or decaying organisms and absorb the products), reproduce using spores

Plantae
Examples: mosses, ferns, flowering plants
Features: eukaryotic, multicellular, cell walls made of cellulose, can photosynthesise, contain chlorophyll, autotrophic (produce their own food)

Animalia
Examples: nematodes (roundworms), molluscs, insects, fish, reptiles, birds, mammals
Features: eukaryotic, multicellular, no cell walls, heterotrophic (consume plants and animals)

Phylogeny

Phylogeny is the study of the evolutionary history of groups of organisms.
It tells us who's related to whom and how closely related they are.
All organisms have evolved from shared common ancestors (relatives).
Closely related species diverged away from each other most recently.

Tip: 'Diverged' just means 'evolved to become a different species'.

Example

Members of the Hominidae family (great apes and humans) evolved from a common ancestor. First orangutans diverged from this common ancestor. Next gorillas diverged, then humans, closely followed by bonobos and chimpanzees. This is illustrated on the phylogenetic tree below...

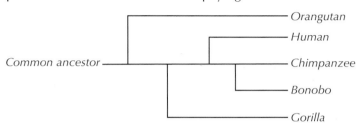

Humans and chimpanzees are closely related, as they diverged very recently. You can see this because their branches are close together. Humans and orangutans are more distantly related, as they diverged longer ago, so their branches are further apart.

Classification systems now take into account phylogeny when arranging organisms into groups.

Figure 2: *Orangutans, chimps and gorillas are all closely related.*

Practice Questions — Application

The diagram below shows a simplified phylogenetic tree for the phylum Chordata:

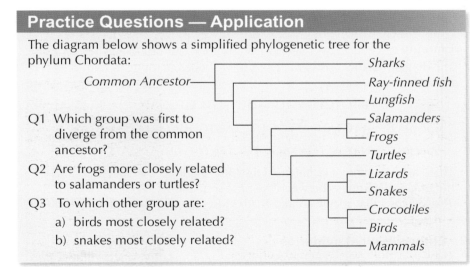

Q1 Which group was first to diverge from the common ancestor?

Q2 Are frogs more closely related to salamanders or turtles?

Q3 To which other group are:
   a) birds most closely related?
   b) snakes most closely related?

Tip: It might surprise you that some species are closely related — but just because you can't see a similarity in their features doesn't mean the phylogenetic tree is wrong.

Practice Questions — Fact Recall

Q1 What is taxonomy?

Q2 The list below shows the eight levels of the taxonomic hierarchy. Complete the list by filling in the blanks:

   ? Kingdom ? Class Order ? ? Species

Q3 Describe how organisms are named using the binomial system.

Q4 Give three characteristics of the kingdom Plantae.

2. The Evolution of Classification Systems

Classification systems aren't set in stone. Like living organisms, they evolve...

Evidence for classification

Early classification systems only used observable features (things you can see) to place organisms into groups. Observable features can be anatomical (structural), e.g. how many legs an organism has, or behavioural, e.g. whether an organism lives in groups. But this method has problems. Scientists don't always agree on the relative importance of different features and groups based solely on physical features may not show how related organisms are.

Example

Sharks and whales look quite similar and they both live in the sea. But they're not actually closely related — sharks are cartilaginous fish (meaning they have skeletons made of cartilage instead of bone), whereas whales are vertebrate mammals (they have a backbone).

Classification systems are now based on observable features along with other evidence. This evidence tells us how similar, and therefore how related, organisms are. The types of evidence taxonomists look at include:

1. Molecular evidence

Gathering molecular evidence involves analysing the similarities in proteins and DNA. More closely related organisms will have more similar molecules. You can compare things like how DNA is stored, the sequence of DNA bases and the sequence of amino acids in proteins from different organisms.

Example

The diagram below shows the DNA base sequence for gene X in three different species...

Species A: ATTGTCTGATTGGTGCTAGTCGTCGATGCTAGGATCG

Species B: ATTGTATGATTGGTGCTAGTCGGCGATGCTAGGATCG

Species C: ATTGATTGAAAGGAGCTACTCGTAGATATAAGGAGGT

There are 13 differences between the base sequences in species A and C, but only 2 differences between the base sequences in species A and B. This suggests that species A and B are more closely related than A and C.

2. Embryological evidence

Gathering embryological evidence involves looking at the similarities in the early stages of an organism's development.

Example

Fish and salamander embryos are more similar than turtle and salamander embryos (see Figure 1). This suggests that salamanders are more closely related to fish than to turtles.

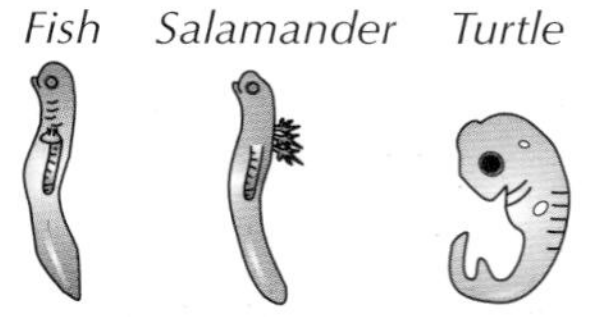

 Fish Salamander Turtle

Figure 1: *Comparison of developing embryos.*

Learning Objectives:
- Be able to discuss the fact that classification systems were based originally on observable features but that more recent approaches draw on a wider range of evidence to clarify relationships between organisms, including molecular evidence.
- Be able to compare and contrast the 'five kingdom' and 'three domain' classification systems.
  Specification Reference 2.3.2

Tip: Molecular evidence is sometimes referred to as biochemical evidence.

Tip: There's more on DNA bases on pages 125-126.

Tip: Cytochrome C is a protein found in almost all living things. Because of this, similarities in the amino acid sequence of cytochrome C are often used to determine relationships between organisms.

Tip: Remember, the more similar organisms are, the more related they are.

3. The fossil record

Studying fossils can provide evidence of how organisms evolved from one another and so how closely related they are. This is part of phylogeny (see page 201).

┌─ Example ─────────────────────────────
Fossils of *Archaeopteryx* (a reptile with feathers that enabled it to fly) provide evidence that birds evolved from dinosaurs.
└──────────────────────────────────────

Tip: Scientists still use observable features, e.g. anatomical ones, to help classify organisms — but they use other evidence too.

Changing the classification of organisms

New technologies (e.g. new DNA techniques, better microscopes) can result in new discoveries being made. Scientists can share their new discoveries in meetings and scientific journals. How organisms are classified is continually revised to take account of any new findings that scientists discover.

(HOW SCIENCE WORKS)

Tip: There's more on how and why scientists share their findings on page 2.

┌─ Example ─────────────────────────────
Skunks were classified in the family Mustelidae until molecular evidence revealed their DNA sequence was significantly different to other members of that family. So they were reclassified into the family Mephitidae.
└──────────────────────────────────────

Five kingdoms vs three domains

The three domain classification system shown on page 199 is relatively new, and was suggested because of new evidence. In the older system the largest groups were the five kingdoms (see page 200) — all organisms were placed into one of these groups. In 1990, the three domain system was proposed. This new system has three domains — large superkingdoms that are above the kingdoms in the taxonomic hierarchy (see Figure 2).

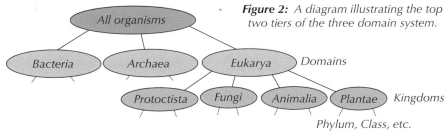

Figure 2: *A diagram illustrating the top two tiers of the three domain system.*

In the three domain system, organisms with cells that contain a nucleus are placed in the domain Eukarya (this includes four of the five kingdoms). Organisms that were in the kingdom Prokaryotae (which contains unicellular organisms without a nucleus) are separated into two domains — the Archaea and Bacteria. The lower hierarchy stays the same — Kingdom, Phylum, Class, Order, Family, Genus, Species. The three domain system was proposed because of new evidence, mainly molecular.

┌─ Example ─────────────────────────────
The Prokaryotae were reclassified into two domains because new evidence showed large differences between the Archaea and Bacteria.
The new evidence included:

Molecular evidence:

▪ The enzyme RNA polymerase (needed to make RNA) is different in Bacteria and Archaea.
└──────────────────────────────────────

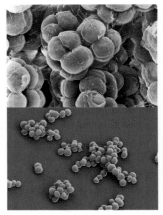

Figure 3: *Electron micrographs of an Archea species (top) and a Bacteria species (bottom). Archea and bacteria often look very similar, but are biochemically different.*

- Archaea, but not Bacteria, have similar histones (proteins that bind to DNA) to Eukarya.

Cellular evidence:

- The bonds of the lipids (see p. 115) in the cell membranes of Bacteria and Archaea are different.
- The development and composition of flagellae (see p. 11) in Bacteria and Archaea are also different.

Most scientists now agree that Archaea and Bacteria evolved separately and that Archaea are more closely related to Eukarya than Bacteria. The three-domain system reflects how different the Archaea and Bacteria are.

Practice Questions — Application

The graph below illustrates the sequence of a small stretch of DNA in 3 different species:

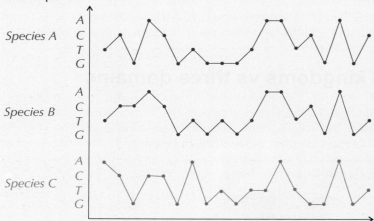

Distance along gene sequence (bp)

Q1 Using the graph, write down the base sequence for this stretch of DNA in each of the three species.

Q2 In how many places do the base sequences of species A and B differ?

Q3 In how many places do the base sequences of species A and C differ?

Q4 Is species A more closely related to species B or species C? Explain your answer.

Q5 To which of the two species is species C most closely related? Explain your answer.

Practice Questions — Fact Recall

Q1 Apart from observable features, give three types of evidence used by scientists to classify organisms.

Q2 Describe the three domain system of classification.

Q3 Describe one piece of evidence that led to Prokaryotes being reclassified.

3. Dichotomous Keys

Despite their tongue-twister of a name, dichotomous keys are a relatively easy and straightforward way of identifying organisms.

What are dichotomous keys?

Dichotomous keys can be used to identify organisms. They provide a way to identify organisms based on observable features (e.g. colour, type of leaves).

They consist of a series of questions, each with only two possible answers. Each answer leads to the name of the organism or another question, and so on, until the organism is identified.

Using dichotomous keys

In the exam you could be asked to use a dichotomous key to identify some organisms.

┌─ **Example** ─────────────────

The table below shows a dichotomous key.
It can be used to identify seaweeds.

1.	Is it bright, grassy green?	Yes	Sea lettuce
		No	Go to 2.
2.	Is it reddish brown?	Yes	Irish Moss
		No	Go to 3.
3.	Does it have a large, root-like structure?	Yes	Kelp
		No	Go to 4.
4.	Does it have air bladders (pockets of air) in the leaves?	Yes	Bladder wrack
		No	Go to 5.
5.	Is the leaf edge saw-toothed?	Yes	Saw wrack
		No	Go to 6.
6.	Is the leaf rolled in at the edges?	Yes	Channelled wrack
		No	Spiral wrack

The diagrams below show four unidentified seaweeds:

Seaweed 1 *Seaweed 2* *Seaweed 3* *Seaweed 4*

- Using the key to identify seaweed 1, the answer to question 1 is yes (it's bright, grassy green) — so it's sea lettuce.

- For seaweed 2, the answers to questions 1, 2 and 3 are no. The answer to question 4 is yes (it has air bladders) — so it's bladder wrack.

- For seaweed 3, answer 1 is no, but answer 2 is yes (it's reddish brown) — so it's Irish moss.

- And for seaweed 4, answers 1, 2, 3 and 4 are no, but 5 is yes (it's got saw-toothed edges) — so it's saw wrack.

Learning Objective:

- Be able to use a dichotomous key to identify a group of at least six plants, animals or microorganisms.

Specification Reference 2.3.2

Tip: Dichotomous keys are useful because anyone can use them — so if you're collecting or studying organisms, you don't need to be an expert to identify what you find.

Exam Tip
Identifying organisms using a dichotomous key is easy marks in the exam — just make sure you take your time and read each question carefully to avoid making silly mistakes.

Practice Question — Application

Q1 The pictures below show six different species of garden bird.
Use the following dichotomous key to identify each one.

1.	Does it have a mainly yellow breast?	Yes	Go to 2.
		No	Go to 3.
2.	Is the top of its head blue?	Yes	Blue tit
		No	Great tit
3.	Does it have red and white markings on its face?	Yes	Goldfinch
		No	Go to 4.
4.	Does it have spots or speckles on its chest and throat?	Yes	Thrush
		No	Go to 5.
5.	Does it have a red patch under its tail?	Yes	Great spotted woodpecker
		No	Chaffinch

Section Summary

Make sure you know...

- That classification is the act of arranging organisms into groups based on their similarities and differences and that taxonomy is the study of classification.

- That organisms can be classified into a taxonomic hierarchy consisting of the following eight groups: domain, kingdom, phylum, class, order, family, genus, species.

- That the binomial system is used to give each organism a two part scientific (Latin) name — the first part is the name of the organism's genus and the second part is the name of its species.

- The defining features of the Prokaryotae (Monera), Protoctista, Fungi, Plantae and Animalia kingdoms.

- That phylogeny is the study of the evolutionary history of groups of organisms (i.e. how closely related they are) and that it can be used to help classify organisms.

- That classification systems were originally based only on observable features, but that scientists now use a range of different evidence (including molecular, embryological and fossil evidence) to classify organisms.

- The similarities and differences between the 'three domain' and 'five kingdom' classification systems.

- That the three domain classification system was introduced because of new molecular evidence.

- How to use a dichotomous key to identify a group of plants, animals or microorganisms.

Exam-style Questions

1   The organism *Halobacterium salinarum* is classified as Archea under the three domain system.

(a)   Fill in the blanks in the table below to show how *H. salinarum* is classified.

Domain	Archea
Kingdom	Euryarcheota
Phylum	Euryarcheota
	Halobacteria
Order	Halobacteriales
	Halobacteriaceae
Species	

(5 marks)

(b)   Under the five kingdom classification system, *H. salinarum* would have been classified as Prokaryotae.

(i)   Give **two** characteristics of the Prokaryotae kingdom.

(2 marks)

(ii)   Explain why the three domain system does **not** contain the Prokaryotae kingdom.

(2 marks)

(iii)   Give **one similarity** between the three domain classification system and the five kingdom classification system.

(1 mark)

2   The **RuBisCo gene** is found in all plants.

When a new species of plant is being classified, this gene is often compared with the gene in other species to determine evolutionary relatedness.

(a)   Describe how a scientist could compare the RuBisCo gene in two different species of plant to determine how closely related they are.

(2 marks)

(b)   Why is the RuBisCo gene useful for determining relationships between plant species?

(1 mark)

(c)   Classification of plants was originally based only on observable features. Explain why taxonomists now consider other evidence when classifying plant species.

(2 marks)

(d)   Plants are classified into the kingdom Plantae.
Name the other **four** kingdoms in the five kingdom classification system.

(4 marks)

3 Fig 3.1 shows the leaves of six different tree species, labelled A to F.

Fig 3.1

(a) (i) Use the following dichotomous key to identify which tree species the leaves belong to. Write your answers in the table below. One has been done for you.

1.	Are the leaves dark green with a cream-coloured edge?	Yes	*Argentea pendula*
		No	Go to 2.
2.	Are there five pairs of leaves arranged around a central stem?	Yes	*Sorbus acuparia*
		No	Go to 3.
3.	Is each leaf split into separate pointed fingers or teeth?	Yes	Go to 4.
		No	Go to 5.
4.	Are the leaves a reddish-orange colour?	Yes	*Acer palmatum*
		No	*Acer pseudoplatanus*
5.	Are the edges of the leaves made up of rounded lobes?	Yes	*Quercus robur*
		No	*Betula pendula*

A	B	C	D	E	F
	Quercus robur				

(5 marks)

(ii) What evidence is there that trees C and E are related?

(1 mark)

(b) Explain why all tree species are given an internationally accepted scientific name.

(1 mark)

1. Variation

Learning Objectives:

- Be able to define the term 'variation'.
- Be able to discuss the fact that variation occurs within as well as between species.
- Be able to describe the differences between continuous and discontinuous variation, using examples of a range of characteristics found in plants, animals and microorganisms.
- Be able to explain both genetic and environmental causes of variation.

Specification Reference 2.3.3

All organisms vary — it's what makes each and every one of us unique.

What is variation?

Variation is the differences that exist between individuals. Every individual organism is unique — even clones (such as identical twins) show some variation. It can occur:

Within species

Variation within a species is called **intraspecific** variation.

┌─ **Example** ─────────────────────────────────────
Individual European robins weigh between 16 g and 22 g and show some variation in many other characteristics including length, wingspan, colour and beak size.

Between species

The variation between different species is called **interspecific** variation.

┌─ **Example** ─────────────────────────────────────
The lightest species of bird is the bee hummingbird, which weighs around 1.6 g on average. The heaviest species of bird is the ostrich, which can weigh up to 160 kg (100 000 times as much).

Continuous variation

Continuous variation is when the individuals in a population vary within a range — there are no distinct categories.

┌─ **Examples** ─────────────────────────────────────

Animals

- Height — humans can be any height within a range (e.g. 139 cm, 175 cm, 185.9 cm, etc.), not just tall or short — see Figure 1.
- Mass — humans can be any mass with a range.
- Milk yield — cows can produce any volume of milk within a range.

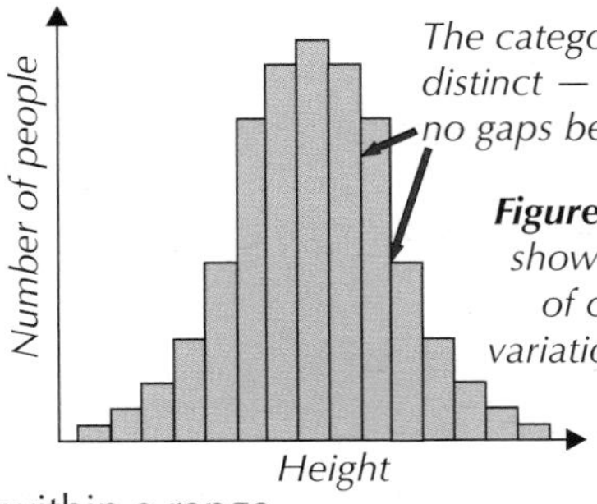

The categories are not distinct — there are no gaps between them.

Figure 1: *Graph to show an example of continuous variation in humans.*

Plants

- Number of leaves — a tree can have any number of leaves within a range.
- Mass — the mass of the seeds from a flower head varies within a range.

Microorganisms

- Width — the width of *E. coli* bacteria varies within a range.
- Length — the length of the flagellum (see p. 11) can vary within a range.

Tip: Don't get inter- and intra-specific variation mixed up. If you're struggling, just remember — int**er** means diff**er**ent species. intr**a** means the s**a**me species.

Tip: Continuous variation can be shown by continuous data. Continuous data is <u>quantitative</u> — this means it has values that can be measured with a number.

Discontinuous variation

Discontinuous variation is when there are two or more distinct categories — each individual falls into only one of these categories, there are no intermediates.

---Examples---

Animals

- Sex — humans can be either male or female.
- Blood group — humans can be group A, B, AB or O (see Figure 2).

Plants

- Colour — courgettes are either yellow, dark green or light green.
- Seed shape — some pea plants have smooth seeds and some have wrinkled seeds.

Microorganisms

- Antibiotic resistance — bacteria are either resistant or not.
- Pigment production — some types of bacteria can produce a coloured pigment, some can't.

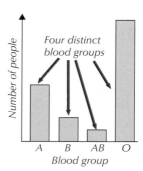

Figure 2: Graph to show an example of discontinuous variation in humans.

Figure 3: Pea seeds can be wrinkled or smooth.

Causes of variation

Variation can be caused by genetic factors, environmental factors or a combination of both.

Genetic factors

Different species have different genes. Individuals of the same species have the same genes, but different versions of them (called **alleles**). The alleles an organism has make up its **genotype**. The differences in genotype result in variation in **phenotype** — the characteristics displayed by an organism.

---Examples---

Variation caused by genetic factors includes:

- Eye colour in humans (which can be blue, green, grey, brown),
- Blood type in humans (O, A, B or AB),
- Antibiotic resistance in bacteria.

You inherit your genes from your parents. This means variation caused by genetic factors is inherited.

Environmental factors

Variation can also be caused by differences in the environment, e.g. climate, food, lifestyle. Characteristics controlled by environmental factors can change over an organism's life.

---Examples---

Variation caused only by environmental factors includes accents and whether people have pierced ears.

Both genetic and environmental factors

Genetic factors determine the characteristics an organism's born with, but environmental factors can influence how some characteristics develop.

- Height — genes determine how tall an organism can grow (e.g. tall parents tend to have tall children). But diet or nutrient availability affect how tall an organism actually grows.

- Flagellum — genes determine if a microorganism can grow a flagellum, but some will only start to grow them in certain environments, e.g. if metal ions are present.

Practice Question — Application

Q1 A twin study was performed to determine whether head circumference is influenced mainly by environmental factors or by genetic factors. 25 pairs of identical twins were selected for the study and the mean difference in the head circumference of each pair was calculated. The same was done for 25 pairs of non-identical siblings and 25 pairs of unrelated individuals. The results are shown on the right.

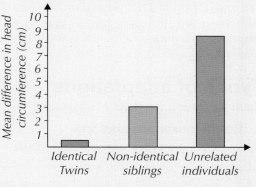

Tip: Identical twins are genetically identical — so any differences in phenotype must be due to environmental factors.

a) Is head circumference an example of continuous or discontinuous variation?

b) Describe the data.

c) Do you think that genetic or environmental factors have a larger effect on head circumference? Explain your answer.

Tip: It's not always clear what the main cause of variation is, so you need to be careful when drawing any conclusions about variation.

A similar study was performed on adults to determine the effects of genetic and environmental factors on activity levels. Pairs of identical twins, pairs of non-identical siblings and pairs of unrelated individuals were asked to wear a pedometer and the mean difference in steps taken per day was recorded. The results are shown on the right.

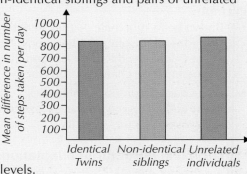

d) Explain what the results show about the role of genetics in determining activity levels.

Practice Questions — Fact Recall

Q1 What is: a) intraspecific variation? b) interspecific variation?

Q2 Describe the difference between continuous variation and discontinuous variation. Give an example of each.

Q3 Give one example of a characteristic that is influenced by both genetic factors and environmental factors.

Learning Objective:

- Be able to outline the behavioural, physiological and anatomical (structural) adaptations of organisms to their environments.

Specification Reference 2.3.3

Tip: It's the alleles that code for the adaptations that get passed on from parents to offspring.

Tip: Organisms that are well adapted to their environment have a <u>selective advantage</u> over less-well adapted organisms.

Figure 1: *When American possums feel threatened, they 'play dead' to escape attack.*

2. Adaptations

Variation gives some organisms an advantage over others...

What are adaptations?

All the variation between and within species means that some organisms are better adapted to their environment than others. Being adapted to an environment means an organism has features that increase its chances of survival and reproduction, and also the chances of its offspring reproducing successfully. These features are called adaptations and can be behavioural, physiological and anatomical (see below).

Adaptations develop because of evolution by natural selection (see page 214). In each generation, the best-adapted individuals are more likely to survive and reproduce — passing their adaptations on to their offspring. Individuals that are less well adapted are more likely to die before reproducing.

Types of adaptations

There are three main types of adaptations that you need to know about.

1. Behavioural adaptations

These are ways an organism acts that increase its chance of survival.

Examples
- Possums sometimes 'play dead' — if they're being threatened by a predator they play dead to escape attack. This increases their chance of survival.
- Scorpions dance before mating — this makes sure they attract a mate of the same species, increasing the likelihood of successful mating.

2. Physiological adaptations

These are processes inside an organism's body that increase its chance of survival.

Examples
- Brown bears hibernate — they lower their metabolism (all the chemical reactions taking place in their body) over winter. This conserves energy, so they don't need to look for food in the months when it's scarce — increasing their chance of survival.
- Some bacteria produce antibiotics — these kill other species of bacteria in the area. This means there's less competition, so they're more likely to survive.

3. Anatomical (structural) adaptations

These are structural features of an organism's body that increase its chance of survival.

Examples
- Otters have a streamlined shape — making it easier to glide through the water. This makes it easier for them to catch prey and escape predators, increasing their chance of survival.
- Whales have a thick layer of blubber (fat) — this helps to keep them warm in the cold sea. This increases their chance of survival in places where their food is found.

Figure 2: *An otter's streamlined body helps it to move easily through water.*

Practice Questions — Application

Q1 The common pipistrelle bat lives throughout Britain on farmland, open woodland, hedgerows and urban areas. It feeds by flying and catching insects in the air.

a) Some adaptations of the common pipistrelle bat are shown in the table below. Put a tick to show whether each adaptation is behavioural, physiological or anatomical.

Exam Tip
Read any information you're given in the exam carefully — it's there to help you answer the question.

		Behavioural	Physiological	Anatomical
Adaptation	Light, flexible wings			
	Male bats make mating calls to attract females			
	Bats lower their metabolism to hibernate over winter			

b) For each of the adaptations in the table above, suggest how it helps the common pipistrelle bat to survive.

Q2 Killer whales are commonly found in the cold seas around the Arctic and Antarctic. They live and hunt in groups called pods, eating a varied diet of fish, seals, sea lions and other whales. Killer whales dive to catch their prey and can reduce their heart rate by up to half whilst diving. A thick layer of blubber (fat) under the whales' skin gives them a smooth, rounded shape.

Using the information given above:

a) Name one behavioural, one physiological and one anatomical adaptation of the killer whale to its environment.

b) For each adaptation, explain how it helps the killer whale to survive.

Tip: Like all whales, killer whales are mammals. They can't breathe underwater, so they have to hold their breath while they dive.

Evolution is the slow and continual change of organisms from one generation to the next. Charles Darwin came up with a neat little theory to explain it...

Darwin's theory

Scientists use theories to attempt to explain their observations — Charles Darwin was no exception. Darwin made four key observations about the world around him.

Darwin's observations:

1. Organisms produce more offspring than survive.

2. There's variation in the characteristics of members of the same species.

3. Some of these characteristics can be passed on from one generation to the next.

4. Individuals that are best adapted to their environment are more likely to survive.

Natural selection

Darwin wrote the **theory of evolution by natural selection** to explain his observations. This is the theory as it stands today:

- Individuals within a population show variation in their phenotypes (their characteristics) due to differences in their alleles.

- Predation, disease and competition create a struggle for survival.

- Individuals with better adaptations (characteristics that give a selective advantage, e.g. being able to run away from predators faster) are more likely to survive, reproduce and pass on the alleles that cause the advantageous adaptations to their offspring.

- Over time, the number of individuals with advantageous adaptations increases.

- Over generations this leads to evolution as the alleles that cause the advantageous adaptations become more common in the population.

Example — peppered moths

Figure 1: *Two colours of peppered moth on tree bark.*

- Peppered moths show variation in colour — there are light ones (with alleles for light colour) and dark ones (with alleles for dark colour).

- Before the 1800s there were more light moths than dark moths.

- During the 1800s, pollution had blackened many of the trees that the moths lived on.

- Dark coloured moths were now better adapted to this environment — they were better camouflaged from predators, so would be more likely to survive, reproduce and pass on the alleles for their dark colouring to their offspring.

- During this time the number of dark moths increased and the number of alleles for dark colour became more common in the population.

Reaction to Darwin's theory

At first, there was some opposition to Darwin's theory as it conflicted with some religious beliefs. Over time the theory has become increasingly accepted as more evidence has been found to support it and no evidence has been shown to disprove it. Evidence increases scientists' confidence in a theory — the more evidence there is, the more chance of something becoming an accepted scientific explanation (see pages 1-2).

Evidence to support evolution

There's plenty of evidence to support evolution, such as...

Fossil record evidence

Fossils are the remains of organisms preserved in rocks. By arranging fossils in chronological (date) order, gradual changes in organisms can be observed that provide evidence of evolution.

┌─ Example ──────────────────────────────

The fossil record of the horse shows a gradual change in characteristics, including increasing size, lengthening of the limbs and hoof development.

Figure 2: Suggested evolution of the horse.

Tip: The evidence supporting evolution isn't always perfect, e.g. there are sometimes gaps in the fossil record. This is because fossils don't always form and when they do, they can be easily damaged or destroyed.

Molecular evidence — DNA

The theory of evolution suggests that all organisms have evolved from shared common ancestors. Closely related species diverged (evolved to become different species) more recently.

Evolution is caused by gradual changes in the base sequence of organisms' DNA. So, organisms that diverged away from each other more recently, should have more similar DNA, as less time has passed for changes in the DNA sequence to occur. This is exactly what scientists have found.

Tip: There's more on DNA base sequences on pages 125-126.

┌─ Example ──────────────────────────────

Humans, chimps and mice all evolved from a common ancestor. Humans and mice diverged a long time ago, but humans and chimps diverged quite recently. The DNA base sequence of humans and chimps is 94% the same, but human and mouse DNA is only 85% the same.

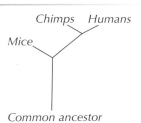

Molecular evidence — proteins and other molecules

In addition to DNA, the similarities in other molecules provide evidence. Scientists compare the sequence of amino acids in proteins, and compare antibodies. Organisms that diverged away from each other more recently have more similar molecules, as less time has passed for changes in proteins and other molecules to occur.

Practice Questions — Application

Q1 The cytochrome C protein is found in almost all living organisms. Suggest how scientists might use cytochrome C to provide evidence for evolution.

Q2 There are many different species of rat snake, all found in different habitats and with slightly different colourings. The black rat snake lives in wooded habitats and has a dark, brown-black colouring (see Figure 3). Describe how natural selection could explain the evolution of a rat snake with black colouring in a wooded habitat.

Figure 3: A black rat snake climbing up a tree.

Speciation

Evolution can lead to speciation — the formation of a new species. A species is defined as a group of similar organisms that can reproduce to produce fertile offspring. Speciation happens when populations of the same species are isolated in some way and evolve to become so different that they can't breed with one another to produce fertile offspring.

Tip: Species can exist as one or more populations, e.g. there are populations of the American black bear in parts of the USA and in parts of Canada.

> ### Example — Darwin's finches
>
> Darwin observed 14 species of finch on the Galapagos Islands — a group of islands in the Pacific Ocean. Each species of finch was unique to a single island. Although the finches were similar, the size and shape of their beaks differed (see Figure 4) — they were adapted to the food sources found on their specific island. Darwin theorised that:
>
> - All the species of finch had a common ancestor.
> - Different populations became isolated on different islands.
> - Each population evolved adaptations to their environment.
> - The populations evolved to become so different that they could no longer breed to produce fertile offspring.
> - They had evolved into separate species.

Tip: Populations of finches became geographically isolated from one another (they ended up on separate islands). They then evolved to become reproductively isolated (i.e. they could no longer breed to produce fertile offspring). This led to speciation.

Figure 4: Examples of the different-shaped beaks found in Darwin's finches.

The evolution of antibiotic resistance

Antibiotics are drugs that kill or inhibit the growth of bacteria. Scientists have observed the evolution of antibiotic resistance in many species of bacteria.

> ### Example
>
> MRSA (methicillin-resistant *Staphylococcus aureus*) is a strain (type) of bacteria that's resistant to the antibiotic methicillin.

The evolution of antibiotic resistance can be explained by natural selection:

- There is variation in a population of bacteria. Genetic mutations make some bacteria naturally resistant to an antibiotic.
- If the population of bacteria is exposed to that antibiotic, only the individuals with resistance will survive to reproduce.
- The alleles which cause the antibiotic resistance will be passed on to the next generation. Over many generations, the population will evolve to become resistant to the drug.

Tip: Mutations are changes to the DNA base code (see p.130). They can produce new alleles, e.g. the alleles for antibiotic resistance.

Testing for antibiotic resistance

You can find out which antibiotics a population of bacteria is resistant to by doing a simple experiment. First, spread a sample of bacteria onto an agar plate. Then place paper discs soaked with the same concentrations of different antibiotics onto the plate and allow the bacteria to grow.

Anywhere bacteria can't grow can be seen as a clear patch on the agar plate. The size of the clear patch tells you how well a particular antibiotic works. The larger the patch, the more the bacteria were inhibited from growing. This can be seen in Figure 5 on the next page.

Tip: This experiment can also be carried out using a multodisc — it's basically one large disc with arms. There's a different antibiotic on the end of each arm. E.g:

Arms   Central disc

Hospitals and clinicians can use tests like these to choose the most suitable antibiotic for treating a patient with a bacterial infection. The tests are cheap, quick and easy to do, and mean that the most suitable antibiotic can be prescribed first time.

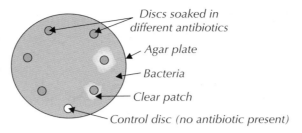

Discs soaked in different antibiotics

Agar plate

Bacteria

Clear patch

Control disc (no antibiotic present)

Figure 5: Antibiotic resistance experiment results.

Figure 6: *Plates testing the resistance of two strains of* S. aureus *bacteria.*

The implications of antibiotic resistance for humans

Infections caused by antibiotic-resistant bacteria (such as MRSA) are harder to treat — some species of bacteria are resistant to a lot of different antibiotics. It may take doctors a while to figure out which antibiotics will get rid of the infection, and in that time the patient could become very ill or die.

There could come a point where a bacterium has developed resistance to all known antibiotics. To prevent this, new antibiotics need to be developed. This takes time and costs a lot of money.

The evolution of pesticide resistance

Pesticides are chemicals that kill pests (e.g. insects that damage crops). Scientists have observed the evolution of pesticide resistance in many species of insect.

Examples

- Some populations of mosquito have evolved resistance to the pesticide DDT.
- Some populations of pollen beetles (which damage the crop oilseed rape) are resistant to pyrethroid pesticides.

The evolution of pesticide resistance can be explained by natural selection:

- There is variation in a population of insects. Genetic mutations make some insects naturally resistant to a pesticide.
- If the population of insects is exposed to that pesticide, only the individuals with resistance will survive to reproduce.
- The alleles which cause the pesticide resistance will be passed on to the next generation. Over many generations, the population will evolve to become more resistant to the chemical.

The implications of pesticide resistance for humans

The implications for humans are pretty similar to those for antibiotic resistance. Crop infestations with pesticide-resistant insects are harder to control — some insects are resistant to lots of different pesticides. It takes farmers a while to figure out which pesticide will kill the insect and in that time all the crop could be destroyed.

If the insects are resistant to specific pesticides (ones that only kill that insect), farmers might have to use broader pesticides (those that kill a range of insects), which could kill beneficial insects. And if disease-carrying insects (e.g. mosquitoes) become pesticide-resistant, the spread of disease could increase.

A population of insects could also evolve resistance to all pesticides in use. To prevent this new pesticides need to be produced. This takes time and costs money.

Tip: A disc that isn't soaked in any antibiotic is included as a negative control (see page 4).

Tip: Different strains of one species of bacteria can be resistant to different antibiotics — one antibiotic won't always kill all of them.

Tip: The pesticide is acting as a selection pressure. Its presence determines which alleles become more common in the population, i.e. the alleles for pesticide resistance.

Tip: Beneficial insects include natural pest predators (e.g. ladybirds) as these feed on pest species, removing them from the crop.

Practice Questions — Application

Q1 Tuberculosis (TB) is a serious respiratory disease caused by bacteria. Some populations of the bacteria have evolved to become resistant to the antibiotic rifampicin, which is commonly used to treat TB.

    a) Suggest how the bacteria that cause TB have evolved to become rifampicin-resistant.

    b) Some populations of the TB-causing bacteria are now resistant to multiple antibiotics. Explain the implications this may have for:

       i) people infected with TB,

      ii) the drug companies that make antibiotics.

Q2 DDT is a chemical insecticide that was first used to kill malaria-carrying mosquitos around the time of WWII. In the 1950s, DDT-resistant mosquitos began to appear in areas of widespread DDT use. Describe how DDT-resistance became widespread in some mosquito populations.

Practice Questions — Fact Recall

Q1 State two observations made by Darwin, that led him to develop his theory of evolution.

Q2 Explain how the following can provide evidence for evolution:
    a) the fossil record,   b) DNA.

Q3 What is the formation of new species known as?

Section Summary

Make sure you know...

- That variation is the differences that exist between individuals and that it can occur within a species (intraspecific variation) or between species (interspecific variation).

- That continuous variation is where the individuals in a population vary within a range — there are no distinct categories.

- That discontinuous variation is where there two or more distinct categories and each individual falls into only one of these categories.

- How to describe the differences between continuous and discontinuous variation using examples from plants, animals and microorganisms.

- That variation can be caused by genetic factors, environmental factors or a combination of both.

- That an adaptation is a feature that increases an organism's chances of survival and reproduction, and also the chances of its offspring reproducing successfully.

- That adaptations can be behavioural, physiological or anatomical (structural).

- The four observations made by Darwin and how these led to his theory of evolution.

- How variation, adaptation and selection all play a role in evolution.

- That fossil evidence, along with DNA and other molecular evidence, provides support for evolution.

- That speciation is the formation of a new species.

- That speciation happens when populations of the same species are isolated in some way, then evolve to become so different that they can't breed to produce fertile offspring.

- How bacteria evolve resistance to antibiotics and the implications this has for humans.

- How insects evolve resistance to pesticides and the implications this has for humans.

Exam-style Questions

1   Fig 1.1 shows the range of wingspans of two different species of bird, both of which live in the same area of woodland.

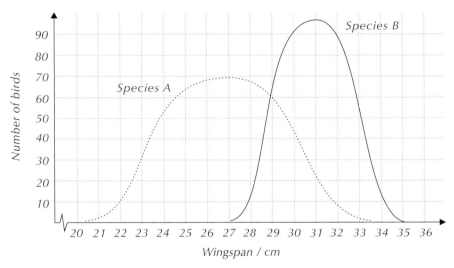

Fig. 1.1

(a)   What is the most common wingspan in birds of species A?

(1 mark)

(b) (i)   Which species shows a greater variation in wingspan?
Explain your answer.

(1 mark)

(ii)   Suggest what may be causing the variation in wingspan between species A and species B. Give a reason your answer.

(2 marks)

(c)   Is variation in wingspan continuous or discontinuous?
Give **three** reasons for your answer.

(3 marks)

(d)   A population of species A becomes isolated from the rest of the species.
If this population remains isolated from the rest of species A for a prolonged period of time, speciation may eventually occur.

(i)   What is meant by the term '**speciation**'?

(1 mark)

(ii)   Suggest how scientists studying species A could find out if speciation has occurred.

(2 marks)

2   Fig. 2.1 shows the use of an anti-aphid pesticide on a farm and
the number of aphids found on the farm over a period of time.

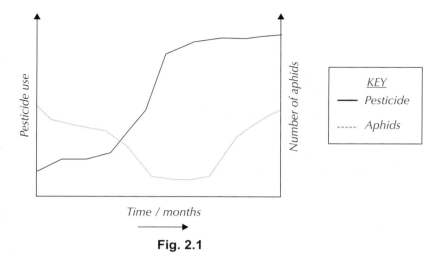

Fig. 2.1

(a) (i)   Describe the changes shown in the data in Fig. 2.1.

(3 marks)

(ii)   Explain how the changes you described in **part i)** may have occurred.

(4 marks)

(b)   Suggest **one** implication these changes may have for the farmer.

(2 marks)

3   The bat *Anoura fistulata* has a very long tongue (up to one and a half times the
length of its body).

The tongue enables the bat to feed on the nectar inside a deep tubular flower
found in the forests of Ecuador.

(a)   The bat's tongue is an **anatomical** adaptation to feeding on deep flowers.

(i)   What is an adaptation?

(2 marks)

(ii)   Give **two** other types of adaptation an organism can have to its environment.

(2 marks)

(b)   Describe how natural selection can explain the evolution of *Anoura fistulata's*
long tongue.

(5 marks)

(c)   Describe the types of evidence that scientists could use to determine how
Anoura fistulata may have evolved from its ancestors **and** explain what this
evidence could show.

(6 marks)

Exam Help

1. Exam Structure

You'll take two exams as part of AS Level Biology. Everything you need to know about them is summarised below.

Unit 1 exam (F211) — Cells, Exchange and Transport
- There are 60 marks to be had.
- It's 1 hour long (so you've got exactly 1 minute per mark).

Unit 2 exam (F212) — Molecules, Biodiversity, Food and Health
- There are 100 marks in total.
- It's 1 hour 45 minutes long (so that's just over 1 minute per mark).

Tip: The unit 1 exam is worth 30% of your AS Level and the unit 2 exam is worth 50%. The other 20% comes from coursework (testing your practical and investigative skills).

2. Command Words

Command words are just the bits of a question that tell you what to do. You'll find answering exam questions much easier if you understand exactly what they mean, so here's a brief summary table of the most common ones:

Command word:	What to do:
Give / Name / State	Give a brief one or two word answer, or a short sentence.
Define	Give the meaning of a word.
What is meant by...	Give the meaning of a word or phrase.
Describe	Write about what something's like, e.g. describe the structure of fish gills.
Explain	Give reasons for something.
Suggest	Use your scientific knowledge to work out what the answer might be.
Compare	Give the similarities and differences between two things.
Evaluate	Give the arguments both for and against an issue, or the advantages and disadvantages of something. You also need to give an overall judgement.

Tip: Read exam questions <u>carefully</u> and do what's asked of you. For example, if a question says 'give two processes' then the examiner will probably only mark the first two things you write.

Exam Tip
When you're reading exam questions, underline the command words. That way you'll know exactly what type of answer to give.

Exam Tip
If you're answering a longer 'compare' or 'evaluate' question make a mental list of the similarities and differences or pros and cons first, so you know what you want your answer to include before you start writing.

Some questions will also ask you to answer 'using the information provided' (e.g. a graph, table or passage of text) — if so, you must refer to the information you've been given or you won't get the marks.

Tip: There are usually two questions in each exam that test QWC — both have one QWC mark available.

Examiners like to know you can write answers that include correct scientific terms and avoid waffle. There are some questions in the exam where extra marks are available for being able to do this.

How to get QWC marks

In each exam there are two marks you can pick up for having good quality of written communication (QWC). The questions are easy to spot because they have a little pencil symbol underneath them and some advice on what to include in your answer.

Exam Tip
The advice next to the pencil symbol tells you what the examiners are looking for to give you the QWC marks, so make sure you pay attention to it. E.g. if it tells you to use information from a table or make it clear how the steps in a process are sequenced, make sure you include these details in your answer.

Examiners like to know you can use the right scientific terms in your answers and spell them correctly. They also need to be able to read your answer easily to give you the marks, so make sure your writing is clear, your answer is in a logical order and your punctuation and grammar are up to scratch.

4. Interpreting Data and Experiment Design

You'll get lots of questions about data in the exam, so you need to be a dab hand at describing a good experiment, describing the data, drawing conclusions from it and commenting on the reliability of the data. It's quite a lot to get your head around, but this will help...

Describing a good experiment

You could be asked to describe an experiment in the exam. You need to plan what you're going to write before you start — roughly jot down the sequence of the experiment. Next you need to describe the sequence of the experiment — what you do first, then second, then third etc. Use the proper names for the equipment and reagents, e.g. spectrophotometer, Benedict's reagent etc. and don't forget to mention any calculation steps, e.g. finding averages. Be specific about what you would do. Finally, if it's a test (e.g. a test for sugar), describe what results you'd expect — e.g. what colour change you'd expect.

Tip: Catalase catalyses the breakdown of hydrogen peroxide into water and oxygen.

┌─ **Example** ───────────────────

Investigating the effect of temperature on catalase activity

To start with, set up test tubes containing the same concentration of hydrogen peroxide. Also set up the apparatus to measure the volume of oxygen produced from each test tube.

Next put each test tube in a water bath set to a different temperature (e.g. 10 °C, 20 °C, 30 °C and 40 °C). Add the same volume of catalase to each test tube and record how much oxygen is produced in the first minute (60 s) of the reaction. A negative control reaction, not containing catalase, should be carried out at each temperature.

Repeat the experiment at each temperature three times, and use the results to find an average volume. Calculate the average rate of reaction at each temperature by dividing the volume produced by the time taken (cm^3/second).

Describing the data

You need to be able to describe any data you're given. The level of detail in your answer should be appropriate for the number of marks given. Loads of marks = more detail, few marks = less detail.

Example 1 — Experiment A

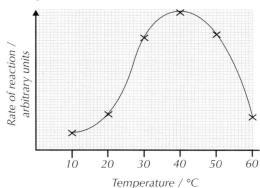

Temperature / °C

Exam Tip
It's easy to get <u>describe</u> and <u>explain</u> mixed up. If you're asked to describe the data, just state the overall pattern or trend. If you're asked to explain the data, you'll need to <u>give reasons</u> for the trend.

Experiment A examined the effect of temperature on the rate of an enzyme-controlled reaction. The rate of reaction for enzyme X was measured at six different temperatures. All other variables were kept constant.

A negative control containing all solutions except the enzyme was included. The rate of reaction for the negative control was zero at each temperature used. The results are shown in the graph above.

Describing the data (2 marks):

The data shows that the rate of reaction increases as temperature increases up to a certain point. The rate of reaction then decreases as temperature increases.

Describing the data (3 marks):

The data shows that the rate of reaction increases as temperature increases from 10 °C up to 40 °C. The rate is fastest between 20 and 30 °C. The rate of reaction then decreases rapidly as temperature increases from 40 °C to 60 °C.

Exam Tip
If you need to describe the data in detail, it's a good idea to include numbers from the graph.

Example 2 — Study B

Study B examined the effect of farm hedgerow length on the number of species in a given area. The number of species present during a single week on 12 farms was counted by placing ground-level traps. All the farms were a similar area. The traps were left out every day, at 6 am for two hours and once again at 6 pm for two hours. The results are shown in the scattergram on the right.

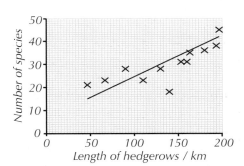

Length of hedgerows / km

Exam Tip
You'll see data presented in all sorts of ways in the exam — scatter graphs, line graphs, bar charts, tables... Make sure you're comfortable interpreting all of them.

Describing the data (1 mark):

The data shows a positive correlation between the length of hedgerows and the number of species in the area.

Exam Tip
If a question is only worth 1 mark, don't waste time writing more than you need to.

Drawing and checking conclusions

You have to be very careful when drawing conclusions in the exam. For results that show a correlation between the variables, remember that this doesn't prove that a change in one causes a change in the other.

Tip: See page 5 for more on correlations and causal relationships.

Example — Study B

The length of the hedgerows shows a positive correlation with the number of species in that area. But you can't conclude more hedgerows cause more species (or that fewer hedgerows cause fewer species). Other factors may have been involved, for example, the number of predators in an area may have decreased or the farmers may have used less pesticide there.

The data should always support the conclusion too. This may sound obvious but it's easy to jump to conclusions. Conclusions have to be precise — not make sweeping generalisations.

Example — Experiment A

A science magazine concluded from this data that enzyme X works best at 40 °C. The data doesn't support this. The enzyme could work best at 42 °C or 47 °C but you can't tell this from the data because increases of 10 °C at a time were used. The rates of reaction at in-between temperatures weren't measured.

Exam Tip
Data questions are fairly common in the exams. You might be given a conclusion for the data and asked to evaluate it — this just means you have to give reasons why it is (or isn't) a valid conclusion.

Commenting on reliability

If the data isn't reliable for whatever reason you can't draw a valid conclusion. Any experiment has to be carried out properly to get reliable results. Here are some of the things you'll need to think about if you're asked to comment on the reliability of an experiment or study in the exam.

1. Size of the data set

For experiments, the more repeats you do, the more reliable the data. The general rule for studies is the larger the sample size, the more reliable the data is.

Exam Tip
If you're asked to design or evaluate a method used in an experiment, you also need to comment on the same things mentioned here.

Example — Study B

Study B is quite small — they only used 12 farms. The trend shown by the data may not appear if you studied 50 or 100 farms, or studied them for a longer period of time.

---

2. Variables

The more variables you control, the more reliable your data is.

Example 1 — Experiment A

In Experiment A, all other variables were controlled, e.g. pH, concentrations, volumes, so the results are reliable and you can be sure the temperature is causing the change in the reaction rate.

Example 2 — Study B

In Study B you're not told if all the other variables were controlled, e.g. you don't know if all the farms had a similar type of land, similar weather, the same crops growing, etc. This means you don't know how reliable the study is — you can't be sure that the factor being investigated (hedgerows) is the only one affecting the thing being measured (number of species).

Tip: Reliability means the results can be consistently reproduced in independent experiments. See pages 3-5 for more info.

3. Data collection

Think about all the problems with the method and see if bias has slipped in. The less bias there is, the more reliable the data.

┌─ **Example — Study B** ─────────────────────────────

In Study B the traps were placed on the ground, so species like birds weren't included. The traps weren't left overnight, so nocturnal animals wouldn't get counted, etc. This could have affected the results.
└─

4. Controls

Controls are needed in order to draw valid conclusions.

┌─ **Example — Experiment A** ─────────────────────────────

The negative control (containing all solutions except the enzyme) showed that the change in reaction rate was caused by the effect of temperature on the enzyme, and not anything else (e.g. the water, or something in the test tube).
└─

5. Repetition by other scientists

For theories to become accepted as 'fact' other scientists need to repeat the work (see page 2). If multiple studies or experiments come to the same conclusion, then that conclusion is more reliable.

┌─ **Example — Experiment A** ─────────────────────────────

If a second group of scientists carried out the same experiment for enzyme X and got the same results, the results would be more reliable.
└─

Analysing the data

Sometimes it's easier to compare data by making a few calculations first, e.g. converting raw data into ratios or percentages.

┌─ **Example** ─────────────────────────────

Three UK hospitals have been trying out three different methods to control the spread of chest infections. A study investigated the number of people suffering from chest infections in those hospitals over a three month period. The table on the right shows the results.

Hospital	Number of cases per 6000 patients		
	Jan	Feb	March
1	60	65	78
2	14	24	55
3	93	96	110

If you just look at the number of cases in the last month (March) then the method of hospital 3 appears to have worked least well, as they have the highest number of infections. But if you look at the percentage increase in infections you get a different picture:

$$\text{Hospital 1: } \frac{(78 - 60)}{60} \times 100 = \frac{18}{60} \times 100 = 30\%$$

$$\text{Hospital 2: } \frac{(55 - 14)}{14} \times 100 = \frac{41}{14} \times 100 = 293\%$$

$$\text{Hospital 3: } \frac{(110 - 93)}{93} \times 100 = \frac{17}{93} \times 100 = 18\%$$

So hospital 3 has the lowest percentage increase, suggesting their method of control is working the best.
└─

Tip: Bias can also come from the people collecting the data. For example, a company testing its own product might report the data in a way that makes it look better than it is.

Tip: There's more on control experiments and control groups on pages 3 and 4.

Exam Tip
You might be asked to evaluate the reliability of an experiment in the exam — or you might be asked to suggest ways to improve its reliability. Either way, keep these 5 points in mind.

Tip: Remember, ratios and percentages are used so you can <u>compare</u> different sets of data fairly.

Tip: To work out a percentage change you need to calculate:

$$\frac{(new \quad original}{value} - \frac{value)}{original \; value} \times 100$$

5. Graph and Table Skills

You should be a dab hand at all things to do with graphs and tables by now, but if you aren't don't worry — here are some tips to help.

Reading values off graphs

If there's a key pay close attention to it — you'll be throwing away easy marks if you don't. If the graph has more than one vertical axis make sure you read off the correct one. Also, always put the units on your answer.

Calculating the gradient of a graph

A little trickier is calculating the gradient of the graph:

$$\text{Gradient} = \frac{\text{Change in Y}}{\text{Change in X}} \qquad \text{Units} = \frac{Y}{X}$$

Example

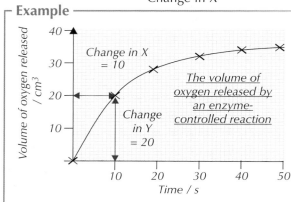

The volume of oxygen released by an enzyme-controlled reaction

If you want to know the rate of a reaction over the first 10 seconds:

Gradient = rate of reaction

$$= \frac{20}{10} = 2$$

$$\text{Units} = \frac{cm^3}{s} = cm^3s^{-1}$$

So, the answer is 2 cm³s⁻¹.

Drawing graphs

Here are a few rules:

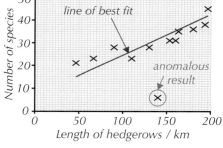

Length of hedgerows / km

- The dependent variable should go on the y-axis (the vertical axis) and the independent on the x-axis (the horizontal axis).

- Always label the axes and include the units.

- If you need to draw a line (or curve) of best fit on a scatter graph, don't just join the points up. Instead, draw the line through or as near to as many points as possible, ignoring any anomalous results.

- To estimate what a result outside the range that you studied might be, just extend the line of best fit then read off the data.

Drawing tables

Tables are useful for organising data. When you draw a table, use a ruler and make sure each column has a heading. The units should be in the column heading, not the table itself.

You usually have to process raw data in some way to make it useful, e.g. by calculating the mean (average).

Farm	Length of hedgerows (km)	Number of species
1	49	21
2	90	28
3	155	30

Answers

Unit 1

Section 1 — Cell Structure

1. Cells and Organelles
Pages 11-12 — Application Questions
Q1 a) Mitochondria — these are the site of aerobic respiration in the cell / where ATP is produced.
You should be able to tell that both organelles are mitochondria by the cristae (folded structures) inside them. Don't be thrown by their slightly odd shapes.
   b) Gogli apparatus — this processes and packages new lipids and proteins. It also makes lysosomes.
   c) Chloroplast — photosynthesis takes place here.
You can clearly see the granum and lamellae in this organelle, which should tell you that it's a chloroplast.
   d) Cilia — used move substances along the cell surface.
Q2 a) nucleolus
   b) cell wall
   c) Image B because there is a large vacuole and a cell wall present. Animal cells don't have either of these structures.

Page 12 — Fact Recall Questions
Q1 A — cell wall, B — cytoplasm, C — mitochondrion, D — nucleus, E — chloroplast, F — vacuole, G — cell membrane, H — ribosome.
Q2 Any three from, e.g. cell wall / plasmodesmata / vacuole / chloroplasts.
Q3 Chromatin/DNA contained in the nucleus controls the cell's activities. The nuclear pores allow substances to move between the nucleus and the cytoplasm. The nucleolus makes ribosomes.
Q4 Any one from: To digest invading cells. / To break down worn out components of the cell.
Q5 The rough endoplasmic reticulum is covered in ribosomes, whereas the smooth endoplasmic reticulum is not.
Q6 It synthesises and processes lipids.
Q7 Golgi apparatus
Q8 centriole
Q9

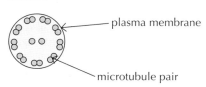
plasma membrane

microtubule pair

2. Organelles Working Together
Page 14 — Application Questions
Q1 Normal Golgi apparatus would look like a group of flattened linear sacs, lined up next to each other, rather than appearing small, round and disconnected.
Q2 E.g. proteins often undergo further processing (e.g. sugar chains are trimmed or more are added) in the Golgi apparatus. If the apparatus is deformed in some way, these modifications might not take place, and so the proteins produced may not function correctly or at all.

Q3 E.g. the cytoskeleton is involved in the transport of vesicles around the cell. Vesicles are used to transport proteins in protein synthesis. If the cytoskeleton is disrupted, proteins may not be transported between the RER and the Golgi apparatus, preventing them from being modified, or between the Golgi and the cell surface, preventing them from being secreted from the cell.

Page 14 — Fact Recall Questions
Q1 The ribosomes on RER make proteins that are excreted or attached to the cell membrane. Proteins produced at the RER are folded and processed there.
Q2 The cytoskeleton supports the cell's organelles, keeping them in position. It also helps to strengthen the cell and maintain its shape. It transports organelles and materials within the cell. It can also cause the cell to move.

3. Prokaryotic Cells
Page 15 — Fact Recall Questions
Q1 Any three from, e.g: prokaryotes are smaller than eukaryotes. / Prokaryotic DNA is circular, eukaryotic DNA is linear. / Prokaryotes don't have a nucleus, eukaryotes do. / In eukaryotes, if a cell wall is present, it is made of cellulose or chitin. The cell wall in prokaryotes is made of a polysaccharide that isn't cellulose or chitin. / Prokaryotes have fewer organelles than eukaryotes and no mitochondria. / Prokaryotes have smaller ribosomes than eukaryotes.
Q2 Any one from, e.g: they both contain ribosomes/DNA/cytoplasm/a plasma (cell surface) membrane. / They may both contain flagella/a cell wall.

4. Studying Cells — Microscopes
Page 17 — Application Questions
Q1 a) length of image ÷ magnification = length of specimen
      8 mm ÷ 3150 = **0.0025 mm**
   b) length of image ÷ magnification = length of specimen
      18 mm ÷ 3150 = **0.0057 mm**
Always make sure you show your working in questions like these — you could pick up some marks for using the correct calculation, even if you end up with the wrong final answer.
Q2 length of specimen × magnification = length of image
   0.00002 mm × 40 = **0.0008 mm**
Q3 First you need to convert 0.023 μm to millimetres by dividing by 1000.
   0.023 μm ÷ 1000 = 0.000023 mm
   magnification = length of image ÷ length of specimen
   0.035 mm ÷ 0.000023 mm = **× 1522**
Q4 length of image ÷ magnification = length of specimen
   13 mm ÷ 7000 = 0.0019 mm
   Then times by 1000 to convert to μm
   0.0019 mm × 1000 = **1.9 μm**
Q5 a) length of image ÷ length of specimen = magnification
      16 mm ÷ 2 mm = **× 8**
   b) length of specimen × magnification = length of image
      3 mm × 50 = **150 mm**
Q6 First you need to convert 10 μm to millimetres by dividing by 1000.
   10 μm ÷ 1000 = 0.01 mm
   length of image ÷ length of specimen = magnification
   10 mm ÷ 0.01 mm = **× 1000**

Page 19 — Application Questions

Q1 *E.coli* bacterium — light microscope, TEM, SEM
nuclear pore — TEM, SEM
human egg cell — light microscope, TEM, SEM
DNA helix — TEM
mitochondrion — light microscope, TEM, SEM
influenza virus — TEM, SEM

Answering this question is a lot easier if you know the maximum resolution for each type of microscope — it could come up in the exam, so make sure you learn it.

Q2 E.g. Team One might use an SEM. HIV is 0.12 µm in diameter, so it needs to be viewed under an electron microscope as these have a higher maximum resolution than light microscopes. Also, the team is looking at surface proteins and SEM images can show the surface of a specimen and can be 3-D. The second team might use a TEM as they want to view the virus's internal structures. A TEM would allow them to do this because it uses thin slices of the specimen material and has a higher maximum resolution than either light microscopes or SEMs.

Page 20 — Fact Recall Questions

Q1 magnification = length of image ÷ length of specimen

Q2 Magnification is how much bigger the image is than the specimen, whereas resolution is how detailed the image is and how well a microscope distinguishes between two points that are close together.

Q3 TEMs use electromagnets to focus a beam of electrons, which is then transmitted through the specimen. Denser parts of the specimen absorb more electrons, which makes them look darker on the image you end up with.

Q4 SEMs scan a beam of electrons across the specimen. This knocks off electrons from the specimen, which are gathered in a cathode ray tube to form an image.

Q5 a) 0.2 µm
b) 0.0001 µm
c) 0.005 µm

Q6 TEM

Q7 TEM
The maximum resolution of a light microscope is 0.2 µm and the maximum resolution of a SEM is 0.005 µm, so you wouldn't be able to see something that was 0.001 µm with either of these.

Q8 To prevent the object being viewed from appearing completely transparent, if light/electrons pass straight through it.

Exam-style Questions — pages 21-22

1 a) i) No. The microscope has a resolution of 200 nm/0.2 µm *(1 mark)*. This means it can't distinguish between objects that are smaller than 200 nm/0.2 µm — such as the ribosomes *(1 mark)*.

If you convert the diameter of the ribosomes and the resolution of the microscope into the same units, (e.g. both nm or both µm) it's easier to see that the ribosomes are too small for the microscope to pick up.

ii) He could expect to see smaller ribosomes in the bacterial cells, 20 nm or less in size *(1 mark)*.

iii) Any two from, e.g. the stomach cell would not have chloroplasts / a vacuole / a cell wall / plasmodesmata *(2 marks)*.

b) length of specimen = length of image ÷ magnification
= 4 ÷ 100 = **0.04 mm/40 µm**
(2 marks for correct answer, 1 mark if only working is correct)

c) New extracellular proteins are made at the ribosomes on the rough endoplasmic reticulum *(1 mark)*. They're then folded and processed (e.g. sugar chains added) at the rough endoplasmic reticulum *(1 mark)* before being transported to the Golgi apparatus in vesicles *(1 mark)*. Here the proteins may undergo further processing (e.g. sugar chains trimmed) *(1 mark)*. The proteins then enter vesicles to be transported to the cell surface, where the vesicles fuse with the plasma membrane and the proteins are secreted *(1 mark)*. *(1 mark for 3 of the following spelled correctly: ribosome(s), rough endoplasmic reticulum, vesicle(s), Golgi apparatus, plasma membrane)*

It might not seem important, but getting the spelling of technical terms right could help you to pick up marks in the exam. If you know your spelling often lets you down, take time to read through your answer when you're done.

2 a) Abnormal mitochondria might not produce as much ATP as normal mitochondria *(1 mark)*. This means the heart tissue may not have enough energy for muscle contraction *(1 mark)*.

b) i) Any two from: abnormal mice have more mitochondria / smaller mitochondria / mitochondria with a smaller/lighter/less dense matrix / mitochondria with fewer cristae. *(2 marks)*

ii) length of specimen is 1.5 µm = 1.5 µm ÷ 1000 = 0.0015 mm
magnification = length of image ÷ length of specimen
= ~23 mm ÷ 0.0015 mm = **× 15333** (allow anything from × 14667 to × 15333 if the length of image measurement was slightly out)
(2 marks for correct answer, 1 mark if only working is correct.)

c) After two years the normal mice show similar symptoms to the abnormal mice, suggesting that the mitochondria degrade with age *(1 mark)*.

3 a) Bacteria are prokaryotic cells, so the penicillin inhibits the synthesis of their cell walls, eventually leading to cell lysis and death *(1 mark)*. Human cells are eukaryotic animal cells, and so have no cell wall, so penicillin antibiotics leave these cells unaffected *(1 mark)*.

b) i) E.g. because electron microscopes have a higher resolution *(1 mark)* so they can be used to look at smaller objects (like bacteria) in more detail *(1 mark)*.

ii) To scatter the electrons that pass through the specimen under the electron microscope *(1 mark)* and create contrast between the different parts of the specimen *(1 mark)* so they're easier to see *(1 mark)*.

c) Any two from, e.g. a prokaryotic cell is smaller than a eukaryotic cell. / There is no nucleus present in a prokaryotic cell. / There are fewer organelles present in a prokaryotic cell. / There are no mitochondria present in a prokaryotic cell. / Ribosomes are smaller in a prokaryotic cell than in a eukaryotic cell. / The DNA in a prokaryotic cell is circular, not linear. / A prokaryotic cell may contain plasmids. *(2 marks)*

Section 2 — Cell Membranes

1. Cell Membranes — The Basics

Pages 25-26 — Application Questions

Q1 a) E.g. to keep the enzymes needed for photosynthesis all in one place/to compartmentalise photosynthesis, making photosynthetic reactions more efficient.

b) E.g. to increase the surface area available for photosynthesis to take place.
c) E.g. to control what substances enter and leave the cell. / To allow cell communication. / To allow cell recognition.

Q2 E.g. using carrier proteins/channel proteins in the membrane.

Q3 E.g. energy-releasing organelles require lots of substances (e.g. nutrients, enzymes, ATP) to travel across their membranes. Some of these substances will require help from proteins to get across the membrane, so these membranes will have a higher protein content.

Q4 Freezing the raspberries will have caused ice crystals to form and pierce the cell-surface/plasma membrane, making the membrane highly permeable when it thawed. This will have caused the red pigment to leak out of the raspberry cells as they defrosted.

Page 26 — Fact Recall Questions

Q1 It allows some molecules through but not others.

Q2 A = glycoprotein, B = glycolipid, C = cholesterol, D = protein channel, E = phospholipid (head)

Q3 'Hydrophilic' means 'attracts water'. Hydrophobic means 'repels water'.

Q4 The centre of the phospholipid bilayer is hydrophobic, so the membrane doesn't allow water-soluble substances through it.

Q5 Some proteins in the membrane allow the passage of large or charged particles that would otherwise find it difficult to cross the membrane.

Q6 a) Helps make the membrane less fluid and more stable. Creates a barrier to polar substances.
b) Stabilise the membrane by forming hydrogen bonds with surrounding water molecules. Act as receptors in cell signalling. Are sites where drugs, hormones and antibodies bind. Act as antigens and allow self-recognition.

Q7 The phospholipid bilayer starts to melt and the membrane becomes more permeable. Water inside the cell expands, putting pressure on the membrane. Channel proteins and carrier proteins in the membrane denature so they can't control what enters or leaves the cell, further increasing the permeability of the membrane.

2. Cell Membranes and Signalling
Page 28 — Application Questions

Q1 The drug is a complementary shape to the membrane-bound receptor — this means it will bind to the receptor, blocking the messenger molecule from doing so. This will prevent the messenger molecule from triggering a response in the cell.

Q2 The mutated receptor is not a complementary shape to the messenger molecule. This means the messenger molecule is unable to bind to it and trigger a response in the target cells.

Q3 The messenger molecule can only bind to receptors with a complementary shape. Different cells have different membrane-bound receptors. Only liver cells have the correct receptor, so only liver cells can respond to the messenger molecule.
The key thing to remember here is that messenger molecules can only bind to membrane-bound receptors that have a complementary shape to their own.

3. Exchange Across Plasma Membranes
Page 31 — Application Questions

Q1 The ink molecules are moving from an area of higher concentration (the original drop of ink) to an area of lower concentration (the surrounding water).

Q2 a) Water molecules will move from the cheek cells into the salt solution.
A -300 kPa solution has a higher water potential (it's less negative) than a -325 kPa solution.
b) Water molecules will move into the apple slices out of the beaker of water.
c) There will be no movement of water molecules as the water potential in both solutions is the same/the solutions are isotonic.

Q3 a) The potato cells have a lower water potential than the sucrose solution, so they gain water by osmosis. This causes the vacuoles to swell and the cell contents to push against the cell wall, making the cells turgid.
b) E.g. The cells in both solutions will become flaccid (limp). This is because they have a higher water potential than the sucrose solutions, so will lose water by osmosis. The cells in solution 3 may lose so much water that they become plasmolysed.

Page 34 — Application Questions

Q1 a) vesicle
b) Exocytosis. A vesicle containing the chemical messenger moves towards the membrane of neurone 1. The vesicles fuse with the membrane and release their contents outside the cell.
c) E.g through a channel protein using facilitated diffusion.

Q2 a) As the rate of sodium ion active transport increases, so does the rate of oxygen consumption.
b) Sodium ion active transport requires energy from ATP. As the rate of active transport increases, the rate of aerobic respiration must also increase in order to produce more ATP, which means the rate of oxygen consumption must increase too.
Remember, ATP is produced by the mitochondria during aerobic respiration — and aerobic respiration uses oxygen.
c) None. Facilitated diffusion doesn't require energy from ATP, so there would be no need for the rate of oxygen consumption to increase.

Page 36 — Application Question

Q1

Transport system	A plant cell taking in water	Calcium ions moving into a cell against a concentration gradient	A muscle cell taking in polar glucose molecules	White blood cell taking in anthrax bacteria
Osmosis	✓	✗	✗	✗
Facilitated diffusion using channel proteins	✓	✗	✗	✗
Facilitated diffusion using carrier proteins	✗	✗	✓	✗
Active transport using carrier proteins	✗	✓	✓	✗
Endocytosis	✗	✗	✗	✓
Exocytosis	✗	✗	✗	✗

Page 36 — Fact Recall Questions

Q1 The net movement of particles from an area of higher concentration to an area of lower concentration.

Q2 It's a passive process.

Answers   **229**

Q3 Molecules that can pass freely through the membrane, e.g. small, non polar molecules (and water).

Q4 In simple diffusion, small, non-polar molecules pass freely through the plasma membrane. Facilitated diffusion uses carrier proteins and channel proteins to aid the movement of large molecules and charged particles through the plasma membrane.

Q5 Osmosis is the diffusion of water molecules across a partially permeable membrane, from an area of higher water potential to an area of lower water potential.

Q6 Water potential is the potential/likelihood of water molecules to diffuse out of or into a solution.

Q7 a) The cell will swell and burst as water moves into it by osmosis.
b) The cell will become turgid (swollen) as water moves into it by osmosis, causing the vacuole to swell and the contents of the vacuole and cytoplasm to push against the cell wall.
c) The cell will become flaccid (limp) as water moves out of the cell by osmosis. The cell may eventually lose so much water that it becomes plasmolysed.

Q8 Similarity: both facilitated diffusion and active transport use carrier proteins to transport molecules across plasma membranes.
Differences: in facilitated diffusion, molecules move down a concentration gradient. In active transport, molecules are moved against a concentration gradient. Facilitated diffusion is a passive process, it doesn't require energy. Active transport is an active process that does require energy.

Q9 a) A molecule attaches to a carrier protein in the membrane. The protein then changes shape and releases the molecule on the opposite side of the membrane.
b) Channel proteins form pores in the membrane for charged particles to diffuse through.

Q10 A cell surrounds a substance with its plasma membrane. The membrane then pinches off to form a vesicle inside the cell, which contains the ingested substance.

Exam-style Questions — pages 38-39

1 a) i) The potential/likelihood of water molecules to diffuse out of or into a solution *(1 mark)*.
ii) The cells in Fig. 1.2 have lost water by osmosis *(1 mark)*. This has caused the cytoplasm and plasma membranes to pull away from the cell walls *(1 mark)*. The cells are plasmolysed *(1 mark)*.
iii) The net movement of water molecules will still be out of the cell by osmosis *(1 mark)*, causing the cell to shrink *(1 mark)*.
b) i) Any five from: In the fluid mosaic model, phospholipid molecules form a continuous double layer/bilayer *(1 mark)*. / The bilayer is fluid because the phospholipids are constantly moving *(1 mark)*. / Cholesterol molecules fit between the phospholipids making the membrane less fluid and more stable *(1 mark)*. / Protein molecules are scattered throughout the bilayer, like tiles in a mosaic *(1 mark)*. / Some protein molecules, called glycoproteins, have a polysaccharide/carbohydrate chain attached *(1 mark)*. / Some lipids, called glycolipids, also have a polysaccharide/carbohydrate chain attached *(1 mark)*. *(1 mark for 3 of the following spelled correctly: phospholipid(s), cholesterol, protein(s), glycoprotein(s), glycolipid(s).)*
Don't let your spelling let you down — one extra mark on each exam paper could make all the difference.

ii) E.g. any two from: Plasma membranes control which substances enter and leave the cell. / Plasma membranes allow recognition by other cells. / Plasma membranes allow cell communication. *(2 marks for 2 correct answers)*

2 a) i) The centre of the phospholipid bilayer is hydrophobic *(1 mark)*. It forms a barrier to the diffusion of water-soluble substances including polar molecules *(1 mark)*. Glucose is a polar molecule, so it can't diffuse directly across the membrane *(1 mark)*.
ii) No. The glucose moves down its concentration gradient/facilitated diffusion is a passive process *(1 mark)*.
b) The movement of molecules against their concentration gradient *(1 mark)* using energy (from ATP) to do so *(1 mark)*.

3 a) In case the cubes did not all start out at exactly the same mass *(1 mark)*.
b) 16% (accept 15-17%) *(1 mark)*
Don't forget that pure water is always 0 kPa.
c) i) The water potential in these three solutions must have been lower than the water potential of the potato cells *(1 mark)* so water moved out of the cells by osmosis *(1 mark)*.
ii) 425 kPa (accept 400 - 450 kPa) *(1 mark)*
The cells won't lose or gain any mass in an isotonic solution, so all you need to do is read the water potential off the graph where the change in mass equals zero.
d) E.g. they could do repeats of the experiment for each concentration of sucrose solution and calculate the mean percentage change in mass *(1 mark)*. / They could repeat the experiment using smaller intervals between the sucrose concentrations *(1 mark)*.
There's more on collecting reliable results in the How Science Works section at the front of this book.
e) Before 12 hours *(1 mark)* because the rate of osmosis will be faster due to the increase in surface area *(1 mark)*.

Section 3 — Cell Division, Diversity and Organisation

1. The Cell Cycle and Mitosis
Page 42 — Application Questions
Q1 a) B
b) C
To answer this you need to quickly go through each stage of mitosis in your head and think about the main thing that's happening, e.g. in metaphase all the chromosomes are in the middle of the cell. Then ask yourself if you can see that in the photo.

Q2 The centromeres are dividing, separating each pair of sister chromatids. The spindles are contracting, pulling chromatids to opposite poles of the cell, centromere first.

Page 42 — Fact Recall Questions
Q1 The process that all body cells from multicellular organisms use to grow and divide.
Q2 interphase
Q3 It's checked for any mutations/errors that may have occurred.
Q4 For growth and for repairing damaged tissues.
Q5 During prophase the chromosomes condense, getting shorter and fatter. The centrioles start moving to opposite ends of the cell, forming the spindle. The nuclear envelope breaks down and chromosomes lie free in the cytoplasm.

Q6 metaphase
Q7 anaphase
Q8 two
Q9 False
Mitosis produces two genetically identical daughter cells.
Q10 Any two from: e.g. In animals, most cells can divide by mitosis. In plants, only cells in meristems can divide by mitosis. / During prophase in animal cells, the spindle forms between centrioles. Plant cells don't have centrioles so the spindle forms without them. / Cytokinesis in animals begins at the edge of a cell, where the cell membrane constricts. Cytokinesis in plants begins in the centre of a cell with a cell plate.

2. Reproduction and Meiosis
Page 46 — Application Questions
Q1 a) Budding, because some of the cells show swellings on their sides.
b) Cell Y swelled on one side, forming a bud on its surface. It underwent interphase — the DNA and organelles replicated ready for the cell to divide. Then cell Y began to undergo mitosis — the replicated DNA, cytoplasm and organelles moved into the bud. Once nuclear division was complete, the budding cell would have contained a nucleus that had an identical copy of cell Y's DNA. Finally, cytokinesis occurred and the bud pinched off from cell Y, to produce cell X.
Q2 A, C, D and F could all be produced by meiosis from this cell. Gametes B and E could not.
Gametes contain one chromosome from each homologous pair. If a gamete contains two chromosomes from the same homologous pair it couldn't have been produced by meiosis.

Page 46 — Fact Recall Questions
Q1 mitosis
Q2 genetically identical
Q3 A — vacuole
B — nucleus (containing DNA)
C — cell membrane
D — cytoplasm
E — cell wall
Q4 The process by which yeast reproduce asexually.
Q5 A pair of matching chromosomes.
Remember that homologous chromosomes are the same size and have the same genes, although they could have different alleles.
Q6 A type of cell division that happens in the reproductive organs to produce gametes.
Q7 E.g. budding produces daughter cells that are genetically identical to the parent cell, meiosis produces daughter cells that are genetically different to the parent cell. Budding produces diploid daughter cells/daughter cells with the same number of chromosomes as the parent cell, meiosis produces haploid daughter cells/daughter cells with half the number of chromosomes as the parent.

3. Stem Cells and Differentiation
Page 50 — Application Question
Q1 E.g. epithelial cells have microvilli, which increase the cell's surface area for absorption of nutrients.
The key thing here is to link what you know about epithelial cells to the information you're given in the question — in this case that they're found in the small intestine. Food is absorbed in the small intestine, so you should be able to work out the answer.

Page 50 — Fact Recall Questions
Q1 An unspecialised cell that can develop into any type of cell.
Q2 The process by which a cell becomes specialised for its job.
Q3 a) i) red blood cells
ii) white blood cells
You could remember that neutrophils are white blood cells by thinking of white as a neutral colour.
b) In the bone marrow.
c) i) Any one from: e.g. erythrocytes have a biconcave disc shape which provides a large surface area for gas exchange. / Erythrocytes don't have a nucleus so there's more room for haemoglobin, the protein that carries oxygen.
ii) Any one from: e.g. neutrophils have a flexible shape which allows them to engulf foreign particles or pathogens. / Neutrophils have a large number of lysosomes in their cytoplasm which contain digestive enzymes to break down engulfed foreign particles or pathogens.
It's dead important that you know the functions and adaptations of erythrocytes, neutrophils, epithelial cells, sperm cells, palisade mesophyll cells, root hair cells and guard cells — you could be asked about any of them in the exam and they're easy marks if you learn them properly.
Q4 The stem cells that form xylem and phloem are found in the cambium. The vascular cambium forms a ring inside the roots. The stem cells divide and grow out from the ring, differentiating as they move away from the cambium.
Q5 a) It allows them to swim to the egg/female sex cell.
b) E.g. they have lots of mitochondria to provide the energy to swim. / The acrosome contains digestive enzymes to enable the sperm to penetrate the surface of the egg.
Q6 a) To carry out photosynthesis.
b) To absorb water and mineral ions from the soil.
Q7 In the light, guard cells take up water (into their vacuoles) and become turgid. Their thin outer walls and thickened inner walls force them to bend outwards, opening the stomata. This allows the leaf to exchange gases for photosynthesis.

4. Tissues, Organs and Systems
Page 53 — Fact Recall Questions
Q1 A group of cells (plus any extracellular material secreted by them) that are specialised to work together to carry out a particular function.
Q2 false
Q3 a) Squamous epithelium is made up of a group of cells/a single layer of flat cells that are specialised to work together to provide a thin exchange surface for substances to diffuse across quickly.
b) Ciliated epithelium is made up of a group of cells/a layer of cells covered in cilia, which are specialised to work together to move a substance along, e.g. mucus in the lungs.
If you're asked why a particular tissue is classified as a tissue in the exam, make sure you include the function of that tissue in your answer.
Q4 E.g. xylem, phloem.
Q5 A group of different tissues that work together to perform a particular function.
Q6 An organ system is where different organs work together to carry out a particular function.
Q7 E.g. the respiratory system. It is an organ system because it is made up of the lungs, trachea, larynx, nose, mouth and diaphragm which work together to carry out gas exchange.

1   a) 12-16 hours and 36-40 hours (**1 mark**), because the
        mass of DNA doubles (**1 mark**).
    b) 24 hours and 48 hours (**1 mark**), because the mass of
        DNA halves / the mass of the cell halves (**1 mark**).
    c) E.g. the cell is growing (**1 mark**) and new organelles and
        proteins are made (**1 mark**). The cell replicates it's DNA
        (**1 mark**) and checks the DNA for errors/mutations
        (**1 mark**).
    d) i) Two (at 24 and 48 hours) (**1 mark**) because the mass
            of the cell and its DNA doubles and halves twice
            (**1 mark**).
       ii) At 72 hours (**1 mark**).
    In graphs with two scales, make sure you match the correct
    line (or bar) to the correct scale before you read off a value.
    e) To prevent mutations being passed onto the daughter cell
        (**1 mark**) which could cause it not to function
        (**1 mark**).
2   a) E.g. it has a large surface area for absorbing water and
        mineral ions from the soil (**1 mark**). The cytoplasm
        contains extra mitochondria to provide the energy
        needed for active transport (**1 mark**).
    b) i) In the cambium (**1 mark**).
       ii) Xylem is a group of cells, including xylem vessel
            cells and parenchyma cells (**1 mark**), that are
            specialised to work together to transport water
            around the plant and support the plant (**1 mark**).
       iii) Each cell type depends on other cells for the
            functions it can't carry out (**1 mark**). This means the
            specialised cells within multicellular organisms must
            cooperate with each other to keep the organism alive
            (**1 mark**).
3   a) Budding in a yeast cell — B
        Mitosis in an animal cell — A
        Mitosis in a plant cell — D
        (**1 mark for each correct answer**)
    b) i) At opposite poles, chromatids uncoil and become
            long and thin again (**1 mark**). A nuclear envelope
            forms around each group of chromosomes, so there
            are two nuclei (**1 mark**). Cytokinesis then occurs/
            the cytoplasm divides (**1 mark**). (**1 mark for 3 of
            the following spelt correctly: chromatids, nuclear
            envelope, chromosomes, cytokinesis.**)
       ii) F (**1 mark**)
       iii) Mitosis is important for growth (**1 mark**), repair
            (**1 mark**), and asexual reproduction (**1 mark**).
    Don't forget that mitosis is not just used for growth and
    repair in multicellular organisms — some single-celled
    organisms (like yeast) use it for asexual reproduction too.
    c) E.g. the daughter cells are genetically different (**1 mark**)
        and contain half the number of chromosomes as the
        parent cell (**1 mark**).

Section 4 — Exchange Surfaces and Breathing

1. Exchange Surfaces
Page 58 — Application Questions
Q1 a) A — surface area = $6 \times 2 \times 2 = $ **24 cm²**
        B — surface area = $(4 \times 4 \times 2) + (2 \times 2 \times 2)$
        $= 32 + 8 = $ **40 cm²**
        C — surface area = $(4 \times 10 \times 5) + (2 \times 5 \times 5)$
        $= 200 + 50 = $ **250 mm²**
    b) A — volume = $2 \times 2 \times 2 = $ **8 cm³**
        B — volume = $2 \times 4 \times 2 = $ **16 cm³**
        C — volume = $10 \times 5 \times 5 = $ **250 mm³**

    c) A — SA:V = $24:8 = $ **3:1**
        B — SA:V = $40:16 = 5:2 = $ **2.5:1**
        C — SA:V = $250:250 = $ **1:1**
Q2 A
    Simplify all of the ratios to 1 in order to compare them, e.g. A
    = 3:1, B = 2.5:1 and C = 1:1 — it's then obvious that A is the
    largest ratio.

Page 58 — Fact Recall Questions
Q1 a) Any two from: e.g. oxygen / nutrients / glucose / water.
    b) E.g. carbon dioxide, urea.
Q2 Some cells are deep within the body so the distance
    between them and the outside environment is too great for
    diffusion to take place quickly. Larger animals have a low
    surface area:volume ratio. This means they don't have a
    large enough area exposed to the environment to be able to
    exchange all the substances they need quickly enough using
    diffusion.

2. The Gaseous Exchange System
Page 61 — Application Questions
Q1 The concentration gradient of oxygen between the alveoli
    and the capillaries will be lower than normal, so the rate of
    diffusion, and therefore gas exchange, will be slower.
Q2 Less air, and so less oxygen, would be inhaled in each
    breath. This means the concentration gradient of oxygen
    between the alveoli and the capillaries will be less steep,
    slowing the rate of diffusion.
Q3 a) The alveoli are enlarged/much larger in the diseased
        lungs than in the healthy lungs.
    b) Having enlarged alveoli means there's a smaller surface
        area for gas exchange, slowing the rate of diffusion of
        oxygen into the blood. So a patient with emphysema
        would have a low level of oxygen in the blood.
    These questions are all asking you to think about factors that
    affect the rate of diffusion across gas exchange surfaces.
    The key things to think about are size of the surface area,
    steepness of the concentration gradients and thickness of
    the exchange surface (or the length of the diffusion pathway).

Page 62 — Fact Recall Questions
Q1 Oxygen diffuses out of the alveoli, across the alveolar
    epithelium and the capillary endothelium, and into
    haemoglobin in the blood.
Q2 The lungs have a large number of alveoli so there is a
    large surface area for gas exchange, which speeds up the
    rate of diffusion. The alveolar epithelium and capillary
    endothelium are only one cell thick, which means there's a
    short diffusion pathway. This speeds up the rate of diffusion
    into the blood. There's also a steep concentration gradient
    of oxygen and carbon dioxide between the alveoli and
    the capillaries, which increases the rate of diffusion. This
    is constantly maintained by the flow of blood and by
    ventilation.
Q3 a) To secrete mucus.
    b) To beat the mucus (plus trapped dust and
        microorganisms) away from the alveoli.
Q4 Elastic fibres help the process of breathing out. On
    breathing in, the lungs inflate and the elastic fibres are
    stretched. The fibres then recoil to help push air out of the
    lungs when exhaling. Elastic fibres are found in the trachea,
    bronchi, bronchioles and alveoli.
Q5 The trachea, bronchi and all but the smallest bronchioles.
Q6 Cartilage in the trachea is found in large C-shaped pieces/
    rings. Cartilage in the bronchi is found in smaller pieces
    and is interspersed with smooth muscle.

3. Breathing
Pages 65-66 — Application Questions
Q1 Accept 0.5 dm³ or 0.55 dm³
Q2 11 breaths per minute
Q3 The air that's breathed out is a mixture of oxygen and carbon dioxide. The carbon dioxide is absorbed by the soda lime and the oxygen gets used up by respiration, so the total volume of gas in the spirometer decreases with time.
Q4 The student's tidal volume has increased from 0.5/0.55 dm³ to 0.7 dm³, and his breathing rate has doubled from 11 breaths per minute to 22 breaths per minute.
Q5 E.g. in the first minute the volume of gas drops from 3.2 dm³ to 2.0 dm³ = **1.2 dm³ / minute**
Here, the oxygen uptake is worked out by using the slope below the trace — but you could have worked it out using the slope above the trace instead.
Q6 That the maximum volume of air he can breathe in or out is 2.85 dm³.

Exam-style Questions — pages 67-68
1 a) i) E.g. simple diffusion across the outer membrane would be too slow *(1 mark)* because multicellular organisms have a low surface area : volume ratio *(1 mark)* and some cells are deep within the body/ too far from the outside environment *(1 mark)*.
       ii) Any two from, e.g. they have many alveoli *(1 mark)* to provide a large surface area for diffusion *(1 mark)*. / The alveolar epithelium and capillary endothelium are each only one cell thick *(1 mark)*, giving a short diffusion pathway *(1 mark)*. / The alveoli have a good blood supply from capillaries *(1 mark)* to maintain the concentration gradients of oxygen and carbon dioxide *(1 mark)*. / The diaphragm and intercostal muscles are involved in ventilation *(1 mark)*, which maintains the concentration gradients of oxygen and carbon dioxide *(1 mark)*. **(Maximum of four marks available.)**
    b) i) E.g. they increase the surface area of the gills *(1 mark)*, which increases the rate of diffusion of oxygen into the gills and carbon dioxide out of the gills *(1 mark)*.
It doesn't matter if you've never come across gaseous exchange in fish before — you know the general adaptations of gaseous exchange surfaces for efficient diffusion, so you just need to apply your knowledge to this particular context.
       ii) Any one from, e.g. the lamellae are very thin *(1 mark)* to provide a short diffusion pathway for oxygen and carbon dioxide *(1 mark)*. / The gills have a good blood supply *(1 mark)* to maintain a steep concentration gradient of oxygen and carbon dioxide *(1 mark)*.
2 a) intercostal *(1 mark)*, contract *(1 mark)*, ribcage *(1 mark)*, volume *(1 mark)*, pressure *(1 mark)*
    b) vital capacity *(1 mark)*
3 a) A person breathes through a tube connected to the oxygen chamber *(1 mark)*. As the person breathes in and out, the lid of the chamber moves up and down *(1 mark)*. These movements are recorded by a pen that writes on a rotating drum, creating a spirometer trace *(1 mark)*.
    b) i) The person breathed out/expired *(1 mark)*.
Watch out here — the spirometer trace shows the volume of gas in the lungs, not the volume of gas in the spirometer. The volume of gas in the lungs will decrease when the person breathes out.

       ii) 14 breaths / minute *(1 mark)*
If the question doesn't tell you what units to give your answer in, just pick sensible ones.
       iii) The trace would slope downwards *(1 mark)*. This is because the volume of gas in the spirometer would decrease over time *(1 mark)*, as oxygen would be used up in respiration *(1 mark)* and carbon dioxide would be absorbed by the soda lime in the spirometer *(1 mark)*.
    c) i) E.g. repeat the measurement several/at least three times and find the mean of the results *(1 mark)*. See if the same measurement could be obtained/ replicated by another observer *(1 mark)*.
There are lots of possible answers here — just use your common sense. (See How Science Works for more on reliability.)
4 a) To beat mucus (plus trapped dust and microorganisms) away from the alveoli *(1 mark)*.
    b) i) Any one from, e.g. to support the trachea *(1 mark)*. / To stop the trachea from collapsing *(1 mark)*.
       ii) the bronchi *(1 mark)*
    c) Any one from, e.g. goblet cells *(1 mark)* — to secrete mucus *(1 mark)*. / Smooth muscle *(1 mark)* — to control the trachea's diameter *(1 mark)*. / Elastic fibres *(1 mark)* — to recoil and push air out of the lungs whilst breathing out/expiring *(1 mark)*.

Section 5 — Transport in Animals

1. The Circulatory System
Page 71 — Fact Recall Questions
Q1 Any two from: multicellular organisms are relatively big. / Multicellular organisms have a low surface area to volume ratio. / A lot of multicellular organisms are very active, so their cells need a constant, rapid supply of glucose and oxygen.
Q2 a) E.g. mammals.
    b) E.g. for mammals: the heart is divided down the middle. The right side of the heart pumps blood to the lungs (to pick up oxygen). From the lungs it travels to the left side of the heart, which pumps it to the rest of the body. When blood returns to the heart, it enters the right side again.
Q3 a) Because blood only passes through the heart once for a complete circuit of the body.
    b) Because blood is enclosed inside blood vessels.
Q4 Because the blood isn't enclosed in blood vessels all the time. Instead it flows freely through the body cavity.

2. Heart Basics
Page 75 — Application Questions
Q1 The left atrium is contracting.
Q2 Closed. The left ventricle is relaxing, so the pressure is higher in the aorta than in the ventricle, forcing the semi-lunar valve shut.
Q3 The left ventricle is relaxing.
Q4 The left atrium is filling up.
At point D, the increase in atrial pressure can't be due to the left atrium contracting because the diagram shows that the left ventricle is relaxing — i.e. the left ventricle doesn't contract next. So you need to think about what happens in the left atrium as the left ventricle is relaxing — it's filling up with blood to prepare for the next atrial contraction.

Q5 Open. The ventricle is relaxing, reducing the pressure in the chamber. The atrium has been filling, increasing the pressure in the chamber. So as the pressure in the atrium becomes higher than that in the ventricle, the atrioventricular valve will open.

Page 75 — Fact Recall Questions
Q1 right side
Q2 a) A — inferior vena cava
    B — left atrium
    C — aorta
    D — right atrium
    E — coronary artery
    F — right ventricle
    G — left ventricle
    H — vena cava
  b) A — pulmonary artery
    B — aorta
    C — inferior vena cava
    D — pulmonary vein
    E — right atrium
    F — semi-lunar valve
    G — right atrioventricular valve
    H — left ventricle
Q3 Because it needs to contract powerfully to pump blood all the way round the body, whereas the right ventricle only pumps blood to the lungs, which are nearby.
Q4 a) semi-lunar valves
  b) They stop blood flowing back into the heart after the ventricles contract.
Q5 An ongoing sequence of contraction and relaxation of the atria and ventricles that keeps blood continuously circulating round the body.
Q6 The volume of the atria decreases and the pressure increases.

3. Electrical Activity of The Heart
Page 79 — Application Questions
Q1 From 1st Q wave to 2nd Q wave:
1.1 − 0.3 = 0.8 s
60 ÷ 0.8 = **75 bpm**
To work out heart rate (in bpm) you need to divide — not multiply — 60 by the length of one heartbeat (in s).
Q2 From 1st Q wave to 2nd Q wave:
1.3 − 0.4 = 0.9 s
60 ÷ 0.9 = **67 bpm**
Q3 ECG B shows a slower heart rate than that of ECG A (67 bpm compared to 75 bpm). ECG B shows a longer interval between contraction of the atria (the P wave) and contraction of the ventricles (QRS complex) than ECG A (about 0.3 s compared to 0.2 s).

Page 79 — Fact Recall Questions
Q1 a) sino-atrial node
  b) It sets the rhythm of the heartbeat by sending regular waves of electrical activity over the atrial walls. This causes the right and left atria to contract at the same time.
Q2 non-conducting collagen tissue
Q3 It conducts waves of electrical activity from the atrioventricular node to the Purkyne tissue.
Q4 It carries the waves of electrical activity into the muscular walls of the right and left ventricles, causing them to contract simultaneously, from the bottom up.
Q5 a) electrocardiogram
  b) E.g. heart problems.

4. Blood Vessels
Page 82 — Application Question
Q1 The water potential of the capillary is higher because there is less albumin in the blood. This means less water is absorbed by osmosis back into the capillary at the vein end of the capillary bed, which leads to an increase in tissue fluid.

Page 82 — Fact Recall Questions
Q1 A — vein, B — capillary, C — artery
Q2 An artery has a thick muscular wall with elastic tissue, and a folded endothelium.
Q3 a) veins
  b) To stop the backflow of blood.
Q4 The fluid that surrounds cells in tissues.
Q5 At the artery end the hydrostatic pressure inside the capillaries is higher than the pressure in the tissue fluid. This means fluid is forced out of the capillaries and into the spaces around the cells, forming tissue fluid.
Q6 lymph vessels
Q7 a) E.g. any two from: blood contains red blood cells, tissue fluid does not. / Blood contains white blood cells, tissue fluid contains very few white blood cells. / Blood contains platelets, tissue fluid usually does not. / Blood contains proteins, tissue fluid contains very few proteins.
  b) E.g. tissue fluid contains very few white blood cells, most white blood cells are in the lymph.

5. Haemoglobin
Page 86 — Application Questions
Q1

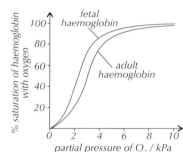

Q2 The dissociation curve for fetal haemoglobin is to the left of the dissociation curve for adult haemoglobin because it has a higher affinity for oxygen than adult haemoglobin. This means fetal haemoglobin takes up oxygen (becomes more saturated) in lower partial pressures of oxygen than adult haemoglobin.
Don't get the dissociation curve for fetal haemoglobin mixed up with a curve showing the Bohr effect, which would be to the right of the normal adult haemoglobin dissociation curve.

Page 86 — Fact Recall Questions
Q1 in red blood cells
Q2 oxyhaemoglobin
Q3 It's the tendency of haemoglobin to bind with oxygen.
Q4 In the alveoli / lungs. This is the site where oxygen first enters the blood so it has the highest concentration of oxygen.
Q5 How saturated haemoglobin is with oxygen at any given partial pressure.
Q6 More oxygen is available to cells during activity.
Q7 It would shift the oxygen dissociation curve right.
Q8 carbonic anhydrase

Q9 a) It splits up to give hydrogen ions and hydrogencarbonate ions.

b) The increase in hydrogen ions causes oxyhaemoglobin to unload its oxygen so that haemoglobin can take up the hydrogen ions.

Exam-style Questions — pages 88-89

1 a) The semi-lunar valves are open *(1 mark)* so the pressure must be higher in the ventricles than the pulmonary artery/aorta *(1 mark)*. This means the blood is moving (from the ventricles) into the pulmonary artery/aorta *(1 mark)*.

If you get a diagram of the heart in your exam that looks a bit different from this, just look to see where the valves are and whether they're open or closed — then you should be able to answer the question.

b) Atrioventricular valves / AV valves *(1 mark)*. They prevent the back-flow of blood into the atria when the ventricles contract *(1 mark)*.

c) i) The ventricle wall should be drawn thicker than the atrium wall, e.g:

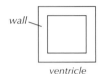

wall

ventricle

(1 mark)

ii) The ventricles have thicker walls than the atria because they have to push blood out of the heart to the lungs or around the body *(1 mark)*, whereas the atria just need to push blood a short distance into the ventricles *(1 mark)*.

2 a) B. During the bike ride the man's respiration rate would have increased, raising the pCO_2 *(1 mark)*. This would have increased the rate of oxygen unloading *(1 mark)*, so the dissociation curve would have shifted to the right *(1 mark)*.

b) i) The Bohr effect *(1 mark)*.

ii) Most of the CO_2 from respiring tissues diffuses into red blood cells and is converted to carbonic acid *(1 mark)* by the enzyme carbonic anhydrase *(1 mark)*. The carbonic acid splits up to give hydrogen ions and hydrogencarbonate ions *(1 mark)*. This increase in hydrogen ions causes oxyhaemoglobin to unload its oxygen *(1 mark)* so that haemoglobin can take up the hydrogen ions *(1 mark)*, forming a compound called haemoglobinic acid *(1 mark)*.

3 a) AVN — B *(1 mark)*, right ventricle — F *(1 mark)*, pulmonary vein — D *(1 mark)*

b) It prevents the waves of electrical activity from being passed directly from the atria to the ventricles *(1 mark)*.

c) There must be a delay so that the atria empty *(1 mark)* before the ventricles contract *(1 mark)*.

To get both marks you need to make two points. It's not enough just to say that there's a delay for the atria to empty, you need to give a full answer.

d) The atrioventricular valve/AVN passes the waves of electrical activity onto the bundle of His *(1 mark)*. The bundle of His conducts the waves of electrical activity to the Purkyne tissue *(1 mark)*. The Purkyne tissue carries the waves of electrical activity into the muscular walls of the right and left ventricles *(1 mark)*. *(1 mark for two of the following spelt correctly: bundle of His, Purkyne tissue, ventricles.)*

4 a) i) X *(1 mark)* because it's an artery *(1 mark)*.

As the blood travels round the circulatory system the pressure of the blood gradually decreases and it is returned to the heart at low pressure via the veins.

ii) E.g. vessel Y contains valves, vessel X doesn't *(1 mark)*. Vessel X contains more elastic tissue than vessel Y *(1 mark)*. Vessel X contains a thicker muscle layer than vessel Y *(1 mark)*.

b) At the start of the capillary bed the (hydrostatic) pressure inside the capillaries is higher than the pressure in the tissue fluid *(1 mark)*. The difference in pressure forces fluid out of the capillaries and into the spaces around the cells, forming tissue fluid *(1 mark)*.

c) E.g. blood contains red blood cells, lymph doesn't *(1 mark)*. Blood contains platelets, lymph doesn't *(1 mark)*.

Section 6 — Transport in Plants

1. Xylem and Phloem

Page 92 — Application Questions

Q1 a) phloem

b) xylem

Q2 a) sieve plate

b) Pit — it allows water and mineral ions to move into and out of the xylem vessels.

Page 92 — Fact Recall Questions

Q1 It would be too slow because plants are multicellular, so have a small surface area to volume ratio.

Q2

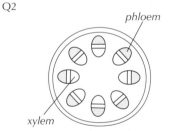

phloem

xylem

If you're drawing both the xylem and the phloem on a diagram remember to label them, so that the examiner knows which is which.

Q3 A — phloem
B — xylem
C — vein

Q4 water and mineral ions
Remember, xylem vessels don't just transport water, they transport mineral ions too.

Q5 lignin

Q6 Via pits in the xylem vessel walls.

Q7 Sucrose/sugars.

Q8 a) living cells

b) Any two from, e.g. they contain a very thin layer of cytoplasm. / They have no nucleus. / They have few organelles.

2. Water Transport
Page 95 — Application Questions
Q1   root hair (cell)
Q2   C
Q3   Casparian strip
Q4   Structure E is the xylem, used to transport water (and mineral ions) to all parts of the plant. If the xylem is blocked some plant cells won't receive enough water and the plant may wilt.

Page 95 — Fact Recall Questions
Q1   Water enters the root from the soil through the root hair cells. It then passes through the cortex, including the endodermis, before it reaches the xylem.
Q2   In the symplast pathway, water moves through the cytoplasm in the root to the xylem. Plasmodesmata connect the cytoplasm of neighbouring cells. In the apoplast pathway water moves through the cell walls of the root. Water diffuses through the cell walls and passes through the spaces between them. However, the apoplast pathway is blocked at the endodermis cell layer by a waxy strip in the cell walls called the Casparian strip. The water then has to take the symplast pathway until it reaches the xylem.
   Be careful not to get the symplast and apoplast pathways mixed up — in the symplast pathway water moves through the cytoplasm.
Q3   The loss of water vapour from a plant's surface/leaves. / The evaporation of water from a plant's surface/leaves.
Q4   The movement of water from a plant's roots to its leaves.
Q5   Adhesion is where water molecules are attracted to the walls of the xylem vessels. It helps water rise up through the xylem vessels.

3. Transpiration
Page 98 — Application Questions
Q1   B. E.g. there is a layer of hairs on the epidermis, which traps moist air around the stomata, reducing the water potential gradient between the leaf and the air, and slowing transpiration down. / The stomata are sunken in pits, which trap water vapour, reducing transpiration by lowering the water potential gradient. / The leaf is curled, which traps moist air. This reduces the water potential gradient between the leaf and the air, slowing down transpiration. This also lowers the exposed surface area for losing water and protects the stomata from wind.
Q2   a) 10 °C — $(15 + 12 + 14) \div 3$ =**13.7 mm**
         20 °C — $(19 + 16 + 19) \div 3$ = **18.0 mm**
         30 °C — $(25 + 22 + 23) \div 3$ = **23.3 mm**
   b) See graph below. The bubble would move approximately 21 mm in 10 minutes at 25 °C.

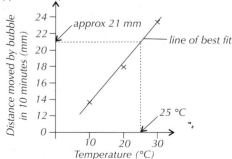

c)
As the temperature increased, the distance moved by the bubble in 10 minutes increased too. This means the rate of transpiration increased with increasing temperatures. At higher temperatures water molecules have more energy so they evaporate from the cells inside the leaf faster. This increases the water potential between the inside and outside of the leaf, making water diffuse out of the leaf faster.

Page 98 — Fact Recall Questions
Q1   gas exchange/photosynthesis
Q2   An increase in wind increases transpiration rate. Lots of air movement blows away water molecules from around the stomata. This increases the water potential gradient, which increases the rate of transpiration.
Q3   E.g. light, temperature and humidity.
Q4   That water uptake by a plant is directly related to water loss by the leaves.

4. Translocation
Page 101 — Application Questions
Q1   E.g. meristems / leaves.
Q2   a) At the roots active transport is used to actively load assimilates into the sieve tubes. This lowers the water potential inside the sieve tubes, so water enters the tubes by osmosis.
    Remember, water always flows from a higher water potential to a lower water potential.
   b) At the sink assimilates are removed from the phloem to be used up. This increases the water potential inside the sieve tubes, so water leaves the tubes by osmosis.

Page 101 — Fact Recall Questions
Q1   It's the movement of dissolved substances/assimilates to where they're needed in a plant.
Q2   In a plant a source is where assimilates/sugars are made, whereas a sink is where assimilates/sugars are used up.
Q3   E.g. If you remove a ring of bark from a woody stem a bulge forms above the ring. If you analyse the fluid from the bulge, you'll find it has a higher concentration of sugars than the fluid from below the ring. This is because the sugars can't move past the area where the bark has been removed — this is evidence that there's a downward flow of sugars.
Q4   Sugar travels to many different sinks, not just to the one with the highest water potential, as the model would suggest. / The sieve plates would create a barrier to mass flow. A lot of pressure would be needed for the dissolved substances to get through at a reasonable rate.

Exam-style Questions — pages 103-104
1   a) i)   Reading off graph, distance moved by bubble in 5 minutes at 1.5 arbitrary units of light intensity = 15 mm
            $15 \div 5 = $ **3 mm/min**
            (2 marks for the correct answer, otherwise 1 mark for showing a calculation of 'distance ÷ time')
      ii)   The greater the light intensity, the greater the distance moved by the bubble in 5 minutes ***(1 mark)***. This means the greater the light intensity, the greater the transpiration rate ***(1 mark)***. This is because the lighter it gets, the wider stomata open ***(1 mark)***.
      iii) E.g. the experiment should be repeated with a light intensity of zero ***(1 mark)***.

b) E.g. when the stomata in a plant open to let carbon dioxide in / when stomata open for gas exchange *(1 mark)* this lets water move out down its water potential gradient *(1 mark)*.

2 a) i) Sieve plate *(1 mark)* — it allows sugars to pass from one sieve tube element to another / it connects cell cytoplasms *(1 mark)*.
   ii) Cell B/the companion cell carries out the living functions for both itself and its sieve tube element *(1 mark)* because the sieve tube element can't survive on its own, e.g. it has no nucleus *(1 mark)*.
   b) *Maximum of 6 marks available:* E.g. active transport is used to actively load the sucrose into the sieve tubes of the phloem at the leaves *(1 mark)*. This lowers the water potential inside the sieve tubes, so water enters the tubes by osmosis *(1 mark)*. This creates a high pressure inside the sieve tubes at the source end of the phloem *(1 mark)*. At the meristems, sucrose is removed from the phloem to be used up *(1 mark)*. This increases the water potential inside the sieve tubes, so water also leaves the tubes by osmosis *(1 mark)*. This lowers the pressure inside the sieve tubes *(1 mark)*. The result is a pressure gradient from the leaves to the meristems *(1 mark)*. This gradient pushes sucrose along the sieve tubes to where it's needed/the meristems *(1 mark)*.

3 a) i) X — xylem *(1 mark)*
      Y — endodermis *(1 mark)*
   ii) The water moves through the apoplast pathway *(1 mark)* until it is blocked by the Casparian strip in the endodermis layer/layer Y *(1 mark)*. Then the water moves through the symplast pathway to the xylem *(1 mark)*.
   Make sure you look carefully at the diagram to work out which part of the cell water is moving through, i.e. is the water moving through the cell wall or the cytoplasm?
   b) Water evaporates from the leaves at the top of the xylem *(1 mark)*. This creates tension which pulls more water into the leaves *(1 mark)*. Water molecules are cohesive so then a whole column of water moves up the xylem *(1 mark)*. Water then enters the stem through the roots *(1 mark)*.
   c) Slower. With more water in the air the water potential gradient between the air and the leaf would be lower *(1 mark)* which would decrease transpiration *(1 mark)*.
   d) The transpiration rate increases during the summer because temperatures are higher during the summer *(1 mark)*. This means water molecules have more energy *(1 mark)* so they evaporate from the cells inside the leaf faster *(1 mark)*. This increases the water potential gradient between the inside and outside of the leaf, making water diffuse out of the leaf faster *(1 mark)*. *(1 mark for two of the following spelled correctly: evaporate, water potential gradient, diffuse.)*

4 Spines — these reduce the surface area for water loss *(1 mark)*.
   Curled leaves — these trap moist air, slowing down transpiration *(1 mark)*.
   Reduced number of stomata — there are fewer places where water vapour can diffuse out of the leaf *(1 mark)*.
   Thick, waxy layer on the epidermis — this reduces water loss by evaporation because the layer is waterproof *(1 mark)*.

Unit 2

Section 1 — Biological Molecules

1. Water

Page 107 — Fact Recall Questions
Q1 Any three from: e.g. it is a reactant in lots of chemical reactions. / It transports substances. / It helps with temperature control. / It is a habitat.
Q2 Because it has a slight negative charge on one side and a slight positive charge on the other.
Q3

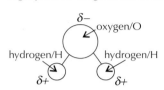

Q4 A weak bond between a slightly positively charged hydrogen atom in one molecule and a slightly negatively charged atom in another molecule.
Q5 E.g.

When drawing a hydrogen bond between two water molecules, make sure you draw it between one hydrogen atom and one oxygen atom.
Q6 Because when water is heated, a lot of the heat energy is used to break the hydrogen bonds between water molecules. This means there is less heat energy available to actually increase the temperature of the water.
Q7 Because it has a high latent heat of evaporation, which means it carries away a lot of heat energy when it evaporates from a surface. This cools the surface and helps to lower the temperature.
Q8 It makes water very cohesive and a good solvent.
Q9 a) B, e.g. because the water molecules are being held further apart in diagram B.
   b) In cold temperatures ice forms an insulating layer on top of water. This means the organisms that live in the water below do not freeze and can still move around.
Q10 The slightly negatively charged ends of the water molecules will be attracted to the positive ion, meaning the positive ion will get surrounded by water molecules.

2. Proteins

Page 109 — Application Questions
Q1 a) E.g.

b) E.g.

c) E.g.

Q2

Page 111 — Fact Recall Questions
Q1 amino acids
Q2 A chain of more than two amino acids joined together.
Q3

You could have drawn your amino group like this;

or your carboxyl group like this;

Both ways are fine and would get you marks in the exam.

Q4 a) condensation
   b) hydrolysis
Q5 peptide
Q6 Hydrogen bonds form between the –NH and –CO groups of the amino acids in the chain. This makes it automatically coil into an alpha helix or beta pleated sheet.
   Don't get the secondary structure of a protein confused with the tertiary structure or quaternary structure. In the tertiary structure, hydrogen bonds form between some of the R groups on the polypeptide chain. In the quaternary structure, hydrogen bonds may form between different polypeptide chains.
Q7 a) tertiary
   b) A — hydrogen bond, B — ionic interaction, C — disulfide bond
   c) When two molecules of the amino acid cysteine come close together, the sulfur atom in one cysteine bonds to the sulfur in the other cysteine.
Q8 It is the way two or more polypeptide chains of a protein are assembled together.
Q9 Haemoglobin is made up of four polypeptide chains — two α chains and two β chains. Each polypeptide chain has a prosthetic group, which is a haem group. Each haem group contains an iron (Fe^{2+}) ion.
Q10 It forms supportive tissue in animals.
Q11 The globular structure of haemoglobin mean that the hydrophilic side chains are on the outside of the molecule and the hydrophobic side chains face inwards. This makes haemoglobin soluble in water, which makes it good for transporting oxygen in the blood.

3. Carbohydrates
Page 113 — Application Questions
Q1 a)

This diagram looks a bit different from other disaccharide diagrams. It's because the OH group needed to form the glycosidic bond is at the top of the galactose molecule rather than the bottom.
   b)

Q2 a)

   b)

Page 114 — Fact Recall Questions
Q1 a)

   b)

Be careful when drawing alpha glucose or beta glucose — it's only the groups on the right-hand side of the molecule that are different between the two types of glucose.
Q2 glycosidic
   There are lots of words similar to 'glycosidic' in biology so make sure you spell it right — you might not get the mark in the exam if you don't.
Q3 a) starch
   b) glycogen
Q4 a) insoluble
   b) It doesn't cause water to enter cells by osmosis, which would make them swell.
Q5 a) A — amylopectin, B — amylose
   b) It has lots of side branches, which means the enzymes that break amylopectin down can get to the glycosidic bonds easily. This means glucose can be released quickly when it is needed.

Q6 Glycogen is made from long, branched chains of α-glucose. It has lots of side branches which means that stored glucose can be released quickly. It's a very compact molecule which makes it good for storage.

Q7 a) cellulose
b) Cellulose is made from long, unbranched chains of β-glucose. These are joined by hydrogen bonds to form microfibrils. Microfibrils are very strong, which means they provide support/strength/rigidity in a cell wall.

Q8
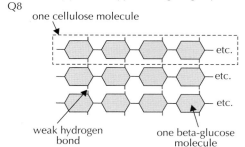
one cellulose molecule

etc.

etc.

etc.

weak hydrogen bond

one beta-glucose molecule

4. Lipids

Page 117 — Fact Recall Questions

Q1 A molecule of glycerol and three fatty acids.
Q2 A saturated fatty acid doesn't have any double bonds between its carbon atoms, an unsaturated fatty acid does.
Q3 A — phosphate group, B — glycerol, C — ester bond, D — fatty acid/hydrocarbon tail
Q4 It has a hydrocarbon ring structure attached to a hydrocarbon tail. The hydrocarbon ring has a polar hydroxyl group attached to it.
Q5 Because they contain lots of chemical energy and they're insoluble.
Q6 a) They make up the bilayer of cell membranes, which controls what enters and leaves a cell.
b) Phospholipid heads are hydrophilic and their tails are hydrophobic, so they form a double layer with their heads facing out towards the water on either side. The centre of the bilayer is hydrophobic, so water-soluble substances can't easily pass through it.
Q7 a) In between the phospholipid molecules.
b) They help to strengthen the cell membrane by making it less fluid and more rigid.

5. Biochemical Tests for Molecules

Page 118 — Application Questions

Q1 Orange juice and goat's milk.
Q2 As a control.
Q3 a) The liquid needs to be alkaline for the test to work.
b) Not added any sodium hydroxide solution. / Not added a high enough concentration of sodium hydroxide solution.

Page 120 — Application Question

Q1 Test 1 — no reducing sugars present, but non-reducing sugars might be present.
Test 2 — non-reducing sugars are present, but reducing sugars are not.
Test 3 — no sugars are present.
Test 4 — reducing sugars are present.

These tests are quite tricky. Think carefully about what sugars have been tested for and what the different colours of the results indicate. Remember that a negative result for a reducing sugar test doesn't rule out non-reducing sugars.

Page 122 — Fact Recall Questions

Q1 a) sodium hydroxide solution
b) copper(II) sulfate solution
c) It would be purple.
Q2 Add Benedict's reagent to a test sample and heat it. Look at the colour of the sample for the result. A positive result would be coloured green, yellow, orange or brick red and a negative result would be blue.
Q3 a) A device that measures the strength of a coloured solution by seeing how much light passes through it.
b) Carry out the Benedict's test on the unknown solution. Remove the precipitate from the solution and use a colorimeter with a red filter to measure the absorbance of the Benedict's solution remaining in the tube. Finally using the calibration curve, read off an estimate for the glucose concentration of the sample.
Make sure you're clear about what goes into the colorimeter — it's what's left in the tube after the precipitate has been removed, not the precipitate itself.
Q4 iodine test

Exam-style Questions — pages 123-124

1 a)

	Observation	Starch present
Plant A	dark, blue-black colour	Yes
Plant B	browny-orange colour	No

(1 mark for each correct answer)

Make sure you emphasise that a positive result would be a dark colour — you won't get a mark in the exam if you just say it turns blue.

b) i) amylopectin *(1 mark)*
ii) Amylose is a long, unbranched chain of α-glucose *(1 mark)*. It has a coiled structure/cylindrical shape *(1 mark)*. These features make it compact meaning it's good for storage *(1 mark)*.
c) i) Any three from: e.g. starch is used to store energy whereas cellulose is used to strengthen cell walls. / Starch is made from α-glucose whereas cellulose is made from β-glucose. / Starch has a compact shape whereas cellulose is a long, straight molecule. / The bonds between the glucose molecules in starch (amylose) are angled whereas the bonds between glucose molecules in cellulose are straight *(3 marks for 3 correct answers)*.
ii)

(1 mark)

You have to flip the glucose molecule on the right-hand side, so that the −OH groups of both glucose molecules are close together — this is where the glycosidic bond forms and a molecule of water is lost.

iii) During hydrolysis reactions *(1 mark)* molecules of water *(1 mark)* break apart the glycosidic bonds *(1 mark)*.

2 a) Shake the liquidised food sample with ethanol for about a minute *(1 mark)* then pour the solution into water *(1 mark)*. Any lipid will show up as a milky emulsion *(1 mark)*.

b) i) E.g. triglycerides are made up of fatty acid molecules with hydrocarbon tails *(1 mark)*, which contain lots of chemical energy *(1 mark)*, making triglycerides good energy storage molecules *(1 mark)*. / The fatty acid tails of triglycerides are hydrophobic *(1 mark)*, which means triglycerides are insoluble *(1 mark)*, making them good energy storage molecules *(1 mark)*. Phospholipids have hydrophilic heads and hydrophobic tails *(1 mark)*, which make up the bilayer of cell membranes *(1 mark)*. The centre of the bilayer is hydrophobic *(1 mark)*, so the membrane acts as a barrier to water-soluble substances *(1 mark)*.
Cholesterol molecules are small and flat *(1 mark)*, so they can interact with the phospholipid bilayer and strengthen the cell membrane *(1 mark)*.
(Maximum of 6 marks from above, plus an extra mark for any 2 complete sentences that link structure to function.)

ii) Cholesterol is soluble in water because it contains a hydroxyl (-OH) group *(1 mark)*, which can form hydrogen bonds with water molecules *(1 mark)*.

3 a) It is the sequence of amino acids in the polypeptide chain *(1 mark)* joined together with peptide bonds *(1 mark)*.

b) ionic *(1 mark)*, cysteine *(1 mark)*, disulfide *(1 mark)*, hydrogen *(1 mark)*, positively *(1 mark)*, negatively *(1 mark)*

c) E.g.

Collagen	Haemoglobin
fibrous protein	**globular protein**
3 polypeptide chains	**4 polypeptide chains**
no haem groups	**haem groups present**

(1 mark per correct row)
When filling in a comparison table like this the statements on each row must be about the same thing, e.g. number of polypeptide chains. You won't get a mark if a row contains two statements that can't be compared.

d) Add a few drops of sodium hydroxide solution to the test sample *(1 mark)*. Then add some copper(II) sulfate solution *(1 mark)*. If protein is present, the solution will turn purple *(1 mark)*. If there's no protein present, the solution will stay blue *(1 mark)*.

Section 2 — Nucleic Acids

1. DNA and RNA

Page 126 — Application Questions
Q1 a) TGACAGCATCAGCTACGAT
b) ACGTGGTACACCATTTAGC
Q2 a) 22
b) 12
c) 12
If there are 34 base pairs in total and 22 of them contain adenine, then the other 12 must contain both cytosine and guanine — it's all to do with complementary base pairing.

Page 127 — Fact Recall Questions
Q1 A = phosphate group, B = deoxyribose (sugar), C = (nitrogenous) base
Q2 adenine, guanine
Q3 Two DNA polynucleotide strands join together by hydrogen bonding between complementary base pairs — A with T and G with C. The antiparallel strands then twist round each other to form the DNA double-helix.

Q4 B/the sugar would be ribose rather than deoxyribose.
Q5 cytosine, uracil
Remember, uracil replaces thymine as a pyrimidine base in RNA.

2. DNA Replication
Page 129 — Application Questions
Q1

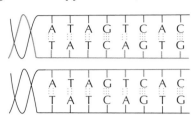

In semi-conservative replication of DNA, each of the new pieces of DNA contains a strand from the original molecule (shown in black in the diagram) and a new strand (green in the diagram).

Q2 a) Because the bases in DNA nucleotides contain nitrogen.
b) i) It's where half of the new molecules of DNA are from the original piece of DNA.
ii) In the bacteria that were grown in heavy nitrogen broth then light nitrogen broth, each DNA molecule contained 50% heavy nitrogen and 50% light nitrogen. This suggests that half of the new strands are from the original heavy nitrogen DNA.
c) It means that the original DNA strand can act as a template for the new strand — free-floating DNA nucleotides can join up with exposed bases on the original strand by complementary base pairing.
d) E.g they could have controlled all the variables, e.g. the other nutrients in the broth. / They could have used a control experiment, e.g. bacteria grown in broth without any nitrogen. / They could have repeated the experiment several times and taken an average of the results. / They could have used a large sample size of bacteria.
If you get a question like this in the exam, try to give specific suggestions about how the results you're being asked about could be made reliable — don't just talk about ways of improving reliability in general.

Page 129 — Fact Recall Questions
Q1 hydrogen bonds
Q2 It joins nucleotides on the new DNA strand together.

3. Protein Synthesis
Page 131 — Application Questions
Q1 a) CATAGACATGGCTGCAGATACTACGGCAGA
b) Gly-Tyr-Gly-His-Arg-Arg-Cys-Tyr-His
Q2 a) i) White
ii) Pink
b) It could change the amino acid sequence of the protein, meaning that the protein does not fold up properly. This could make the enzyme's active site the wrong shape, making the enzyme non-functional.

Exam-style Questions — page 132
1 a) Deoxyribose sugar *(1 mark)*, a phosphate group *(1 mark)* and a (nitrogenous) base *(1 mark)*.
b) i) The DNA will lose its double helix structure/the two DNA strands will unravel *(1 mark)*. This is because the double helix/two DNA strands are held together by hydrogen bonding between the base pairs *(1 mark)*.

ii) adenine *(1 mark)*, guanine *(1 mark)*

If you get a question in the exam that says, 'Name two...' don't hedge your bets and write down three or four possible answers — any wrong answers will cancel out the correct answers and you won't pick up any marks at all.

c) i) unzips *(1 mark)*, template *(1 mark)*, complementary *(1 mark)*, adenine *(1 mark)*, DNA polymerase *(1 mark)*

ii) semi-conservative replication *(1 mark)*

2 a) The sugar in RNA is ribose not deoxyribose *(1 mark)*. Uracil replaces thymine as a base in RNA *(1 mark)*. RNA is usually single-stranded as opposed to double-stranded *(1 mark)*.

b) mRNA carries a complementary copy of a gene/section of DNA *(1 mark)* out of the nucleus to the ribosomes (in the cytoplasm) *(1 mark)*.

c) i) A sequence of DNA nucelotides that codes for a protein/polypeptide *(1 mark)*.

ii) E.g if the sequence of DNA nucleotides changes, it could affect the amino acid sequence *(1 mark)*. This could mean the protein does not fold up properly/ its 3D shape changes *(1 mark)*. This could mean a different/non-functional protein is produced *(1 mark)*.

Section 3 — Enzymes
1. Action of Enzymes
Page 135 — Fact Recall Questions
Q1 A substance that speeds up a chemical reaction without being used up in the reaction itself.

Q2 a) intracellular
b) extracellular
Remember, intracellular enzymes are found inside cells, so extracellular enzymes are found outside cells.

Q3 The enzyme's tertiary structure.

Q4 An enzyme-substrate complex.

Q5 An enzyme can only bind with a substrate that has a complementary shape to its active site.

Q6 a) B
b) The activation energy needed for the reaction with the presence of an enzyme.

Q7 Activation energy is needed to start a chemical reaction. The activation energy is often provided as heat. With the presence of an enzyme, the activation energy required to start a reaction is lowered. Therefore not as much heat is needed, so the reaction can take place at lower temperatures than it could do without an enzyme.

Q8 The substrate has a complementary shape to the active site. This means they fit together the same way that a key fits into a lock. They form an enzyme-substrate complex and catalyse the reaction.

Q9 In the 'lock and key' model the active site has a fixed shape that is complementary to the substrate, but in the 'induced fit' model the substrate has to make the active site change shape slightly to allow the substrate to bind tightly.

2. Factors Affecting Enzyme Activity
Page 138 — Application Questions
Q1 a) i) C — the enzyme is still active at 80 °C. This means the bacteria can live at very high temperatures and therefore is hyperthermophillic.

ii) A — the enzyme is active at temperatures between 0 and 17 °C. This means the bacteria can live at very cold temperatures, so is psychrotropic.

b) A — There would be no enzyme activity at all as the enzyme would be denatured at temperatures over 17 °C.
B — There would be some enzyme activity but the rate of reaction would gradually decrease until temperatures of around 70 °C were reached. At this point the enzyme would be denatured and there would be no further enzyme activity at higher temperatures.
C — There would be an increasing amount of enzyme activity. The rate of reaction would gradually increase as the temperature increased.

Q2 a) A — The rate of reaction is higher in relation to the hydrogen peroxide concentration. This is because there are more catalase molecules present, which means the hydrogen peroxide molecules will collide more frequently with the active sites.

b) The curves flatten out at the saturation point. All the active sites are full, so increasing the hydrogen peroxide concentration won't increase the rate of reaction any further.

Page 139 — Application Questions
Q1 Any one from: e.g. the rate at which galactose is produced. / The rate at which glucose is produced. / The rate at which lactose is used up/disappears.

Q2 Any three from: e.g. temperature / pH / volume of solution / lactose concentration.

Q3 E.g. measure the rate of the reaction using sterile water with no lactase/enzyme present.
If you've struggled with any of these questions it might help to take a look back at the How Science Works section.

Page 139 — Fact Recall Questions
Q1 At higher temperatures there is more kinetic energy, so molecules move faster. This makes the substrate molecules more likely to collide with the enzymes' active sites. The energy of these collisions also increases, which means each collision is more likely to result in a reaction.

Q2 A very high temperature makes the enzyme's molecules vibrate more. This vibration breaks some of the bonds/ hydrogen bonds and ionic bonds that hold the enzyme in shape. The active site changes shape and the enzyme and substrate no longer fit together. The enzyme is denatured.

Q3 e.g. pH

Q4 At first, increasing the enzyme concentration increases the rate of the reaction. This is because the more enzyme molecules there are in a solution, the more likely a substrate molecule is to collide with an active site and form an enzyme-substrate complex. The rate of reaction continues to increase until the substrate concentration becomes a limiting factor. At this point the rate of the reaction levels off.

Q5 The rate of reaction stays constant. All active sites are occupied so increasing the substrate concentration has no effect.

3. Cofactors and Inhibitors
Page 142 — Application Questions
Q1 a) Ethanol has a similar shape to methanol. This means it will act as a competitive inhibitor, binding to the active site of alcohol dehydrogenase and blocking methanol molecules. This means lower levels of methanol will be hydrolysed so the toxic product (formaldehyde) won't build up to fatal levels.

b)

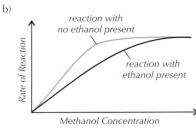

reaction with
no ethanol present

Rate of Reaction

reaction with
ethanol present

Methanol Concentration

Your curve should be lower than the rate of reaction without
any ethanol present. The reaction won't stop completely as
some of the methanol molecules will still bind with the active
sites. The plateau should be later as the reaction won't reach
its maximum rate until the methanol concentration is much
higher. The curve should start at zero.

Q2 a) A non-competitive inhibitor, because it binds to the
enzyme away from the active site.
b) The rate of the reaction decreases because there are
more inhibitor molecules present, which bind to
glycogen phosphorylase molecules and alter the shape of
their active sites. This means there are fewer active sites
in the solution able to bind with glycogen, so the rate of
the reaction slows down.
c) i) B. Increasing the concentration of the substrate
won't make any difference to the rate of the reaction
as enzyme activity will still be inhibited.
ii) A. Increasing the concentration of the enzyme will
mean there are more active sites available for the
substrate so the rate of the reaction increases.

Pages 142-143 — Fact Recall Questions

Q1 A non-protein substance that binds to an enzyme and
activates it.
Q2 The coenzyme is used by an enzyme and is changed during
the reaction. A second enzyme then uses the changed
coenzyme. During this reaction the coenzyme is changed
back to its original form.
Q3 a) Away from the active site.
b) At the active site.
Q4 A non-competitive inhibitor molecule binds to the enzyme
away from the active site. Its presence alters the shape of
the active site meaning that substrate molecules can no
longer bind here. This prevents enzyme activity.
Q5 a) Weak, hydrogen or ionic bonds.
b) Strong, covalent bonds.
Q6 E.g. cyanide is an non-competitive inhibitor of cytochrome c
oxidase. Cyanide molecules bind to cytochrome c oxidase
away from the active site. This causes the active site to
change shape so the substrate molecules can no longer
bind to it. / Malonate is a competitive inhibitor of succinate
dehydrogenase. Malonate molecules have a similar
shape to the substrate, so they compete with the substrate
molecules to bind to succinate dehydrogenase's active site.
They block the active site, so no substrate molecules can
fit in it. / Arsenic is a non-competitive inhibitor of pyruvate
dehydrogenase. Arsenic molecules bind to pyruvate
dehydrogenase away from the active site. This causes the
active site to change shape so the substrate molecules can
no longer bind to it.
Don't fret if you've given a different example of a poison here.
Just make sure when you mark it that it's spelt correctly and
that you've clearly described how it works.

Exam-style Questions — pages 144-145

1 a) i) They lower it (1 mark).
ii) In synthesis reactions, attaching to the enzyme holds
the substrate molecules close together, reducing any
repulsion between them (1 mark). In breakdown
reactions, fitting into an enzyme's active site puts a
strain on the bond in the substrate, causing it to break
more easily (1 mark).
b) i) Catechol and oxygen have a complementary shape
to catecholase's active site (1 mark) so they bind to
the enzyme's active site to form an enzyme-substrate
complex (1 mark). Catechol and oxygen cause
the active site to change shape slightly (1 mark) so
they bind more tightly to the enzyme (1 mark). The
enzyme-product complex is formed (1 mark) and
then benzoquinone and water are released from
catecholase (1 mark).
(1 mark for either linking the complementary
shapes of the active site and the substrates with the
formation of an enzyme-substrate complex, or for
linking the change in the shape of the active site to
the substrates binding more easily to the enzyme).
ii) The 'lock and key' model (1 mark). In this model the
active site does not change shape (1 mark).
c) In a fridge. At cooler temperatures the catechol, oxygen
and catecholase molecules have less kinetic energy than
they would at room temperature (1 mark). This makes
the substrate molecules/catechol and oxygen less likely
to collide with the catecholase active sites (1 mark).
Also, the energy of the collisions is lower, meaning each
collision is less likely to result in a reaction (1 mark).
Therefore, in a fridge the rate of the reaction would be
lower/benzoquinone would be produced more slowly,
so the apple would brown more slowly (1 mark). Accept
reverse theory, i.e. more kinetic energy at higher
temperatures.
d) i) Copper is an inorganic cofactor (1 mark) which
binds to catecholase (1 mark) and helps it form an
enzyme-substrate complex with catechol and oxygen
more easily (1 mark).
Even though the question doesn't tell you what type of
cofactor copper is, you can work out that it must be inorganic
because copper is a metal.
ii) E.g. inorganic cofactors don't directly participate
in the reaction but organic cofactors do (1 mark).
Inorganic cofactors aren't used up or changed during
the reaction but organic factors are changed/recycled
(1 mark).
e) E.g. there would be less copper to bind to catecholase
(1 mark) so fewer enzyme molecules would be able to
form enzyme-substrate complexes (1 mark). This would
decrease the rate of the reaction, slowing the browning
of the apple (1 mark).
2 a) i) (1 mark for a value between pH 4 and pH 5)
ii) pH 1 and pH 9 (1 mark). There is no reaction at
these pH levels (1 mark).
iii) The H+ and OH- ions found in acids and alkalis
can break the weak ionic bonds/hydrogen bonds
that hold the enzyme's tertiary structure in place
(1 mark). This changes the shape of the active site
(1 mark) so it is no longer complementary in shape
to the substrate/will not bind to the substrate to
catalyse the reaction (1 mark).
Remember, it's the change in shape of the active site that
means the reaction can't be catalysed.
iv) E.g. temperature (1 mark) and substrate
concentration (1 mark).

b) i) A. The rate at which diglycerides and fatty acids are produced/the reaction rate is higher without the presence of orlistat *(1 mark)*.
   ii) Molecules of orlistat have a similar shape to triglycerides *(1 mark)*. They bind to the active sites of gastric lipase and block the entry of triglycerides *(1 mark)*. This means the reaction that produces diglycerides and fatty acids can't take place as quickly *(1 mark)*.

Section 4 — Diet and Food Production

1. A Balanced Diet
Page 148 — Application Questions
Q1 Person A — BMI = $110 \div 1.58^2 = 110 \div 2.5 = $ **44.0**
Person B — BMI = $53 \div 1.54^2 = 53 \div 2.37 = $ **22.4**
Person C — BMI = $95 \div 1.62^2 = 95 \div 2.62 = $ **36.3**
Even if a calculation looks simple, take your time — it's easy to make a mistake if you rush.
Q2 Person A, Person C
Q3 No, because their BMI doesn't take into account the additional weight caused by being pregnant.

Page 149 — Application Questions
Q1 Person 1. They have the highest level of LDLs at 4.9 mmol/L, which increase blood cholesterol level, and the lowest level of HDLs at 1.0 mmol/L, which lower blood cholesterol level. This suggests Person 1 has the highest blood cholesterol level. High blood cholesterol increases the build up of fatty deposits/atheromas in the artery walls at places where they've been damaged. This can cause atherosclerosis and lead to CHD.
Q2 a) E.g. eat less saturated fat because saturated fat raises LDL level and Person 2's LDL level (3.5 mmol/L) is above the desirable level (≤ 3 mmol/L). Eat more polyunsaturated fat because polyunsaturated fat raises HDL level and Person 2's HDL level (1.0 mmol/L) is below the desirable level (≥ 1.2 mmol/L).
   b) Effect of statins: 3.5 mmol/L – 1.8 mmol/L = **1.7 mmol/L**. Effect of plant stanol esters: 10% of current LDL level = $(3.5 \div 100) \times 10 = 0.35$ mmol/L. So 10% reduction = 3.5 mmol/L – 0.35 mmol/L = **3.15 mmol/L**. They would benefit most from using statins.
You may be asked to do simple calculations like this in the exam so make sure you have your calculator.

Page 149 — Fact Recall Questions
Q1 A balanced diet is a diet that gives you the right amount of all the nutrients you need (carbohydrates, fats, proteins, vitamins and mineral salts) plus fibre and water.
Q2 Not having enough food, having an unbalanced diet/having too much or too little of a nutrient, malabsorption.
Q3 E.g. eating too much sugary or fatty food and getting too little exercise. / Having an underactive thyroid gland.
Q4 Any two from: e.g. Type 2 diabetes / arthritis / high blood pressure / coronary heart disease / cancer.
Q5 a) A guide to help decide whether someone is underweight, a normal weight, overweight or obese.
   b) Because it doesn't take into account how much of a person's body mass is made of up fat.
Q6 Substances composed of both protein and lipid.
Q7 A diet high in saturated fat raises LDL level, so more cholesterol is transported to the blood, increasing total blood cholesterol. This increases the build up of fatty deposits in artery walls (atheromas), which causes atherosclerosis and increases the risk of CHD.

Make sure you spell atherosclerosis right in your exam — you might lose marks if you put a similar word like <u>arterio</u>sclerosis by mistake.
Q8 To reduce blood cholesterol when the level is too high.
Q9 A high salt intake can cause high blood pressure which can damage artery walls. Damaged walls have an increased risk of atheroma formation, which causes atherosclerosis and increases the risk of CHD.

2. Increasing Food Production
Page 152 — Application Questions
Q1 Select the chickens that produce the most eggs. Breed the chickens together. From the offspring produced select the ones that produce the most eggs and breed them together. Continue until a population of chickens is generated that produces lots of eggs.
Q2 The chickens that have been bred together are likely to be closely related. This means they have a low genetic diversity, so they may be more susceptible to the Gumboro virus.

Page 152 — Fact Recall Questions
Q1 Because plants are at the start of all food chains.
Q2 a) Fertilisers increase crop yields by providing plants with the minerals they need to grow. They're used to replace minerals used up during crop growth, so that a lack of minerals doesn't limit the growth of the next crop.
   b) Pesticides kill pests that feed on crops. This means fewer plants are damaged or destroyed, increasing food production.
Q3 Any three from e.g. they fight/prevent diseases in animals so the animals can use more energy to grow. / They increase the growth rate of animals. / They increase the size of animals when mature. / They make it less likely diseases will pass from animals to humans.
Q4 A process that involves humans selecting which strains of plants or animals to reproduce together in order to increase productivity.
Q5 Plants or animals with useful characteristics that will increase food production are selected. These are then bred together and the offspring with the best characteristics are selected. These are then bred together and the process continued over several generations until a plant or animal with the useful characteristics is produced.
Q6 Any two from: e.g. it can produce high-yielding animals and plants. / It can be used to produce animals and plants that have increased resistance to disease, so farmers have to use fewer drugs and pesticides. / Animals and plants can be bred to have increased tolerance of bad conditions, e.g. drought or cold.

3. Microorganisms and Food
Page 155 — Application Questions
Q1 Any three from: e.g. it may look different to normal. / It may have a strange smell. / It may have a different texture to normal. / It may not taste like it should.
Q2 The salt used in salted eggs inhibits the growth of microorganisms by interfering with their ability to absorb water by osmosis. Salt lowers the water potential of the water outside the microbial cells, causing them to lose water. This can slow the growth of/kill the microorganisms, preserving the eggs.
Q3 Vinegar has a low pH. This denatures enzymes in microorganisms, preventing them from functioning properly and inhibiting the microorganisms' growth. This means the eggs are preserved for longer.

Q4 Pasteurisation involves heating the eggs to a very high temperature. This can denature enzymes and kills any microorganisms present, preventing poisoning by *Salmonella*.

Page 155 — Fact Recall Questions

Q1 E.g. bread is made by mixing yeast, sugar, flour and water into a dough. The yeast turn the sugar into ethanol and carbon dioxide — it's the carbon dioxide that makes the bread rise. / Wine is made by adding yeast to grape juice. The yeast turn the sugar in the grape juice into ethanol/ alcohol and carbon dioxide. / Cheese is made by adding bacteria to milk. The bacteria turn the sugar in the milk into lactic acid, which causes the milk to curdle. An enzyme is then used to turn the curdled milk into curds and whey. The curds are separated off and left to ripen into cheese. / Yoghurt is made by adding bacteria to milk. The bacteria turn the sugar in the milk into lactic acid, causing the milk to clot and thicken into yoghurt.

Q2 Advantages — any two from: e.g. populations of microorganisms grow rapidly under the right conditions, so food can be produced quickly. / Microorganisms can grow on a range of inexpensive materials. / The microorganisms' environment can be artificially controlled so you can grow food anywhere and at any time of the year. / Optimum conditions for the growth of microorganisms are easy to create. / Some of the food made using microorganisms often lasts longer in storage than the raw product they're made from.
Disadvantages — e.g. there's a high risk of food contamination. Small changes in temperature or pH can easily kill the microorganisms.

Q3 The deterioration of a food's characteristics, e.g. its appearance, taste, texture or odour.

Q4 Microorganisms multiply and secrete enzymes which break down molecules in the food, e.g. proteins are broken down into amino acids, fats into fatty acids and carbohydrates into more simple sugars. It's this breakdown of molecules in food that causes the food to spoil.

Q5 Adding sugar inhibits the growth of microorganisms by interfering with their ability to absorb water by osmosis.

Q6 Freezers keep food below −18 °C. This slows down enzyme controlled reactions taking place in microorganisms and freezes the water in the food, so the microorganisms can't use it.

Q7 irradiation

Exam-style Questions — pages 157-158

1 a) i) Subject 1's intake of all nutrients was below the recommended daily intake *(1 mark)*.
   ii) Because subject 3's energy intake (3150 kcal) is much higher than the recommended intake (2500 kcal) *(1 mark)*. Subject 3's sugar/carbohydrate intake (480 g) is much higher than the recommended intake (312.5 g) *(1 mark)*. Subject 3's total fat/saturated fat intake (110 g/42 g) is also much higher than the recommended intake (< 97 g/< 30.5 g) *(1 mark)*.
   If you're asked to use evidence from a source provided in the question, make sure you include figures or data where you can.
   iii) Any two from: e.g. Type 2 diabetes / arthritis / high blood pressure / CHD / cancer *(2 marks for 2 correct answers)*.

b) i) The body regulates its blood cholesterol level using lipoproteins *(1 mark)*. The role of low density lipoproteins/LDLs is to transport cholesterol from the liver to the blood *(1 mark)* so they increase blood cholesterol when the level is too low *(1 mark)*. The role of high density lipoproteins/HDLs is to transport cholesterol from the blood to the liver *(1 mark)* so they reduce blood cholesterol level when the level is too high *(1 mark)*. *(1 mark for a correct link between LDLs and a raised blood cholesterol level or between HDLs and a lowered blood cholesterol level.)*
   ii) He has the greatest intake of saturated fat, which increases LDL level and therefore blood cholesterol level *(1 mark)*. He also has the lowest intake of polyunsaturated fat, which increases HDL level and lowers blood cholesterol level *(1 mark)*.

c) His salt intake (9.7 g) is much higher than the recommended daily intake (6 g) *(1 mark)*. A diet high in salt can cause high blood pressure *(1 mark)*. This can increase the risk of damage to artery walls, which increases the risk of atheroma formation *(1 mark)*. This can lead to atherosclerosis/narrowing and hardening of the artery walls and increase the risk of CHD *(1 mark)*.

d) E.g. they may not be able to absorb the nutrients from digestion into their bloodstream properly *(1 mark)*.

2 a) i) Breed 1 grows from 8 kg to 106 kg/by 98 kg between week 4 and week 22 *(1 mark)*. Breed 2 grows from 8 kg to 76 kg/by 68 kg between week 4 and week 22 *(1 mark)*. Breed 3 grows from 4 kg to 57 kg/by 53 kg between week 4 and week 22 *(1 mark)*.
   ii) Breed 1 — weight at 22 weeks = 106 kg. $(64 ÷ 100) × 106$ kg = **67.8 kg** *(1 mark)*. Breed 2 — weight at 22 weeks = 76 kg. $(73 ÷ 100) × 76$ kg = **55.5 kg** *(1 mark)*. Breed 3 — weight at 22 weeks = 57 kg. $(66 ÷ 100) × 57$ kg = **37.6 kg** *(1 mark)*.

b) i) Breed 1 and Breed 2 *(1 mark)*, because Breed 1 has the highest growth rate and Breed 2 has the highest meat yield *(1 mark)*.
   For this question you need to find the breed(s) of pig that have the most desirable characteristics.
   ii) Any two from: e.g. it can cause health problems in the pigs. / It reduces genetic diversity. / It could make the pigs more susceptible to disease *(2 marks for 2 correct answers)*.

c) i) E.g. antibiotics treat or prevent diseases caused by bacteria *(1 mark)*. Giving antibiotics to the pigs means they spend less energy fighting diseases so they can use more energy to grow, increasing food production *(1 mark)*. / Antibiotics could promote the growth of the pigs by influencing bacteria in the pigs' guts *(1 mark)*, allowing them to digest food more easily *(1 mark)*.
   Remember, if you're asked to explain something you need to give reasons — so for example, writing just "antibiotics increase an animal's growth" wouldn't have answered this question.
   ii) E.g. using antibiotics in farming can increase the chance of bacteria becoming antibiotic resistant *(1 mark)*. Animals naturally have some bacteria in their body which are useful and could be killed by the antibiotics *(1 mark)*. The antibiotic may be present in animal products which humans consume, so it could also have unwanted affects in our bodies *(1 mark)*.

d) By destroying/damaging the microorganisms' DNA
(1 mark).

Section 5 — Health and Disease

1. Defining Health and Disease
Page 160 — Application Questions
Q1 a) non-infectious
   b) chronic
Q2 a) infectious
   b) acute

Page 160 — Fact Recall Questions
Q1 Health is a state of physical, mental and social well-being, which includes the absence of disease and infirmity (weakness of body or mind).
Q2 Disease is a condition that impairs the normal functioning of an organism.
Q3 A pathogen is an organism that can cause disease.
A parasite is an organism that lives on or in another organism (the host) and causes damage to that organism.
Q4 a) An acute disease usually only causes a problem for a short period of time and the symptoms usually appear rapidly. A chronic disease is much more persistent (you can have it your whole life), and the symptoms often appear very slowly, but get progressively worse as time goes on.
   b) Acute disease: e.g. a cold
Chronic disease: e.g. chronic bronchitis / diabetes

2. The Immune System
Page 163 — Application Questions
Q1 With fewer T lymphocytes, fewer pathogens are killed directly. Also, with fewer T lymphocytes in the blood there are fewer cells to be activated by pathogen antigens presented by phagocytes. This means that fewer B lymphocytes are activated, so fewer antibodies are produced against the pathogens. With fewer antibodies, pathogens can survive longer in the body so opportunistic infections can cause problems.
Q2 Antibodies will be generated against antigens on the surface of *S. pyogenes*. These will then bind to antigens on the surface of heart cells because the antigens are so similar in shape. The immune system would then attack the heart cells and cause rheumatic fever.
The command word in this question is 'suggest', so you're not expected to know the exact answer. You're expected to use what you know about the immune system to come up with a possible explanation.

Page 163 — Fact Recall Questions
Q1 The skin and mucous membranes.
Make sure you spell 'mucous' correctly in the exam — you could lose marks if it looks like you've confused the membrane with the sticky stuff secreted by cells to trap pathogens ('mucus').
Q2 The body's reaction to a foreign antigen.
Q3 The molecules found on the surface of cells.
Q4 Phagocytosis is the engulfment of pathogens.
Q5 When activated by antigens presented by phagocytes, some T lymphocytes (helper T cells) release substances to activate B lymphocytes, some attach to antigens on pathogens and kill the cell and some become memory T cells. The function of plasma cells is to produce antibodies.

Q6
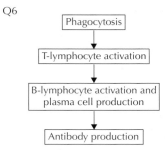

Q7 E.g. helper T cells release substances that bind to receptors on B lymphocytes. This activates the B lymphocytes — the helper T cells are signalling to the B lymphocytes that there's a pathogen in the body.

3. Antibodies
Page 165 — Application Question
Q1 The antibodies in the antivenom bind to the toxins in the poison. This prevents the toxins from affecting human cells, so the toxins are neutralised (inactivated). The toxin-antibody complexes are then phagocytosed and destroyed.

Page 165 — Fact Recall Questions
Q1 a) The variable region is complementary to a particular antigen and forms the antigen binding site.
   b) The hinge region allows flexibility when an antibody binds to an antigen.
   c) The constant region allows the antibody to bind to receptors on immune system cells.
Q2 Antibodies have two antigen binding sites. This is useful because it means that antibodies can bind to more than one pathogen at a time, so they can agglutinate the pathogens (clump them together).
Q3 Agglutinating groups of pathogens. Binding to and neutralising toxins produced by the pathogen. Binding to receptors on the pathogen and preventing it from entering host cells.

4. Primary and Secondary Immune Responses
Page 167 — Application Questions
Q1 Mouse A had 10 units, Mouse B had 10 000 units.
Q2 Mouse B was already immune. You can tell this because the immune response was much quicker and stronger than the immune response of Mouse A.
Q3 a) Day 20
   b) The mouse's memory B lymphocytes rapidly divided and produced the antibody needed to bind to the antigen. The mouse's memory T lymphocytes rapidly divided into the correct type of T lymphocytes to kill the cell carrying the antigen.

Page 167 — Fact Recall Questions
Q1 The primary response is slow because there aren't many T lymphocytes that can bind to the pathogen's antigens and there aren't many B lymphocytes that can make the right antibody to the antigens. The secondary response is faster because there are already memory T and B lymphocytes present that recognise the antigen and rapidly produce the right antibody to it.
Q2 Immunity doesn't always last forever because memory B and T lymphocytes have a limited life-span. If the person is not exposed to the pathogen again, eventually all of the memory cells will die and the person will no longer be immune.

Q3 E.g. the primary response happens the first time a pathogen invades, the secondary response happens the second time a pathogen invades. / The primary response involves B and T lymphocytes, the secondary response involves memory cells. / There are symptoms with a primary response, but not with a secondary response.

5. Immunity, Vaccinations and Developing Drugs
Page 170 — Application Questions
Q1 75% (accept answers in the range of 74-76%)
Q2 1000 cases
Q3 The number of cases decreased in a fluctuating pattern from a peak of around 6000 cases in the early 1960s to a peak of nearly 2000 cases around 1975. This is because more people were directly protected by the vaccine, and some people were protected by herd immunity.

Page 170 — Fact Recall Questions
Q1 Active immunity is the type of immunity you get when your immune system makes its own antibodies after being stimulated by an antigen.
Passive immunity is the type of immunity you get from being given antibodies made by a different organism — your immune system doesn't produce any antibodies of its own.
Q2 Vaccines contain antigens that cause your body to produce memory cells against a particular pathogen. This makes you immune.
Q3 Herd immunity is where unvaccinated people are protected because the occurrence of the disease is reduced by the number of people who are vaccinated.
Q4 The influenza virus can change the antigens on its surface, so every year there are new strains of influenza circulating in the population.

6. Infectious Diseases
Page 174 — Application Questions
Q1 a) Malaria is transmitted by mosquitoes. DEET repels insects including mosquitoes, so wearing DEET impregnated clothing reduces the chance of getting bitten by a mosquito. This means there is less chance of acquiring the malaria parasite.
   b) E.g. sleep under a mosquito net / take anti-malarial drugs / spray insect repellent around their accommodation.
Q2 Mistakes made by reverse transcriptase may introduce mutations in the DNA. This could cause changes in the antigens on the surface of the virus. If the antigens on the surface of the virus change, the vaccine will stop working.
Remember: antigens are proteins, so they're coded for by DNA base sequences. Mutations (changes) in a DNA base sequence can alter the protein that gets produced.
Q3 a) Increased poverty could mean, e.g. less money to spend on healthcare, so fewer people are diagnosed and treated / less money to spend on drugs so fewer people are treated / more people living in over-crowded conditions so there is more spread of the disease by droplet-transmission.
   b) HIV causes a loss of white blood cells and a deterioration of the immune system. This will make people more susceptible to infection by TB as there will be fewer white blood cells to fight off the bacteria.

Page 174 — Fact Recall Questions
Q1 *Plasmodium*
Q2 TB spreads by 'droplet infection' — when an infected person coughs or sneezes, tiny droplets of saliva and mucus containing the bacteria are released from their mouth and nose. These droplets are then breathed in by other people.
Q3 HIV stands for human immunodeficiency virus. It causes AIDS (Acquired Immunodeficiency Syndrome).
Q4 E.g. using barrier contraceptives/condoms, screening blood donor volunteers, not sharing hypodermic needles, taking antiviral drugs during pregnancy.

7. Smoking and Disease
Page 177 — Fact Recall Questions
Q1 An atheroma is a fibrous plaque formed from the build up and hardening of white blood cells, lipids and connective tissue. An atheroma forms when the arterial wall gets damaged and LDL enters and collects in the arterial wall. The build up of LDL triggers an immune response, so white blood cells also move into the area. Over time, more white blood cells, lipids and connective tissue build up and harden forming the atheroma at the site of damage.
Q2 An atheroma partially blocks the lumen of an artery and restricts blood flow.
Q3 E.g. carbon monoxide in cigarette smoke irreversibly combines with haemoglobin, reducing the amount of oxygen transported in the blood. This reduces the amount of oxygen available to tissues, including the heart. Nicotine in cigarette smoke makes platelets (cells involved in blood clotting) sticky, increasing the chance of blood clots forming. If clotting happens in the coronary arteries it could cause a heart attack. The presence of atheromas also increases the risk of blood clots forming (and smoking also increases the risk of atheroma formation).
Q4 Cigarette smoke contains many carcinogens (chemicals that can cause a cell to become cancerous). These carcinogens may cause mutations in the DNA of lung cells, which could lead to uncontrolled cell growth and the formation of a malignant (cancerous) tumour.
Q5 The long-term inflammation of the mucous membranes that line the bronchi.
Q6 The tar in cigarette smoke causes a build up of mucus, which leads to infection and inflammation. Inflammation attracts phagocytes to the area. The phagocytes produce an enzyme that breaks down elastin. Loss of elastin means the alveoli can't recoil as well and leads to the destruction of the alveolar walls.

8. Evaluating Evidence about Smoking and Disease
Page 179 — Application Questions
Q1 Male deaths due to COPD increased from just over 10 per 100 000 people in 1946 to almost 80 per 100 000 in 1972. It then slowly decreased to about 40 per 100 000 by 1998.
Q2 E.g. between about 1948 and 1969 there doesn't seem to be any correlation between female deaths from COPD and tobacco consumption. After this year the number of female deaths from COPD increases as tobacco consumption decreases (there's a negative correlation). This isn't enough to say that COPD in women is not caused by smoking though. Tobacco consumption in women might have risen while tobacco consumption in the overall population was decreasing, but you can't tell from this data. Also, female deaths from COPD could be increasing for other reasons, e.g. industrial causes, even if tobacco consumption is still a cause of the disease.

1   a) *Mycobacterium tuberculosis* *(1 mark)*
    b) i) The number of reported TB cases in the UK increased overall, from about 6750 cases in 2000 to about 9000 cases in 2009 *(1 mark)*.
        ii) 9000 − 7250 = 1750
             (1750 ÷ 7250) × 100 *(1 mark)* = **24.1%** *(1 mark)*
        iii) E.g. although the number of TB cases has risen by about 33% between 2000 and 2009, it doesn't necessarily mean this trend will continue *(1 mark)*. The graph shows the number of reported cases of TB, but the newspaper refers to the number of cases of TB — it may be that the reason for the increasing trend is just because more cases of TB are being reported (i.e. there's not an increase in overall number of cases) *(1 mark)*. The graph shows the number of reported cases of TB in the UK but the newspaper refers to the number of cases of TB in England, so this prediction doesn't fit the data shown in the graph *(1 mark)*.

Always read questions carefully — the introduction mentions that the graph shows the number of reported cases of TB in the UK. You'll miss this if you skim over the introduction and look at the graph first.

    c) E.g. the UK has high standards of hygiene *(1 mark)* and living conditions which are relatively uncrowded *(1 mark)*. This means people are less likely to contract TB through droplet infection/via infected people coughing or sneezing *(1 mark)*. The UK has a (BCG) vaccine available to prevent people contracting TB *(1 mark)*. The UK has antibiotics to treat people with the disease *(1 mark)*. *(Maximum of four marks available.)*

2   a) i) When a phagocyte recognises the antigens on a pathogen *(1 mark)*, the cytoplasm of the phagocyte moves around the pathogen, engulfing it *(1 mark)*. The pathogen is now contained in a phagocytic vacuole inside the phagocyte *(1 mark)*. A lysosome fuses with the phagocytic vacuole *(1 mark)* and the lysosomal enzymes inside the lysosome break down the pathogen *(1 mark)*. The pathogen is then absorbed into the cytoplasm *(1 mark)*. *(1 mark for the sequence of steps described in the correct order.)*
        ii) Receptors on the surface of T lymphocytes bind to the antigens presented by phagocytes, activating the T lymphocytes *(1 mark)*. When B lymphocytes, which are covered in antibodies, meet an antigen with a complementary shape they bind to it *(1 mark)*. This, along with substances released from T lymphocytes/helper T cells, activates the B lymphocytes *(1 mark)*. The B lymphocytes then divide into plasma cells *(1 mark)*. The plasma cells then produce antibodies specific to the antigen *(1 mark)*.
    b) After the first infection their T lymphocytes and B lymphocytes produced memory cells *(1 mark)*. When they were exposed for a second time these memory cells divided into plasma cells and the correct type of T lymphocytes to quickly destroy the virus *(1 mark)*.
    c) The neuraminidase and haemagglutinin antigens on the Asian flu strain were different from the antigens on the Spanish flu strain *(1 mark)*, so any memory cells created against H1N1 would not detect H2N2 *(1 mark)*. So the immune system would have to start from scratch and carry out a primary immune response if exposed to Asian flu *(1 mark)*.

Make sure you use scientific terminology in your answer, e.g. 'antigens' and 'primary immune response'.

    d) To make people immune to more than one strain of flu *(1 mark)*.
3   a) i) Vaccines contain antigens *(1 mark)* which activate T lymphocytes *(1 mark)*. The antigens and T lymphocytes activate B lymphocytes, some of which differentiate into memory B lymphocytes *(1 mark)*.
        ii) They will benefit from herd immunity *(1 mark)*. If most people in a community are vaccinated the disease becomes extremely rare *(1 mark)*. This means people who haven't been vaccinated are less likely to get the disease because there's no-one to catch it from *(1 mark)*.
    b) i) Variable region *(1 mark)* — forms the antigen binding site *(1 mark)*.
           Hinge region *(1 mark)* — allows flexibility when the antibody binds an antigen *(1 mark)*.
           Constant region *(1 mark)* — allows binding to receptors on immune system cells *(1 mark)*.
        ii)

Agglutinating pathogens	✓
Killing pathogens directly	
Neutralising toxins	✓
Activating memory T lymphocytes	
Mutating pathogen DNA	
Stopping pathogens binding cells	✓

(1 mark for each correct answer, if more than three boxes are ticked remove 1 mark for each incorrect answer).

4   a) E.g. the walls of the alveoli have been destroyed in the diseased alveoli *(1 mark)*. Destruction of the alveolar walls reduces the surface area of the alveoli *(1 mark)*, so the rate of gaseous exchange would decrease *(1 mark)*.
    b) i) E.g. tar *(1 mark)*.
        ii) When an individual has emphysema the walls of the alveoli become less elastic/break down *(1 mark)*. As a result the alveoli can't expel air as well/the surface area of the alveoli is reduced *(1 mark)*. This reduces the rate of gas exchange in the alveoli. *(1 mark)*. The lack of oxygen reaching the cells leaves sufferer feeling tired *(1 mark)*.

Section 6 — Biodiversity

1. Investigating Biodiversity

Pages 185-186 — Application Questions

Q1 a) Any one from, e.g. she could sweep the net through the same depth of water. / She could make sure her net stays in the water for the same length of time for each sample. / She could take samples at the same time of day. / She could use the same net/type of net for each sample.

Standardise just means 'make the same' — so the question is asking for ways the environmental officer could collect each sample in the same way.

    b) Any one from, e.g. she could take lots of samples and calculate an average/mean. / She could make sure that fish can't escape from the net before she counts them and that individuals aren't counted more than once.
Q2 a) Pond A because the population sizes of the species are more similar than in pond B.

b) i) Pond A

$$D = 1 - \left(\left(\frac{3}{18}\right)^2 + \left(\frac{5}{18}\right)^2 + \left(\frac{2}{18}\right)^2 + \left(\frac{3}{18}\right)^2 \right. $$
$$\left. + \left(\frac{1}{18}\right)^2 + \left(\frac{4}{18}\right)^2\right)$$
$$= 1 - \left(0.0278 + 0.0772 + 0.0123 + 0.0278 + \right.$$
$$\left. 0.00309 + 0.0494\right)$$
$$= 1 - 0.198$$
$$= \mathbf{0.802}$$

ii) Pond B

$$D = 1 - \left(\left(\frac{13}{54}\right)^2 + \left(\frac{5}{54}\right)^2 + \left(\frac{7}{54}\right)^2 + \left(\frac{2}{54}\right)^2 \right.$$
$$\left. + \left(\frac{18}{54}\right)^2 + \left(\frac{9}{54}\right)^2\right)$$
$$= 1 - \left(0.0580 + 0.00857 + 0.0168 + 0.00137 + \right.$$
$$\left. 0.111 + 0.0278\right)$$
$$= 1 - 0.224$$
$$= \mathbf{0.776}$$

If you have to calculate Simpson's Index of Diversity in the exam, always show your full working out. You can pick up a mark for showing you understand the equation if nothing else.

c) Yes, because they both have a fairly high index of diversity. This means the populations are stable and capable of coping with change.

Page 186 — Fact Recall Questions

Q1 a) The variety of living organisms in an area.
b) The area inhabited by a species.
c) A group of similar organisms able to reproduce to give fertile offspring.

Q2 Habitat diversity — the number of different habitats in an area. Species diversity — the number of different species and the abundance of each species in an area. Genetic diversity — the variation of alleles within a species (or a population of a species).

Q3 It avoids bias in the results and makes it more likely that the sample is representative of the population as a whole.

Q4 a) The number of different species in an area.
b) It's a measure of the relative abundance of each species in an area.

Q5 The total number of organisms in one species. The total number of all organisms.

Q6 That a habitat is highly diverse, making it stable and able to cope with change.

2. Global Biodiversity

Page 189 — Application Questions

Q1 Any one from, e.g. the two teams may have used different techniques to make their estimates. / Relatively little is known about some groups of organisms. The second team may have taken this into account in producing their estimate, while the first team may not. / Some parts of the world, like tropical rainforests, are largely unexplored and the second team might have taken this into account in producing their estimate, while the first team might not.

Q2 a) Sea surface temperature fluctuated around the average between 1950 and approximately 1978, then there was a steady increase between 1978 and 2000, up to just over 0.3 °C greater than the average. Subtropical plankton species were found in the sea south of the UK in 1958-1981. By 2000-2002 their distribution had moved further north along the west coast of the UK and Ireland to the Arctic Ocean.

b) E.g. there could have been factors other than temperature involved, e.g. overfishing could have removed plankton predator species.
Just because the difference in average temperature and the distribution of plankton have both changed over the same time period doesn't mean to say that one caused the other — there could be other factors involved. Remember, correlation and cause aren't the same thing (see page 5).

Q3 E.g. the extreme weather events may decrease biodiversity because the barley crop failure may have disrupted food chains. Changing the crop could decrease biodiversity by disrupting food chains as some existing species will be left without food/changing the crop could increase biodiversity by providing a new food source for other species.

3. Biodiversity and Conservation

Page 192 — Application Questions

Q1 E.g. Hedgerows are wildlife corridors — they enable organisms to move between different habitats safely. If they're removed, species can become isolated and the availability of food and nesting sites for many species will be reduced, lowing biodiversity. / Removing the hedgerows may cause the disruption of food chains. The plants and animals in the hedgerows may be eaten by other species which will lose a food source if the hedgerows are removed. This could reduce the populations of those species, lowing biodiversity.

Q2 E.g. the hedgerows are home to hedgehogs. These are a natural form of pest control which may be lost if the hedgerows are removed. This means the farmer may have to spend more money on pesticides.

Q3 The more crop varieties that are used, the less chance there is of the whole crop being destroyed by a disease/pest.

Pages 194-195 — Application Questions

Q1 a) i) Any one from, e.g. both the Northern Quoll and its habitat are conserved which means that larger populations can be protected than with ex *situ* conservation. / In situ conservation is less disruptive than removing Northern Quoll from their habitats. / The chances of the Northern Quoll population recovering are greater than with ex *situ* methods.

ii) Any one from, e.g. it can be used to protect individual Northern Quolls in a controlled environment — things like predation and hunting can be managed more easily than in in *situ* conservation. / It's possible to reduce competition between Northern Quoll and other animals in ex *situ* conservation but not in in *situ* conservation. / It's easier to check on the health of Northern Quoll and treat them for diseases in ex *situ* than in in *situ* conservation. / It's easier to manipulate breeding e.g. through the use of reproductive hormones and IVF, in ex *situ* than in in *situ* conservation.

b) In situ conservation would involve eradicating the cane toads. Without the cane toads to eat the sugarcane pests, the yield of the sugarcane crops could fall, lowering farmers' income from the crop / forcing the farmers to spend more money on pesticides.

Q2 a) The biodiversity of the site will be estimated. The impact of the development on the site's biodiversity will be explored. The EIA will identify ways that the biodiversity can be conserved, any threatened or endangered species, and any laws relating to their conservation.

b) i) E.g. the plant may provide us with new products in the future.

ii) E.g. relocate the plant species to another area. / Store its seeds in a seed bank.

Page 195 — Fact Recall Questions

Q1 a) Any two from: e.g. conserved plants and animals may provide food and drink/clothing/drugs/fuels/industrial materials for trade.

b) Any two from: e.g. conservation of biodiversity may help to prevent the disruption of food chains/nutrient cycles/ the loss of habitats/climate change (by preserving natural CO_2 stores).

c) Any two from: e.g. some people believe that we should conserve species because they believe it's the right thing to do/organisms have a right to exist/humans have a moral responsibilty to conserve biodiversity for future human generations.

Q2 Many fruit and vegetable crops are pollinated by insects such as bees and butterflies. The higher the diversity of insects the more pollinators there are. The majority of our food comes from only a few species of plants, so if a disease or pest affects these few species, our food supply is at risk. The more crop varieties that are used, the less chance there is that all the crops will be destroyed. Many species are used as food sources for humans and livestock. The more different species there are the more possible sources there are to choose from. Plant varieties are needed for cross-breeding. Wild plants can be bred with domesticated plants to produce new varieties with, e.g. increased disease resistance/faster growth/increased ability to cope with climate change. A number of animals are natural predators of crop pests, e.g. slugs. The more of these organisms there are the fewer pests there will be.

Q3 The protection and management of species and habitats.

Q4 a) Conservation on site. / Protecting a species in its natural habitat.

b) Any two from: e.g. establishing protected areas such as national parks and nature reserves. / Controlling or preventing the introduction of species that threaten local biodiversity. / Protecting habitats. / Restoring damaged areas. / Promoting particular species. / Giving legal protection to endangered species.

Q5 a) Conservation off site. / Protecting a species by removing part of the population from a threatened habitat and placing it in a new location.

b) Any one from e.g. usually only a small number of individuals can be cared for. / It can be difficult and expensive to create and sustain the right environment. / It is usually less successful than *in situ* methods as many species can't breed in captivity or don't adapt to their new environment when moved to a new location.

Q6 An international agreement that aims to develop international strategies on the conservation of biodiversity and how to use animal and plant resources in a sustainable way.

Q7 An agreement designed to increase international cooperation in regulating trade in wild animal and plant specimens.

Exam-style Questions — pages 197-198

1 a) It's an assessment of the impact a development project might have on the environment *(1 mark)*.

b) Wood

$$D = 1 - \left(\left(\frac{15}{101} \right)^2 + \left(\frac{18}{101} \right)^2 + \left(\frac{17}{101} \right)^2 + \left(\frac{19}{101} \right)^2 + \left(\frac{9}{101} \right)^2 \right.$$
$$\left. + \left(\frac{8}{101} \right)^2 + \left(\frac{7}{101} \right)^2 + \left(\frac{8}{101} \right)^2 + \left(\frac{0}{101} \right)^2 \right) \textit{ (1 mark)}$$

$= 1 - (0.0221 + 0.0318 + 0.0283 + 0.0354 + 0.00794 + 0.00627 + 0.00480 + 0.00627 + 0)$
$= 1 - 0.143$ *(1 mark)*
= 0.857 *(1 mark)*

Town

$$D = 1 - \left(\left(\frac{1}{41} \right)^2 + \left(\frac{3}{41} \right)^2 + \left(\frac{2}{41} \right)^2 + \left(\frac{1}{41} \right)^2 + \left(\frac{1}{41} \right)^2 \right.$$
$$\left. + \left(\frac{2}{41} \right)^2 + \left(\frac{20}{41} \right)^2 + \left(\frac{6}{41} \right)^2 + \left(\frac{5}{41} \right)^2 \right) \textit{ (1 mark)}$$

$= 1 - (0.000595 + 0.00535 + 0.00238 + 0.000595 + 0.000595 + 0.00238 + 0.238 + 0.0214 + 0.0149)$
$= 1 - 0.286$ *(1 mark)*
= 0.714 *(1 mark)*

c) Both areas have a relatively high index of diversity/an index of biodiversity close to 1 *(1 mark)*. This means that both areas have a relatively high biodiversity *(1 mark)* and so are likely to be fairly stable habitats that are able to withstand change *(1 mark)*.

d) Any two from: e.g. the red squirrels could be relocated to a safer area. / The red squirrels could be bred in captivity and reintroduced into the wild elsewhere. / The remaining woodland could be made a protected area. *(1 mark for each correct answer up to a maximum of 2 marks.)*

There are lots of possible right answers here — just apply your scientific knowledge to the situation and make two sensible suggestions.

2 a) i) The total number of species on Earth *(1 mark)*.

ii) E.g. A large proportion of the species on earth are undiscovered, so some estimates may not have taken these into account *(1 mark)*. The different researchers may have used different techniques to come up with their estimates *(1 mark)*. Not much is known about some groups of organisms, so some estimates may not have taken them into account *(1 mark)*. Estimates of biodiversity change as researchers find out new things, and the estimates might have been made at different times *(1 mark)*.

There are 4 marks available for this question, so make sure you make four distinct points in your answer.

b) *Maximum of 6 marks available*: E.g. climate change could cause changes in weather conditions/rainfall/ the timing of the seasons/the frequency of flood and drought *(1 mark)*. This could make land available that was previously unavailable suitable for farming *(1 mark)*, which could increase biodiversity *(1 mark)*. It could mean that different crops will need to be grown *(1 mark)*. This could disrupt food chains, removing a source of food for some species *(1 mark)*, which could decrease biodiversity *(1 mark)*. Climate change could also lead to extreme weather events that cause crop failure *(1 mark)*. This could disrupt food chains and cause a decrease in biodiversity *(1 mark)*. *(Plus 1 mark for a clear, correct link made between climate change, changing patterns of agriculture and the impact this might have on global biodiversity.)*

It tells you in the question to make the link between climate change, changing patterns of agriculture and the impact on global biodiversity clear — if you don't make the link between all three of these obvious, e.g. you only talk about how climate change affects agriculture, you won't get the extra mark for Quality of Written Communication.

   c) Any three from, e.g. the higher the diversity of insects, the more crop pollinators there are *(1 mark)*. / The more different species there are, the more food sources there are for humans and livestock *(1 mark)*. / The more pest predators there are, the fewer pests there will be *(1 mark)*. /The more crop varieties that are used, the less chance there is that all our crops will be destroyed by, e.g. disease *(1 mark)*. / The greater the variety of wild plant species there are, the more opportunities to cross-breed crop plants to produce new varieties with improved characteristics *(1 mark)*.

3 a) The number of different species *(1 mark)* and the abundance of each species in an area *(1 mark)*.

   b) Any two from, e.g. the sample was biased/not collected at random/the sample was only collected from one area *(1 mark)*. All the samples were collected on the same day/at the same time *(1 mark)*. / The student's method only collected insects that live on the ground *(1 mark)*.

   c) Any one from, e.g. that one or two species dominate the habitat *(1 mark)*. / That insect diversity is low *(1 mark)*.

   d) E.g. use the same sampling method/set up the pitfall traps in the same way *(1 mark)*.

Section 7 — Classification

1. Classification Basics

Page 201 — Application Questions
Q1 sharks
Q2 salamanders
Q3 a) crocodiles
     b) lizards

Page 201 — Fact Recall Questions
Q1 The study of classification.
    Definitions are easy marks in the exam — make sure you know the definitions for classification, taxonomy and phylogeny off by heart.
Q2 Domain, Phylum, Family, Genus
Q3 Each species is given a two-part Latin name. The first part is the genus name and the second part is the species name.
Q4 Any three from, e.g. eukaryotic / multicellular / cell walls made of cellulose / can photosynthesise / contain chlorophyll / autotrophic.

2. The Evolution of Classification Systems

Page 204 — Application Questions
Q1 Species A: TCGACGTGGGTAATCGAGC
      Species B: TCCACGTGTGTAATCGAGT
      Species C: ACGCCGAGTGTTATGGAGT
Q2 3
    Take your time with questions like this. Once you've got your answer, recount it to make sure it's right.
Q3 7
Q4 Species B. There are fewer base differences in the DNA when comparing A and B than A and C.
Q5 Species B. There are only 6 base differences between species C and B. This is fewer than for species C and A so species C and B are more closely related.

Page 204 — Fact Recall Questions
Q1 molecular evidence, embryological evidence, the fossil record
Q2 In the three domain system, organisms with cells that contain a nucleus/eukaryotes are placed in the domain Eukarya. Organisms without a nucleus/prokaryotes are separated into two domains — Archea and Bacteria.
Q3 Any one from, e.g. the RNA polymerase enzyme is different in Bacteria and Archea. / Archea have similar histones to Eukarya, but Bacteria don't. / The bonds of the lipids in the cell membranes of Bacteria and Archea are different. / The development and composition of flagellae are different in Bacteria and Archea.

3. Dichotomous Keys
Page 206 — Application Question
Q1 A = Blue tit, B = Thrush, C = Chaffinch, D = Great spotted woodpecker, E = Great tit, F = Goldfinch

Exam-style Questions — pages 207-208
1 a)

Domain	Archea
Kingdom	Euryarcheota
Phylum	Euryarcheota
Class	Halobacteria
Order	Halobacteriales
Family	Halobacteriaceae
Genus	*Halobacterium*
Species	*salinarum*

     (1 mark for each correct answer)
   b) i) Any two from, e.g. no nucleus *(1 mark)* / unicellular *(1 mark)* / less than 5 µm *(1 mark)*
      ii) Under the three domain system, organisms that would be in the Prokaryotae kingdom are split into two separate domains/Archea and Bacteria *(1 mark)*. This is because of new evidence/molecular evidence that showed large differences between the two domains/Archea and Bacteria *(1 mark)*.
      iii) Any one from, e.g. the Protoctista/Plantae/Fungi/Animalia kingdom is present in both systems *(1 mark)*. / Four out of five kingdoms are present in both systems *(1 mark)*. / The hierarchy below domain (e.g. kingdom, phylum, class, order, family, genus, species) stays the same *(1 mark)*.
2 a) E.g. he/she could analyse the DNA base sequences of the genes *(1 mark)*. The more similar the base sequences, the more closely related the plant species *(1 mark)*.
   b) It is present in all plants so any two species of plant can be compared by looking at RuBisCo *(1 mark)*.
   c) E.g. scientists don't always agree on the relative importance of different features *(1 mark)*. Groups based solely on physical features may not show how related organisms are *(1 mark)*.
   d) Prokaryotae/Monera, Protoctista, Animalia, Fungi *(1 mark for each correct answer, only credit if spelt correctly)*
    When you know the answer, it's a real shame to lose out on the marks just because your spelling lets you down — so make sure you put the effort in and learn how to spell these words.
3 a) i) A = *Sorbus aucuparia* *(1 mark)*, C = *Acer palmatum* *(1 mark)*, D = *Betula pendula* *(1 mark)*, E = *Acer pseudoplatanus* *(1 mark)*, F = *Argentea pendula* *(1 mark)*.

ii) They are members of the same genus (*Acer*) *(1 mark)*.
b) To avoid the confusion of using common names *(1 mark)*.

Section 8 — Evolution

1. Variation

Page 211 — Application Questions

Q1 a) continuous
Head circumference can take any value within a range, so it's continuous data. This indicates that head circumference is an example of continuous variation.
b) The mean difference in head circumference is approximately 0.5 cm for identical twins, 3 cm for non-identical siblings and 8.5 cm for unrelated individuals. So the mean difference in head circumference is much larger for unrelated individuals than for either identical twins or non-identical siblings.
c) The data suggests that genetic factors have a larger effect on head circumference, because the mean difference in head circumference is much larger for unrelated individuals than for either identical twins or non-identical siblings. However, the mean difference for identical twins wasn't zero, so environmental factors appear to play some role.
d) The mean difference in the number of steps taken is between 800 and 900 for all three sample groups. Identical twins and non-identical siblings show the lowest difference and unrelated individuals the highest but the margins are very small. This suggests that environmental factors play a more important role than genetic factors in determining activity level when measured by the number of steps taken per day.

Page 211 — Fact Recall Questions

Q1 a) Variation within a species.
b) Variation between different species.
Q2 Continuous variation is when the individuals in a population vary within a range — there are no distinct categories, e.g. height in humans. Discontinuous variation is when there are two or more distinct categories and each individual falls into only one of these categories — there are no intermediates, e.g. blood group in humans.
Q3 E.g. height in humans/plants / whether a microorganism grows a flagellum.

2. Adaptations

Page 213 — Application Questions

Q1 a) Light flexible wings = anatomical. Male bats make mating calls to attract females = behavioural. Bats lower their metabolism to hibernate over winter = physiological.
b) E.g. light, flexible wings — allow the bat to fly after insects, increasing its chances of catching prey and so surviving. Mating calls — increase the bat's chance of finding a mate and reproducing successfully. Hibernation — saves the bat's energy when food is scarce and so increases the bat's chances of surviving.
Q2 a) Behavioural adaptation — e.g. hunting in groups/pods. Physiological adaptation — reducing heart rate whilst diving.
Anatomical adaptation — a thick layer of blubber.

b) E.g. Hunting in groups/pods helps killers whales to hunt food successfully, increasing their chances of survival. Reducing heart rate whilst diving helps the whales conserve oxygen, so they can last for longer underwater without breathing. This increases their chances of catching prey and so surviving.
A thick layer of blubber keeps them warm, so increases their chances of surviving in cold seas. / A think layer of blubber gives them a streamlined shape, so helps them to move more easily through water to catch their prey, increasing their chances of survival.
The important thing about all adaptations is that they increase an organism's chance of surviving and reproducing successfully.

3. Evolution

Page 215 — Application Questions

Q1 E.g. scientists could compare the amino acid sequence of cytochrome C in different organisms. Cytochrome C is present in almost all living organisms, so it suggests that we all evolved from a common ancestor. The more similar the amino acid sequence of cytochrome C in different organisms, the more recently the organisms diverged away from one another.
Q2 Some individuals in the population have an allele for darker colouring that helps them to blend into their environment (wooded areas) better. This is beneficial because it helps them to avoid predators and sneak up on prey. So these individuals are more likely to survive, reproduce and pass on the allele for darker colouring. After some time most organisms in the population will carry the allele for darker colouring.
Whatever adaptation you're asked about in the exam, make sure you get the phrase, 'it helps the organism to survive, reproduce and pass on their alleles' into your answer.

Page 218 — Application Questions

Q1 a) There was variation in the bacterial population that causes TB. Genetic mutations made some bacteria naturally resistant to rifampicin. When the bacteria were exposed to rifampicin, only the rifampicin-resistant ones survived to reproduce. The alleles for rifampicin resistance were then passed on to the next generation. Over many generations, the population evolved to become rifampicin-resistant.
b) i) E.g. it could take doctors longer to figure out which antibiotics will get rid of their TB, during which time the patient could become very ill or die.
ii) E.g. it means that the drug companies have to keep developing more antibiotics, which takes time and costs money.
Q2 Some individuals in the population had an allele that gave them resistance to DDT. The population was exposed to DDT, killing the mosquitoes without the resistance allele. Individuals with the resistance allele survived, reproduced and passed on the allele to the next generation. After many generations most organisms in the population carried the allele for DDT resistance.

Page 218 — Fact Recall Questions

Q1 Any two from, e.g. organisms produce more offspring than survive. / There's variation in the characteristics of members of the same species. / Some characteristics can be passed on from one generation to the next. / Individuals that are best adapted to their environment are more likely to survive.

Q2 a) By arranging fossils in chronological (date) order, gradual changes in organisms can be observed that provide evidence of evolution.

b) Scientists can analyse DNA base sequences. The theory of evolution suggests that all living organisms evolved from a common ancestor, so organisms that diverged away from each other more recently should have more similar DNA than those that diverged less recently (as less time has passed for changes in the DNA sequence to occur).

Q3 speciation

Exam-style Questions — pages 219-220

1 a) 27 cm *(1 mark)*

b) i) Species A because it has a bigger range of wingspans than species B *(1 mark)*.

ii) Species A and species B live in the same environment *(1 mark)*, so the difference in wingspan is probably a result of genetic factors *(1 mark)*.

c) Continuous, because individuals can have a wingspan of any value within a range *(1 mark)*, there are no distinct categories *(1 mark)* and the values are quantitative/can be measured with a number *(1 mark)*.

d) i) The formation of a new species *(1 mark)*.

ii) E.g. they could try to breed members of the isolated population with other members of species A *(1 mark)*. If the organisms can't interbreed to form fertile offspring, a new species has been formed *(1 mark)*.

2 a) i) At first, as the use of the pesticide increases, the number of aphids falls *(1 mark)*. After a period of time, the number of aphids plateaus and pesticide use increases less steeply *(1 mark)*. The number of aphids then begins to increase *(1 mark)*.

ii) E.g. the number of aphids fell as they were being killed by the pesticide *(1 mark)*. Random mutations may have occurred in the aphid DNA, resulting in pesticide resistance *(1 mark)*. Any aphids resistant to the pesticide were more likely to survive and pass on their alleles *(1 mark)*. Over many generations, the number of aphids increased as those carrying pesticide-resistant alleles became more common *(1 mark)*.

b) E.g. if the aphids are resistant to lots of other pesticides as well as this one, it might take the farmer a long time to find one that works *(1 mark)* — in that time the entire crop could be destroyed *(1 mark)*. / If the insects are resistant to specific pesticides, farmers might need to use broader pesticides *(1 mark)*, which might kill beneficial insects *(1 mark)*.

3 a) i) A feature of an organism that increases its chances of survival and reproduction *(1 mark)* and also the chances of its offspring reproducing successfully *(1 mark)*.

ii) behavioural *(1 mark)*, physiological *(1 mark)*

b) Individuals within the *Anoura fistulata* population showed variation in their phenotypes *(1 mark)* due to differences in their alleles *(1 mark)*. The bats with long tongues were more likely to survive, reproduce and pass on their alleles *(1 mark)*. Over time the number of individuals with a long tongue increased *(1 mark)*. Over generations this led to evolution as the alleles that caused the long tongue became more common in the population *(1 mark)*.

Always try to use the correct scientific language in your answers — here you should be talking about organisms passing on 'alleles' not 'features' or 'characteristics'.

c) *Maximum of 6 marks available:* E.g. fossil evidence *(1 mark)* could show gradual changes in *Anoura fistulata*'s ancestors over time *(1 mark)*. *Anoura fistulata*'s DNA base sequences could be compared with its ancestors' DNA base sequences *(1 mark)*. This would show how recently *Anoura fistulata* and each of its ancestors diverged away from a common ancestor *(1 mark)*. Organisms that diverged away from each other more recently should have more similar DNA than those that diverged less recently *(1 mark)*. *Anoura fistulata*'s proteins could be also be compared with its ancestors' proteins *(1 mark)*. This would show how recently *Anoura fistulata* and each of its ancestors diverged away from a common ancestor *(1 mark)*. Organisms that diverged away from each other more recently should have more similar proteins than those that diverged less recently *(1 mark)*.

Glossary

A

Activation energy
The energy that needs to be supplied before a chemical reaction will start.

Active immunity
The type of immunity you get when your immune system makes its own antibodies after being stimulated by an antigen.

Active site
The part of an enzyme where a substrate molecule binds.

Active transport
Movement of molecules and ions across plasma membranes, against a concentration gradient. Requires energy.

Accurate result
A result that is really close to the true answer.

Adaptation
A feature of an organism that increases its chances of survival and reproduction, and also the chances of its offspring reproducing successfully.

Affinity for oxygen
The tendency a molecule has to bind with oxygen.

Allele
An alternative version of a gene.

Alveolus
A microscopic air sac in the lungs where gas exchange occurs.

Amino acid
A monomer of proteins.

Anomalous data
Measurements that fall outside the range of values you'd expect or any pattern you already have.

Antibiotic
A chemical that kills or inhibits the growth of bacteria.

Antibiotic resistance
When bacteria are able to survive in the presence of antibiotics.

Antibody
A protein produced by B lymphocytes in response to the presence of a pathogen.

Antigen
A molecule found on the surface of a cell. A foreign antigen triggers an immune response.

Apoplast pathway
A route that water takes through a plant root to the xylem, through cell walls.

Asexual reproduction
A form of reproduction where the parent cell divides into two daughter cells (by mitosis). The daughter cells are genetically identical to the parent cell.

Assimilate (in a plant)
A substance that becomes incorporated into the plant tissue, e.g. sucrose.

Atheroma
A fibrous plaque caused by the build up and hardening of white blood cells, lipids and connective tissue.

Atherosclerosis
The hardening of arteries due to the formation of atheromas in the arterial wall.

Atrioventricular node (AVN)
A group of cells in the heart wall that are responsible for passing waves of electrical activity from the SAN on to the bundle of His.

Atrioventricular (AV) valve
A valve in the heart linking the atria to the ventricles.

B

B lymphocyte
A type of white blood cell involved in the immune response. It produces antibodies.

Balanced diet
A diet that provides the right amount of all the nutrients needed to maintain health.

Benedict's test
A biochemical test for the presence of sugars.

Bias
When someone intentionally, or unintentionally, favours a particular result.

Binomial system
The nomenclature (naming system) used for classification, in which each organism is given a two-part scientific (Latin) name.

Biodiversity
The variety of living organisms in an area.

Biuret test
A biochemical test for the presence of polypeptides and proteins.

Bohr effect
An effect by which an increase of carbon dioxide in the blood results in a reduction of haemoglobin's affinity for oxygen.

Budding (in yeast)
A form of asexual reproduction.

Bundle of His
A group of muscle fibres in the heart, responsible for conducting waves of electrical activity from the AVN to the Purkyne tissue.

C

Carrier protein
A protein that carries molecules across a plasma membrane.

Casparian strip
A waxy strip in the cell wall of an endodermis cell.

Catalyst
A substance that speeds up a chemical reaction without being used up itself.

Causal relationship
Where a change in one variable causes a change in the other.

Cell cycle
The process that all body cells in multicellular organisms use to grow and divide.

Cell signalling
The process by which cells communicate with each other.

Cell wall
A rigid structure that surrounds the plasma membrane of some cells, e.g. plant cells. Supports the cell.

Cellulose
A polysaccharide made of long, unbranched chains of β-glucose.

Centriole
A small, hollow cylinder, containing a ring of microtubules. Involved with the separation of chromosomes during cell division.

Centromere
The point at which two strands of a chromosome are joined together.

Channel protein
A membrane protein that forms a pore through which ions or small, polar molecules move.

Cholesterol
A lipid (fat) containing a hydrocarbon tail attached to a hydrocarbon ring and a hydroxyl group.

Chloroplast
A small, flattened organelle present in plant cells. The site of photosynthesis.

Chromatid
One 'arm' of a double stranded chromosome.

Chronic bronchitis
The long-term inflammation of the mucous membranes that line the bronchi.

Ciliated epithelium
A layer of cells covered in cilia, found in animals (e.g. in the trachea or the lungs).

Cilium
A small, hair-like structure found on the surface membrane of some animal cells. Used to move substances along the cell surface.

Classification
The act of arranging organisms into groups based on their similarities and differences.

Climate change
A significant long-term change in an area's climate.

Closed circulatory system
A circulatory system where the blood is enclosed inside blood vessels.

Coenzyme
An organic cofactor.

Cofactor
A non-protein substance that binds to an enzyme and activates it. It can be organic or inorganic.

Collagen
A fibrous protein that forms supportive tissue in animals.

Companion cell
A type of plant cell located next to a sieve tube element in phloem tissue, which carries out living functions for itself and the sieve cell.

Competitive inhibitor
A molecule with a similar shape to that of a substrate, so it competes with the substrate to bind to the enzyme's active site.

Complementary base pairing
Hydrogen bonds between specific pairs of bases on opposing polynucleotide strands, e.g. A always pairs with T and C always pairs with G.

Concentration gradient
The path from an area of higher concentration to an area of lower concentration.

Condensation reaction
A reaction that releases a small molecule (e.g. water) when it links molecules together.

Conservation
The protection and management of species and habitats.

Control experiment
An extra experiment set up to eliminate the effect of some variables that can't be controlled.

Control group
A group in a study that is treated in exactly the same way as the experimental group, apart from the factor you're investigating.

Control variable
A variable you keep constant throughout an experiment.

Correlation
A relationship between two variables.

Coronary heart disease (CHD)
When the coronary arteries have lots of atheromas in them, which restricts blood flow to the heart.

Cytokinesis
The process by which cytoplasm divides during mitosis in eukaryotic cells.

Cytoskeleton
The network of protein threads contained in a cell.

Denatured
The point at which an enzyme no longer functions as a catalyst.

Dependent variable
The variable you measure in an experiment.

Differentiation
The process by which a cell becomes specialised.

Diffusion
The net movement of particles from an area of higher concentration to an area of lower concentration.

Dipeptide
A molecule formed from two amino acids.

Disaccharide
A molecule formed from two monosaccharides.

Disease
A condition that impairs the normal functioning of an organism.

Disulfide bond
A bond formed between two sulfur atoms, which links together two cysteine amino acids in a polypeptide chain.

DNA (deoxyribonucleic acid)
A nucleic acid containing deoxyribose sugar. Stores genetic information in cells.

DNA polymerase
An enzyme that joins together the nucleotides on a new strand of DNA during DNA replication.

Double-blind trial
A study involving a control group and an experimental group where neither the scientists involved nor the participants know which group the participants are in.

Double circulatory system
A circulatory system where blood passes through the heart twice for each complete circuit of the body.

Emphysema
A chronic lung disease involving the breakdown of the alveoli.

Emulsion test
A biochemical test for the presence of lipids.

Endangered species
A species whose population is so low that they could become extinct.

Endocytosis
The process by which a cell surrounds substances with a section of its plasma membrane and takes them into the cell.

Enzyme
A globular protein that speeds up the rate of chemical reactions.

Enzyme-product complex
The intermediate formed when a substrate has been converted into its products, but they've not yet been released from the active site of an enzyme.

Enzyme-substrate complex
The intermediate formed when a substrate molecule binds to the active site of an enzyme.

Erythrocyte
A red blood cell.

Eukaryote
Organism made up of a cell (or cells) containing a nucleus, e.g. animals and plants.

Evolution
The slow and continual change of organisms from one generation to the next.

***Ex situ* conservation**
Protecting a species by removing part of the population from a threatened habitat and placing it in a new location.

Exchange organ
An organ (e.g. the lungs) specialised to exchange substances.

Exocytosis
The process by which a cell secretes substances using vesicles.

Facilitated diffusion
The diffusion of particles through carrier proteins or channel proteins in the plasma membrane.

Fair test
A test in which only the independent variable has been allowed to affect the dependent variable.

Fibrous protein
An insoluble, rope-shaped protein.

Flaccid plant cell
A plant cell which is limp due to lack of water.

Flagellum
Like a cilium, but longer, it sticks out from the cell surface and is surrounded by the plasma membrane. Used to move the cell.

Fluid mosaic model
Model describing the arrangement of molecules in a cell membrane.

Food spoilage
The deterioration of a food's characteristics, e.g. its appearance, taste, texture or odour.

Gas exchange surface
A boundary between the outside environment and the internal environment of an organism, over which gas exchange occurs.

Gene
A sequence of DNA nucleotides that codes for a protein (polypeptide).

Genetic diversity
The variation of alleles within a species (or a population of a species).

Genotype
All the alleles an organism has.

Globular protein
A soluble, round and compact protein.

Glycogen
A polysaccharide made from a long, very branched chain of α-glucose.

Glycolipid
A lipid which has a polysaccharide (carbohydrate) chain attached.

Glycoprotein
A protein which has a polysaccharide (carbohydrate) chain attached.

Glycosidic bond
A bond formed between monosaccharides.

Golgi apparatus
A group of fluid-filled flattened sacs. Involved with processing and packaging lipids and proteins, and making lysosomes.

Habitat
The area inhabited by a species.

Habitat diversity
The number of different habitats in an area.

Health
A state of physical, mental and social well-being, which includes the absence of disease and infirmity (weakness of body or mind).

Helper T cell
A differentiated form of a T lymphocyte which releases substances that activate B lymphocytes.

Herd immunity
Where unvaccinated people are protected because the occurrence of the disease is reduced by the number of people who are vaccinated.

High density lipoprotein (HDL)
A lipoprotein mainly composed of protein that transports cholesterol from body tissues to the liver.

Homologous pair
A pair of matching chromosomes — each chromosome contains the same genes but different alleles.

Hydrogen bond
A weak bond between a slightly positively charged hydrogen atom in one molecule and a slightly negatively charged atom in another molecule.

Hydrolysis
A chemical reaction that uses a water molecule when it breaks bonds between molecules.

Hydrophilic
Attracts water.

Hydrophobic
Repels water.

Hypothesis
A specific testable statement, based on a theory, about what will happen in a test situation.

Immune response
The body's reaction to a foreign antigen.

Immunity
The ability to respond quickly to an infection.

In situ conservation
Protecting species in their natural habitat.

Independent variable
The variable you change in an experiment.

Infectious disease
A disease that can be passed between individuals and is caused by infection with a pathogen or parasite.

Iodine test
A biochemical test for the presence of starch.

Ionic interaction (in a protein)
A weak attraction between a negatively charged R group and a positively charged R group on different parts of the molecule.

Latent heat of evaporation
The heat energy required to change a liquid to a gas.

Lipoprotein
A substance composed of both protein and lipid which transports cholesterol around the body.

Low density lipoprotein (LDL)
A lipoprotein mainly composed of lipid that transports cholesterol from the liver to the blood.

Lymph
Excess tissue fluid that has drained into lymph vessels.

Lysosome
A round organelle that contains digestive enzymes.

Magnification
How much bigger an image from a microscope is compared to the specimen.

Malnutrition
A condition caused by having too little or too much of some nutrients in the diet.

Mass flow hypothesis
The best supported theory for how translocation works.

Mean
The average of the values collected in a sample.

Meiosis
A type of cell division where a parent cell divides to create four genetically different haploid cells.

Membrane-bound receptor
A molecule (often a glycoprotein or glycolipid) that acts as a specific, complementary receptor for a messenger molecule in cell signalling.

Memory cell
A B or T lymphocyte which remains in the body for a long time and initiates a secondary immune response if a pathogen is re-encountered.

Meristem
Mitotically active tissue found in the growing parts of plants (e.g. the roots and shoots).

Mitochondrion
An oval-shaped organelle with a double membrane. The site of aerobic respiration.

Mitosis
A type of cell division where a parent cell divides to produce two genetically identical daughter cells.

Model (scientific)
A simplified picture of what's physically going on.

Monomer
A small, basic molecular unit, e.g. amino acids and monosaccharides.

Monosaccharide
A monomer of carbohydrates.

Mucous membrane
A membrane which protects body openings that are exposed to the environment (e.g. the mouth).

Mucus
A sticky substance that traps pathogens and contains antimicrobial enzymes.

Natural selection
The process whereby an allele becomes more common in a population because it codes for an adaptation that makes an organism more likely to survive, reproduce and pass on its alleles to the next generation.

Neutrophil
A white blood cell.

Non-competitive inhibitor
A molecule that binds to an enzyme away from its active site. This changes the shape of the active site so the substrate can no longer bind.

Nucleotide
The monomer that makes up polynucleotides — consists of a pentose sugar, a phosphate group and a nitrogenous base.

Nucleus
A large organelle surrounded by a nuclear envelope. Contains DNA which controls the cell's activities.

Obesity
A condition whereby an individual is 20% (or more) over their recommended body weight.

Open circulatory system
A circulatory system where the blood isn't enclosed in blood vessels all the time — it flows freely through the body cavity.

Optimum pH
The pH at which the rate of an enzyme-controlled reaction is at its fastest.

Optimum temperature
The temperature at which the rate of an enzyme-controlled reaction is at its fastest.

Organ
A group of different tissues that work together to perform a particular function.

Organ system
A group of organs that work together to perform a particular function.

Organelle
A part of a cell, e.g. the nucleus.

Osmosis
The diffusion of water molecules across a partially permeable membrane, from an area of higher water potential to an area of lower water potential.

Oxygen dissociation curve
A curve on a graph that shows how saturated with oxygen haemoglobin is at any given partial pressure.

P

pCO₂
Partial pressure of carbon dioxide — a measure of carbon dioxide concentration.

pO₂
Partial pressure of oxygen — a measure of oxygen concentration.

Parasite
An organism that lives on or in another organism (the host) and causes damage to that organism.

Partially permeable membrane
A membrane that lets some molecules through it, but not others.

Passive immunity
The type of immunity you get from being given antibodies made by a different organism.

Pathogen
An organism that can cause damage to the organism it infects (the host).

Peer review
Where a scientific report is sent out to peers (other scientists) who examine the data and results, and if they think that the conclusion is reasonable it's published.

Peptide bond
A bond formed between the amino group of one amino acid and the carboxyl group of another amino acid.

Pesticide resistance
When pests, e.g. insects, are able to survive in the presence of pesticides.

Phagocyte
A type of white blood cell that carries out phagocytosis, e.g. a macrophage.

Phagocytosis
The engulfment of pathogens.

Phenotype
The characteristics displayed by an organism.

Phloem
A tissue in plants that transports sugars (e.g. sucrose) from their source to their sink.

Phospholipid
A lipid containing one molecule of glycerol attached to two fatty acids and a phosphate group. Main component of the plasma membrane.

Phylogeny
The study of the evolutionary history of groups of organisms.

Placebo
A dummy pill or injection that looks exactly like the real drug, but doesn't contain the drug.

Plasma cell
A type of B lymphocyte that produces antibodies.

Plasma membrane
The membrane found on the surface of animal cells and just inside the cell wall of plant cells and prokaryotic cells. Regulates the movement of substances into and out of the cell.

Plasmodesmata
Channels in plant cell walls for exchanging substances between neighbouring cells.

Plasmolysis (plant cells)
The pulling away of the cytoplasm and plasma membrane from the cell wall due to lack of water.

Polar molecule
A molecule with a slight negative charge on one side and a slight positive charge on the other.

Polymer
A large, complex molecule composed of long chains of monomers, e.g. proteins and carbohydrates.

Polynucleotide
A molecule made up of lots of nucleotides joined together in a long chain.

Polypeptide
A molecule formed from more than two amino acids.

Polysaccharide
A molecule formed from more than two monosaccharides.

Precise result
A result taken using sensitive instruments that measure in small increments.

Prediction
See hypothesis.

Pressure filtration
The process by which substances move out of capillaries into the tissue fluid, at the artery end of a capillary bed.

Primary defence
A defence that helps prevent pathogens and parasites from entering the body. E.g. the skin.

Primary immune response
The immune response triggered when a foreign antigen enters the body for the first time.

Prokaryote
Single-celled organism without a nucleus or membrane-bound organelles, e.g. bacteria.

Purkyne tissue
Fine muscle fibres in the heart that carry waves of electrical activity into the muscular walls of the right and left ventricles.

Reliable evidence
Evidence that can be consistently reproduced in independent experiments.

Resolution
How well a microscope distinguishes between two points close together.

Ribosome
A small organelle that makes proteins.

RNA (ribonucleic acid)
A type of nucleic acid, similar to DNA but containing ribose instead of deoxyribose sugar and uracil instead of thymine.

Rough endoplasmic reticulum (RER)
A system of ribosome-covered membranes enclosing a fluid-filled space. Involved in protein synthesis.

S

Sample size
The number of samples in the investigation, e.g. the number of people in a drug trial.

Secondary immune response
The immune response triggered when a foreign antigen enters the body for the second time.

Selective breeding
A process that involves humans selecting which strains of plants or animals to reproduce together in order to increase productivity.

Semi-conservative replication
The process by which DNA molecules replicate. The two strands of a DNA double helix separate, each acting as a template for the formation of a new strand.

Semi-lunar (SL) valve
A valve in the heart linking the ventricles to the aorta and pulmonary artery.

Sexual reproduction
A form of reproduction where two gametes join together at fertilisation to form a zygote, which divides and develops into a new organism.

Sieve tube element
Living plant cells that form the tube for transporting assimilates through a plant.

Single circulatory system
A circulatory system where blood only passes through the heart once for each complete circuit of the body.

Sink (in a plant)
Where assimilates (e.g. sucrose) are used up.

Sino-atrial node (SAN)
A group of cells in the wall of the right atrium that set the rhythm of the heartbeat by sending regular waves of electrical activity over the atrial walls.

Smooth endoplasmic reticulum (SER)
Similar to rough endoplasmic reticulum, but with no ribosomes. Involved in lipid synthesis.

Source (in a plant)
Where assimilates (e.g. sucrose) are produced.

Specialised cell
A cell adapted to carry out specific functions.

Speciation
The formation of a new species.

Species
A group of similar organisms able to reproduce to give fertile offspring.

Species diversity
The number of different species and the abundance of each species in an area.

Species evenness
A measure of the relative abundance of each species in an area.

Species richness
The number of different species in an area.

Specific heat capacity
The energy needed to raise the temperature of 1 gram of substance by 1 °C.

Squamous epithelium
A single layer of flat cells lining a surface found in animals (e.g. in the alveoli).

Starch
A carbohydrate molecule made up of two polysaccharides — amylose and amylopectin.

Stem cell
An unspecialised cell that can differentiate into any type of cell.

Stroke
A rapid loss of brain function due to a disruption in the blood supply to the brain.

Substrate
A substance that interacts with an enzyme.

Surface area : volume ratio
An organism's or structure's surface area in relation to its volume.

Symplast pathway
A route that water takes through a plant root to the xylem, through the cytoplasm of cells.

T lymphocyte
A type of white blood cell involved in the immune response. Some types activate B lymphocytes and some kill pathogens directly.

Taxonomy
The study of classification.

Theory
A possible explanation for something.

Tidal volume
The volume of air in each breath.

Tissue
A group of cells (plus any extracellular material secreted by them) that are specialised to work together to carry out a particular function.

Translocation
The movement of assimilates to where they're needed in a plant.

Transpiration
The evaporation of water from a plant's surface.

Triglyceride
A lipid containing one molecule of glycerol attached to three fatty acids.

Turgid plant cell
A cell which is swollen with water.

Ultrastructure (of a cell)
The details of a cell's internal structure and organelles that can be seen only under an electron microscope.

Vaccination
The administering of a vaccine containing antigens to give immunity.

Vacuole
An organelle that contains cell sap (a weak solution of sugar and salts).

Valid conclusion
A conclusion that answers the original question and uses reliable data.

Variable
A quantity that has the potential to change, e.g. weight, temperature, concentration.

Variation
The differences that exist between individuals.

Vesicle
A small fluid-filled sac in the cytoplasm. Transports substances in and out of the cell and between organelles.

Vital capacity
The maximum volume of air that can be breathed in or out.

Water potential
The likelihood of water molecules to diffuse into or out of solution.

Xerophytic plant
A plant that is adapted to live in dry climates.

Xylem
A tissue in plants that transports water and mineral ions.

Acknowledgements

OCR Specification reference points are reproduced with the permission of OCR.

Data acknowledgements

Graph of whooping cough and vaccine uptake on page 170 from Health in Scotland 2000, CMO Annual Report, September 2001. This information is licensed under the terms of the Open Government Licence http://www.nationalarchives.gov.uk/doc/open-government-licence/ (accessed November 2011).

Data used to construct the graph on page 178 from R. Doll, R. Peto, J. Boreham, I. Sutherland. Mortality in relation to smoking: 50 years observations on male British doctors. BMJ 2004; 328: 1519

Graph of tobacco consumption and death rates for COPD on page 179 © Australian Institute of Health and Welfare 2011. Source: AIHW: de Looper M & Bhatia K 2001: Australian Health Trends 2001. AIHW Cat. No. PHE 24. Canberra: AIHW; the National Mortality Database.

With thanks to the HPA for permission to use the graph on page 180, adapted from Tuberculosis in the UK: Annual report on tuberculosis surveillance in the UK, 2010. London: Health Protection Agency Centre for Infections, October 2010.

Data used to construct the graph of global sea temperature on page 189 reproduced with kind permission from NASA Goddard Institute for Space Studies.

Diagram showing the distribution of subtropical plankton on page 189 reproduced with kind permission from Plankton distribution changes, due to climate changes - North Sea. (February 2008). Hugo Ahlenius, UNEP/GRID-Adrenal Maps and Graphics Library. http://maps.grida.no/go/graphic/plankton-distribution-changes-due-to-climate-changes-north-sea.

Photograph acknowledgements

p 1 **Dr Jeremy Burgess**/Science Photo Library, p 3 **Monty Rakusen**/Science Photo Library, p 4 **Cordelia Molloy**/Science Photo Library, p 8 **Omikron**/Science Photo Library, p 9 (top) **Biophoto Associates**/Science Photo Library, p 9 (bottom) **Martin M. Rotker**/Science Photo Library, p 10 (top) **Science Photo Library**, p 10 (middle) **Don W. Fawcett**/Science Photo Library, p 10 (bottom) **Biology Pics**/Science Photo Library, p 11 (top) **Don W. Fawcett**/Science Photo Library, p 11 (bottom left) **Dr David Furness, Keele University**/Science Photo Library, p 11 (bottom right) **Science Photo Library**, p 12 (left) **Dr Karl Lounatmaa**/Science Photo Library, p 12 (right) **Prof. P. Motta/Dep. of Anatomy/University "La Sapienza", Rome**/Science Photo Library, p 13 **Dr Torsten Wittmann**/Science Photo Library, p 14 **Jeurgen Berger**/Science Photo Library, p 15 **Ami Images**/Science Photo Library, p 17 (top) **Steve Gschmeissner**/Science Photo Library, p 17 (middle) **NIAID/CDC**/Science Photo Library, p 17 (bottom) **CNRI**/Science Photo Library, p 18 (Fig. 1 top) **Herve Conge, ISM**/Science Photo Library, p 18 (Fig. 1 bottom) **Dr. Fred Hossler/Visuals Unlimited, Inc.**/Science Photo Library, p 18 (Fig. 2 top) **Science Photo Library**, p 18 (Fig. 2 bottom) **Pasieka**/Science Photo Library, p 19 (Fig. 5) **Jack Bostrack, Visuals Unlimited**/Science Photo Library, p 19 (Fig. 6) **CDC**/Science Photo Library, p 22 **CNRI**/Science Photo Library, p 23 **Dr Don Fawcett**/Science Photo Library, p 24 **Russell Kightley**/Science Photo Library, p 25 **Martyn F. Chillmaid**/Science Photo Library, p 31 (top, upper) **J.C. Revy, ISM**/Science Photo Library, p 31 (top, lower) **J.C. Revy, ISM**/Science Photo Library, p 31(bottom) **Andrew Lambert Photography**/Science Photo Library, image on p 32 © **The Science Picture Company**, p 34 **Don Fawcett**/Science Photo Library, p 38 (left and right) **J.C. Revy, ISM**/Science Photo Library, p 40 **Pr. G Gimenez-Martin**/Science Photo Library, p 41 (all) **Pr. G Gimenez-Martin**/Science Photo Library, p 42 (top) **Dr. Robert Calentine, Visuals Unlimited**/Science Photo Library, p 42 (middle) **Steve Gschmeissner**/Science Photo Library, p 43 **London School of Hygiene & Tropical Medicine**/Science Photo Library, p 44 **Eye of Science**/Science Photo Library, p 45 (top) **Power and Syred**/Science Photo Library, p 45 (bottom) **Pr. G Gimenez-Martin**/Science Photo Library, p 46 **Science Vu, Visuals Unlimited**/Science Photo Library, p 47 (left) **Paul Gunning**/Science Photo Library, p 47 (right) **Dr. Tony Brain**/Science Photo Library, p 48 **Steve Gschmeissner**/Science Photo Library, p 49 (Fig. 6) **Eye of Science**/Science Photo Library, p 49 (Fig. 7) **Steve Gschmeissner**/Science Photo Library, p 49 (Fig. 8) **Dr Keith Wheeler**/Science Photo Library, p 49 (Fig. 9) **Microfield Scientific Ltd**/Science Photo Library, p 50 (top) **Dr Jeremy Burgess**/Science

Photo Library, p 50 (middle) **Steve Gschmeissner**/Science Photo Library, p 51 **Steve Gschmeissner**/Science Photo Library, p 52 **Eye of Science**/Science Photo Library, p 53 **Carolina Biological Supply Co/Visuals Unlimited, Inc.**/Science Photo Library, p 55 **Power and Syred**/Science Photo Library, p 57 (bottom) **William Weber**/Science Photo Library, p 59 **Science Vu, Visuals Unlimited**/Science Photo Library, p 61 **Dr Keith Wheeler**/Science Photo Library, p 61 **Manfred Kage**/Science Photo Library, p 61 (Fig. 8) **Dr. Richard Kessel & Dr. Gene Shih, Visuals Unlimited**/Science Photo Library, p 61 (Fig. 9) Science Photo Library, p 62 **Sinclair Stammers**/Science Photo Library, p 64 **John Thys/Reporters**/Science Photo Library, p 67 **Dr Keith Wheeler**/ Science Photo Library, p 68 **Dr. Richard Kessel & Dr. Gene Shih, Visuals Unlimited**/Science Photo Library, p 72 **Kevin Curtis**/Science Photo Library, image on p 73 © **The Science Picture Company**, p 76 **Simon Fraser/ Coronary Care Unit/Hexham General Hospital**/Science Photo Library, p 77 **BSIP VEM**/Science Photo Library, p 78 **Dr P. Marazzi**/Science Photo Library, p 80 (top) **Biophoto Associates**/Science Photo Library, p 80 (bottom) **Ralph Hutchings, Visuals Unlimited**/Science Photo Library, p 82 **Ed Reschke, Peter Arnold Inc.**/ Science Photo Library, p 91 (top) **Eye of Science**/Science Photo Library, p 91 (bottom) **Dr Keith Wheeler**/ Science Photo Library, p 92 (top) **Herve Conge, ISM**/Science Photo Library, p 92 (Fig. A) **J.C. Revy, ISM**/ Science Photo Library, p 92 (Fig. B) **Power and Syred**/Science Photo Library, p 93 **Microfield Scientific Ltd**/ Science Photo Library, p 98 (left) **Eye of Science**/Science Photo Library, p 98 (right) **Power and Syred**/Science Photo Library, p 107 (left and right) **Clive Freeman/Biosym Technologies**/Science Photo Library, p 111 (top) **Laguna Design**/Science Photo Library, p 111 (bottom) **Animante4.Com**/Science Photo Library, p 114 **Biophoto Associates**/Science Photo Library, p 118 **Andrew Lambert Photography**/Science Photo Library, p 119 (Fig. 5) **Andrew Lambert Photography**/Science Photo Library, p 120 **Martyn F. Chillmaid**/Science Photo Library, p 121 (top and bottom) **Andrew Lambert Photography**/Science Photo Library, p 126 **Science Photo Library**, p 134 **Clive Freeman, The Royal Institution**/Science Photo Library, p 140 **Jeff Daly, Visuals Unlimited**/Science Photo Library, p 146 **Mauro Fermariello**/Science Photo Library, p 148 **BSIP VEM**/Science Photo Library, p 151 (Fig. 2) **Michael P. Gadomski**/Science Photo Library, p 152 **Scott Sinklier/Agstockusa**/Science Photo Library, p 153 **Eye of Science**/Science Photo Library, p 154 (top) **Astrid & Hanns-Frieder Michler**/Science Photo Library, p 154 (bottom) **Cordelia Molloy**/Science Photo Library, p 159 (top) **A. Dowsett, Health Protection Agency**/Science Photo Library, p 159 (bottom) **Eye of Science**/Science Photo Library, p 160 **Kenneth Eward/ Biografx**/Science Photo Library, p 161 **Science Photo Library**, p 162 **Dr Olivier Schwartz, Institute Pasteur**/ Science Photo Library, p 164 (top) **Phantatomix**/Science Photo Library, p 164 (bottom) **Science Photo Library**, p 165 **NIBSC**/Science Photo Library, p 169 (top) **Simon Fraser**/Science Photo Library, p 169 (bottom) **CNRI**/ Science Photo Library, p 170 **Dr Jeremy Burgess**/Science Photo Library, p 171 (top) **Biodisc, Visuals Unlimited**/Science Photo Library, p 171 (bottom) **Juergen Berger**/Science Photo Library, p 172 (top) **Mauro Fermariello**/Science Photo Library, p 172 (bottom) **Du Cane Medical Imaging Ltd**/Science Photo Library, p 173 **Thomas Deerinck, NCMIR**/Science Photo Library, p 175 **Pasieka**/Science Photo Library, p 176 (top) **Zephyr**/Science Photo Library, p 176 (bottom) **Du Cane Medical Imaging Ltd**/Science Photo Library, p 177 **Biophoto Associates**/Science Photo Library, p 178 **Antonia Reeve**/Science Photo Library, p 181 (left) **Eye of Science**/Science Photo Library, p 181 (right) **Dr. Fred Hossler, Visuals Unlimited**/Science Photo Library, p 183 **Nigel Cattlin**/Science Photo Library, p 187 **Philippe Psaila**/Science Photo Library, p 188 (top) **Nancy Sefton**/ Science Photo Library, p 188 (bottom) **Mike Boyatt/AGstockUSA**/Science Photo Library, p 191 **Simon Little**, p 193 (top) **Dr P. Marazzi**/Science Photo Library, p 193 (bottom) **Paul Shoesmith**/Science Photo Library, p 194 (top) **John Reader**/Science Photo Library, p 194 (bottom) **B. G Thomson**/Science Photo Library, p 200 (Prokaryotae) **A.B. Dowsett**/Science Photo Library, p 200 (Protoctista) **Michael Abbey**/Science Photo Library, p 203 (top and bottom) **Eye of Science**/Science Photo Library, p 206 (Image A) **John Devries**/Science Photo Library, p 206 (Image B) **Dr P. Marazzi**/Science Photo Library, p 206 (Image C) **Duncan Shaw**/Science Photo Library, p 206 (Image D) **Leslie J Borg**/Science Photo Library, p 206 (Image E) **Brian Gadsby**/Science Photo Library, p 206 (Image F) **John Devries**/Science Photo Library, p 208 (Image A) **George Bernard**/Science Photo Library, p 208 (Image B) **Gustoimages**/Science Photo Library, p 208 (Image C) **Rachel Warne**/Science Photo Library, p 208 (Image D) **Colin Varndell**/Science Photo Library, p 208 (Image E) **Pascal Goetgheluck**/Science Photo Library, p 208 (Image F) **Geoff Kidd**/Science Photo Library, p 210 **Wally Eberhart, Visuals Unlimited**/ Science Photo Library, p 212 (top) **David M Schleser/Nature's Images**/Science Photo Library, p 212 (bottom) **Duncan Shaw**/Science Photo Library, p 214 **Michael W. Tweedie**/Science Photo Library, p 215 **John Serrao**/ Science Photo Library, p 217 **Sotiris Zafeiris**/Science Photo Library.

Index

Q

quality of written communication (QWC) marks 222
quaternary structure of proteins 110

R

random sampling 183
reducing sugars 119
reliability 3, 224, 225
resolution 17, 18
respiratory system 52
ribcage 59, 63
ribose sugar 127
ribosomes 9, 15, 130
Rio Convention on Biodiversity 194
RNA (ribonucleic acid) 127, 130
    function 127, 130
    structure 127
root cortex 93
root hair cells 49, 93
rough endoplasmic reticulum (RER) 9

S

salt 148
salting 154
sample sizes 4, 224
sampling 182, 183
saturated fatty acids 115
scanning electron microscopes (SEMs) 18
scientific journals 2
secondary response 166, 167
secondary structure of proteins 109
selective breeding 151, 152
semi-conservative replication 128
semi-lunar (SL) valves 73
sexual reproduction 44
sieve plates 91
sieve tube elements 91
Simpson's Index of Diversity 184, 185
sinks (in translocation) 99
sino-atrial node (SAN) 76
skin 161

smoking 175-179
    evaluating evidence about 178-179
smooth endoplasmic reticulum (SER) 9
smooth muscle (in the airways) 61, 62
sources of medicines 170
sources (in translocation) 99
specialised cells 48-50
specialist exchange organs 58
speciation 216
species 182, 199
species diversity 182
species evenness 184
species richness 184
sperm cells 49
spirometer traces 65
spirometers 64
squamous epithelium tissue 51
staining microscope samples 18, 19
starch 113
stem cells 47, 48
stents 176
stomata 94
strokes 176
sugar-phosphate backbone 125
surface area : volume ratios 57
symplast pathway 93

T

T lymphocytes 162, 163
table skills 226
target cells 27
taxonomic hierarchies 199
taxonomy 199
telophase 41
tension (in plant water transport) 95
tertiary structure of proteins 110
theories 1
thymine 125
tidal volume 64
tissue fluid 80-82
tissues 51, 53
toxins 165
trachea 59
translocation 99
transmission electron microscopes (TEMs) 18

transpiration 94, 96
transpiration stream 94
transport systems
    in multicellular animals 69
    in multicellular plants 90
triglycerides 115, 116
tubercles 172
tuberculosis (TB) 172, 174
turgid cells 31

U

unsaturated fatty acids 115
unspecialised cells 47
uracil 127

V

vaccination 168, 169
vacuoles 8
validity 5
variable regions (antibodies) 164
variables 3, 224
variation 209-211
vectors 171
veins 80
ventilation 63
ventricles 72-74
vesicles 10
vital capacity 64
vitamins 146

W

water 105-107
water potential 30, 81, 93
water transport through plants 93-95

X

xerophytic plants 97, 98
xylem 48, 51, 90, 91

Y

yeast 43